INTERNATIONAL SALES LAW

United Nations Convention on Contracts for the
International Sale of Goods

Convention on the Limitation Period in the International
Sale of Goods

Commentary by:
Prof. Dr. jur. Dr. sc. oec. Fritz Enderlein
Prof. Dr. jur. Dr. sc. oec. Dietrich Maskow

Oceana Publications
New York * London * Rome

Library of Congress Cataloging-in-Publication Data

Enderlein, Fritz

[Internationales Kaufrecht, English]

International sales law : United Nations Convention on Contracts for the International Sale of Goods : Convention on the Limitation Period in the International Sale of Goods : commentary / by Fritz Enderlein, Dietrich Maskow.

Includes the text of the conventions.

Includes bibliograhical references and index.

ISBN 0-379-20418-5

1. Export sales contracts. 2. Commercial agents. 3. Conflict of law--Sales. I. Maskow, Dietrich. II. United Nations Convention on Contracts for the International Sale of Goods (1980). 1992. III. Convention on the Limitation Period in the International Sale of Goods (1974). 1992. IV. Title.

K1030.4.E5313 1992

341.7'53--dc20

92-27786

Manufactured in the United States of America

CONTENTS

TABLE OF ABBREVIATIONS

AALCC	Asian African Legal Consultative Committee
ABGB	Allgemeines Bürgerliches Gesetzbuch, Austria
AcP	Journal"Archiv für die civilistische Praxis", Tübingen
AJCL	"American Journal of Comparative Law", San Francisco
AW-Dok.	Journal "Dokumentationen zur Außenwirtschaft"
AW-Dokumente	Supplement "Dokumente" to "Dokumentationen zur Außenwirtschaft"
BBl.	Bundesblatt, Switzerland
BGB	Bürgerliches Gesetzbuch of 18 August 1896, RGBl. p. 195
BGBl.	Bundesgesetzblatt
C.c.	Code civil (France)
CC	Codice civile (Italy)
CISG	United Nations Convention on Contracts for the International Sale of Goods of 11 April 1980, Official Records, Documents of the Conference and Summary Records of the Plenary Meetings and of the Meetings of the Main Committees, United Nations, New York, p. 178 fol
CMEA	former Council for Mutual Economic Assistance
DDR-AW	Journal "DDR-Außenwirtschaft"
DPCI	Journal "Droit et pratique du commerce international", Paris, New York, Barcelona, Milan
EC	European Communities
ECE	Economic Commission for Europe

ECE Arbitration Arbitration clauses of the Economic Commission clauses of the United Nations for Europe, in: E/ECE/25 - E/ECE/TRADE/81

EEC European Economic Community

Factoring Convention UNIDROIT Convention on International Factoring, in: Final Act to the Diplomatic Conference for the Adoption of the Draft UNIDROIT Conventions on International Factoring and International Financial Leasing done at Ottawa, 28 May 1988, Annex II

Hamburg Rules Convention on the Transportation of Goods by Sea (Hamburg Rules) of 30 March 1978, UN Document A/CONF.89/13, 30 March 1978, Annex I

HfÖ former College for Economics "Bruno Leuschner", Berlin

HGB German Handelsgesetzbuch (Code of Commercial Law) of 10 May 1897, RGBl. p. 210

ICLQ "The International and Comparative, Law Quarterly", London

IECL International Encyclopedia of Comparative Law, Tübingen etc.

INCOTERMS International Commercial Terms, ICC Publication No. 460 INCOTERMS

Intr. remarks Introductory remarks

IPRax Journal "Praxis des internationalen Privat- und Verfahrensrechts", Bielefeld

KfA GDR Chamber of Foreign Trade

Leasing Convention UNIDROIT Convention on International Financial Leasing, in: Final Act to the Diplomatic Conference for the Adoption of the Draft UNIDROIT Conventions on International Factoring and International Financial Leasing done at Ottawa, 28 May 1988, Annex I

Limitation Convention	Convention on the Limitation Period in the International Sale of Goods of 14 June 1974 in the version of the Protocol of 11 April 1980, United Nations Conference on Prescription (Limitation) in the International Sale of Goods, New York, 20 May - 14 June 1974, Official Records, Documents of the Conference and Summary Records of the Plenary Meetings and of the Meetings of the Main Committees, United Nations, New York, 1975, p. 101 fol; United Nations Conference on Contracts for the International Sale of Goods, Vienna, 10 March - 11 April 1980, Official Records, Documents of the Conference and Summary Records of the Plenary Meetings and of the Meetings of the Main Committees, United Nations, New York 1981, p. 191 fol
NJW	Weekly "Neue Juristische Wochenschrift", Munich/Frankfort on the Main
O.R.	Official Records of the relevant United Nations Conferences, see pages 19 and 389
OAS	Organization of American States
OR	Obligationenrecht (Switzerland)
Paris Convention	Paris Convention for the Protection of Industrial Property of 20 March 1883
Quebec draft	The Quebec Civil Code, Vol. I, Draft Civil Code 1977
PICC	Principles for International Commercial Contracts, in: UNIDROIT 1989, Study L-Doc. 40, Rev. 4
PIL	Private International Law
RabelsZ	Rabels Zeitschrift für ausländisches und internationales Privatrecht, Tübingen
Recueil des Conventions	Recueil des Conventions/Collection of Conventions (1951 - 1988), Publication de la Conférence de La Haye de Droit International Privé
RGBl.	Reichsgesetzblatt

RiA	until December 1967 "Recht im Außenhandel", supplement to the journal "Außenhandel"; from January 1968 to June 1973 "Recht in der Außenwirtschaft", supplement to the journal "Sozialistische Außenwirtschaft"; from October 1973 "Recht im Außenhandel", supplement to the journal "DDR-Außenwirtschaft"; starting 1 July 1983 supplement to "Dokumentationen zur Außenwirtschaft"
RIW	Journal "Recht der Internationalen Wirtschaft", Heidelberg
SG	Schiedsgericht (Berlin Court of Arbitration)
SGA	Sale of Goods Act
SuR	Journal "Staat und Recht"
UCC	Uniform Commercial Code (USA)
ULF	Uniform Law on the Formation of Contracts for the International Sale of Goods of 1 July 1964
ULIS	Uniform Law on the International Sale of Goods of 1 July 1964
UN	United Nations Organization
UNCITRAL	United Nations Commission on International Trade Law
UNCITRAL YEARBOOK	United Nations Commission on International Trade Law, Yearbook, New York
UNCTAD	United Nations Conference on Trade and Development
UNIDROIT	Institut international pour l'unification du droit privé (International Institute for the Unification of Private Law)
Uniform Customs and Practices	Uniform Customs and Practices for Documentary Credits, Rev. 1983, International Chamber of Commerce, Paris, Publication No. 400, 1983

Uniform Rules Uniform Rules for Collections, Rev. 1978, International Chamber of Commerce, Paris, Publication No. 322, 1978

Vienna Treaty Convention Vienna Convention on the Law of Treaties of 23 May 1969, UN Document A/CONF.39/27 of 23 May 1969

WIPO World Intellectual Property Organization

EXPLANATION OF ABBREVIATED BIBLIOGRAPHICAL REFERENCES

Basedow

J. Basedow, Das amerikanische Pipeline-Embargo vor Gericht. Übersetzung des Urteils vom 17. September 1982 (Fall SENSOR) sowie Anmerkungen dazu in: RabelsZ, 1983/1, p. 140 fol

BB

C. M. Bianca/M. J. Bonell, Commentary on the International Sales Law. The 1980 Vienna Sales Convention, Milan 1987

Beinert

D. Beinert, Wesentliche Vertragsverletzung und Rücktritt, Schriften zum deutschen und europäischen Zivil-, Handels- und Prozeßrecht, Vol. 90, Bielefeld 1979

Bergsten/Miller

E. E. Bergsten/A. J. Miller, "The Remedy of Reduction of Price", AJCL, 1979/2/3, p. 255 fol

Bonell

M. J. Bonell "Some critical reflections on the new UNCITRAL draft Convention on the international Sale", Uniform Law Review, 1978/II, p. 2 fol

Bonell, DPCI

M. J. Bonell, "La nouvelle Convention des Nations Unies sur les contrats de vente internationale de marchandises", DPCI, 1981/3, p. 7 fol

Bonell, Uniform Rules

M. J. Bonell, "Is it feasible to Elaborate Uniform Rules Governing the Relations between Principal and Agent?", Uniform Law Review, 1984/I, p. 52 fol

V. Caemmerer

E. v. Caemmerer, "Probleme des Haager einheitlichen Kaufrechts", AcP 1978, p. 121 fol

CISG Kommentar, 1985

F. Enderlein/D. Maskow/M. Stargardt Konvention der Vereinten Nationen über Verträge über den internationalen Warenkauf. Konvention über die Verjährung beim internationalen Warenkauf. Protokoll zur Änderung der Konvention über die Verjährung beim internationalen Warenkauf, Berlin 1985.

Charlesworth	Charlesworth's Mercantile Law, 14th ed. by C. M. Schmitthoff and D. A. G. Sarre, London 1984
Date-Bah, Perspective	S. K. Date-Bah, "The Convention on the International Sale of Goods from the Perspective of the Developing Countries", in: La Vendita Internazionale, Milan 81, p. 23 fol
Date-Bah, Standpoint	S. K. Date-Bah, "Problems of the Unification of International Sales Law from the Standpoint of Developing Countries", in: Problems of Unification, p. 39 fol
David	R. David, Arbitration in International Trade, Deventer 1985
Dölle	H. Dölle (Editor), Kommentar zum Einheitlichen Kaufrecht, Munich 1976
Doralt	P. Doralt (Editor), Das UNCITRAL-Kaufrecht im Vergleich zum österreichischen Recht, Vienna 1985
dti	United Nations Convention on Contracts for the International Sale of Goods. A consultative document, Department of Trade and Industry, London, June 1989
Dubrovnik	P. Sarcevic/P. Volken (Editors), International Sale of Goods: Dubrovnik Lectures (11-13 March 1985), New York/London/Rome (Oceana) 1986
Enderlein, Ausarbeitung	F. Enderlein, "Zur Ausarbeitung einer Konvention über den Abschluß internationaler Kaufverträge durch die UNCITRAL", RiA, 32. Beilage zur DDR-AW, 1977/52, p. 1 fol
Enderlein, Interpretation	F. Enderlein, "Die Interpretation internationalen Einheitsrechts", RiA, 32. Beilage zu AWDok., 1987/52, p. I fol
Enderlein, Standpoint	F. Enderlein, "Problems of the Unification of Sales Law from the Standpoint of the Socialist Countries", in: Problems of Unification, p. 26 fol

Engler

H. Engler, "Zum Inkrafttreten der UN-Konvention über das Recht des internationalen Warenkaufs", RiA, 109, Beilage zu AW-Dok., 1989/17, p. I fol

Eörsi, Convention

G. Eörsi, "A propos the 1980 Vienna Convention on Contracts for the International Sale of Goods", AJCL, 1983/2, p. 333 fol

Eörsi, Unification

G. Eörsi, "Two Problems of the Unification of the Law of Agency", Law and International Trade, Recht und Internationaler Handel, Festschrift für Clive M. Schmitthoff zum 70.Geburtstag, Frankfort on the Main, 1973, p. 83 fol

Farnsworth

E. A. Farnsworth, "Damages and Specific Relief", AJCL, 1979/2/3, p. 247 fol

Farnsworth, Standpoint

E. A. Farnsworth, "Problems of Unification of Sales Law from the Standpoint of the Common Law Countries", in: Problems of Unification, p. 3 fol

Freiburg

Einheitliches Kaufrecht und nationales Obligationenrecht. Referate und Diskussionen der Fachtagung Einheitliches Kaufrecht, Freiburg im Breisgau am 16./ und 17. 2. 1987, Baden-Baden, 1987

Garro

A. M. Garro, "Reconciliation of Legal Traditions in the U.N. Convention on Contracts for the International Sale of Goods", The International Lawyer, 1989/2, p. 443 fol

Handbuch 1

F. Enderlein (editor), Handbuch der Außenhandelsverträge, Band 1, Der Außenhandelskaufvertrag, Berlin and Heidelberg 1986

Handbuch 2

F. Enderlein (editor), Handbuch der Außenhandelsverträge, Band 2, Anlagenvertrag, Montagevertrag, Lohnveredlungsvertrag u.a., Berlin and Heidelberg 1987

Handbuch 3

F. Enderlein (editor), Handbuch der Außenhandelsverträge, Band 3, Transport, Spedition, Lagerung, Kontrolle, Versicherung, Berlin and Heidelberg, 1984

Handbuch 4
F. Enderlein (editor), Handbuch der Außenhandels-verträge, Band 4, Kooperation, Kompensation, Gesellschaft, Konsortium, Berlin 1983

Hellner
J. Hellner, "The UN Convention on International Sale of Goods - an Outsider's View", in: JUS INTER NATIONES, Festschrift für Stefan Riesenfeld, Heidelberg 1983, p. 71 fol

Herber
R. Herber, Wiener UNCITRAL Übereinkommen über den internationalen Kauf beweglicher Sachen, Schriftenreihe: Ausländisches Wirtschafts- und Steuerrecht, Vol. 59, Cologne 1981

Herber, Rules
R. Herber, "The Rules of the Convention Relating to the Buyer's Remedies in Cases of Breach of Contract", in: Problems of Unification, p. 104 fol

Hillmann
R. Hillmann, "Article 29 (2) of the UnitedNations Convention on Contracts for the International Sale of Goods: A New Effort at Clarifying the Legal Effect of 'No Oral Modification' Clauses", Cornell International Law Journal, 1988/3, p. 449 fol

Honnold
J. Honnold, Uniform Law for International Sales under the 1980 United Nations Convention, Deventer/Netherlands, Antwerp, Boston, London, Frankfurt 1982

Huber
U. Huber, "Der UNCITRAL-Entwurf eines Übereinkommens über internationale Warenkaufverträge", RabelsZ, 1979, p. 423 fol

Kahn
P. Kahn, "La Convention de Vienne du 11 avril 1980 sur les contrats de vente internationale de marchandises, Revue internationale de droit comparé, 1981/4, p. 951 fol

Kahn, Caractères
P. Kahn, "Convention de Vienne du 11 avril 1980. Caractères et domaine d'application",„DPCI, 1989/3, p. 385 fol

Kindler P. Kindler, "Die Anwendungsvoraussetzungen des Wiener Kaufrechtsübereinkommens der Vereinten Nationen im deutsch-italienischen Rechtsverkehr", RIW, 1988/10, p. 776 fol

König D. König, "Voraussehbarkeit des Schadens als Grenze vertraglicher Haftung - zu Art. 82, 86, 87 EKG", in: G. Leser, Das Haager Einheitliche Kaufgesetz und das deutsche Schuldrecht, Kolloquium zum 65. Geburtstag von Ernst v.Caemmerer, Karlsruhe 1973, p. 75 fol

Kötz H. Kötz, "Gemeineuropäisches Zivilrecht", in: Festschrift für Konrad Zweigert, Tübingen 1981, p. 481

Lando, International Encyclopedia International Encyclopedia of Comparative Laws, Vol. III, Private International Law, Chapter 24, Contract, The Hague/Tübingen 1976

Lausanne Wiener Übereinkommen von 1980 über den internationalen Warenkauf. Lausanner Kolloquium vom 19. und 20. November 1984, Zurich 1985

Liebold, Haftung H. Liebold, Die Haftung für schadensverursachende Waren im internationalen Handel - Ausgewählte Fragen -, Aktuelle Beiträge der Staats- und Rechtswissenschaft, H. 236, Potsdam-Babelsberg 1981

Liebold, Produktenhaftung H. Liebold, "Zum Problem der Produktenhaftung in den kapitalistischen Industrieländern", RiA, 46. Beilage zu DDR-AW, 1980/16, p. 1 fol

Loewe R. Loewe, Internationales Kaufrecht, Wien 1989

Madl/Vékas F. Madl/L. Vékas, The Law of Conflicts and Foreign Trade, Budapest 1987

Magnus U. Magnus, "Währungsfragen im Einheitlichen Kaufrecht. Zugleich ein Beitrag zu seiner Lückenfüllung und Auslegung", RabelsZ, 1989/1, p. 116 fol

Prager

M. Prager, Verkäuferhaftung und ausländische gewerbliche Schutzrechte. Die Haftung des Verkäufers beweglicher Sachen für deren Freiheit von gewerblichen Schutzrechten oder Urheberrechten nach dem UN-Kaufrechts-Übereinkommen vom 11. April 1980, Pfaffenweiler 1987

Problems of Unification

Problems of Unification of International Sales Law, Working Papers Submitted to the Colloquium of the International Association of Legal Science, Potsdam, August 1979, New York/London/Rome 1980

Réczei

L. Réczei, "The Rules of the Convention Relating to its Field of Application and to its Interpretation", in: Problems of Unification, p. 53 fol

Richter

R. Richter, Transportdokumente und Warenpapiere im Außenhandel, KfA, Informationen, Reihe C,,Nr. 16, Berlin 1979

Roth

P. M. Roth, "The Passing of Risk", AJCL, 1979/2/3, p. 291 fol

Schlechtriem

P. Schlechtriem, Einheitliches UN-Kaufrecht. Das Übereinkommen der Vereinten Nationen über internationale Warenkaufverträge - Darstellung und Texte, Beiträge zum ausländischen und internationalen Privatrecht, Bd. 46, Tübingen 1981

Schlechtriem, Einheitliches Modell

Einheitliches Kaufrecht - wissenschaftliches Modell oder praxisnahe Regelung? Schriftenreihe: Juristische Studiengesellschaft Karlsruhe, H. 138, Heidelberg/Karlsruhe 1978

Schlechtriem, Kaufrecht

P. Schlechtriem, "Einheitliches Kaufrecht, Erfahrungen mit den Haager Kaufgesetzen - Folgerungen für das Wiener UN-Kaufrecht", Österrei-chisches Recht der Wirtschaft, 1989/2a, p. 43 fol

Schlechtriem/ Magnus

P. Schlechtriem/U. Magnus, Internationale Rechtsprechung zu EKG und EAG. Eine Sammlung belgischer, deutscher, italienischer, israelischer und niederländischer Entscheidungen zu den Haager Einheitlichen Kaufgesetzen, Baden-Baden, 1987

Siehr	K. Siehr, "Der internationale Anwendungs bereich des UN-Kaufrechts", RabelsZ, 1988/3 -4, p. 587 fol
Sono, UNCITRAL	K. Sono, UNCITRAL, The United Nations Commission on International Trade Law, New York 1986, p. 67 fol
Spruchpraxis, 1954 - 1968	Aus der Spruchpraxis des Schiedsgerichts bei der Kammer für Außenhandel der Deutschen Demokratischen Republik (1954 - 1968), Kammer für Außenhandel der DDR, Berlin 1979
Strohbach	H. Strohbach, Handbuch der internationalen Handelsschiedsgerichtsbarkeit, Berlin 1990
Tallon	D. Tallon et autres, La détermination du prix dans les contrats, Paris 1989
Thieffry	J. Thieffry, "Les nouvelles règles de la vente internationale", DPCI, 1989/3, p. 369 fol
UNIDROIT	International Uniform Law in Practice, Acts and Proceedings of the 3rd Congress on Private Law held by the International Institute for the Unification of Private Law, UNIDROIT, Rome, - 10 September 1987, Rome/Dobbs Ferry, NY 1988
van der Velden	F. J. A. van der Velden, "Indications of the Interpretation by Dutch Courts of the United Nations Convention on Contracts for the International Sale of Goods", 12th International Congress of Comparative Law
van der Velden, Koopvertrag	F. J. A. van der Velden, Het Weense Koopvertrag en sign Rechtsmiddeln, Deventer 1988
Vékas	L. Vékas, "Zum persönlichen und räumlichen Anwendungsbereich des UN-Einheitskaufrechts", IPRax, 1987/6, p. 342 fol
Völter/Wagner	J. Völter/H. Wagner, "Einheitliches Recht für internationale Kaufverträge", Wirtschaftsrecht, 1980/3, p. 141 fol

Winship   P. Winship, "Private International Law and the U.N.
                         Sales Convention", Cornell International Law Review,
                         1988/3, p. 487 fol

Winship,   P. Winship, "Commentary on Professor Kastely's
Commentary   Rhetorical Analysis", Northwestern Journal of
                         International Law and Business, 1988/3, p. 623 fol

PREFACE

1. The need for the unification of law and the genesis of the United Nations Convention on Contracts for the International Sale of Goods and of the Convention on the Limitation Period in the International Sale of Goods

1.1. The need for and problems involved in the unification of law

It is generally acknowledged that the existence of different national legal systems impedes the development of international economic relations with complicated problems arising from the conflict of laws. For a long time efforts have been made to overcome the contradiction between the character of contracts on the international sale of goods and the regulation of these contracts by the individual State under the domestic rules of civil and trade law by drafting uniform rules at the international level. Not only does the fact that the international sale of goods is provided for by each individual State constitute a serious obstacle, but the additional fact that most of those individual rules do not take into consideration the particularities and specific traits of international economic relations is a considerable obstruction as well.

In order to alleviate this situation, first, rules should be drafted which meet the specific character of international economic relations, i.e. rules which are adequate to the relations to be governed, and, second, it is a task for all States which participate in international trade and should be tackled and solved jointly on the basis of equality. (C. F. Enderlein, "The Law of International Trade: A new Task for National Legislators or a new lex mercatoria?" in: New Directions in International Trade Law, Dobbs Ferry 1977, Vol. II, 448.)

Work on the unification of sales law started in the 1920s, but not until 1972 did the laws on sale adopted at a diplomatic conference in The Hague in 1964 (Uniform Law on The International Sale of Goods and Uniform Law on the Formation of Contracts for the International Sale of Goods) enter into force between a few States (the parties to those laws were at the time Belgium, the FRG, Gambia, Britain, Israel, Italy, Luxembourg, the Netherlands and San Marino).

The results obtained so far in the unification of law, be it in the field of conflict of laws or of substantive law, clearly show that "joint law-making" in international economic relations is an extremely difficult task. Success could be achieved, therefore, above all in those areas where objective requirements forced a solution, as in the international transport of goods.

And it became obvious that a unification of law is not impossible to achieve at a global level. The adoption in Vienna in 1980 of the CISG and the earlier adoption in New York of the 1974 Limitation Convention have proved to be a considerable success and are a demonstration that the international community of States is capable of solving complex tasks when it is guided by the principles of peaceful coexistence and the idea of equality of all States. Just like any achievement in the unification of law, the aforementioned two Conventions, which are to be commented on in the present work, are the result of many compromises.

Any unification of law is dependent on a certain readiness for compromise on the part of the States involved. Compromising is both a problem of substance and form with the chances for compromise being better in regard to form. But a compromise cannot be achieved in respect of each and every issue. Hence, the Convention as a whole constitutes a compromise in that all States either gave in or prevailed.

One problem involved with comprise is to decide by which yardstick to measure the proposed solutions. One's own rules cannot serve as a measure for what compromise is possible in regard of a uniform regulation at the international level, for the same functions can very well be fulfilled using different legal structures.

The limits of compromise solutions are determined by certain minimum functions to be implemented by way of the unification of law. The equality, for instance, of the parties involved in commercial relations must not be questioned, and a balanced relationship between the parties' rights and obligations must exist.

1.2. On the genesis of the Conventions

The above-mentioned Hague Conventions of 1964 were basically the result of the work of some Western countries. Apart from reservations concerning their substance, this was one of the main reasons that the Conventions *a priori* did not have a chance of being adopted worldwide. This followed from an analysis made on the basis of comments by governments, which was submitted by the Secretary-General of the United Nations to the third session of UNCITRAL in 1970 (A/CN.9/31). UNCITRAL, after having been founded, considered it as one of its primary tasks, to revise the Hague uniform sales law and to draft rules which all States of the world, irrespective of their economic and social systems, and of their level of development, could accede to. At its first session in 1968 it decided to give priority to the following topics:

(a) international sale of goods;
(b) international payments; and
(c) international commercial arbitration (c. UNCITRAL Yearbook, Vol. I: 1968 - 1970, 78).

At the second session of the Commission in 1969 a specific working group was established which consisted of 14 members and whose task it was to submit proposals for amending the existing sales law conventions and drafting new ones. At the same time, another working group of 7 was founded. This group was to prepare suggestions for an internationally uniform regulation of the issues of limitation which arose in the context of the international sale of goods (ibid. 99 fol).

In 1977, the working group on the sale of goods in 1977 submitted the complete draft of a convention on the international sale of goods (CISG) to the tenth session of UNCITRAL (c. F. Enderlein/J. Volter, "Ergebnis der Arbeit der UNCITRAL für ein einheitliches Recht über den internationalen Warenkauf", RiA, 31th supplement to AW documents, 1977/51, 5 fol). In 1978 the group then presented the eleventh session of UNCITRAL with the draft of a convention on the formation of contracts for the international sale of goods (CFS) (F. Enderlein, "Zur Ausarbeitung einer Konvention über den Abschluss internationaler Kaufverträge durch die UNCITRAL", RiA 32nd supplement to DDR-AW, 1977/52, 1 fol). Both drafts were integrated into one single draft, consisting of relatively independent parts, at the eleventh session of the Commission.

The draft consolidated by UNCITRAL was then debated in two committees and the plenary at a diplomatic conference held in Vienna from 10 March to 11 April 1980. Representatives of 62 States and 8 international organizations attended the conference.

About 300 amendments were submitted to the UNCITRAL draft; only a few of them were considered in the final text. On 11 April 1980 the CISG was adopted without a vote against, however, several abstentions were made. (The documents of the conference are published in: United Nations Conference on Contracts for the International Sale of goods, Official Records, New York 1981, A/CONF. 97/19.)

Already some years earlier, a diplomatic conference that had been held in New York from 20 May to 14 June 1974 had adopted the Convention on the Limitation Period in the International Sale of

Goods. (The documents of that conference are contained in: United Nations Conference on Prescription (Limitation) in the International Sale of Goods, Official Records, New York 1975, A/CONF. 63/16.)

The question has been raised on several occasions whether or not it was right to deal with the problems of limitation before the problems involved in the international sale of goods were tackled. Seen from today's perspective, it would certainly have been better to have dealt with limitation in the context of the issues of international sale of goods and, if possible, integrate them into one uniform convention (even a separate accession could have been considered, just as it was done in regard to Parts II and III).

At that time, it was an important concern of UNCITRAL to prove that the expectations placed in the Commission were justified and that it had been possible to make progress in the unification of law.

The following chart depicts the present situation (as of 28 April 1992) in regard to the signature and ratification and/or accession to the CISG:

State	Signature	Ratification Accession Approval Acceptance	Entry into force
Argentina		19 July 1983	1 Jan. 1988
Australia		17 March 1988	1 April 1989
Austria	11 April 1980	29 Dec. 1987	1 Jan. 1989
Belarus		9 Oct. 1989	1 Nov. 1990
Bulgaria		9 July 1990	1 August 1991
Chile	11 April 1980	7 Febr. 1990	1 March 1991
China	30 Sept. 1981	11 Dec. 1986	1 Jan. 1988
Czechoslov.	1 Sept. 1981	5 March 1990	1 April 1991
Denmark	26 May 1981	14 Febr. 1989	1 March 1990
Ecuador		27 Jan. 1992	1 Febr. 1993
Egypt		6 Dec. 1982	1 Jan. 1988
Finland	26 May 1981	15 Dec. 1987	1 Jan. 1989
France	27 August 1981	6 August 1982	1 Jan. 1988

Germany[1]	26 May 1981	21 Dec. 1989	1 Jan. 1991
Ghana	11 April 1980		
Guinea		23 Jan. 1991	1 Febr. 1992
Hungary	11 April 1980	16 June 1983	1 Jan. 1988
Iraq		5 March 1990	1 April 1991
Italy	30 Sept. 1981	11 Dec. 1986	1 Jan. 1988
Lesotho	18 June 1981	18 June 1981	1 Jan. 1988
Mexico		29 Dec. 1987	1 Jan. 1989
Netherlands	29 May 1981	13 Dec. 1990	1 Jan. 1992
Norway	26 May 1981	20 July 1988	1 August 1989
Poland	28 Sept. 1981		
Romania		22 May 1991	1 June 1992
Russian Federation[2]		16 August 1990	1 Sept. 1991
Singapore	11 April 1980		
Spain		24 July 1990	1 August 1991
Sweden	26 May 1981	15 Dec. 1987	1 Jan. 1989
Switzerland		21 Febr. 1990	1 March 1991
Syrian Arab R.		19 Oct. 1982	1 Jan. 1988
Uganda		12 Febr. 1992	1 March 1993
Ukraine		3 Jan. 1990	1 Febr. 1991

[1] The Convention was signed by the former German Democratic Republic on 13 August 1981, ratified on 23 February 1989 and entered into force on 1 March 1990.

[2] The Russian Federation continues, as from 24 December 1991, the membership of the former Union of Soviet Socialist Republics (USSR) in the United Nations and maintains, as from that date, full responsibility for all the rights and obligations of the USSR under the Charter of the United Nations and multilateral treaties deposited with the Secretary-General.

USA	31 August 1981	11 Dec. 1986	1 Jan. 1988
Venezuela	28 Sept. 1981		
Yugoslavia	11 April 1980	27 March 1985	1 Jan. 1988
Zambia		6 June 1986	1 Jan. 1988

1.3. Purpose of the commentary

The present commentary is to acquaint companies and factories with UNCITRAL sales law so as to enable them, when shaping and implementing their contracts, to better meet the new challenges arising with the entry into force of the Conventions.

The main purpose of the commentary, however, is to explain to the reader how the individual provisions of the CISG and the Limitation Convention are to be conceived and which importance should be attached to them; also, how the conventions should be interpreted and which interpretation can reasonably be expected.

The authors of the present commentary have for many years been involved in work on the unification of law. F. Enderlein was a member of the government delegation of the former GDR to the tenth and eleventh sessions of UNCITRAL and to the 1974 diplomatic conference in New York. At the 1980 Vienna Conference he was the Secretary of the Second Committee and represented the United Nations Office of Legal Affairs. D. Maskow was a member of the government delegation of the former GDR to the 1980 Vienna Conference and has had a considerable share in the work of the First Committee.

Both during the drafting of the CISG and the Vienna Conference the idea of such a commentary was repeatedly suggested. A relevant commentary would indeed be of great help to judges and arbitrators. But the discussion within UNCITRAL, and at the diplomatic conferences made, it clear that the project of an official commentary could not be realized because its preparation and adoption would take an additional period of time as long as that needed for drafting and adopting the Conventions themselves. As a consequence, there will be no official commentaries relating to the CISG and the Limitation Convention. The commendable commentaries by the Secretariat of UNCITRAL (c. Official Records) refer to the respective drafts and do not always reflect the views of the Commission's Member States.

Commenting is thus left up to science, and it is has already become obvious that there will be different views in regard to interpretation. At the time this commentary went to press there were already several national commentaries in existence (c. v. Caemmerer/Schlechtriem, Kommentar zum Einheitlichen UN-Kaufrecht, CISS, Munich 1990; J. Honnold, Uniform Law for International Sales, Deventer 1982; Z. Stalev, Vienskata konvenciha zu mezdunarodna prodazba na stoki: kratak kommentar, Sofia 1981; J. Vilus, Kommentar Konvencije Ujedinjenih Nacija o medunarodnoj prodaji robe, Zagreb 1981). Also an international commentary, in which D. Maskow participated, has been published: Bianca/Bonell, Commentary on the International Sales Law. The 1980 Vienna Sales Convention, Milan 1987). Several national and international conferences have also dealt with the International Sales Convention and its interpretation. In this context see also the list of abbreviations of the quoted publications.

A supreme international instance lacking, diverging interpretations of the Conventions by national courts - a problem of all international uniform laws - will not fail to appear. Hence even greater need for reciprocal information on the interpretation and application of the Conventions - an objective to which the present commentary is committed.

On the part of UNCITRAL it was thought how the Secretariat, with the assistance of national correspondents, could gather all court decisions and arbitral awards to be expected in regard of the conventions and how to disseminate the relevant information. It was decided to collect all decisions in the original language in the Commission's Secretariat and to make them available if requested. A short summary of each decision will be translated into the six official languages of the United Nations. These summaries will be published as regular United Nations documents.

The Limitation Convention was adopted in the Chinese, English, French, Russian and Spanish languages, with each version being equally authentic. In the case of the CISG a further official language - Arabic - was added. All versions in other languages are considered to be translations.

The sub-titles of the individual paragraphs of the two Conventions, which are put in brackets, are not part of the official texts. They were added to facilitate orientation for the reader of this commentary.

2. General problems of the CISG

2.1. Convention instead of uniform law

Whereas ULIS and ULFC have been adopted in the form of uniform laws which States adhering to the special <u>conventions</u> for their introduction are bound to incorporate into their national law, the CISG has been shaped in the form of a convention. It contains in one document rules governing the relations between parties to contracts of sale as well as the international law instruments to put them into force. The CISG thus follows a new trend in the formal arrangement of a universal standardization of law that was already given expression in the conventions on prescription, agency, factoring and leasing.

Prevailing opinions also expects meritorious rules of a contractual convention to be incorporated into the domestic law of the Contracting States, so that they become binding on their legal subjects. Yet, there is a *difference with uniform laws* insofar as this incorporation elucidates the international character of the respective rule, underlines its special position in domestic law, and furthers an interpretation and application which is orientated to the standardization of law. So it aims at an international harmony of decisions and represses a legal practice coined by national concepts, to which jurisdiction tend in the case of uniform laws (for examples c. Volken/Freiburg, p. 86).

An apparent expression thereof is that the use of the convention form provides, in cases of discrepancies, for an *interpretation pursuant to the authentic text* and not according to a translation into another language.

Incorporation into domestic law is effected *by promulgating* the adopted convention and not by enacting a special law. There exists a somewhat simplified procedure in some countries. In the USA, for instance, the Senate can decide on its own, whereas uniform laws suppose a decision by both Houses of Congress (Winship, Commentary, p. 626).

The strengthening of the international character of contractual norms may even be more effectively achieved, in the authors' view, if one dispenses with the auxiliary construction of an integration into domestic law, and rather proceeds from the assumption that domestic law renounces its own regulations and their use for the benefit of the convention and to the extent of its scope. When a State becomes party to a convention containing authoritative rules for its legal subjects, we would prefer to interpret that the rules become *directly binding* on its legal subjects *as international rules*. Such a construction is even favoured whenever domestic law refers to international norms, and Mjullerson starts from this point ("Über die Beziehungen zwischen Völkerrecht, Internationalem Privatrecht und nationalem Recht", Sowjetskoje gossudarstwo i prawo, 1982/2, p. 80 fol). This reference may clear up matters, however it does not seem to us a *conditio sine qua non*, for it implies making the direct application of international norms dependent on national law, a practice being still widespread. However, this is not to be desired, for the very reason that it would lead to a situation where some countries apply international treaty norms as integral part of their domestic law system whereas other countries directly apply them as international law.

2.2. The Convention as a contribution to standardizing international trade law

The CISG refers to *international contracts of sale* as it ensues from its title and Article 1. Consequently, it leaves the domestic law of sales untouched. This approach is, at present, the only possible one as the domestic sales law is marked by targets of economic and social policy which result in very different legal solutions. Hence follows, that standardization comprising domestic matters as well, seems to be out of the question, at least on an international scale (see also Bonell/BB, p. 8). It would also hardly be desirable as it does not take sufficient account of the special features of international matters, evidenced by the fact that international economic treaties tie together different economic systems (with their respective civil, commercial, and foreign trade law regulations). Different currencies and issues that reach beyond borders must also be taken into consideration. This requires specific techniques in trade and the stipulation of special obligations (viz. the preservation of the goods - Article 86 fol). Certainly, these peculiarities tend to diminish in trade between integrated communities. Yet, they have not at all disappeared there. The special treatment of the individual consumption sphere which can be occasionally found in connection with the evolution of consumer protection leads, in addition, to a differentiated contract law, temporarily rendering an all-out standardization more difficult.

By aiming for a standardization of the rules in the most important practical field of international economic relations between enterprises on a universal level, namely contracts of sale, the CISG creates an international uniform law of sales, or, as will call it henceforth, an *"international sales law"*. It represents a decisive component of the growing international trade law, which itself is a weighty building block in setting up a legal regulation of international economic relations, i.e. *international economic law*. But the CISG realizes only a *partial legal standardization*. Higher legal security and lucidity of the legal conditions of international trade caused by it will be none the less more beneficial to trade, the more States adhere to it and the more one succeeds in standardizing border matters. This is done by creating *supporting conventions* (Article 7, note 7). In a wider sense, conventions in the field of transport and currency circulation are to be considered as supporting conventions. In this way a growing stock of norms of international trade law, which calls ever more urgently to be conceived as a unity by science and to be interpreted as such in applying the law, is formed in this regard see also van der Helden, esp. p. 18 fol). Finally, this requires that the further development of a stock of norms must take into consideration what has been achieved, and create new regulations which fit to it as far as possible.

2.3. International sales law and national law

The shaping of an international trade and sales law involves manifold disturbances of growth. They depend on different interests of the States conditioned by contradictions and/or differences in their socio-economic structures, economic development and foreign trade system, but also by their cultural and legal traditions. For those reasons, no settlement could be reached on a number of issues (see for instance subjects mentioned in Article 4). Therefore, it will be necessary to apply *national law in addition to standardized law* for a relatively long period of time. So, it has to be determined what problems are to be ruled by international sales law, and what problems are to be given over to national law. This is not a question of a conflict of laws in the traditional sense, for the limits of legal spheres are to be determined rather than those of national laws; and the national sphere consists of the individual national legal systems among which a choice must be made in a conflict of laws.

The question as to *what relations are covered by the international sales law* is determined by the CISG itself, as it:

> defines its scope *ratione materiae* in a general way or, in a positive or negative manner, with regard to certain legal institutions (Articles 1 to 5);

tries, in a general way, to mark off its scope from national law, and thus indicates possibilities and limits of an extensive interpretation (Article 7 - in this respect one could speak of a vertical rule in case of a conflict of laws);

> refers to national law in either direct or, even more, indirect manner (Article 20, paragraph 2; Articles 30, 42, 54 and 78);

> settles problems and, consequently, supersedes national law.

In general, the international sales law *takes precedence over the national law of the Contracting States*. In this sense it should be interpreted in a tenable but broad manner (Magnus, esp. p. 121). Yet, there are cases where it recedes in favour of individual regulations of certain States, either by virtue of the CISG directly, or by virtue of a reservation made by a State which objects to the stipulations of the Convention (see Article 9 in connection with Article 12). In the latter case, the consequences of a declaration of reservation are only, according to a widely held opinion (c. Article 1, note 2), in the non-application of the convention norm to the affected contracts. It is in the first case that the rules of a particular State are positively called to apply in lieu of the stipulations of the Convention, i.e. the prescriptions of *Lex fori*. Above all, the CISG may be superseded, pursuant to Articles 90 and 94, by international or national rules.

It is possible, in principle, that the international sales law determines, together with its delimitation from national law, the national law to be applied. If need be, it also decides upon the traditional *question of a conflict of laws*. In regard to the CISG, one did not like to complicate the already delicate settlement of the substantive and legal problems by raising the conflict of laws problem. However, a new special supporting convention has been made for that purpose (Hague Convention on the Law Applicable to Contracts for the International Sale of Goods, 1986). Also, the CISG itself settles problems of conflict of laws by some of its provisions which bear not only secondary character. Among them are, besides Article 28, to some extent Article 20, paragraph 2, and Article 42, paragraph 1, subpara. (a).

On the one hand, the gradual shaping of the international sales law obliterates the traditional problem of the conflict of law, as far as the standardization extends with regard to subject and territory. On the other hand, it creates the problem of determining the boundaries of international and national law, simply because trade law does not yet from an integrated system (Introductory remarks 2, Chapter I). The combined application of norms of both spheres to the same subject matter causes a special form of *cleavage of statutes*. Such evolutionary problems can and must be put up with during a longer transitional period. In most cases, however, one will manage with the standardized rules.

2.4. The structure of the Convention

The structure of the Convention (see Völter/Wagner, p. 142) follows the usual pattern by defining, in its introductory part, the *sphere of application* (Articles 1 to 6). The follow the *general provisions* (Articles 7 to 13) which refer to the stipulations regarding the formation of the contract (Part II) as well as its contents (Part III). Here, the points are the interpretation of the Convention and the conduct of the parties, trade customs and usages, and establishment and problems of form. According to the typical structure of contractual arrangements, including conventions, there follows the regulation regarding the *formation of the contract* (Articles 14 to 24). When Part II was set up, some solutions were conditioned by the legal policy decision to enable parties to omit Part II or Part III when adhering to the Convention. Therefore, it was not recommendable to interlace the questions of formation and the questions of modification and termination by agreement. The latter are now regulated by Article 29 under the general provisions for the sale of goods (Article 29, note 1.2.). Actually, Chapter I of Part II comprises very heterogeneous subjects that have been combined mainly for pragmatical rather than for theoretical reasons. Here we find also, in part, general provisions relating to breaches of contract (Articles 25, 26 and 28) and stipulating the rights of both buyer and seller. Of course, their inclusion in Chapter V would have been possible and, eventually, even more expedient.

The core of the regulation of part III is formed by Chapters II and III, regarding the *obligations of the seller and the buyer respectively*. They have been set up symmetrically, so far as the peculiarities of the performances of both parties allowed for it. In the respective introductory articles, the obligations of the parties are regulated, preceded by their summing-up (with the exception of the obligation of the seller to confer property - Article 4, subpara. (b)). At this, the obligations of the seller take the larger space, because they are more multifarious, and because special attention has to be given to the conformity of the goods with the contract and to the rights and claims of third parties. Hereupon, the rights of the other party, in case of being violated of its rights, are set down.

Chapter IV deals with the *passing of risk* as a special problem. Thus, disturbances which affect the implementation of the contract from outside, but for which none of the parties is responsible (as they are chiefly disturbances which occur during transport), are classed with the parties risk spheres. Thus, the parties are being enabled to prepare for it by obtaining insurance policies.

Chapter V refers to the *risks to the contract and special breaches of contract* respectively, and stipulates, in more detail, some of the *legal consequences of breaches of contract* (Section II, Section V). In this context, some stipulations governing the consequences of an avoidance of the contract may also be applied, so far as the statutory conditions are given, to an avoidance by agreement or a unilateral avoidance not pursuant to a breach of contract. Chapter V also lays down special legal consequences of breaches of contract in principle (Section III).

Specific legal consequences of breaches of contract are also stipulated by Section VI regarding the preservation of the goods. Since they do not primarily concern the contract violator, but the party aggrieved in its rights, certain particularities in substance result. In between, Section IV, relates to exonerating circumstances, which determine the subjective part of breaches of contract (above all the exclusion of a generally presupposed liability with regard to damages), viz. objective liability with possible exoneration. So, if one proceeds on the assumption that the regulation of *breaches of contract* mainly comprises mainly of three elements:

-   statutory breaches;

-   subjective factors; and

-   legal consequences;

The subject matters are regulated by Section III of Chapters II and III and by Section I of Chapter V, respectively. The definition of subjective factors, insofar as they are relevant, results from Section IV of Chapter V. In one part, the legal consequences are treated together with the statutory provisions on breaches, as in cases where there are claims to adequate performance, i.e. late performance, substitute performance, repair, and price reduction. In the other part, they are precisely set down in Chapter·V. This concerns particularly claims to compensation for losses suffered (damages) and anticipated termination of contract. Some of these claims (preservation of the goods, interests(are only founded by Chapter V.

The concluding Part IV contains the *questions of international law* that have become integral parts of the Convention, due to the nature of the document.

Though the structure of the Convention reveals several absurdities, it must altogether be seen as a success, because, for all its originality, it can be intellectually recollected. This result has been achieved by adjusting the efforts to the *typical time course* of an international contract of sale (i.e. formation, obligations of the parties, passing of risk), as well as by a *logical designing* of the Convention (obligations of the seller, obligations of the buyer, common provisions regarding the obligations of both of them). This emphasis presupposes, however, that the business process is conceived in a highly abstract manner. The legal contents of the regulation as a structural principle is thereby thrust into the background.

2.5. The structure of the CISG norms

The norms of the Convention are predominantly regulatory norms. In a smaller portion (apart from the international law rules of Part IV), they are in the nature of metanorms, which do not directly determine the commercial conduct of the parties, but the sphere of application of the regulation (Articles 1 to 6) and its interpretation (Article 9). According to the requirements of it subject matter, the Convention contains predominantly norms for reciprocal conduct.

We also find in the text of the CISG isolated *target norms*, which are characterized by the fact that they prescribe the result to be attained by the addressee of the norm, but leave it to him to choose the means, to wit, the concrete modes of conduct. In this manner, Article 54 determines the acts which form part of the obligation to pay the purchase price. Article 60, subpara. (a), and Article 70 also belong to this category. In view of the various possible and admissible modes of conduct in international trade, the conduct to be adopted in a definite situation cannot always be prescribed in detail. The use of this structure of norms serves as a means to secure the necessary flexibility of the regulations. Thus, as a consequence, the space of discretion is enlarged for both the parties and the adjudicating body.

It is apparent, with regard to other international contractual conventions, like the Hamburg Rules and the Convention on International Multiple Transport of Goods, that the CISG uses only a few formally independent *legal definitions*. Yet, there is quite a number of rules which represent definitions as to their contents, and we therefore threat them as such. But, more often they are shaped in the form of norms of conduct, i.e. operational rules (for instance Article 9, paragraph 2; Articles 30 and 53). The existing definitions (for example Articles 10, 13 and 24) appear largely in context with the respective practical issue, and we desist from giving a catalogue.

A typical structural principle of the norms of the CISG is seen in the fact that the character of the whole regulation as a compromise is reflected by the individual norms, by combining different principles, e.g. as rules or exceptions, from which the various legal systems proceed (Article 16 - for details see Maskow, Hauptzüge, p. 546 fol).

2.6. Formation of terms

It may be realized that there is an endeavour to use such terms whose corresponding words or expressions in other languages do not have a definite legal significance attributed to them, and which are, consequently, non-technical in a legal sense and become legal terms by the CISG only. Terms to be so classified are "avoidance of the contract" (Articles 49 and 64), "to deliver" (Articles 30 and 33), "to hand over" (Article 31, subpara. (a); and Article 32, paragraph 1), "to take delivery" (Articles 53 and 60), and "to take over" (Article 60). The formation of terms in this manner favours an *original interpretation of the Convention* that is based upon its contents and does not refer to the significance of these terms in the national legal system (note 3 of Article 7). In view of the high differentiation in national legal languages, this goal could not consistently be reached, as new adequate terms may not be found for all legal problems, or the originality obtained is lost again with the translation. Furthermore, there is no safe protection against a nationally coloured interpretation (D. Tallon "Questions de langage à propos des textes d'unification de la vente immobilière", Prace z prawa cywilnego, Warsaw, 1987, p. 403). But the terms cited as examples are not entirely unknown in the national legal languages. However, in interpreting the Convention one should, insofar, depart from their originality. Thus they get a new meaning by the CISG. This phenomenon can also be observed within the law of a particular State, when the same term is used by different branches of the law.

Already, it ensues from the originality of the formation of terms that the precise and detailed legal contents of the *terms* has still to be defined in the process of the application of the Convention. This implies, **a priori**, that the terms are vague in a certain manner. Yet, their uncertainty is limited by the fact that often one can link up with their meaning in common or commercial language in order to determine their contents more precisely. Though one must state that the CISG often uses term where this is not easily possible, as, for instance, with "reasonable person" (Article 8, paragraph 2; Article 25), and "unreasonable inconvenience" (Articles 34, 37; and Article 48, paragraph 1). The precise contents may not only differ from Article to Article, but also in applying one and the same Article to different subject matters. Terms, the contents of which result from the relations to which they are applied, allow for a large degree of *flexibility*, appropriate to the variety of subjects presented with international contracts of sale. Thus, the disadvantage of a lesser anticipation is compensated for. The use of vague terms occasionally shows the smallest common denominator of the negotiating States and conceals different conceptions as to content.

The vagueness of the terms correlates with their *abstract character* and influences the CISG as a whole. It is shown by the relevancy of general principles, for one part (esp. Article 7, paragraph 2). Apart from good faith (Article 7, paragraph 1), the principles are not even characterized by terms. For the other part, concrete legal situations are conceived in relatively abstract terms. Typical in this regard are the term "breach of contract" and the differentiation made, in its context, between fundamental and other breaches (Article 25). The term "acceptance of an offer" in Article 18, paragraph 2, is also very abstractly seized. Not only has the consistent use of such terms tightened the text of the Convention, in comparison with ULIS, but it may also facilitate the application of the law, as the regulation has become more easily surveyed, and subtle distinctions, which are hardly related to factual consequences, have been waived. The individual decisions do not become more foreseeable in this way. At any rate, this will change when, after a longer period of time, relevant jurisdiction is firmly established.

2.7. Summary valuation of the system of the CISG

Our explanations under ciphers 2.4. to 2.6. have shown that the method applied to the Convention is based on a thorough *theoretical grasp of the structure* of international sales of goods which is reflected by the high degree of abstraction of the Convention altogether, and also by its norms and terms. There is a guarantee that the legal problems of international contracts of sale are seized in a relatively comprising and flexible way. Whether the abstractions made are the right ones, is a matter of content that will have to be referred to, in general (cipher 2.8.) and in detail, in the course of commenting.

2.8. Summary valuation as to the content of the CISG

In order to evaluate the *Convention* as to its content, it must, above all, be stressed that the CISG is *directed towards the needs of international trade* and does not chiefly aim for a standardization of national regulations on sale, set up to meet domestic requirements. For example, the international character of the Convention is expressed by the authoritative rules governing its interpretation (Article 7), the weight it allots to trade usages, its consideration of the main forms of international sales of goods (Part III, Chapter II), and the preservation of the goods (Part III, Chapter V, Section VI). It is pointed out that the CISG, in comparison with ULIS, is more orientated toward the trade in machinery than in raw material (Hellner, Dubrovnik, p. 337 fol).

As unconventional or even modern as the CISG may appear in solving traditional problems (for examples see Bonell/BB, p. 13 fol), it is predominantly cautious in regard to new legal phenomena. This applies to dealing with the process of negotiating the contract, the pre-contractual relations, the influence of administrative measures on contracts, and change of circumstances. Altogether, the

Convention represents a balance between a modernization of the law of sales and the status quo.

The CISG will not relieve the parties of the *individual formation of the contract*. This is not only due to the fact that it has left or had to leave open a number of questions, but rather certain provisions call for an individual agreement. Therefore, the Convention often refers to the contract itself. It is up to the parties to make arrangements which answer the particularities of the deal, correspond to the foreign trade regulations of the countries involved, and endeavour to bring to bear their respective interests. For that reason, auxiliary means of contract formation, like general conditions of individual enterprises, conditions of branches and sets of clauses (IN-COTERMS, model contracts, guides) which are issued by international, regional or universal governmental organizations will also preserve their value within the framework of the Convention. Of course, in some cases, an appropriate adaption will be expedient. Insofar as such documents have a bearing on the relations of the parties, by virtue of the contract, they will even rank before the CISG, because in the relation between the Convention and the contract, the letter has priority.

In our view, the CISG has taken into *account* both the *interests* of seller and buyer *in a well balanced manner*. This is also admitted by representatives of the developing countries (Date/Bah, Perspective, p. 37 fol) who, at the Diplomatic Conference, carried through a series of modifications, seen from the perspective of the buyer of plants, machinery and finished products.

Summing up, it may be said that the CISG seizes those basic problems of the international sale of goods which can be regulated at present, and it solves them in a way that meets the requirements. The Convention thus effects - to resume the statement made in valuating its method (cipher 2.7.) - a scientific generalization which is just in principle. So far, the question raised by Schlechtriem (Einheitliches Modell), as to whether the uniform law of sales represents a scientific model or a regulation close to practice, may be answered as follows: The CISG comprehends practice related rules within a new scientific model or under a new method. But this answer involves that, whenever the addressees of the provisions are neither jurists nor legal specialists in the international law of sales, understanding is affected by a certain *discrepancy between contents and method*. It is our impression that the contents of the CISG is closer to commercial practice than its methodical presentation. This contradiction can only be overcome by an effort of legal propaganda.

Some constructions which are not familiar to the German lawyer are due to the influence of common law. At any rate, this should not be overstated, as Thieffry does (esp. p. 378 fol).

2.9. On the introduction of the Convention

It lies in the very nature of the standardization of law that practically any party to the comprised international economic contracts is confronted, though to a different extent, with *conceptions that are* new and *unfamiliar* to it, and that will first be met with skeptically. The addressees of these rules have to acquaint themselves with the new regulations. Business conditions and other documents have to be adapted and the ensuing business practices have to be developed. The pros and cons of the new regulation are not immediately comprehensible and, above all, they cannot be weighed against each other. This is one the reasons why the Hague Uniform Laws did not find striking success (Kahn, UNIDROIT, p. 359 fol), however, the perspective of the CISG is seen more favourably (ibid. p. 375; see also Herber, UNIDROIT, p. 514).

These *difficulties*, which *will be overcome* in a few years, should not detain the States and the parties to international economic contracts to adopt and to apply the Convention, which, as far as theoretical considerations allow to foretell, meets the requirements of the international sales law. The advantage of a standardization of law will prove worthwhile in the end. Those who make the effort, contribute to further the evolution of international trade law, for the CISG should be a starting point for far-reaching endeavours. (In the same sense, D. Tallon, "La résolution du contrat pour inexécution imputable au débiteur:...", Recht in Ost und West, Tokio, 1988, p. 597).

A.

COMMENTARY ON THE UNITED NATIONS CONVENTION ON CONTRACTS FOR THE INTERNATIONAL SALE OF GOODS OF 11 APRIL 1980**

Preamble

The States Parties to this Convention[1],

Bearing in mind the broad objectives in the resolutions adopted by the sixth special session of the General Assembly of the United Nations on the establishment of a New International Economic Order[2],

Considering that the development of international trade on the basis of equality and mutual benefit is an important element in promoting friendly relations among states[3],

Being of the opinion that the adoption of uniform rules which govern contracts for the international sale of goods and take into account the different social, economic and legal systems[4] would contribute to the removal of legal barrier in international trade and promote the development of international trade[5],

Have agreed as follows:

1. Opinions differ in the legal systems as to the legal importance of preambles. In the Eastern European countries preambles, in general, define in a binding way the social function of the respective legal act. That definition is then decisive when it comes to interpreting such act. In common law countries, however, where skepticism prevails in regard to general principles, they play a negligible role. Honnold, in his commentary, does not even comment on the CISG preamble, and Evans (BB, 25) is very skeptical about it. Loewe does not want to refer to it in the interpretation of specific provisions.

**United Nations Conference on Contracts for the International Sale of Goods, Vienna, 10 March - 11 April 1980, Official Records, Documents of the Conference and Summary Records of the Plenary Meetings and of the Meetings of the Main Committees, United Nations, New York 1981, p. 178.

The preamble of the Convention, which was drafted at the diplomatic conference, was not the subject of substantive discussion (O.R., 219 fol). This might be an indication that no particular importance was attached to it. It would, however, be inappropriate to dismiss the preamble from the start as insignificant from a legal point of view. The principles it contains can be referred to in interpreting terms or rules of the Convention, such as the term of "good faith" (Article 7, paragraph 1) or the rather frequent and vague term "reasonable".

It could also be used to fill gaps because those principles can be counted among, or have an influence on, the basic rules underlying the Convention (Article 7, paragraph 2). The spirit of the preamble should also be taken account of when agreed *texts of sales contracts* are to be *interpreted*.

All in all and in spite of the reservations to follow, the preamble can be used, in a cautious way, to *put restraint on* the immense *liberty* the parties have *to dispose of the Convention* (Article 6). In so doing, a referral to national law, which would otherwise be necessary, can be avoided.

2.1. Reference is made here to the Declaration on the Establishment of a New International Economic Order of 1 May 1974, 3201 S-VI (resolutions 220 fol) and to the Programme of Action on the Establishment of a New International Economic Order of 1 May 1974, 3202 S-VI (ibid 234 fol). Both resolutions contain political-economic principles which aim to eliminate the developing countries' economic backwardness.

2.2. The first part of the preamble should be understood as including the CISG into the efforts for the *establishment of a New International Economic Order* and making it a component of those endeavours. Hence the altruism that Winship, Commentary (625), deduces from the preamble. But the Convention can make only a moderate contribution towards that objective. This can be inferred from the fact that trade measures, which are expressed in foreign trade regulations, have a much greater influence on the international flow of goods that the unified sales law (in this sense Date-Bah, Standpoint, 40). Furthermore, the Convention can exercise only a limited influence because it can be altered in general and disposed of (Article 6).

Experience has shown that *reference to current documents* in a Convention which comes into force only eight years after its adoption and which is to exist for decades entails quite a few problems. We believe that a general reference to the New International Economic Order, as it is included in the preamble of the Convention on Agency, is more appropriate. We do not see any disadvantage in even renouncing such reference, as is done in the preambles to the Factoring and Leasing Conventions, for requirements which go beyond those mentioned under note 3 cannot clearly be deduced from the New International Economic Order and applied to contractual relations. It is, therefore, sufficient, to make only general mention of it.

3. Emphasis is place here on two of the particularly important principles of international trade, "equality" and "mutual benefit", which should also govern the relations between States and the process of shaping the New International Economic Order. They expressly refer to the relations between States. However, it is exactly this part of the preamble which is relevant for *commercial relations* as well, for equal and mutually beneficial relations between States in this context have to be specified in the respective commercial relations, including sales contracts.

4. In the quarterly meetings before the holding of the diplomatic conference agreement could be reached in that the different legal systems were taken into consideration in the Convention. As a result of those discussions, the Convention has the character of a compromise. This can be seen from both the substantive solutions and the regulation methods used (Preface 2.5. and Maskow, Hauptzüge, 546 fol).

5. The idea that the unification of law would promote international trade, as it is expressed here in an exaggerated way ("...removal of legal barriers"...), is the underlying motif of any efforts to achieve uniform laws in this field (c. Preface 1.1, 2.2, 2.3.). From this wording it can be deduced, in our view, that legal problems should, whenever possible, be solved in line with the Convention. Doubts, however, should always be removed in applying the provisions of the Convention, as is stipulated in Article 7, paragraph 2.

Part I

SPHERE OF APPLICATION
&
GENERAL PROVISIONS

Chapter I

SPHERE OF APPLICATION

Introductory remarks

1. Article 1 above all defines the sphere of application of the Convention in terms of persons involved and territory, the substantive coverage of the Convention being an essential vehicle for that purpose since the Convention deals with contracts (Article 1, note 1) for the sale of goods (Article 1, note 2). For that matter a rough description of the substantive sphere of application is given at the outset. The international character of the Convention is defined through identification (contracts concluded between parties having their place of business in different States (Article 1, notes 3 and 4), hence international sales contracts); the sphere of application in terms of persons involved being the result of that identification. The territorial sphere of application is defined in Article 1, paragraph 1, subparas. (a) and (b) in that a connection is established between a regulated relationship and Contracting States, using two very different methods (Article 1, notes 5 and 6; also Introductory remarks 2). As a result, the territorial sphere of application reaches as far as it covers the above relationship.

The substantive sphere of application of the Convention thus depends on the type of contract involved. It is restricted in Article 2, and explained more precisely and/or extended in Article 3. Articles 4 and 5 restrict the subject matter in selected points excluding specific aspects of rules for sales contracts. The sphere of application of the Convention in terms of time follows from Article 100.

2. In explaining, in a doctrinal legal fashion, the grounds for the determination of the Convention's substantive sphere of application and, as deduced from the former, of the sphere of application in terms of persons involved and territory, most authors start from the theory of autonomy of the will of the parties in forming contracts under the Convention (Secretariat's commentary, O. R., 15; Schlechtriem, 9; Jayme/BB, 28; Vékas, 342; Winship, 520) stressing, partly, that the provisions on the sphere of application are themselves private international law (Loewe/Doralt, 13) and/or constitute unilateral conflict-of-law norms (Huber, 422). Few of them, however, consider a conflicts rule theory which is based on the assumption that, first, and under private international law, it shall be identified which country's law is decisive and then, on the basis of the provisions on the sphere of application of the Convention, it

shall be decided whether the Convention or domestic law shall be applied (von Mehren Report, 191). Such considerations are relevant in regard to Article 1, paragraph 1, subpara. (b) (Winship, 520), but otherwise are not convincing. It was considered necessary to expressly stipulate in ULIS and ULFC that the rules of private international law are excluded as a matter of principle (Article 2 and/or 1, paragraph 9). This is quite understandable if there is a model law (Introductory remarks, 2.1.). The conventions relating both uniform laws permitted, in each case in Article IV, a reservation in solving a presumable conflict between the former sales agreement under private international law and the uniform laws (regarding the genesis see in extenso Vékas 342 fol). In the case of a convention, however, such considerations are, *a priori*, irrelevant in our view.

We hold that the provisions governing the sphere of application can be regarded as vertical norms of conflict. While norms of conflict usually occur between domestic laws existing at the same level, a distinction should be made between the domestic laws and international law (in our opinion to be imagined as being above the former). In so doing, the sphere of application is defined positively and negatively by way of inclusion and exclusion. This becomes particularly obvious where the Convention refers back directly to domestic law, as is done in Article 7, paragraph 2. A vertical norm of conflict can, however, be linked with a horizontal norm, not only when it serves to answer the question whether national or international law is to be applied, but also which national law is to be applied (as in Article 28). And finally, it should be pointed out that there are also (horizontal) conflict rules which refer to the relations between different conventions. In this context we speak of delimitation norms, e. g. Article 90.

When one, as we do, makes a distinction between horizontal and vertical norms of conflict, then the question arises of what is their relationship. Here we clearly express our preference for vertical norms of conflict. Therefrom results a functional interpretation which is guided by the underlying idea of unifying the law. That underlying idea is not least to overcome uncertainties in reference to horizontal norms of conflict and to avoid that they be reintroduced through the backdoor. When a State decides in favour of a convention, it does so in regard to the provisions contained therein with respect to the sphere of application as autonomous norms. There is no question of horizontal conflict rules since because of the existence of uniform norms there is no longer a need to chose between different legal systems (similarly Vékas, 343). Nor is there the problem of delimiting uniform conflict-of-law rules in the field of sales contracts (part IV of this book) and the CISG. Article 90 is in our view not relevant insofar as it refers only to agreements under substantive law (and only those belong to the subject matter of the Convention) and not to conflict-of-law arrangements (Article 90, note 4).

3. Regarding application in regard to CMEA relations compare Introductory remarks 2.2.

Article 1

(Sphere of application)

(1) This Convention applies to contracts of sale[1] of goods[2] between parties whose places of business[3] are in different States[4]:

(a) when the States are Contracting States[5]; or

(b) when the rules of private international law lead to the application of the law of a Contracting State[6].

(2) The fact that the parties have their places of business in different States is to be disregarded whenever this fact does not appear either from the contract or from any dealings between or from information disclosed by, the parties at any time before or at the conclusion of the contract[7].

(3) Neither the nationality of the parties[8] nor the civil or commercial character of the parties or of the contract[9] is to be taken into consideration in determining the application of this Convention.

1. The description of what is a contract of sale, whose existence is the first decisive criterion for the application of the Convention, follows in particular from the provisions on the obligations of the seller (Article 30) and of the buyer (Article 53). Both taken together could be conceived as a definition of the contract of sale. Article 3 extends the scope of application of the Convention to some contracts which are not purely sales contracts.

Whether the so-called linked operations are also covered by the Convention's scope of application is not expressly clarified. At present those operations, above all in East-West economic relations, to which, however, they are not limited, include the following main forms of contracts: counter-purchase, buyback and barter, of which exists no uniform definition at all. It is widely held (Documents of the ECE TRADE/WP.5/R.4/Rev.1, Ziff. 8 fol for counter-purchase and TRADE/WP.5/R.5 for buyback) thatat least the two first mentioned forms of bound transactions are understood to be such where separate contracts are often concluded in both directions; provided that further prerequisites are met those are no doubt governed by the Convention.

There are problems in regard to genuine barter which, in present-day world trade, is relatively seldom. An overwhelming number of arguments in our view speaks in favour of applying the Convention also in this case (Loewe, 27, seems to have a different view). Any partner is to be considered here both as buyer and seller, though with regard to different performances - in respect of the obligations to deliver, to hand over documents, to acquire title in the goods and to take delivery.

It has to be admitted, however, that Article 53 expressly mentions the obligation to pay the price and that also the following provisions require payment of money. Difficulties could arise in regard to the provisions concerning the synallagmatic connection between performance and counter-performance (Article 58); and to that extent it is understandable that Huber (419) holds a different opinion. Those difficulties should be overcome in shaping the contract; and, according to our experience, this is actually done. The opinion substantiated in the genesis of ULIS, namely that the uniform law is not to be applied to barter (Herber/Dölle, 9) does not, as we believe, have to be applied in regard to the CISG.

The Convention cannot be applied to leasing contracts even if they contain a purchase option (Volken/Freiburg, 113 holds a different view). For such contracts there is a specific convention in the form of UCIF, even if it has not yet entered into force. This does not, however, exclude that in the case of financial leasing in regard to the sales contract between the seller and the lessor, the CISG is applied if the required conditions are met. Then the CISG is applied to the relations between the lessor and the lessee to the extent to which the conditions of the delivery contract affect the former (e.g. Articles 10 to 12, Factoring Convention).

Neither does the Convention apply, as a matter of principle, to agency agreements with commercial dealers (Herber/Freiburg, 103). We believe, however, that it is valid for those sales contracts which are concluded on the basis of the dealer contract (e.g. through delivery on call).

As to investment contracts compare Article 3, note 7.

2. The *goods* referred to are conceived as movable assets; and the common-law tradition sets great store by noting that they have to be corporeal as well (Honnold, 88). A reflection of this position was the exclusion of electricity from the Convention's scope of application. Hence sales of immovable property and legal assets (e.g. sales of industrial property rights) are not covered by the Convention's field of application. The results of scientific and technological research (e.g. projects, construction documents etc.), however, can well be the substance of sales contracts in the meaning of the Convention (Article 3, note 7). The term "goods" in the sense of the Convention is limited by Article 2, subparas. (d), (e) and (f); but then again extended in Article 3.

3. Concerning the notion "place of business" compare Article 10, note 2.

4. Reference is made here to the second decisive criterion for the Convention's application: the internationality of the contract. The inclusion of the requirement of transboundary transportation following the ULIS model, as was requested by Volken (Freiburg, 92 fol) citing examples which would cause problems, would have produced legal complications and lack of clarity in terms of substance.

5.1. *Restrictions* follow from Article 90 and, insofar as the States concerned have made relevant declarations, also from Article 94.

5.2. The Convention does not apply, *per se*, to the relations between parties from different territorial units of States having several relevant legal systems (Jayme/BB, 30).

6.1. This rule enables the Convention to be applied also to contracts between parties of whom one, or in exceptional cases even two, does *not* have his *place of business in a Contracting State*. This is valid where the decisive rules of private international law refer to the law of a Contracting State.

We hold that in the event of such reference the *CISG should be applied at once* without checking the private international law of the State to whose law reference is made (so convincingly Winship, 521 fol with reference to views contradicting one another; in favour of reference back or forth Loewe/Lausanne, 15).

6.2. What matters here are the rules of private international law which determine the law to be applied to sales contracts. In many instances this applies to arbitral tribunals. The national conflict-of-law rules in most cases permit a broad *party autonomy in terms of conflicts of law* (Lando, International Encyclopedia, 24 fol) of which the parties to international economic contracts make use frequently. As a consequence, the further connecting factors like the right of the seller's country and, having the same result, the right to characteristic performance are diminished in their practical significance.

Important *arbitration rules*, like those thought for ad hoc arbitration courts, e.g. the UNCITRAL arbitration rules (Article 33, paragraph 1) or the ECE arbitration rules (Article 38) or even those for international arbitral tribunals (ICC Rules of Conciliation and Arbitration, Publication of the International Chamber of Commerce No. 447, Paris 1987, Article 13, paragraph 3), while giving absolute priority to the choice of law by the parties, in the absence of it concede to the arbitrators the right to decide for themselves which are to be the decisive conflict-of-law rules and thus which is the substantive law.

The *main cases* to which this rule could apply will be those where the parties have chosen the law of one Contracting State, if only one or even none of them belongs to a Contracting State, and where because of the conflict-of-law rules of one Contracting State that State's own law is applied to a contract in which at least one of the parties is from a non-contracting State.

6.3. This rule may also place an obligation on *courts and arbitral tribunals in non-contracting States* to apply the Convention if they invoke the law of a Contracting State on the basis of the conflict-of-law rules that are decisive for them (see also Siehr, 610 fol). That State, in acceding to the Convention, has expressed that the provisions of the Convention are the decisive norms of its law in regard to international sales contracts. Since foreign law is to apply in the same way as in the State where it is in force, foreign arbitral institutions have to accept that decision. Concerning modifications in the context of a reservation (note 6.4.) compare Article 95, notes 1 and 2.

6.4. At the diplomatic conference the FRG voiced reservations against this rule, *inter alia*, because according to the decisive private international law the conclusion and the content of the contract could be *connected differently* (O. R., 236 fol). Huber (423) declared a special way of connecting the formation of a contract as incompatible with the meaning of Article 1, paragraph 1, subpara. (b). This is incomprehensible since even a participation in the Convention can be limited to the conclusion of a contract or to the purchase of goods. We could well imagine the Convention to be applied only to the extent to which the decisive private international law refers to it: e.g. only in regard to the formation of the contract (there we are in agreement with the Norwegian delegate; O. R. 237).

Czechoslovakia and the former GDR, referring to their special legislation concerning international economic contracts, were in favour of deleting this rule (O. R., 237 fol).

Such interest in having the rule deleted was finally taken into consideration insofar as Article 95 provides for a *reservation* in respect of Article 1, paragraph 1, subpara. (b).

7.1. In that case the Convention does *not* apply *for either party* Loewe/Doralt, 14). This rule is to prevent that a party who, because of the facts known to him believed the contract to be a domestic one, all of a sudden is confronted with the fact that it is an international contract to which the CISG applies.

7.2. Under the common law view, one of the essential applications of this paragraph is the case of agency of an i.e. indirectly acting as an agent which under continental European law is expressed through the legal institute of the commission (Secretariat's Commentary, O. R., 15; Honnold, 78; but also Jayme/BB, 31). A condition for this situation is that the applicability of the CISG in the case of a sales contract between an agent and a third party is derived from the status of the principal and the third party and, therefore, does not apply if the foreign capacity of the principal in the sense of the rule is not obvious to the third party. This is certainly true of the common law and may also be true in respect of the Member States of the Agency Convention which in Article 2, paragraph 2, provides for indirectly acting as an agent. Continental European laws would in this case regularly assume that the sales contract between the agent and the third party is valid and judge by their status whether the CISG is the applicable law.

8. Hence, what matters is the *place of business* (Article 10). In the case of legal persons neither the nationality of the actual owner nor the law on which they are based, nor other criteria are relevant.

9. The notion of international sales contract had to be freed from the possible influence of different national differentiation which already, in regard to the scope of application, could prevent the uniform application of law. The criteria cited can only be examples by which it is to be generally expressed that the *term "international sales contract"* can only be interpreted on the basis of the Convention. The latter, however, gives a differentiation which is comparable to some of the national rules that have been rejected (Article 2, subpara. (a) and note 2 to that Article).

Article 2

(Exclusions from Convention)

This Convention does not apply to sales[1]:

(a) of goods bought for personal, family or household use[2], unless the seller, at any time before or at the conclusion of the contract, neither knew or ought to have known that the goods were bought for any such use[3];

(b) by auction[4];

(c) on execution or otherwise by authority of law[5];

(d) of stocks, shares, investment securities, negotiable instruments or money[6];

(e) of ships, vessels, hovercraft or aircraft[7];

(f) of electricity[8].

1. There are three types of *restrictions* in this article:

- those based on the purpose for which the goods were purchased, (subpara. (a)),

- those based on the type of sales contract, (subparas. (b) and (c)),

- those based on the kinds of goods sold, (subparas. (d), (e) and (f)).

2. This generally refers to a non-commercial purpose (similar view held by Huber, 421 fol). Those contracts are mostly excluded from the Convention's scope of application which in many countries are regarded as civil law contracts (in contrast to trade law contracts). That criterion, however, is not applied with regard to the character of the parties to a contract, which would have to be defined, but rather, to the purpose of the goods.

In many countries special laws have been enacted which are directed against *clauses in general business conditions* by which the legal rights, in particular of the buyer, are limited. Such legislation is above all aimed at consumer contracts which, irrespective of any national differences, meet the very definition of the contracts excluded here.

Insofar the relationship between the CISG and the mandatory domestic consumer protection rules does not have to be determined.

The legislation aimed against an abuse of general business conditions is not necessarily limited to consumer contracts and can, where it reaches beyond them, achieve importance also for *international economic contracts*. Since the CISG does not regulate those problems and also from its underlying principles the prohibition of abuses of general business conditions can hardly be deduced, it cannot be excluded that the relevant norms of the applicable law chosen on the basis of the decisive rules of private international law can be invoked in addition whenever a gap under Article 7, paragraph 2, is found. Contradictions that may exist between the CISG and the mandatory domestic law should, in our view, be settled in favour of the Convention (see Schlechtriem, 14; also as the Convention is the more recent and more specific law). This includes that the parties can make relevant arrangements, and the Contracting States must leave them that much freedom within the scope of application of the CISG (Herber/Doralt, 36). We believe that this is justifiable also because the structure in regard to parties to international economic contracts is generally more balanced than in the case of national ones. Should domestic protection rules, however, affect the validity of contracts or clauses they will generally supersede the CISG under Article 4, subpara. (a). There is a trend in publications to attach growing importance to this provision.

3.1. The purpose of the goods will in general be recognizable from the *circumstances of the transaction*, e.g. retail sale, sale through mail order firms, etc. If the goods, contrary to the purpose at the time of the purchase, are used for commercial purposes, the Convention will not apply because late changes in purpose are irrelevant (Honnold, 86).

If, however, the circumstances of the transaction are such that an *intended industrial use* of the goods suggests itself (e.g. a wood-working machine for industrial purposes is ordered directly from the foreign manufacturer) the CISG is applied also in the exceptional case that the goods are destined for personal purposes (e.g. for use in one's own personal workshop), unless the seller knew or ought to have known this, e.g. because of an indication by the buyer (Loewe/Lausanne, 17). The Convention applies, however, to a contract which seems to be a consumer contract but is not (ibid).

In regard to whether the seller "knew" or "ought to have known", what matters again is the *time* of the conclusion of the contract (Secretariat's Commentary, O. R., 16; Khoo/BB, 37). It is not sufficient to gain this knowledge only when, for instance, the machine is being installed.

3.2. At the diplomatic conference (O. R., 238 fol) *problems related to the burden of proof* have played a role in this context. The view was also held that the Convention should not decide questions of burden of proof, but rather, this should be left to the courts as matters of procedural law (O. R., 295 fol; Khoo/BB, 39). It is no doubt correct that in formulating most of the provisions of the CISG the questions of burden of proof have not specifically been taken into account. Chances are that checking the Convention's text for them will not be successful. This should, however, not be made into a problem. The Convention should be invoked to the extent to which is solves such questions, and this is what it does in this place. Therefore, the usual methods of interpretation arc to be used.

A typical constellation in this case could be, as Khoo (BB/40) rightly notes, that the buyer wishes to prevent application of the CISG in order to enjoy the domestic protection laws which are more favourable to him. The buyer will have to prove that he has bought the goods for personal use, and the seller will have to prove that he did not even have to have knowledge of it (Honnold, 87; Khoo, ibid).

4. As a reason for this exception it was indicated that there are often *specific rules* for auctions under applicable domestic law (Secretariat's Commentary, O. R., 16). Already Réczei (Problems of Unification, 70) has justly objected that the rules for auctions are mostly created by the very institutions which hold such auctions; and the participants in the auction are obliged to accept those conditions. This specific form of party agreement could be complemented by the Convention as decisive law.

Already at present, the rules for auctions could naturally determine the CISG as the subsidiary applicable law (opting in).

5. Such sales are excluded because they are governed by special and mostly *mandatory rules* in numerous countries.

6. This exception can be explained by the existence of mandatory domestic rules of which only *foreign exchange control regulations* shall be mentioned here.

The negotiable instruments referred to here include bills of exchange, cheques and shares; but *not*, however, the *documents relating to the goods* (see also Secretariat's Commentary, O. R., 16; Honnold, 88), i.e. documents of title. The buyers of such papers are basically the buyers of the goods to which those refer. That such purchases should not be excluded follows, *inter alia*, from the fact that the documents mentioned in Articles 34 and 58, paras. 1 and 2, which relate to the goods and/or allow to have disposal of the goods are, in particular but not exclusively, documents relating to the goods.

7.1. The reasons given for this exception were, above all, *registration requirements* and the existence of specific rules for the sale of ships in some countries according to which ships are treated as immovable property (Secretariat's Commentary, O. R. 16). But the problems of title, which are the first to be affected in this context, are left out of the Convention (Article 4, subpara. (a)). Besides, the latter does not apply to aircraft. The argument mentioned by the FRG representative, that sales contracts for ships are of a very specific nature (O. R., 240 fol) could be invoked in regard to many other types of contracts which are not excluded from the Convention. Kahn (958) also justifies the exclusion referring, *inter alia*, to Article 3, paragraph 2, though he wants to have the Convention applied to contracts for the setting up of plants (not in agreement Huber, 419).

7.2. A distinction between the terms *"ships" and "vessels"* is not easy to make. For this reason, Honnold (89) wants to exclude any ship from the scope of application as is doubtlessly done in the case of seagoing (Schlechtriem, 16), hovercraft and aircraft. It should, therefore, be recommended to the parties in cases of doubt to expressly agree when to apply the Convention.

8. The reason given here that electricity in many legislations is *not* considered to be *a good* (compare O. R., 16) is theoretically not convincing because the Convention may create its own definition of a good. It should be admitted, however, that in light of the strong centralization of electricity trade contracts can be elaborated in

great detail. But this would not exclude application of the Convention's general provisions.

Article 3[1]

(Contracts for services or for goods to be manufactured)

(1) Contracts for the supply of goods to be manufactured or produced are to be considered sales[2] unless the party who orders the goods undertakes to supply a substantial part[3] of the materials necessary for such manufacture or production[4].

(2) This Convention does not apply to contracts in which the preponderant part of the obligations[5] of the party who furnishes[6] the goods consists in the supply of labour or other services.

1. Given the difficulties in interpreting this article because of the vague terms used (notes 3 and 5) it is recommended that the parties use the following *clause* when wishing to apply the Convention:

"The contract is subject to the United Nations Convention on Contracts for the International Sale of Goods. Specific problems relating to services which are not covered by the Convention are subject to the law of the ... 's country. That same law also applies under Article 7 of the Convention to complement it."

2. The *inclusion of contracts on the delivery of goods* to be manufactured (machines, manufactured goods) or produced (agricultural produce, raw materials) at the time of conclusion of the contract, in sales contracts means that the CISG can be applied also to certain contracts which are considered to be *works contracts*.

3. The CISG uses here a vague term which permits flexibility but also creates uncertainty. The term "a substantial part" should be defined using *criteria of value* (Honnold, 92 and Khoo, BB, 42). Substantial is not "preponderant" as in Article 2, it may even be less than one half. We doubt, however, that 15 per cent will suffice, as believes Honnold. When the relevant proportional value is to be calculated, a complementary criterion could be to assess the importance of supplies of parts of the goods for the purpose of manufacture. Only if those are substantial for determining, for instance, the technical parameters of a machine to be delivered, a portion of less than one half of the value could be considered sufficient to exclude

the Convention. In this case, it should not be substantially lower, otherwise it should be above that portion.

The *order* has to be *free of charge*. When the seller acquires parts from the buyer which become part of the machine, there will be a sales contract irrespective of their proportional value.

The provision of *technical drawings* etc. has no influence on the character of a sales contract in the meaning of the Convention. This follows not only from the failure of a motion submitted by Britain and aiming towards the opposite (O. R., 84 fol), but can be deduced, above all, from Article 42, paragraph 2, subpara. (b) which regulates a specific problem related to it.

4. This serves to exclude particularly *processing upon contracts,*and several other types of work contracts from the scope of application of the CISG.

5. The criteria of what is to be considered the preponderant part of the obligations are similar to those explained in note 3. But the "preponderant" part is bigger than a substantial part and has to mean more than half. A proposal by Britain, which aimed at adopting a merely quantitative, value related approach (major part of the value), did not meet with the approval of the Conference (O. R., 84 fol).

6. The notion "seller" was not used because the partner in question was not a seller in this case, or rather not exclusively (O. R., 242).

7. The opposite conclusion would be that the CISG is to apply also to contracts *which do not exclusively have the character of a sales contract*. Therefore, regular contracts containing an obligation of assembly fall under the scope of the Convention.

There are problems when it comes to applying the Convention to *contracts for the setting up of plants*. Kahn (955 fol) is in favour of that solution in relation to turn-key contracts, while Herber (Freiburg/103), referring to ULIS jurisdiction, is considerably more cautious in aiming towards the same direction. The UNCITRAL Legal Guide on Drawing Up International Contracts for the Construction of Industrial Works, New York 1988, points to the fact that the Convention can be applied in regard to some works contracts and recommends agreements (303 fol). We endorse this position (in detail see Brand/Maskow, Der internationale Anlagenvertrag, Berlin 1989, 78 fol). We do not understand why Honnold (89 fol) excludes building contracts (which have much in common with contracts for the setting up of plants even if more is manufactured at a construction site) from the scope of the Convention. His argumentation is based on the common law interpretation of the term "goods". This is not necessarily the Convention's interpretation of the term; and furthermore, it has been extended by Article 3 (and not restricted, as Honnold (75) affirms in another place). The situation in respect of the application of the CISG to contracts for the setting up of plants and other combined contracts is different from what the Secretariat's Commentary (O. R., 16 fol) and Schlechtriem (17) believe, but is, as Kahn (956) correctly explains, *to be decided pursuant to the CISG* and not to applicable domestic law, since the latter is applicable only to the extent to which the former is unable to apply.

From the fact that the CISG is applicable to certain contracts containing elements that are alien to sales it may be concluded that *regulations* of the Convention *which are not typical for sales apply to the contract generally* (see also Honnold, 93) e.g. the general provisions, the rules for the formation of the contract, the rights in case of breach of contract, and exemptions. Specific rules concerning the rights and obligations of the parties, which do not have the character of a sales contract (e.g. conditions of stay of experts) would, if need be, have to be drawn from national law (frequently the contracts sufficiently provide for them). Where there are contradictions between the CISG and the national rules for non-sales elements (e.g. when the national law to be applied to assembly contracts permits ordinary unilateral termination which is unknown under the CISG) the Convention will supersede that domestic law because it applies to the largest part of the performance anyway.

When the terms "labour" and "other services" are used to characterize non-sales obligations, then this is obviously done to express that *human labour* as such is owed, irrespective of whether it has a form giving effect or not. If it is only the result of labour which is owed, like in many contracts on the preparation of scientific and technological results (project contracts), then there exists a sales contract in the sense of the CISG in any case.

This also has to be taken into account when the preponderant part of obligations is defined. "Labour" or "other services" include, above all, assembly work, supervision, control, storage, after-sales services and maintenance.

Article 4[1]

(Substantive coverage of Convention)

This Convention governs only the formation of the contract of sale and the rights and obligations of the seller and the buyer[2] arising from such a contract. In particular[4], except as otherwise expressly provided in this Convention[3], it is not concerned with:

(a) the validity of the contract[5] or of any of its provisions[6] or of any usage[7];

(b) the effect which the contract may have on the property in the goods sold[8].

1.1. Any legal relationship involves a host of legal relations so that it is covered in its entirety only by the respective national system of law. In the case of international legal relationships there are also other national legal systems and internationally agreed rules which are relevant. Since unification of law can only be achieved step by step there are inevitably *problems of delimitation* between unified and national law (Introductory remarks 2.3.). The Convention solves them, positively, in giving a definition of its scope of application so that the space left free can be covered by domestic law (or other conventions), and, negatively, in excluding certain aspects from its field of application.

1.2. The scope of application of the CISG is determined not only by the legal relations it involves, but also by the depth and comprehensiveness in which these relations are regulated (Maskow, Convention, 50).

As to the *depth of regulation*, i.e. the concreteness and detail with which the relations covered by the Convention are actually regulated, it is, in particular, Article 7, paragraph 2, which provides a general guideline. The first sentence of Article 4 covers the *comprehensiveness of the regulation*, i.e. the extent to which the problems falling under the substantive scope of application of the Convention are covered.

2. The *substantive scope of application* of the CISG is once again summarized and described in a general way in this place, using terms which have been explained more precisely in the preceding articles. It is basically pointed to what is indeed governed by the Convention, i.e. the content of Parts II and III. Those parts can also serve to flesh out what is understood by the conclusion of the contract of sale and the rights and obligations of its parties (Honnold, 96).

In accordance with the principle of an interpretation that is favourable to the Convention (Introductory remarks 2.3.) the terms used here should be broadly interpreted. Many of the aspects of a sales contract, which are mentioned separately in Article 12 of the Hague Convention on the Law Applicable to Contracts for the International Sale of Goods 1986 apart from the rights and obligations of the parties, according to the Convention clearly fall under those terms. This is true of the interpretation and performance of the contract, (subparas. (a) and (b)); the time from which the buyer has the right to the fruits and use of the goods and/or the risk passes to him, (subparas. (c) and (d)); the consequences of non-performance; and the different ways of expiration of obligations and the loss of rights after the expiration of a time-limit, (subparas. (f) and (g)). Concerning the voidness and ineffectiveness of the contract, (subpara. (h)), compare note 4.

Other problems covered by the contract's statute in the meaning of the Hague Convention on the Law Applicable to Contracts for the International Sale of Goods 1986, namely the validity and effectiveness of reservation clauses on property and the limitation (Article 12, subpara. (e) and (g)), are not regulated by the CISG and therefore do not belong to the rights and obligations of the parties in the specific sense of Article 4.

3.1. The discussion in note 2 has already shown that the *terms* which describe the substantive scope of application of the Convention in a positive or negative manner have *to be identified* under the CISG and not under domestic law or other conventions. This problem is of specific relevance when it comes to finding out whether the CISG expressly provides otherwise, i.e. regulates specific aspects of a problem, which is generally excluded. It is quite obvious, however, that no express, even if anonymous, rejection of certain national concepts can be demanded (similarly Schlechtriem, 19) as is indeed known under the CISG (e.g. Article 45, paragraph 3 and Article 61, paragraph 3; but there are quite a number of other articles which at least can be seen in this light). It is sufficient that the CISG contains other options to settle the problem. Here the general principles under Article 7, paragraph 2, are insufficient. But when was such express provision made? Schlechtriem (19), in our view, is basically right in believing that national law on validity will not apply when the CISG provides a *functionally adequate solution* to the problem which has been settled nationally by questioning the validity of the contract, e.g. no rescission in the case of error on the character of a person under domestic law (119 (2), German BGB), if the problem can be solved pursuant to Article 71 (Article 8, note 3.4.). Honnold (97) holds a similar view, but even goes beyond and believes that the crucial question is whether the domestic rule is invoked by the same operative facts that invoke a rule of the Convention. If this is the case, the domestic law is dispensed by the Convention. Practice must show whether or not such a far-reaching general formula will prove its worth. The idea should be supported nevertheless. Heiz ("Validity of Contracts Under the United Nations Convention on Contracts for the International Sale of Goods, April 11, 1980, and Swiss Contract Law", Vanderbilt Journal of Transnational Law, Volume 30, (1987), 639 fol) has explained on the basis of this argumentation that Article 24, paragraph 1, clause 4 OR in most cases would not apply apart from the Convention in regard to an important error on a fact which by the person who erred was considered as belonging to the very foundations of a contract. Thus he chose an example that is similar to the one Schlechtriem mentioned. As a result, the view could crystallize, with respect to error on the character, that the relevant national rules as a matter of principle should not be invoked apart from the CISG. According to the opposite view, at least under Austrian law, rescission of an error is to be judged by 871 fol Austrian ABGB if this is the applicable law, because according to the latter, lack of intention is equal to defect in validity. This is clearly voiced by Lessiak ("Kaufrechtsabkommen und Irrtumsanfechtung", Juristische Blätter 1989, p. 487 fol, as above p. 496).

3.2. When the CISG itself proceeds on the assumption that *certain facts do not constitute a reason for nullifying a contract* (although they do under domestic law) then this includes, in our view, an express and different provision (express does not explicitly mean direct). This refers, for instance, to contracts without agreement on price (Article 55, notes 1 and 2) or certain grounds for failure (Article 79, note 13.6.).

4.1. Apart from those mentioned in subparas. (a) and (b) there are many other problems which are relevant to sales contracts and *which in part directly relate to the rights and obligations of the parties*, which are not and/or not directly provided for. Those include agency (authority), limitation, calculation of periods (individual aspects are, however, provided in the CISG - e.g. in Article 20), plurality and change in Contracting Parties, claims for liquidated damages and the amount of interests. *Domestic law* is invoked to the extent provided for in Article 7, paragraph 2. Also, unless conventions like the Limitation Convention (Part II) and, at a later date, the Agency Convention (Part IV) apply.

4.2. Another problem, which can only be mentioned briefly, here follows from the possible *concurrence between claims that derive from the contract of sales law and those that fall under the law of torts.*

Theoretically there is no doubt that in the context of sales contracts there can emerge rights under the law of torts which are not covered by the Convention and have, therefore, to be deduced from domestic law. Problems arise, however, in cases where the same fact may entail consequences both under the CISG and the domestic law of torts. This relates, in particular, to *cases of product liability*(Article 5). But the concurrence in regard to rights goes much further. This is also to be seen in connection with the broad term of breach of contract used in the Convention which is, in our view, expressed, above all, in Article 45, paragraph 1 and Article 61, paragraph 1 and not so much in Article 74 which does flesh out the consequences. We hold that in regard to this specific question (generally in note 2), the rules of the Convention should supersede domestic law. Schlechtriem (Borderline, 473 fol) makes an attempt to solve the problem by way of making a distinction between contractual and other interests with the contractual and their respective obligations being decided in accordance with the Convention. Since the qualification of the interests must not be characterized by domestic rules, they would have to be guided by the Convention. That is why we are afraid that not much will be gained by Schlechtriem's attempts because in the long run they will lead back to the question of the rights and obligations of the seller and the buyer under the Convention. We believe that it is still too early to try to make the general principles more precise; first a consensus will have to be achieved in regard to the categories of main cases.

Insofar as the Convention is invoked it must, in our view, be applied as it is, i.e. it *excludes claims under the domestic law of torts.* We, therefore, cannot join Khoo (BB, 47) who believes that the Convention would not want to take away rights from the parties which they would otherwise have. The Convention very well replaces existing rights by certain other rights.

We do not consider as sufficient other provisions regarding the competence for tort claims (Schlechtriem apparently believes otherwise, Borderline 475) in order to justify application of domestic law in regard to that. It would also be extremely problematic to limit the consequences of such application by interpreting that law in the light of the CISG because the recognized methods of interpretation will not yield sufficiently certain results in this context.

5.1. Concerning the validity of contracts a distinction is made between formal and substantive validity. *Formal validity* may depend on keeping with provisions on form. The Convention provides for this so that domestic law will apply only in exceptional cases, namely when a reservation is made against the freedom of form (compare Articles 11, 12 and 29, note 2). Hence, this rule above all relates to the *substantive validity* of the contract. It is, however, pointed out that a distinction between provisions of validity as to substance and such relating to form can often be doubtful (Herber/Doralt, 41). In our view, obligations should be prevented from being re-introduced through the backdoor, by declaring certain form requirements to be substantive.

The validity of the contract in terms of substance depends on *fulfilment of specific contract law provisions*, which for instance could be aimed at fighting unfair behaviour that is contrary to normal commercial conduct (fraud, threat, profiteering). In this context, such situation should be mentioned where the rights and obligations of the parties are grossly imbalanced and where the contract is declared invalid by virtue of law for those and other reasons (e.g. impossibility of performance). By 1972 UNIDROIT had already submitted a draft convention on the validity of international sales contracts (ETUDE XVI/B, Doc. 22, U.D.P. 1972) which was examined in the process of preparing the CISG, but was not included (Enderlein, Ausarbeitung, 3 fol). As to the effects on validity it does not matter whether or not the relevant contracts are invalid by virtue of law or voidable (directly by the parties or the judge at the request of the parties) (Schlechtriem, 18 fol; Honnold, 97), nor does it matter whether invalidity is absolute or can be remedied by procuring a (governmental) approval. Validity or invalidity of a contract are governed by the applicable national law.

In regard to the contractual validity, the *statute of the contract* is applied in general, i.e. the law which under the decisive conflict-of-law rules (Introductory remarks 2.3., Article 1, note 6.2. and Part IV of the Hague Convention on the Law Applicable to Contracts for the International Sale of Goods) governs contracts.

The substantive validity of international sales contracts can furthermore depend on *norms of an economy-managing or economy-controlling character*. In such case, each State will apply his *own domestic rules* without invoking conflict-of-law rules. This is also true of courts and arbitral tribunals (however with restrictions, above all in the case of international arbitral tribunals), provided that the relationship to be judged is substantially related to the State in question. Other States, which are related in such a way, demand at the same time that their relevant rules be invoked. But apart from some provisions in conventions there is no general obligation to take foreign public prohibitions and permissions requirements into account. (On the overall problem see Lando, International Encyclopedia, 112 fol).

The parties to the contract, however, have to *consider the existence of those rules*. Were they do not do so, the course of the transaction would slacken if the State which had prescribed the prohibitions or permissions requirements had a real influence on that process. Article 54 of the Convention is based on the same assumption.

5.2. The examples given for validity requirements should have made clear that, on the one hand, it was indeed not possible insofar to bring about broad unification and that, on the other, the States could not renounce the inclusion of a relevant reservation in regard to national law. Concerns are, therefore, not unfounded that those provisions could turn out to be the "black hole" which *shortens the scope of application of the CISG* (Winship, Commentary, 636). Indications of that kind are already given in publications (examples in note 6.2.). This trend can be countered at present by scientific efforts at the international level which are aimed at a narrow interpretation of the possibility to declare void under domestic law specific clauses or usages (note 6.1.) and at a broad interpretation of other express provisions of the Convention (note 3), but against which Lessiak expresses himself (loc sit, note 3.1., p. 492 fol).

6.1. In regard to specific contract provisions, the same considerations apply as for the contract as a whole (note 5). In addition, the question should be asked how the contract in its entirety is to be treated when *only some provisions* are declared *void*. It has to be answered pursuant to domestic law.

6.2. There are legislative rules in a number of countries to prevent abuse of *general business conditions*. Those are, in part, limited to consumer sales. At least the British Unfair Contract Terms Act of 1977 to a large extent exempts international sales contracts. Insofar the problem is irrelevant. But other provisions of that kind relate completely or to a lesser degree to international sales contracts in the meaning of the Convention (regarding the legal situation in several countries see H. Rudolph/G. Neumann/P.-M. Petzow, Allgemeine Geschäftsbedingungen und Vertragsgestaltung, Berlin 1985, p. 31 fol). Herber (Doralt, 36) rightly pointed to the fact that the Contracting States' domestic law within the Convention's scope of application has to grant autonomy to conclude contracts unless such protective provisions can be regarded as obstacles to the contract's effectiveness. This presupposes, in our view, that the relevant provisions, whether they are part of specific legislative acts or of general contractual rules, can clearly be recognized as referring to the validity of the contract and do not have to be re-interpreted as such.

We also believe that the problem of to what extent of domestic law contradict the validity of specific contractual provisions, which from time to time is raised in publications (see also note 3 of Article 6), has to be solved in a similar way. While Winship ("International Sales Contracts Under the 1980 Vienna Convention", Uniform Commercial Code Journal, 1984/1, p. 66 fol) seems to understand "mandatory" rules of law to be the international mandatory rules of the *Lex fori* in the meaning of Article 7, paragraph 2, ECE Convention 1980, Magnus (133) obviously sees this problem in a larger perspective. We hold that mandatory rules of domestic law should not be interpreted as contradicting the validity of specific contractual provisions in the meaning of the CISG (it appears that Thieffry, 383, believes the same, while Kahn, Caractères, 399, leaves open the possibility of a broader interpretation of national law). This is unequivocal insofar as the CISG itself contains rules for this (note 3.1.). In regard to the area beyond, which is covered by the general principles of Article 7, paragraph 2, one should be very careful. Mandatory national rules should be invoked at most if they provide for the voidness of contrary stipulations not just implicitly. Typically, international mandatory norms are formulated clearly so that one can assume that they will prevail more often than normal mandatory rules of domestic law. Generally, there is still a *large degree of uncertainty* in this matter, but Hellner (Dubrovnik, 361) seems to be right in admitting that the unification of control in regard to standard terms of contract, that he would find desirable, might be very difficult to attain.

7. Basically, recognition of a specific conduct as *usage and non-validity* exclude each other. It is nonetheless possible that certain countries consider as void internationally recognized usages or such usages which are agreed between the parties.

8. It is a fact that the Convention mentions problems of title in providing in Article 30 for the obligation of the seller to pass title in the goods, and also indirectly in Article 41, stipulating that the goods delivered have to be free from third party rights or claims (see furthermore Article 42). *It is, however, up to the applicable domestic law to determine the time and conditions of such passing of title.*

These problems are extremely complex so that they could not be solved with the CISG. Even the attempt at regulating one partial problem, namely the protection of the *bona fide* purchaser of movable property by means of a uniform law whose draft had been prepared in the framework of UNIDROIT (UNIDROIT Yearbook, 1967-68, vol. 1, 222 fol), was not successful.

Article 5

(Exclusion of seller's liability for death or personal injury)

This Convention does not apply to the liability of the seller for death or personal injury caused by the goods to any person[1].

1.1. This rule relates to *products liability*. This term refers to the liability of the manufacturer and/or importer, seller and/or supplier for personal injury, damages and further possible damages to property which have been caused by defective goods. In a number of States this kind of liability has developed into an independent legal institute. While it is based in some countries (e.g. FRG) on the law of torts, it is construed in others (e.g. France) as falling under the law of contracts. There is also a combination of both (USA, Britain) (Liebold, Produktenhaftung, 1 fol). By enacting the guideline of the Council of the European Communities of 25 July 1985 for the alignment of the Member States' legal and administrative rules on liability for defective products (ABl. EG No. L 210/29-33), the obligation was placed on those States to put into effect relevant and generally mandatory liability norms under the law of torts (Liebold, "Zur Vereinheitlichung des Produktenhaftungsrechts der EG-Staaten durch die EG-Produktenhaftungsrichtlinie", RiA, 112, Beilage zu AW-Dok., 1989/27, p. II).

This article clearly stipulates that national law and/or possibly other conventions apply to *liability for personal* injury caused by the goods sold. It is not relevant in this context whether it is the buyer himself, his employees, other Contracting Parties in the purchaser chain or third parties who suffer such personal injury. What is relevant, however, is whether or not it was the defect in the goods sold which caused the injury. Provided that is so, the buyer can, as a result, claim damages under national law (Schlechtriem, 20) also by way of recourse where they will typically appear as claims for damages.

1.2. Proposals to exclude products liability for damages or injuries *other than personal injury*, as in damages in property, were not successful. It seems that in spite of the opposite view of the Norwegian delegate (O. R. 245) the reverse conclusion has to be drawn from that situation that they come under the Convention. The arguments put forward against the proposal to exclude products liability in the case of such damages (set-back for the unification of law, difficulties in distinguishing claims) only serve to emphasize this. Therefore, in our view, claims from products liability for damages other than personal injury in the relationship between the Contracting Parties must be considered as part of the Convention and in general as being regulated by it (in particular because of the provisions on quality and the rights of the buyer). This is clearly the dominating view expressed in publications (Schlechtriem, 20 fol; Honold, 101 fol; Stoll/Freiburg, 259; Khoo/BB, 50; Herber/Doralt, 38).

Only occasionally is it affirmed that the Convention is not to apply to product liability (M. Ndulo, "The Vienna Sales Convention 1980 and the Hague Uniform Laws on the International Sale of Goods 1964: A Comparative Analysis", ICLQ, vol. 38 (1989), p. 5). There is no room for other claims under the law of torts (Stoll, 259, believes differently) because the Convention, even if only indirectly, has given a qualification of its own, and the possibility of an alternative application of national law cannot be made dependent on the qualification of that legal institute in domestic law (also note 4.2. of Article 4). It is exactly such attempts which Article 7 is directed against. However, it is not excluded that product liability claims from non-personal injury, which cannot be regarded as breaches of contract, are judged under the national law of torts. Naturally, third parties can assert claims from product liability as a result of damages other than personal injury under the applicable rules directly against the responsible person (manufacturer, seller). Given the typical constellation of international sales contracts this will not be the standard case. A third party will, in most cases, prefer to address his immediate partner, *inter alia*, because the latter is more easily accessible for him (in general he is from the same country).

Insofar as a case of product liability causes personal injury and other damages, both aspects are to be judged invoking different rules. Such *duplication* is in no way unusual in regard to issues which are subject to unification of law.

Article 6

(Exclusion, variation or derogation by the parties)

The parties may exclude[1] the application of this Convention or, subject to article 12[2], derogate from or vary the effect[3] of any of its provisions.

1.1. The Convention, by virtue of law, applies to all sales contracts which come under its sphere of application. The parties may, however, *exclude it as a whole*, i.e. including Part II regarding the formation of the contract. This may facilitate the adoption of the Convention by certain States because it allows those business circles which cannot get to like it or, at least, not at once to evade it and/or grants them a longer period of adaptation, thus building down possible resistance. Honnold (105) points out that this degree of freedom for the parties in concluding a contract was made possible by excluding certain, meaning those governed by nationally mandatory rules, transactions and issues from the Convention.

1.2. While Article 3, sentence 2 ULIS provided that the exclusion can be express or implicit, the CISG does not say anything about how this should be done. The Convention can be excluded by expressly declaring so in the offer and also in the acceptance, which then, however, as a rule would take on the character of a counter-offer (Huber, 426 fol; Bonell/BB, 54 fol). But the view is overwhelmingly held that there is also a possibility of *implicitly excluding it* in its entirety (Bonell/BB, 55 mentioning further proof). By no longer mentioning such implied exclusion it was to be prevented that requirements for it were set too low (as already mentioned in the Secretariat's Commentary, O. R. 17) or that a hypothetical party will were construed in this sense (Huber, 425 fol). There must, however, be relatively clear indications (see also note 1.3.) that such an exclusion is indeed wanted. In regard to the Convention in its entirety this will, in our view, rather seldom be the case in practice.

Under the meaning of Article 7 and of Article 3 of the preambular part the *Convention is to apply if there is doubt*.

1.3. If the Contracting Parties have agreed invoking the *law of one Contracting State*, this does not, as is correctly believed by a majority, mean exclusion of the Convention (among others Schlechtriem, 22; Herber/Doralt, 42; Herber/Freiburg, 104; Bonell, 56). Loewe, 24, speaks up in favour of exploring the party will). In regard to the case most likely to occur in practice, given under Article 1, paragraph 1, subpara. (a), Vékas (346) expresses himself in favour of the opposite assumption. When a State participates in the Convention the latter can be assumed to be part of his domestic law so that additional reference to it could be considered as superfluous at first, and/or for the reference to make sense, as an exclusion of the CISG. But the application of the Convention does in no way make the application of the other parts of the national law irrelevant (Article 4, note 3; Article 7, note, 11). Therefore, it must be recommended to the parties to determine the national law that is applicable in addition to the Convention (Article 3, note 11) so that they can avoid the uncertainties involved in determining that law, using the conflict-of-law norms. When the parties agree on a shortened form expressing that a specific national law is to apply, then it would clearly amount to a wrong interpretation of their intention to consider this as an exclusion of the Convention. There is also a trend to reject such an exclusion in the FRG's jurisdiction in regard to Article 3 ULIS which is similar to Article 6 of the Convention. The 41 decisions collected by Schlechtriem (Magnus, 123 fol) on this matter are very illustrative and instructive. The interpretation preferred here is also supported by the fact that two proposals (Canada, Belgium), which aimed toward the opposite direction (O. R., 86), were clearly rejected. Agreement on the application of the law of a non-Contracting State will quite often amount to an exclusion of the Convention (Bonell/BB, 56). However, it remains to be explored here whether it should not be referred to in addition.

If the parties wish to safely *exclude application of the Convention*, they do so best in agreeing to invoke the law of a specific State under exclusion of the CISG (similarly now Winship, "International Sales Contracts under the 1980 Vienna Convention", Uniform Commercial Code Law Journal, 1984/1, p. 65, reacting to views cited in said place which reject the possibility of an implied exclusion). It is not advisable to exclude the Convention without replacement since in that case, the applicable domestic law will have to be determined by mostly using the rather vague conflict-of-law rules.

Reference made in the contract *to specific national rules,* e.g. in modifying them, can be considered as excluding the Convention as a whole only when they appear to be an expression of the parties' conviction that the Convention should not apply. This may follow, for instance, from the terminology used or from the system of the contract, while the contrary can occur when the rules invoked refer to such issues which are not regulated by the Convention anyway. On no account can the exclusion of the Convention be deduced merely from agreement of such terms of contract which contradict specific CISG provisions because deviating individual exclusions are indeed compatible with the CISG (note 2; but not in agreement Bonell/BB, 56).

2. This reservation serves to emphasize the rule given in the last sentence of Article 12 (Article 12, note 4).

Bonell (BB, 62) has drawn attention to the fact that there are *further Articles* (in particular Article 4) which must not be *excluded* because this would amount to nonsense. We agree in respect of the result, but there is no question of nonsense in this context; this is very well a matter of interpretation. At the time of the diplomatic conference the generally expressed convictions, including the above-mentioned rejection of the Canadian proposal (note 1.3.) had in no way been sensitized toward prohibiting the exclusion and even less the modification of Article 4 of which particularly subpara. (a) is of interest here. In the meantime, the general convictions have been correctly changed, and now legislative omissions have to be compensated by interpretational efforts.

3.1. When the contract is governed by the CISG, the *mandatory rules* of the otherwise applicable national law will be left out of the framework of the Convention's substantive scope of application. To start with, they are replaced by the Convention's provisions. The parties retain, however, the right to modifications. They can make agreements which are in contradiction to the mandatory rules of domestic law (different view on the very similar Article 3 ULIS, Herber/Dölle, 22 and on the result of the present rule also Bonell/BB, 54; evading Honnold, 112). This follows, in our view, also from the fact that a Canadian proposal which was aimed at declaring the exclusion of certain basic obligations (good faith, care) inadmissible was rejected by a large majority (O. R., 86). Most national laws, however, do not contain many mandatory rules under the substantive scope of application of the Convention. The freedom of the parties to make their own arrangements generally meets the needs of international commercial relations. Transactions which are subject to large restrictions in many countries, essentially are excluded from the sphere of application of the Convention (in particular Article 2, subpara. (a), but also Article 4).

Given the growing efforts of fighting *grossly unjust contractual practices* in international economic relations, it would, however, not have been superfluous to take precautions in order to secure certain basic requirements. We are now faced with the expected attempts (CISG Commentary 1985, 45) to invoke the national law instead (*inter alia* Bonell/BB, 60, and note 6.2. of Article 4). Once the dam has broken down to national law, the latter enters without encountering obstacles; and there is a risk that safeguards will be invoked which go beyond the requirements of international trade. As a result, the success of the unification of law is diminished.

Grossly unjust agreements, which deviate from the CISG, can - under Articles 7, 8 and 9, and possibly under the preambular paragraph - only be interpreted restrictively. They can be declared void only under *domestic law* pursuant to Article 4, subpara. (a), whose possibilities should, however, not be abused.

3.2. Considering the discussion held at the diplomatic conference (O. R., 252 fol) the Convention can be interpreted in such a way that its application to such contracts which are not covered, can be agreed. In this case the substantive and territorial, and hence personnel and time *scope of application*, can be *extended*. Such an agreement can be made expressly or implicitly, but in the latter case it has to be sufficiently clear. The mandatory rules of the applicable domestic law, however, are not affected by this (Honnold, 109; Bonell/BB, 62). This follows from the fact that a proposal by the former GDR, aiming toward expressly empowering the parties to agree an extended application of the Convention, was rejected. The reason given for the decision was that a circumvention of mandatory national rules was to be prevented in this way (O. R. 252 fol). The Agency Convention provides for a broadened application by virtue of a relevant declaration by a State (Article 30). An agreed application of the Convention beyond the territorial scope of application is considered possible, including the possibility of superseding the otherwise applicable domestic law (Siehr, 611 fol).

Chapter II

GENERAL PROVISIONS

Article 7[1]

(Interpretation of Convention and relationship with national law)

(1) In the interpretation of this Convention[2], regard is to be had to its international character[3] and to the need to promote uniformity in its application[4] and the observance of good faith[5] in international trade[6].

(2)[7] Questions concerning matters governed by this Convention[8] which are not expressly settled in it are to be settled in conformity with the general principles on which it is based[9] or, in the absence of such principles[10], in conformity with the law applicable by virtue of the rules of private international law[11].

1. This rule is one of the *most discussed* rules of the CISG. One of the subjects of the XIIth International Congress on Comparative Law (Australia 1986) was dedicated to this issue, and it also played an important role at the Third UNIDROIT Congress on private law (Rome 1987) (International Uniform Law in Practice, Rome/New York 1988, in particular the second item, ibid, p. 163 fol, Enderlein giving the general report, Interpretation). We have to confine ourselves here to explaining some basic ideas.

2.1. During the preparation and the holding of the diplomatic conference (O. R., 87) there was an intensive debate regarding the extent to which the principles for interpretation as developed in Article 1, in particular the principle of good faith, were relevant for the *interpretation of the Convention* and for the relationship between the parties, and possibly even for the conclusion and realization of the contract. Norway suggested (O. R., 87) to consider the observance of good faith at the end of what is now Article 8, paragraph 3, making it clear that the principle would apply to the declarations of the parties and thus the contract. Italy (ibid) expressed even further-reaching considerations, suggesting that in including this principle and that of international co-operation in a separate article, reference should be made more to the conduct of the parties, not just at the time of performance, but also at the time of the conclusion of the contract, rather than to the interpretation of the Convention or of the contract. In the context of discussing these two proposals (O. R. 255 fol), which were finally rejected (O. R., 87), it became evident that, as in the case of Article 6, the majority of delegations were cautious not to permit that unjust contracts may be avoided or corrected by way of the CISG. Neutral arguments, such as non-clarity of the principle, no need for its inclusion, were given at the conference mainly to explain the motives for the rejection. These arguments were put forward in another context more clearly by the American delegate Farnsworth (Problems of Unification, 18 fol). In regard to the growing restriction of party autonomy in the industrialized countries (P.-M. Petzow, Rechtsfragen der Verantwortlichkeit aus vor- und nachvertraglichen Abreden in den intersystemaren Wirtschaftsbeziehungen, doctoral thesis B, HfÖ 1989, 73 fol) the situation has changed over the past ten years since the adoption of the Convention (loc sit, 35).

Although the present-day wording refers to the Convention, no strict distinction can be made between the interpretation of the Convention and the agreement of the parties. When certain principles are applied in interpreting the Convention's provisions, they must have an *effect on agreements between the parties to which the Convention is applied*. It is exactly for party agreements that the principle of good faith must acquire particular importance, for it has to be assumed, in regard to the Convention's provisions, that they observe that principle. This is not always true of party agreements. A provision would have a limited effect if it did not also refer to the interpretation of party agreements. Even though this might have been the intention of some delegations, the final Convention has to be interpreted as a whole and in such a way that each and every of its provisions acquires a meaning. Eörsi (Convention, 348 fol), who had expressed his opinion already in 1983, recognized the limited role of the principle of good faith and regretted it (reserved also Honnold/Freiburg, 144). Quite a number of well-known authors in the meantime voiced their belief that the principle of good faith also addresses the parties and their conduct, and refers to agreements between them (Bonell/BB, 84 giving further examples; Kahn, 961; Ziegel, National Report of Canada on item I.C. of the XIIth International Congress on Comparative Law, 18). Some of the authors want to achieve this in deducing good faith from a number of provisions as being a general principle underlying the Convention, which then is applied in accordance with Article 7, paragraph 2 (note 10.1.) (Honnold, 125; C. Samson, National Report of Canada and Quebec on item I.C. of the XIIth International Congress on Comparative Law, 34; Bonell/BB, 85; Kahn, Caractères, 398, also sees the connection). Others refer to the closely related basic principle under which one would have to behave according to the standards of a "reasonable man" which they consider implemented in the Convention (Schlechtriem, 25). We share the conviction of Winship

(Commentary, 635) that the criticism, which seeks to broaden the effect of good faith, will in the course of time lead to the recognition of a general obligation of the parties to behave accordingly.

2.2. *In interpreting* the Convention a *distinction* has to be made between Parts I to III, on the one hand, and Part IV, on the other (Honnold, 134 fol). While the classical methods of interpretation under international law are applied to Part IV, the other parts of the Convention are to be interpreted in accordance with the emerging new method under the international uniform law. The latter is governed by such rules of the international uniform law as have just been commented on, and absorbs elements of the methods of interpretation under international law as well as a synthesis of methods which have developed in the national laws (in detail see Maskow, "On the Interpretation of the Uniform Rules of the 1980 UN Convention on Contracts for the International Sale of Goods", in: National Reports for the XIIth International Congress of Comparative Law, Potsdam-Babelsberg 1986, p. 5 fol). Scientific analysis makes its own contribution to that matter.

3. To have regard to the *international character* of the Convention means, above all, not to proceed in interpreting it from national juridical constructions and terms (Introductory remarks 2.6.). This does not only refer to judges but also to the parties which in settling their differences of opinion first and foremost have to interpret the applicable rules. The meaning of terms and rules thus has to be concluded from the context and the function they have (Introductory remarks 2.6.). If reference to other materials is necessary, then those should primarily be international documents, above all those documents which have a connection to the CISG, such as preparatory documents, including protocols; and possibly the Limitation Convention and the Agency Convention. Usages can, in the meaning of Article 9, also be relevant in determining what is in conformance with the international character of the Convention. Likewise, in international trade this can be widely recognized non-governmental codifications, e.g. the INCOTERMS, the Uniform Rules and Practices for Documentary Credits and the Uniform Rules for Collections. This can be done independently of the degree by which they are already regarded as codification of usages. Surely, the rules of the PICC project under preparation in the framework of UNIDROIT can be used in this sense.

This also includes that the *legal institutes have to be qualified* in accordance with the common will of the Contracting States as expressed in the Convention; meaning that once a specific issue has been legally solved under the Convention, there will be no room left for functionally equivalent, but differently construed national rules to be applied.

We believe that it is not generally recommendable to determine the origin of certain provisions and to interpret those rules according to the *law of their origin*, as Thieffry (378 fol) seems to have in mind.

4. Since the CISG is *applied* by the deciding organs *in a decentralized fashion*, there is a great risk that those organs reach differing solutions, which could reduce the results of the unification of law. Disharmony in decisions cannot be excluded even if the international character of the CISG under Article 3 is strictly observed; additional efforts are required. Those efforts could include the taking into account of decisions which already exist in other countries when looking for a solution pursuant to the Convention. This is a method which was widely used in foreign trade arbitration in regard to the General Conditions of Delivery of Goods/CMEA and has helped making the finding of a decision more objective. In other countries foreign rulings are taken into consideration to a growing extent, but in differentiated form, as can be seen from the reports to the XIIth International Congress on Comparative Law on item I.C.1. (summarizing Honnold/Freiburg, 120 fol). What matters here is not a prejudicial effect of rulings by foreign courts or arbitrational tribunals and not that the decision taken by an organ, which by accident was entrusted first to deal with a specific legal issue, is attached a particularly great importance; rather, the existing material in regard to relevant rulings has to be taken account of when giving the reasons for a decision. A basic prerequisite for this is to make the decisions taken in respect of the CISG known in an appropriate form (Introductory remarks 1.3.).

5. *Observance of the principle of good faith* means to display such conduct as is normal among businessmen. Hence, no exaggerated demands can be made, and observance of good faith does in no way necessarily include the establishment of material justice between the contracting parties. It is exactly these concerns which give reason to attribute to the principle of good faith only a limited role. Assuming that the provisions of the Convention are themselves an expression of good faith, the underlying principles of the Convention, to be explained below (note 9), have to be also conceived as manifestations of this principle. In applying the Convention to the agreements of the parties, the former has to be interpreted in such a way that the conduct prescribed coincides with the principle of

good faith, so that deviating conduct must be qualified as unlawful. This means, for instance, that unjust clauses are interpreted, in the case of doubt, in favour of the disadvantaged party. However, a contract with clear wording cannot be modified in this way. When judging what is conduct based on the principle of good faith, the usages and practice in concluding contracts cannot be left out of consideration (Article 9, note 8).

6. National *measures* for a conduct based on good faith are thus only relevant insofar as they are also the recognized measure for international trade.

7. Paragraph 2 also clarifies the relationship between the *Convention and domestic law* (Introductory remarks 2.3.). Since the laws can of necessity only be unified step by step, it remains unfinished work for now and cannot at once solve all legal issues involved in a concrete manifestation; as it is in this case international contracts of sale. The underlying idea of the unification of law is served best when such gaps are closed by way of supporting and complementary conventions (Introductory remarks 2.2.).

Another possibility would be to close the gaps within the substantive scope of application on the basis of the *principles governing the respective convention*. This, however, requires a particularly exact formulation of the substantive scope of application. And this is the road followed by ULIS in Article 17. An analysis of the consequences of such rule nonetheless has clearly established the problems involved (Mertens/Rehbinder, 143 fol; Dölle, XXXVI). They result, above all, from the fact that not all problems falling under the substantive sphere of application of the Convention, which are, however, not expressly regulated by it, can be solved in this way and/or that divergent solutions can be expected. But there were sufficient voices welcoming the ULIS principle and requesting a development of it under the CISG in order to promote the achievement of uniformity in international trade law (Bonell, 2 fol).

A third variant would be to immediately pass on to *national law* whenever gaps became apparent, as was done in 122, sec. 1 of the General Conditions of Delivery of Goods/CMEA. This was, however, no obstacle for arbitral tribunals to fill gaps also from within the General Conditions of Delivery of Goods/CMEA (Kemper/Strohbach/Wagner, 62 fol).

And finally, those methods can be combined.

For the sake of completeness it must be pointed out that there are *parallel methods of gap-filling*: 1. the (possibly broadened) interpretation of the contract (Article 8, in a way also Article 7, paragraph 1); and 2. recourse to usages and other practices (Article 9).

At the diplomatic conference Italy made an attempt to have recourse to domestic law excluded and, in the event of lacking general principles under the Convention, to have the parties attain a solution invoking the national law of both parties. Czechoslovakia suggested to immediately apply domestic law in the absence of a rule under the Convention. Bulgaria, in the same breath, wanted to have the conflict-of-law problem regulated in the sense of the law of the place of business of the seller (O. R., 87). A *compromise proposal by the former GDR* (O. R., 257), providing a combined solution, was eventually adopted.

8. Pursuant to Article 4 the Convention governs "the formation of the contract of sale and the rights and obligations of the seller and the buyer", i.e. the substance of the contract. Hence, a very broad scope of problems is addressed. Insofar as Article 4, subparas. (a) and (b) and Article 5 expressly declare the *non-applicability of the Convention* to certain matters, it is inadmissible to decide on the basis of its underlying general principles. We favour a broad interpretation of the words commented here which also leads to a relatively wide scope of application of the Convention. W. C. Vis ("Aspectos de los contratos de compraventa internacional de mercaderías no comprendidos por la Convención de Viena de 1980, Anuario Jurídico, 1983/X, p. 11 fol), who at the time of the holding of the Conference was director of the International Trade Law Branch, opts in favour of a narrow interpretation. He fears a reduction of legal security because of the insufficient predictability of the principles. We do not see such risk because of the very fact that a broad interpretation does not necessarily have to lead to invoking the general principles.

9.1. Gaps should be *closed* in the first place *from within the Convention*. This is in line with the aspiration to unify the law which, in a way, is established in the Convention itself (paragraph 3 of the preambular part, Article 7, paragraph 1) as one of its underlying principles. Such gap-filling can be done, as we believe, by applying such interpretation methods as extensive interpretation and analogy. The admissibility of analogy is directly addressed in the wording contained in the CISG because it is aimed at obtaining, from several comparable rules, one rule for a not expressly covered fact and/or a general rule under which the fact can be subsumed. When one interpretation reaching this far beyond the wording of the law is expressly approved by the Convention's text, then this must all the more apply to an extensive interpretation. But it seems as though the Convention goes one step further permitting decisions which themselves go beyond analogy and reach into the area of a *creative continuation of the development of the law*. It also appears to be admissible under the Convention that decisions can be the result of principles which the Convention itself formulates and which do not necessarily have to be reflected in individual rules. Such principles include (similarly Bonell/BB, 80) good faith (Article 7, paragraph 1), contract autonomy (Article 6) and the principle of dispatch (Article 27).

The *conduct of a reasonable person* is relevant in the CISG in several contexts (c. Article 8, paragraph 2, Article 25), in that reasonable conduct is expected from one of the Contracting Parties or from a potential Contracting Party (Article 16, paragraph 2, subpara. (b); Article 35, paragraph 2, subpara. (b)). Article 44 permits a reasonable excuse, and Article 79 mentions conducts which "could not reasonably be expected".

Other formulations, too, like the reference to comparable circumstances (e.g. Article 55) or to a reasonable period of time for performance (e.g. Article 63, paragraph 1), aim at declaring as binding *normal commercial conduct* in international trade and using it as a yardstick for the parties' conduct. Thus this yardstick can be used for those cases for which it has not expressly been declared binding. Taking it as a basis can, therefore, be considered as a general principle of the Convention. This includes also the principle of good faith (Article 7, note 5).

Another criterion to be conceived as a general principle of the Convention, at least when it comes to assessing the scope of the legal consequences which are linked to non-conformance or failure of a party and/or to the overall legal consequences, can be the *predictability of effects* (Article 25; Article 35, paragraph 2, subpara. (b); Article 42, paragraph 1, subpara. (a) and Article 74; and in a way also Article 79, paragraph 1).

It appears in a largely generalized form in Article 80, but is recognizable also in the concrete rules of Article 8, paragraph 3; Article 29, paragraph 2; Article 35, paragraph 3; Article 40; Article 41, first sentence; Article 43, paragraph 2; Article 47, paragraph 2; Article 48, paragraph 2, second sentence; and Article 63, paragraph 2.

The *obligation* of the parties *to co-operate* in performing the contract, in particular in the case of disturbances, with the aim of minimizing the effect of such disturbances on the party who caused it or at whose place it occurred, can be synthesized from a number of articles (Article 34, second sentence; Article 37; Article 48, paragraph 1; Article 85 fol; and also Article 77).

We also count the *principle of specific performance* (subject to Article 28) among the general principles of the Convention. This follows above all from the provisions governing the rights in the case of breach of contract (Articles 46 - 52; Articles 62 - 65).

The discussion held so far has shown that there is *gratifying agreement* with regard to the principles contained in the CISG (in particular the summary of the principles established from the national reports on item I.C.1. to the XIIth International Congress on Comparative Law, see Honnold/Freiburg, 139 fol, which are largely congruous with the ones developed above). However, agreement on principles does not yet mean agreement on their application.

9.2. It is, in our view, *not* possible to obtain the Convention's general principles from an *analysis prepared by comparison of the laws* of the most important legal systems of the Contracting States (similarly van der Velden, National Report of the Netherlands to the XIIth International Congress on Comparative Law, 0013) as it was supported, in some cases, in regard to Article 17 ULIS (e.g. Wahl/Dölle, 139) and is occasionally advocated also for the CISG (Bonell/BB, 81). This also follows from the impossibility to choose, on the basis of objective criteria, the most important of the legal systems of the countries which were involved in preparing the Convention. The wording of the Convention does in no way support the application of this methods. Where such need arises, domestic law will have to be invoked.

9.3. If priorities can be established under the admissible methods of interpretation, the *method closest to the wording* should in our view be preferred, e.g. analogy before deduction from general principles. Hellner (78) also points to the paramount importance of the Convention's wording for its interpretation.

10. An overburdening of the first alternative under Article 7, paragraph 2, would certainly not serve the unification of law. One will have to assume, in particular, that *entire legal institutes*, which are missing in the Convention, cannot be construed from its principles (examples given in Article 4, note 4.1.). This refers, no doubt, also to penalties. It is, however, not excluded in our view that solutions for problems provided for under the Convention, e.g. the reasons for

exemption (Article 79 fol), will also apply in regard to legal institutes which are not included in the Convention, like exemptions from penalties.

11. The *conflict-of-law issue* itself is not decided under the Convention (Introductory remarks 2.3.; Article 1, note 6). As decisive as the statute of sales contracts is, special connecting factors might apply. We cannot join Kahn (Caracteres, 398), who advised to renounce the complementary reference to national law because this would heighten the legal uncertainty.

Article 8[1]

(Interpretation of conduct of a party)

(1) For the purposes of this Convention statements made by and other conduct of a party[2] are to be interpreted according to his intent where the other party knew or could not have been unaware[3] what that intent was.

(2) If the preceding paragraph is not applicable[4], statements made by and other conduct of a party are to be interpreted according to the understanding that a reasonable person of the same kind as the other party would have had in the same circumstances[5].

(3) In determining the intent of a party or the understanding a reasonable person would have had[6], due consideration is to be given to all relevant circumstances[7] of the case including the negotiations[8], any practices[9] which the parties have established between themselves, usages[10] and any subsequent conduct of the parties[11].

1. While Article 7 deals with the interpretation of the Convention, which, however, has its effect on the interpretation of the agreements between the parties (Article 7, note 2), Article 8 governs the interpretation of statements and the otherwise legally relevant conduct of the parties. It does not refer only to *offer and acceptance* (Articles 14 and/or 18) and other acts done before the conclusion of the contract, withdrawal or revocation of an offer (Article 15, paragraph 2; Article 16, paragraph 1) and rejection of an offer (Article 17), but also to acts which are committed during the *realization* and with the objective of *terminating the contract*, e.g. notice of defects (Article 39, paragraph 1), notice of third party rights or claims (Article 43, paragraph 1), assertion of claims because of breach of con-

tract and related claims, including the right to performance (e.g. Article 46, paragraph 1; Article 62), damages and claims for compensation of expenses incurred (Article 45, paragraph 1, subpara. (b); Article 61, paragraph 1, subpara. (b) in relation to Article 74 fol; Article 85; Article 86, paragraph 1)), mitigation of loss (Article 52), suspension of performance of obligations (Article 71, paragraph 1), avoidance of contract (Article 49, paragraph 1; Article 64, paragraph 1; Article 72, paragraph 1; Article 73), and restitution of supplies and expenses in the case of avoidance of contract (Article 81, paragraph 2). In specific cases (Article 52), even acceptance is an act which is to be interpreted under Article 8. And finally, the setting of an additional period for delivery (Article 47, paragraph 1; Article 63, paragraph 1) has to be mentioned. Apart from these most important examples, under the CISG numerous such acts, provided for in the contract or not, can emerge in connection with a possible modification or avoidance of the contract when claims for breach of contract are asserted. Their interpretation is also governed by Article 8.

2.1. The statements or other conduct, - as can be seen from the further text of the Article, - are such acts by which the *intent of the respective party* is to be expressed ("according to his intent"). This condition is given in general when the statement is made, unless the latter is of a purely informational character (e.g. communication that the goods have been dispatched). In this context there can be problems of interpretation, e.g. where the communication is considered to be an obligation and opinions diverge on whether this obligation was fulfilled through a specific act. Article 8, by analogy, would also apply to such a case.

2.2. Above all, in the context of the *other conduct* of a party, a distinction can be made between such conduct which is to express a legal intent (examples in Article 18, note 2) and mere acts of performance where this is not so. The rules of interpretation of Article 8 refer to the first-mentioned case, are however, applicable analogously to the mere acts of performance insofar as there is a need for interpretation. A party may in any case express his intent by a *statement* which is forwarded to the other party. There are cases where this is expressly prescribed (Article 26). Where this is not the case and/or where it is expressly permitted that a party can express his intent also by other conduct (Article 18, paragraph 1), a statement is not necessary but recommendable because it is as a rule clearer and can, therefore, be interpreted more easily.

In some cases, above all in the event of *information* which at the same time expresses an intent, the need for a statement is in the nature of things (non-conformity claim).

2.3. Article 8 relates directly only to the acts (legal acts - referred to below also as acts) of a party and contains no provision for the *interpretation of contracts*. Insofar as contracts are based on corresponding unilateral acts by the parties, there will be no problems. This also holds true where a party accepts the contract offer made by the other party, for instance, by signing it. When the contract, however, is contained in a joint document of the parties, it cannot be generally determined which party made a specific statement becoming part of the document. Basically, each party has then made a statement relating to the entire substance of the contract document so that the general rule can be applied, as in the case of corresponding individual statements of intent, i.e. the relevant clause is interpreted first as the statement of the one party and then as the statement of the second party (so already in the Secretariat's Commentary, O. R., 18; Farnsworth/BB, 101), their identity resulting in a common intent. Honnold (137) wants to apply here only paragraph 3, which seems inconsistent to us.

3.1. Hereby, the subjective theory or *theory of intent* of the conclusion of a contract has found its way into the Convention. It is the intent of the party undertaking the legal act which is decisive. Such intent has an effect only when the other party is actually or supposedly aware of it. At the conclusion of the contract it becomes the common intent of both parties, if the other party accepts it. The fact that acceptance refers to the offer has, of course, an influence on its interpretation (because, e.g. an offer provides a substantive frame). The unequivocal cases are covered here, while otherwise paragraph 2 applies. When one party *clearly expresses* his intent through a legal act, the addressee cannot pretend to have insufficient knowledge of that intent. The same applies when the acting party has not clearly expressed his intent, or even *disguised* it, but the addressee knew of the real intent. It would, however, be up to the acting party to prove this. In this context, the factors mentioned in Article 3 will be of particular relevance. Such proof is made easier for him by a certain objectiveness in regard to the knowledge of the other party which is based on the fact that it suffices that the other party "could not to have been unaware". This notion is supposed to objectivize even more than "ought to have known" (O. R., 260). It follows from paragraph 1 that in the case of fictitious transactions the real substance is decisive. This does, however, not say anything about the validity of such transactions for it is the prohibitive norms of national law declaring contracts void which can be invoked here (Article 4, subpara. (a)).

The *decisive time* is, in our view, the moment when the conduct is displayed and/or taken note of. According to Farnsworth (BB, 98) this should be the moment when the conduct has its effect. That opinion, as we believe, is concurrent with ours, but is less clear and gives, therefore, might cause difficulties of interpretation.

3.2. Of particular importance are statements which are legal acts. To recognize the intent expressed by them, the *language* in which they are formulated is of considerable relevance. Without being able to discuss this issue in detail (for a detailed explanation see Reinhart/Dölle, 97 fol), we hold that one should proceed from the following principles:

- When a party reacts in substance to a statement it has to be generally assumed that he has understood it, unless the contrary can be deduced from the content of his reaction.

- When the reply to a statement is formulated in the same language as the statement itself or in the language of the country of the statements recipient or in a language which is customary in the relations between the countries where the parties have their places of business, it has to be assumed that the statement has been understood by the other party.

- Similar principles apply to statements made in the process of the performance of contracts, the language of the contract being of particular importance.

- Statements which are not made in a language which has possibly been agreed in the contract or which are made in a language which is not customary at all in the country of the recipient, even as business language, do not attain legal effect.

3.3. In some cases the CISG makes *assumptions on the interpretation of statements* (Article 9, paragraph 2; Article 48, paragraph 3; Article 55 fol). Since in such cases neither the party making the statement can refer to having meant the statement differently nor the statement's addressee can refer to having interpreted it differently, these assumptions practically have the effect of dispositive rules, although they are in part the result of lack of agreement. The parties, therefore, have to clearly show that through their action they wish to express an intent other than that assumed by law. This will regularly require a statement.

3.4. Since the CISG ignores problems of validity (Article 4, subpara. (a)) and the problems of rescission touch upon the validity, the rescission because of a defect in intent, notably a mistake, lies as a matter of principle outside the scope of application of the CISG (Honnold, 141; Farnsworth/BB, 102). The CISG does, however, apply if it contains rules which are functionally equivalent to the rescission pursuant to domestic laws (c. note 6 of Article 4). Cases of *slips, transference and faulty transmission* are also covered by the legal institute of rescission and are outside the Convention's sphere of application. Insofar as the addressee of the statement knew of the intent of the party making the statement, or could not have been unaware of it, the statement is effective according to the intent of the party making the statement (e.g. the price is to be indicated as amounting to Swiss francs 50,000 instead of Swiss francs 500,000, Secretariat's Commentary, O. R., 18). A special problem of faulty transmission is covered by Article 27.

4. This refers to a situation where the intent of the acting party cannot be recognized from his action according to the relevant criteria or where the addressee of the action did not know the intent of the acting party and cannot be purported to have been aware of it, i.e. the individual intent or also the common individual *intent cannot be determined*.

5. The criteria mentioned here link subjective with objective elements in a way that one can speak of a *type-related objectivization*.

The *subjective element* relates to a person of the same type as the other party, hence the addressee of the action. The same type can be defined by different criteria whose cumulative application can amount to a relatively strong individualization. Such criteria include the kind of work done by the party's enterprise (e.g. a factory or a trading firm); the country in which he has his decisive place of business (including the language spoken there); the business forms customary in that country; and also (Farnsworth/BB, 99) the knowledge and experience of prior dealings between the parties. Another subjective element is added by the reference to the same circumstances, which is described in an exemplary way in precise terms under paragraph 3 (notes 7 - 11). Such circumstances can be a certain situation of the market; but they can also express that more simplified forms of business transactions are applied (e.g. sales contracts in the framework of an agency contract on a dealer basis); that statements are given under special conditions (trade fair transactions); or that specific links have been established between the parties' interests (e.g. counter-transactions).

The *objective element* refers to a situation where the conduct of a reasonable person is made the yardstick (note 6). But in assessing how such person would behave, the subjective and objective elements of each case have to be taken into account. Only an unreasonable, e.g. professionally incompetent conduct or such conduct that is contrary to good faith of the addressee of the legal act would have to be left out of consideration.

As a result, according to Farnsworth (BB, 99), more *reasonable solutions* will prevail. An objectivized interpretation can, therefore, very well result in an act producing a legal effect which does not correspond to the intent of the acting person (Schlechtriem, 26, in our view unjustly considers this case as not provided for). The latter will then have to rely on rescission (note 3.4.).

6. The criteria mentioned below serve, first, to determine the *intent of a party*. The mere subjective element is thus left, and the intent of a party is in a way objectivized. But from this it follows that a secret reservation of a party is irrelevant, at least when the other party is not aware of it. Secondly, these criteria are supposed to help determine the *view of a reasonable person*. Those criteria also play a role in determining whether the *other party* could not have been unaware of the intent of the acting party, because in this context the measure of a reasonable person is to be applied.

7. The *relevant circumstances* are described below in an exemplary fashion, but they also include the kind of circumstances mentioned in note 5. To give due consideration to these circumstances means to determine their specific influence on the issue to be decided.

8. This refers in particular to documents and oral statements which have been exchanged by the parties in the *process of preparing the contract*, but are not expressed in the documents which brought about the contract. Unlike Honnold (142 fol) and in agreement with Farnsworth (ibid.), we believe that possible national rules, which exclude the negotiations on the contract from the interpretation, are superseded by the CISG because the latter contains a specific rule to this (Article 4, second sentence).

9. *Established practices* are practices or exercises which have developed between specific, in general two, parties over a longer period of time in similar business relations (Article 19, note 11). They refer to individual, not expressly regulated aspects of the contract; like for instance, to the way in which documents are presented and include the tendering of account, the notification of consignments, the regulation of non-conformity and other claims.

10. Compare Article 9, note 1.

By contrast to Article 9, note 2, *national practices* can also, according to the certainly correct view of Schlechtriem (26), be related to as they attain relevance in international transactions.

11. This serves, - even if in a very cautious way, - to express a prohibition of the *venire contra factum proprium* (*prohibition to contradict one's own conduct*) (similarly Huber, 430). If a party thus expresses through his conduct that he interprets the contract in a specific way, he can later not rely on the opposite interpretation.

Article 9

(Usages and established practices)

(1) The parties are bound by any usage[1] to which they have agreed[2] and by any practices which they have established between themselves[3].

(2) The parties are considered[4], unless otherwise agreed, to have impliedly made applicable to their contract[5] or its formation[6] a usage[7] of which the parties knew or ought to have known[8] and which in international trade is widely known[9] to, and regularly observed[10,11] by, parties to contracts of the type involved in the particular trade concerned.

1.1. It is not generally defined in the CISG what *usages* are. Insofar as reference is made to such usages which the parties have agreed to, this is of no relevance since agreed rules are binding for the parties in any case and independent of their character. This is true also of national usages and rules whose legal character is disputed. If, however, usages have been agreed whose validity is excluded under national law, they are not binding (Article 4, subpara. (a), which expressly mentions usages; c. also Article 4, note 6). Paragraph 2 defines those usages which are binding for the parties even though they were not agreed.

1.2. If usages are agreed, they *will prevail over the Convention*, just like all agreements between the parties (Article 6). This holds true also when the agreement is assumed under paragraph 2. Such is the view expressed overwhelmingly in publications (already Junge/Dölle, 47 on Article 9 ULIS which has a very similar content; Honnold, 149; Loewe/Lausanne, 19; Bydlinski/Doralt,76; Bonell/BB, 104) and there are only rare instances where this issue is considered unsolved (Garro, 479). The opinion of the majority is supported by the fact that a Czechoslovak proposal to consider only such usages as valid in the case of fictitious agreements, which are not contrary to the Convention, did not succeed (O. R., 89). Should there be contradictions between usages, agreed usages will prevail over fictitiously agreed ones, as can be concluded from the introductory half-sentence of paragraph 2. Agreed usages, in general, refer only to the post-conclusion stage of the contract, i.e. to the contract performance. Insofar as there are frame contracts or other agreements between the parties, whose effect reaches beyond the individual contract, they can also relate to the conclusion of the contract.

2. This formulation expresses that there has to be an *agreement between the parties*. Such agreement can be an implied one. But the assumption that there is implied agreement must not be stretched too far because paragraph 2 would loose its function and the additional requirements mentioned thereunder could be evaded. A combination of both provisions by Bonell/BB, 107, seems rather unconvincing.

3. Concerning the term "established practices" compare Article 8, note 9. It is derived from US law (Art. 1-205 UCC).

Practices, which can be interpreted as implied agreement between the parties and which frequently modify original agreements, should be considered as having *priority* in their relationship with agreed usages (so believes also Goldstajn/Dubrovnik, 99). They are generally better geared to the particularities of a concrete relationship because they are of an individual and thus more specific character. FRG jurisdiction, in line with the thus far identical (English) text of ULIS, has recognized a usage of fairness of the parties which deviates from the provisions on the time, form and content of a lack of conformity notice (OLG Düsseldorf in: Schlechtriem/Magnus, 167 fol).

4. This somewhat strange juridical construction of a *fictitious agreement* constitutes a compromise between those States whose aim was to have a normative validity of usages, hence validity brought about directly by virtue of law, and those which would have wanted to permit only the application of agreed usages. But in the end, the result in its substance comes close to a normative validity, which is even strengthened by the fictitious character of an agreement, because on grounds of party autonomy the agreement is on top of the hierarchy of the sources determining the substance of a contract (note 1.2.). A number of developing countries voiced some concern at this solution because they were not involved in estab-

lishing those usages; and so did some Eastern European countries (summarizing Garro, 476 fol).

5. The obvious idea to be expressed here is that the usages are to be applied to those stages of contract performance which *follow the conclusion of the contract*, i.e. are to serve the interpretation of the contract.

6. The fictitious agreement of usages thus also extends to the *formation of the contract* and can insofar only be deduced, apart from overlapping agreements, from relations the parties enter into at the time of starting preparation for a contract. The CISG proceeds here, as a matter of exception, from the existence of pre-contractual obligations. But fiction cannot reach beyond the substantive scope of application of the Convention (Article 4) and does, therefore, not cover subjects excluded by it.

7. It seems that using the term "usages" *no additional features*, except for the ones mentioned below, are to be required for the rules which become binding by virtue of fiction. This also serves to prevent the risk of an interpretation of the term "usages" under national law and related differences of opinion on whether specific rules are to be regarded as usages. The term "usages" is autonomous and can, therefore, be interpreted as broadly as possible (Bonell/BB, 111). It is not required that a usage be ancient or of long standing (Honnold, 148; Bonell/BB, 113). It seems questionable to us whether the measure of good faith should be used to determine to what extent usages are to be considered, as Bonell (ibid.) indicates. Even if one, as we do, does not want to limit this principle to the interpretation of the Convention, this does not mean it should be turned into the criterion for the validity of rules to be followed otherwise. (The situation is different in interpreting practices - note 5 of Article 7). After all, a Chinese proposal requiring usages to be reasonable (O. R., 89 fol) was rejected so that the necessary corrections have to be left to a large extent to the rules of validity of national law. Insofar as there are customary rights which meet the criteria of paragraph 2, they would have to be considered as a usage in the meaning of the CISG. The same goes for local customs which are accepted internationally as being valid for that trading place (similarly Honnold, 148; Bonell/BB, 109; more reserved Schlechtriem, 28).

8. This feature is *largely redundant* (critical also Huber, 428, and the Indian delegate at the diplomatic conference, O. R., 266, who both go still further, and Bydlinski/Doralt, 77) because, if usages fulfil the requirement described in note 9, the parties have to recognize them as a rule. Only in very rare, exceptional cases one will be able

to permit that a party invokes that he did not know, nor ought to have known, the rules which meet the remaining requirements (e.g. a factory which regularly does not participate in transactions abroad buys, as an exception, a machine abroad which is traded according to international usage). On the other hand, it is not sufficient that the parties positively know certain rules, but that those rules are not widely known for the individual characteristics must be cumulative.

9. This criterion is the most relevant of all. It will be assumed, in any case, that such usages are widely known in international trade which are known to the relevant business circles in the majority of countries which also belong to different groups of countries, hence in particular developed and developing countries. In a concrete case it may, however, suffice that the usages are known in the relevant *business circles of* those *States* where the parties have their places of business. But they must be known there as rules governing international trade and not just domestic transactions.

The applicable usages need not generally be valid for all contracts; it is a sufficient but also necessary requirement that they relate to *sales contracts of the respective kind.* The types of sales contracts, i.e. the subcategories, are divided according to the goods sold. Accordingly, the usages for trade in machinery and plants; raw materials or specific raw materials; foodstuffs etc. are applied to the respective contract. But the type of contract can also be determined according to whether the contract is one for single delivery or for delivery by instalments; whether it is a short-term or long-term contract; whether delivery is against cash or credit; or whether it is a tender or a direct transaction. The category of goods traded is also an important criterion for the determination of the decisive branch; but here also other requirements are to be considered like, e.g. the use of the goods sold (sales to re-sellers - e.g. dealers - on the one hand, and to final consumers, on the other).

10. Contrary to the view held be Huber (428), we do not consider this characteristic superfluous, but rather very important. It may very well occur, for instance, that specific rules, which are applied in industrialized countries, are *known but not applied* in developing countries. Their agreement can then not be assumed, except for contracts between parties from industrialized countries.

11. When a rule meets the requirements explained under notes 8 - 10 their application is fictitiously agreed. Since this refers to the INCOTERMS, the Uniform Customs and Practices for Documentary Credits and the Uniform Rules for Collections, they are applied without taking a decision on whether they are usages at all. The

above-mentioned rules are *rules of interpretation* which require a specific stipulation in the contract (use of a specific trade term, of specific conditions of payment). If it is not determined at the same time which is the decisive interpretation; e.g. merely FOB, named port of shipment, then it is governed by the INCOTERMS and not by national usages or laws. Part of the problems with which Article 9, paragraph 3 ULIS deals (interpretation of expressions, clauses or forms), which in spite of relevant requests at the diplomatic conference did not find its way into the CISG (O. R., 89 fol), can be solved in this way (similarly Secretariat's Commentary, 19). Article 8, paragraph 2 can also be consulted in this context (Schlechtriem, 29).

Article 10

(Place of business)

For the purpose of this Convention[1]:

(a) if a party has more than one place of business[2], the place of business is that which has the closest relationship to the contract and its performance[4], having regard to the circumstances known to or contemplated by the parties[3] at any time before or at the conclusion of the contract;

(b) if a party does not have a place of business, reference is made to his habitual residence[5].

1. It is important to determine the *decisive place of business* in order to find out whether the sales contract in question comes under the sphere of application of the Convention at all (c. Article 1). But a number of other articles also refers directly or indirectly to the place of business (e.g. Art. 12; Art. 18, paragraph 2; Art. 20, paragraph 1; Art. 24; Art. 31, subpara. (c); Art. 42, paragraph 1, subpara. (b); Art. 57, paragraph 1, subpara. (a); Art. 69, paragraph 2).

2. The *term* "place of business" is *not defined* in the CISG. For an establishment to be regarded as a place of business it is not necessary for that establishment to be a legal person. It can, for instance, be also a business of an individual. However, the mere incorporation in a specific State would already create a place of business. Insofar as no legal person was created, certain facts have to be given: the establishment must have existed for a certain time, it must have an address and probably also an office, and it must have a certain competence. Temporary travel groups, therefore, do not form a place of business. As to production facilities, the former will, how-

ever, generally apply insofar as they enter into contracts which refer to the provision of the facility. Such production facilities can, however, not be regarded as place of business if employees working there conclude contracts for the mother company, e.g. agree modifications of a contract for whose performance the facility was built.

3. The circumstances which are contemplated by the parties must at least be known so that the latter criterion would have been sufficient. The relevant *circumstances must be known* to both parties at the latest *at the conclusion of the contract.* If they are not, they will have no influence on the determination of the decisive place of business. "Ought to have known" is not sufficient in this case.

4. In regard to the *criteria* which have *to be taken into account* and weighed against each other, the details given by the parties themselves on the contract partnership should gain decisive importance. Normally, they are incorporated in the contracts. Further clues could be deduced from the permanent working place of the employee authorized to conduct contractual negotiations, the terms of payment, a distinction possibly made in the contract between contract partnership and performance of the contract, or from the correspondence in general or on specific issues etc. Less meaningful in this regard is the place of manufacture or destination of the goods. We tend to interpret "the closest relationship" more in the legal than in the factual sense because we consider the commercial management of the transaction as being the decisive factor.

5. The alternative envisaged here can only apply in the case of natural persons who rarely are parties to international sales contracts in the meaning of the CISG (in particular the exception in Article 2, subpara. (a)). The *habitual residence* of a natural person is where that person actually stays most of the time (at the time of the preparation and conclusion of the contract), if it can be concluded from the circumstances of that stay (e.g. renting of an apartment) that the stay is intended for a certain duration. This last criterion can, however, not be taken into consideration when there is another permanent residence (if considered in a larger time frame).

Article 11

(Form of contract)

A contract of sale need not be concluded in or evidenced by writing and is not subject to any other requirement as to form[1]. It may be proved by any means, including witnesses[2].

1.1. Basically, it is declared that international sales contracts, which fall under the CISG, *need not be* concluded in *writing*. The CISG determines here, as a matter of exception the validity of sales contracts, including such which under the applicable national law would be void because of lack of a required form, (Article 4, subpara. (a)). This is true independent of the nature of the requirement and of the purposes it is supposed to serve (Rajski/BB, 123). Article 96, however, opens up the possibility for a reservation. A reservation under the above-mentioned Article would entail the legal consequences indicated under Article 12. Many authors consider the removal of the writing requirement for sales contracts on movable goods as an achievement of western legal systems to speed things up, whereas the former socialist countries are believed to attach great importance to certainty, predictability and lack of surprises (e.g. Garro, 461; S. G. Zwart, "The New International Law of Sales: A Marriage between the Socialist, Third World, Common and Civil Law Principles", The North Carolina Journal of International Law and Commercial Regulative, 1988/1, 116). It is difficult for us to understand, however, why in the age of telex, and now even telefax, the speed, with which oral contracts would be concluded, should be considerably higher. On the contrary, modern international trade is not possible without storing information outside the heads of the people involved, including information concerning the conclusion of a contract. Therefore, in a broad sense, almost all contracts are formed in writing. It is no wonder, therefore, that it was in particular the western side which tried to save the writing requirement in certain cases (note 5.1. of Article 4; also note 1.2. at the end). We hold, nonetheless, that it is correct to proceed from the principle of freedom of form, - even though in practice it is relied upon only exceptionally. We do so to *prevent dishonoured contractual relationships*. Where the contract is the result of a correspondence, it happens quite often that there is no reaction to the last statement, which leads to the conclusion of a contract, although it contains modifications which transform it into a counter-offer (Article 19). In such event there will be no contract since the written form is required, even though the parties have performed. The written form requirement of the General Conditions of Delivery of Goods/CMEA (4) has in such cases often led to difficult situations.

1.2. Form prescriptions under foreign trade regulations, e.g. in the area of approval of goods and foreign exchange flows, are not affected by Article 11 insofar as the sanctions envisaged therein remain effective, e.g. punishment in the event of violating those prescriptions. But they do not attain any effectiveness in the relations between the parties to the sales contract. The contract remains valid (Secretariat's Commentary, O. R., 20; Honnold, 153).

Other *State regulations,* e.g. ministerial orders, and also internal company rules which prescribe that international sales contracts are to be concluded in writing are treated similarly.

1.3. The rule refers to the formation of the contract and thus to acts which lead to a contract. In regard to other *legal acts* the CISG generally does not prescribe a specific form unless it follows from the nature of the act (e.g. statement - Article 8, note 2.2., which can be done orally, - Article 24, Article 21, paragraph 1, but not by conduct implying an intent). Contradictory regulations under domestic law, which insofar are still scarcer, have to come second.

2. It is here expressly noted that the exclusion of *proof by witnesses,* as may be envisaged in domestic legal systems, is not effective within the Convention's scope of application.

Article 12

(Effect of declarations relating to form)

Any provision of article 11, article 29 or Part II of this Convention that allows[1] a contract of sale or its modification or termination by agreement or any offer, acceptance or other indication of intention to be made in any form other than in writing does not apply[2] where any party has his place of business in a Contracting State which has made a declaration under article 96 of this Convention[3]. The parties may not derogate from or vary the effect of this article[4].

1. The possible exclusion of any form requirement does *not* refer *to all indications of intention* and even less to all legal acts which come under the Convention's scope of application, but only to the conclusion of the contract (Art. 11), agreed avoidance of contract (Art. 29) and to all indications of intention ("or other indication of intention") which Part II of the Convention on the conclusion of a contract provides for. The decisive indications of intention of Part II, like offer and acceptance, will be expressly mentioned below. The freedom of form in the case of a reservation does, for instance, not apply to the withdrawal of an offer (Art. 15., paragraph 2) and the revocation of an offer (Art. 16, paragraph 1). National form requirements should, however, be seldom. *Indications of intention* which are mentioned *in other parts of the Convention* (except for Art. 11 and 29), are however, also in the context of a reservation not governed by form requirements which may exist under national law (note 3). This is true, as was made clear at the Conference by a precise statement (O. R., 272 fol), of the statement according to which the contract is made void

(Art. 26) and of the notice of lack of conformity (Art. 39, paragraph 1).

2.1. Article 12 provides for the consequences which follow from a *reservation* for the contractual relations of the parties. The seeming duplication of the rule was called for because Article 96 includes only the admissibility under international law of the reservation, hence only relates to the relations between States.

2.2. The Convention merely states that the named provisions concerning freedom of form (note 1) do not apply in the case of a reservation when the party has his place of business in a State making a reservation. There is *no positive provision as to the form*. This corresponds to the one-sidedness of a reservation which has the effect that no agreement is brought about between the State making the reservation and the other State. As is widely believed, the applicable provisions as to form have to be taken from the applicable national law in this case (Art. 1, note 6) (Schlechtriem, 30, 32; Honnold, 156; Loewe/Lausanne, 20; Rajski/BB, 126 fol). The written form, therefore, is a condition for the validity of a contract only when it is prescribed by the applicable domestic law. Consequently, when a sales contract is concluded in a non-written form between a party from a reservation State and a party from a non-reservation State, that contract is valid no less than if it is governed by the law of the non-reservation State which does not provide for the relevant contract to be made in writing. But also the opinion to the contrary has found renowned champions (note 10 of Art. 96).

3. The *declaration* under Article 96 must state that the provisions contained in Article 12, which allow a contract of sale to be made in any form other than writing, do not apply where a party has his place of business in the State making the declaration.

4. *Article 12* does thus contain the *sole mandatory rule* of the Convention (but compare Article 6, note 2). The exclusion of the Convention as a whole, however, is hereby not precluded (Article 6) because in that case national law is invoked from which the respective rules as to form are to be deduced (Art. 29, notes 1.3. and 5).

Article 13

(Writing)

For the purposes of this Convention "writing" includes telegram and telex[1].

1. This rule, without any doubt, refers to cases where the Convention itself relates to the written form, e.g. in Article 29, paragraph 2. It seems to be appropriate, however, to invoke it also when interpreting a *writing requirement under national law* (Article 12, note 2). Although the use of the Convention for such interpretation of the national law leads to a strange entanglement of the two, it may be considered as covered by the introductory part of this Article for it refers to an interpretation of the national law to the extent to which it is to be applied as an exception within the substantive scope of application of the Convention. The *definition given here of the written form is valid also for a contractually agreed written form.*

By contrast, it seems to us to go too far to turn this rule as Schlechtriem does (32 fol) generally into a *"uniform objective standard for form requirements"*. When the national law to be invoked as an exception prescribesfurther-reaching form requirements than mere writing (authentication, e.g. at consulates; certification, affixing of seal or stamp), those will certainly not be removed by Article 13. The rule includes *machine-readable data carriers* for being regarded as "writing". They certainly exist objectively and independently of the parties and are durable, thus meeting essential criteria for writing requirements to be substantiated. There are, however, concerns in regard to the recognizability of the content of their declaration by the other party which speak against recognizing them as written form. Similar considerations are relevant as they were made in respect of languages (Art. 8, note 3.2.). We, therefore, believe that machine-readable data carriers can be considered as indications of intention in the meaning of the CISG only if their content is recognizable to the addressee. In that case they also constitute written declarations or communications.

The Factoring Convention adopted in 1988 already considers further possibilities formulating: "notice in writing includes, but is not limited to telegrams, telex and any other telecommunication capable of being reproduced in tangible form" (Art. 1, paragraph 4, subpara. (b)) This refers in the first place to *telefax* and does not address the special problems of recognizability of machine-readable data carriers. It is said furthermore and expressly in the Factoring Convention that a notice in writing need *not be signed*, but must identify the person by whom or in whose name it is given (Art. 1, paragraph 4, subpara. (a)). A signature by a machine would, for instance, be sufficient. It seems to us that in the light of the discussion at the diplomatic conference (O. R., 269), Article 13 can also be interpreted in this sense, as Rajski (BB, 129) already does, even without reference to the Factoring Convention.

We can, however, not agree with his view expressed in the same place that telegram and telex are *less strong evidence* than the traditional written form. This does, in our view, not depend on the category of document, but rather on such factors as the processing remarks, the role it has played in commercial intercourse between the parties, like reference to it, etc.

Part II
FORMATION OF THE CONTRACT

FORMATION OF THE CONTRACT

Introductory remarks

1. While the 1964 Hague Conventions dealt separately with the formation and the terms of international sales contracts, the CISG integrates both, thus avoiding parallel provisions as well as problems related to the mutual reference with regard to the interpretation of the Conventions (Schlechtriem, 34). As suggested, in particular by Scandinavian States, *Parts II and III became independent to a certain extent* so that they can be ratified separately (Art. 92).

2. From among the States that are parties to the CISG, only Denmark, Finland, Norway and Sweden have made use so far of the reservation under Article 92. In the case of a contract between parties from Germany and a Scandinavian State, Part II would be applied by German courts only under the preconditions of Article 1, paragraph 1, letter (b), if German law were applied generally. Article 1, paragraph 1, subpara. (a) would not be taken into account because the Scandinavian States are not parties to the Convention with regard to Part II.

3. Part II sums up the most important provisions for the formation of a contract. However, *other parts as well contain provisions which are relevant for the formation of a contract*. This refers, in particular, to Article 4 and Articles 6 to 13. From Article 7, for instance, it can be inferred that in the case of problems related to interpretation, particularly concerning probable gap-filling, domestic law must not be applied immediately.

4. Part II is structured in such a way that Articles 14 to 17 deal with the offer, Articles 18 to 22 with the acceptance of the offer, Article 23 with the moment of the conclusion of the contract and Article 24 with questions of definition.

5. The rule underlying the formation of a contract is a *compromise between States Parties having different legal traditions*. The main controversy referred to the question of whether a contract should be formed with the dispatch or receipt of the statement of acceptance. Here the continental European thinking based on Roman legal traditions has prevailed, in which the receipt of the statement of acceptance is the prerequisite for the formation of a contract. Whereas, the Anglo-American doctrine found its way into the Convention through the general possibility to revoke the offer.

Other essential points of discussion referred to the determinability of the price and the relationship between Articles 14 and 55; the formation of a contract outside the traditional scheme of offer and acceptance, and, finally, the inclusion of the general business conditions (battle of forms). As regards the latter questions, no generally acceptable solutions could be found.

6. The rules under Part II of the CISG are based largely on the Uniform Law on the Formation of Contracts for the International Sale of Goods concerning movable goods (ULF) and, compared to the latter, constitute an improvement with regard to a number of issues. To leave room for other considerations, a comparison with the ULF (c. Rehbinder/Freiburg) will be omitted in this commentary. It will have to be taken into consideration, however, that courts of those countries which were parties to the Hague Conventions will resort to decisions regarding the ULF when it comes to interpreting the CISG insofar as the old rules were retained (see the excellent compilation by Schlechtriem/Magnus).

7. Obviously, there have been no major practical differences with regard to the formation of a contract for there are not many relevant judgements (Rehbinder/Freiburg, 150). Schlechtriem (Kaufrecht, 46) points to the "noticeable discrepancy between the efforts made by scientists to cope with supposed problems, on the one hand, and questions which, on the other hand, turned out to be relevant for practical purposes because of the number of court decisions that have become necessary."

8. The *ruling concerning the formation of a contract* under Part II of the CISG is aimed at the formation of sales contracts, but it does *not specifically relate to sales in its entirety*. A large number of existing provisions could also be applied to the formation of other international commercial contracts. Insofar, Part II could form the "core of a unified general contract law" (c. Hoffmann/Lausanne, 79). Also a study group of UNIDROIT, which deals with the drafting of general contractual rules, used Part II of the CISG as the foundation for their work (c. PICC).

Article 14

(Offer)

(1) A proposal[2] for concluding a contract[3] addressed to one or more specific[4] persons constitutes an offer[1] if it is sufficiently definite[7] and indicates the intention[5] of the offeror to be bound in case[6] of acceptance. A proposal is sufficiently definite[7] if it indicates the goods[8] and

expressly or implicitly[11] fixes or makes provision[12] for determining the quantity[9] and the price[10].

(2) A proposal other than one addressed to one or more specific[4] persons is to be considered merely as an invitation to make offers, unless the contrary[13] is clearly indicated by the person making the proposal.

1. An offer is defined as a *proposal* for the conclusion of a contract if it is addressed to one or more specific persons, expresses the *intention* of the offeror *to be bound* and contains certain minimum terms. A statement of acceptance can also be an offer if it goes beyond the terms of the offer, differs greatly from that one or is given belatedly (c. Articles 19 and 21). Any successive proposal constitutes an offer. The decisive "offer" is always the declaration which preceded final acceptance (Eörsi/BB, 136 fol). Here the CISG follows the traditional treatment of the conclusion of a contract which does not fully meet the requirements of today's world of business, especially when it comes to the conclusion of sales contracts covering major and technically complicated objects.

In many instances the question is raised, therefore, of how to deal with contracts which do not fit into the scheme of offer and acceptance (e.g. see Doralt, 60; examples are given also by Schlechtriem, 34).

2. An offer is not defined as a statement but rather as a proposal. Sometimes the *dispatch of goods* can constitute such a proposal. It may be recalled here that the written form is not mandatory for the conclusion of a sales contract.

3. The proposal has to be aimed at *concluding a contract*, i.e. it should cause the conclusion of a contract merely by accepting it. Inquiries for possible deliveries or proposals for negotiations on a sale do therefore not constitute an offer.

4. *Newspaper advertisements* and similar *acts of publicity* or *public tenders* do *not* constitute *an offer*. Proposals addressed to the public at large are mere invitations to make offers. Even if brochures, catalogues or circulars, for instance to all mechanical engineering companies, are addressed to specific persons, there will mostly be a lack of the intention to be bound (c. note 5). If there is such intention to be bound and if circulars or catalogues are addressed to specific persons, those acts could constitute an offer, the number of addressees being of no consequence (Eörsi/-Lausanne, 45); also Sono/Dubrovnik, 119).

5. A proposal is aimed at concluding a contract only when it expresses the intention of the offeror to be bound. The *offer is one of the two statements of will* which lead to the conclusion of a contract. Hence the relationship under a contract is a relationship of intention. The intention to be bound is not excluded because of the fact that the contract is to be concluded under a condition. A proposal for the conclusion of a contract does not automatically contain the intention to be bound; it may also be aimed at taking up negotiations on a sale. This could be the case in particular if the proposal at first only contains the category and quantity of the goods (c. note 7). If there is the intention to be bound, lacking provisions could be complemented by *jus dispositivum* (Sono/Dubrovnik, 120). Some formulations in the offer might cause doubt as to the intention to be bound. In some instances the intention to be bound can be seen from the clarity with which the goods are specified (Eörsi/BB, 140). As far as the intention to be bound is the result of an error, question of validity are touched upon which do not come under the CISG. *Non-binding offers do not contain an intention to be bound.*

6. It is expressly stipulated here that the intention to be bound must refer to the contract to be concluded. If the offer is not accepted, there will be no binding. The intention to be bound does not refer to the offer itself. (As to the binding nature of the offer compare Article 15 fol).

7. The *minimum content* should include the *description of the goods as well as the quantity and the price* (c. Article 55). The goods can be indicated both individually and as a category. Insufficient and not a category in this sense are collect names, e.g. woodworking machinery. It is not necessary for the offer to indicate the quality, its packaging (Article 35) as well as the place or date of delivery (Articles 31 and 33). If the offer contains relevant information, however, those are to be considered as being material (Article 19, paragraph 3).

The second sentence of paragraph 1 had been particularly disputed both during the preparation and the holding of the Vienna Conference (O. R., 92) because such "minimum terms" do not suffice in many practical cases, and a relevant proposal is then not definite enough to constitute an offer (c. note 5). One has to proceed, however, on the assumption that the offeror will not express an intention to be bound unless he himself believes that the proposed parts of the contract are sufficient. If, on the contrary, the offeree considers those parts as insufficient, he may add the relevant amendments to his statement (c. Article 19).

8. The *mere indication of the goods may not always suffice*, but rather calls for a certain specification depending on the category of the goods (Eörsi/Lausanne, 46).

9. The *quantity does not have to be determined from the outset*. Reference to all the requirements or total output of the goods should be acceptable (O. R., 21). Any quantity may also be offered; the determination can be done through acceptance (Eörsi/Lausanne, 46). The quantity may also be determined by naming the requirements for a certain purpose or the amount of money available for it (Eörsi/BB, 141).

10. While the price belongs here to the minimum content of an offer, Article 55 concedes that a contract may also be validly concluded if the price has not been fixed expressly or implicitly and nothing has been agreed that would make provision for its determination.

Thus there is a contradiction between Articles 14 and 55, which has been duly reflected in various sources (Bydlinski/Doralt, 62 fol; Schlechtriem, 37 fol; Rehbinder/Freiburg, 158; Eörsi/BB, 141). Article 55 presupposes the existence of a valid contract which pursuant to Article 14 simply cannot exist. It seems to us that the price problem has been over-emphasized in the discussion because Article 14, in the extreme, permits that nothing be said about the price but that the possibility of determining it is implied.

The *determination of the price* necessarily *includes the currency*, whereas agreement on the terms of payment is not necessary (c. Articles 54 and 57 fol).

11. This rule of implicitly agreeing on the quantity and price was very much disputed at the Vienna Conference (O. R., 275, 292) for many delegations feared a misuse by (economically more powerful) sellers. Whether or not one can proceed on an implicit agreement on quantity and price certainly depends in the first place on the intention of the parties themselves (Article 8, paragraph 1) as well as on the usage of the parties and the established practices in the relevant branches (Article 9).

12. Quantity and price can be fixed later on the basis of objective factors (requirements, output and/or offer of the competition, stock market or market prices). It may, however, also be left to one of the parties (list price) or a third person to fix quantity and price (Schlechtriem/Doralt, 187); Schlechtriem, 37; Eörsi/Lausanne, 47).

13. The contrary means that the offeror wants to be bound also towards *non-specific persons*, e. g. in formulating "as long as stocks last". Commercial practices may be of importance in this respect, too.

Article 15

(Time of effect of offer; withdrawal of offer)

(1) An offer becomes effective^1 when it reaches^2 the offeree.

(2) An offer, even if it is irrevocable^3, may be withdrawn^4 if the withdrawal^6 reaches the offeree before or at the same time^5 as the offer.

1. An *offer* has only a *limited life-span*. It becomes effective at a specific date, later it ceases to be effective. Neither before (if e.g. the offeree is informed of the offer by a third person) nor afterwards can it be accepted. (Concerning late acceptance, however, compare Article 21.)

Also a binding offer is not binding before it becomes effective (Honnold, 165).

It is a *precondition* for the offer *to be effective* in order to be accepted. From the offer and acceptance being effective it does, however, not follow automatically that the contract is effective. A conditional contract only becomes effective if and when that condition is fulfilled (Eörsi/BB, 148).

2. It is a *precondition* for the offer to become effective that it *reaches the offeree*; it needs to be received. The withdrawal of the offer (Article 15, paragraph 2), the revocation of the offer (Article 16, paragraph 1), the rejection of the offer (Article 17) and the acceptance (Article 18, paragraph 2) also become effective when they are received. Here the CISG follows the rule of receipt. By contrast, Articles 26 and 27 are based on the dispatch rule. Also, the rejection or approval of a late acceptance under Article 21 becomes effective with dispatch. The subject here is the risk of transmission, which in each case should be assumed by the party which in deviating from the normal procedure gave rise to a statement (Bydlinski/Doralt, 65). The offer will, however, not become effective in spite of its reaching the offeree if a *withdrawal* reaches the addressee earlier or at the same time.

Receipt of an offer does not mean that the addressee has to be aware of its content. It suffices that the offer reaches the area of receipt or disposal of the addressee. (As to the definition of "reaches" see Article 24).

3. According to the CISG an offer is not always irrevocable, but only under certain conditions (c. Article 16, paragraph 2). As a *basic principle* it is *revocable* under Article 16, paragraph 1. An offer is irrevocable, for instance, if the offeror himself has declared it firm, binding or irrevocable.

4. Even an *irrevocable offer may be withdrawn*. Hence, the CISG distinguishes between revocation (Article 16, paragraph 1) and withdrawal which is possible only until the offer has become effective. An offer which has not yet become effective is withdrawn, while the offer which has become effective is revoked. The difference consists thus in whether the offer is dropped before it becomes effective or afterwards. As to everyday language, revocation and withdrawal are identical anyway. The English language uses here two verbs, one of Latin and one of Germanic origin (revoke - withdrawn) which have the same meaning. If there is only one verb for this in one language, a translation should be difficult (Eörsi/BB, 147, 149).

Incidentally, the rule of withdrawal as contained in the CISG corresponds to the rule of withdrawal in many legal systems.

5. According to the continental European law no revocation is possible after the offer reaches the offeree. According to the CISG the *possibility of withdrawal ends*; however, the *possibility of revocation commences* pursuant to Article 16.

6. The withdrawal does not have to be in the same form as the offer, i. e. offer by letter, withdrawal by telex or telegram. Withdrawal can also be declared by telephone even if otherwise the written form is required.

Article 16

(Revocability of offer)

(1) Until a contract is concluded[2] an offer may be revoked[1] if the revocation reaches[3] the offeree before he has dispatched[4] an acceptance.

(2) However, an offer cannot be revoked[5]:

(a) if it indicates, whether by stating a fixed time[7] for acceptance or otherwise[6], that it is irrevocable;

(b) if it was reasonable for the offeree to rely[8] on the offer as being irrevocable and the offeree has acted in reliance on the offer[9].

1. Here we are dealing with a principle that is taken from the Anglo-American legal family: the *principle of revocability of the offer*. The binding to an offer is an exception there. This rule is the most important deviation from the rule that governs the conclusion of contracts under German law.

The CISG, however, makes some major exceptions to the principle of revocability so that principle is put into question again (c. notes 4 and 5). According to W. v. Marschall, who refers to E. v. Caemmerer (Freiburg, 174), an offer is, therefore, irrevocable as a rule. Rehbinder (Freiburg, 177), however, talks of a "feeble assumption of revocability". Sono draws attention to the fact that the Convention meets practical needs and should not be considered as being a compromise between Common Law and other legal systems, but rather brings to light the common basis of the two (K. Sono, "Restoration of the Rule of Reason in Contract Formation: Has There Been Civil and Common Law Disparity?", Cornell International Law Journal, 1988/3, p. 478).

2. *Revoking* is *only possible before the conclusion of the contract*. The contract is concluded when the acceptance becomes effective (Article 23). The date when the acceptance becomes effective is determined by Article 18, paragraphs 2 and 3. Consequently, only in the case of oral negotiations or in the case of acceptance by conduct implying an intent can the offer be revoked up until the conclusion of the contract. When acceptance is given in writing, the possibility of revoking is further limited (c. note 4). *Revoking* is thus as a rule not possible up until the conclusion of the contract but *only until the statement of acceptance is dispatched*. If the offeror revokes his offer, he has to be aware that it may be too late to do so because the offeree by this time may have already dispatched his statement of acceptance (Eörsi/BB,160).

3. For the *revocation* of an offer to become effective it *needs to reach the offeree* just as does the offer itself (Article 15, paragraph 1). (As to the definition of "reach" compare Article 24).

4. Should the offeree receive a revocation even before he accepted the offer, he could no longer accept the offer because it is terminated. On the other hand, a revocation remains ineffective if the offeree has already dispatched a statement of acceptance even though a contract has not yet been formed. In this case, the offeror does not have the possibility to revoke his offer until the conclusion of the contract. The purpose of this rule is to *cut short the time available for revocation* (Eörsi/BB, 156).

5. *Two important exceptions* are made here to the principle of revocability of an offer, which to a large extent annul the principle itself: First, an offer can express not only that it is irrevocable (see note 6); and, second, an offer can be made out in such a way that the offeree could consider it as irrevocable (note 8).

According to Eörsi (BB, 156) the two exceptions, as stipulated under (a) and (b), refer to identical situations both in Civil Law and Common Law language.

If an offer is revoked, even though the revocation is not admissible, then that revocation is not effective and the offer can still be accepted. In that case, however, the offeree has to take non-fulfilment of the contract by the offeror into account and has the obligation to reduce the damages under Article 77 (Honnold, 176).

One rule suggested by the former GDR concerning precontractual liability (e.g. unjustified breaking off of negotiations when through reliance on the conclusion of the contract project costs were incurred; A/Conf. 97/C.1/L.95) was not adopted.

6. An *offer* is *doubtlessly irrevocable* only if the offeror expressly defines it as firm, binding or as irrevocable (Eörsi(Lausanne, 48).

7. Whether or not the *determination of a time limit for acceptance* leads automatically to irrevocability, or whether additional statements by the offeror are necessary, was strongly disputed at the Vienna Conference (O. R. 278) since that determination can have *different meanings*. It may mean that the offer should be binding and irrevocable, or, as under Anglo-American law, that the offer lapses thereafter. It was, therefore, not stipulated that a time limit for acceptance should automatically mean irrevocability (Honnold, 171). In the CISG the time limit for acceptance is only an indication (Rehbinder/Freiburg, 158; Schlechtriem, 40). Bydlinski (Doralt, 67) would like the time limit for acceptance to be sufficient, just as according to the ULF the time limit for acceptance meant irrevocability. Thus the *fixing of a time limit for acceptance alone does not suffice*. The offer is not yet irrevocable if it states a fixed time for acceptance but only

if that statement of a fixed time is to express irrevocability (Eörsi/BB, 157). In interpreting the intention of a party (c. Article 8), the origin of the parties is also to be taken into consideration. If both come from the Anglo-American legal order then, in the case of the mere statement of a time limit for acceptance, a court having recourse to Article 9 would come to the conclusion that the offer is not irrevocable.

8. Reference is made here to the *protection of* the *good faith* of the offeree (Rehbinder/Freiburg, 160). It is not sufficient that the addressee of an offer relies on the irrevocability of that offer. Rather, he should reasonably be able to rely on it, i. e. another party in the same situation should have reached the same conclusion, *and* he must have become active. The irrevocability of the offer may be the result of circumstances, e. g. the ordering of replacement parts in the case of an accident. However, the offeree will under certain circumstances rely on the offer also if the acceptance of the offer requires time- and cost-consuming investigations (O.R., 22) or if he has informed the offeror that he will participate in a tender, the offeror thus to be the sub-contractor (Honnold, 172). Eörsi (BB, 159) raises the question of whether an analogous situation is possible in that the offeror, e.g. because of his conduct in previous negotiations, may rely on the other party accepting an offer.

9. Such act could be, for instance, the participation in a tender on the basis of the offer (Honnold, 171) or the conclusion of contracts with third parties or also the preparation of production or other measures, provided such acts or conduct were considered as normal in the branch concerned, or were supported by previous negotiations, or could be foreseen by the offeror (Eörsi/BB, 159). It should be taken into account that the offeree in any case has to make a decision in favour of acceptance within the period fixed for acceptance (c. Article 18).

Article 17

(Termination of an offer by rejection)

An offer[5], even if it is irrevocable[2], is terminated[1] when a rejection[3] reaches[4] the offeror.

1. Except for oral offers, one can in general proceed on the assumption that an *offer remains valid for a certain time*. After this time, which is either fixed by the offeror or is considered as being reasonable under the circumstances (Article 18, paragraph 2) has expired, the offer lapses. The offer, however, also lapses if it is rejected. The offeror becomes free even if the time which he has declared binding

for his offer has not yet expired. The addressee of the offer can therefore not reject it in the first place and then, within the original time frame, accept it nonetheless.

Whether or not the offer lapses in the event of death, bankruptcy or incapability to do business, is left open by the CISG in contrast to Article 11 ULF.

2. *Any offer is terminated with its rejection*, irrespective of whether it was revocable or irrevocable.

3. An offer is *rejected* not only *when* an offeree rejects it but also when he accepts the offer with material modifications. Such an "acceptance" constitutes a new offer (Article 19, paragraph 1). The rejection of an offer often is pronounced not only at the end of the time limit for acceptance (then the offer would lapse anyway) but during that time. In the interest of the possible conclusion of a contract, not every inquiry should be interpreted as being a rejection.

4. The *offer is terminated when* its *rejection reaches* the *offeror* (as to the time of "reaching", c. Article 24). Consequently, if the offeree accepts the offer, for instance by telex, before his letter containing a rejection has reached the offeror, a contract is made (Honnold, 179).

Article 18

(Acceptance; Time of effect of acceptance)

(1) A statement[1] made by or other conduct[2] of the offeree indicating assent to an offer is an acceptance. Silence or inactivity does not in itself[3] amount to acceptance.

(2) An acceptance of an offer becomes effective[4] at the moment the indication of assent[5] reaches[6] the offeror. An acceptance is not effective[7] if the indication of assent does not reach the offeror within the time he has fixed[8] or, if no time is fixed, within a reasonable time[9], due account being taken of the circumstances of the transaction, including the rapidity of the means of communication employed by the offeror. An oral offer[10] must be accepted immediately unless the circumstances indicate otherwise[11].

(3) However, if, by virtue of the offer or as a result of practices which the parties have established between themselves or of usage[13], the offeree[12] may indicate assent by performing an act, such as[14] one relating to[15] the dispatch of the goods or payment of the price, without notice[16] to the offeror, the acceptance is effective[17] at the moment the act is performed, provided that the act is performed within the period of time laid down in the preceding paragraph.

1. Generally, a contract is made by way of *two corresponding statements of intention*: the offer and the acceptance. But in case there is agreement between the parties (e.g. by way of signing a document) there will also be a contract, even if offer and acceptance are not identifiable (Rehbinder/Freiburg, 166; c. also Article 14, note 1).

The statement of acceptance does not expressly have to declare acceptance of the offer; it is necessary that assent to the offer be expressed by the offeree. The statement or conduct is interpreted pursuant to Article 8. The *statement must express assent to the offer*. The mere *acknowledgment of receipt* of the offer is *thus not sufficient*, neither is an expression of interest in it (Farnsworth/BB, 166).

The offeror may prescribe the form of the answer, e. g. by telex. This is of importance when it comes to interpreting the time limit for acceptance (c. note 8).

2. The offeree may also express his *assent through conduct implying an intent*, e. g. dispatch the urgently needed replacement parts or open a letter of credit in the amount of the price. The act which is to express assent to an offer has to refer clearly to the offer. It also suffices that the offeree commences manufacture of the goods (s. Farnsworth/BB, 166) or performs the purchases required (O. R., 24). As to these examples, one fails to see why the offeree should not inform the offeror of his decision to accept the offer. After all, for both parties clarification is needed as regards the conclusion of the contract (Sono/Dubrovnik, 124). Only such conduct can, in our view, be judged to be an acceptance which becomes directly effective towards the other party.

If pursuant to Article 96 a reservation were made concerning the written form, assent through conduct implying an intent would be excluded (c. note 12).

3. There need not be a reaction to goods that were not ordered. *Silence* does *not* mean *acceptance* in this case. However, the offeree may have an obligation to preserve the goods (c. Article 85; Schlechtriem, 40).

The offeror cannot force the offeree to react in writing, for instance: "Consider your silence as assent." Conversely, the offeree may, if he wants to enter into a contract, keep silent and consider the contract as concluded (Farnsworth/BB, 172).

Silence could express acceptance if usages and practices that exist between the parties (Article 9) called for expressly rejecting an offer. In the case of longstanding business relations, silence for reason of good faith (c. Article 7) may mean acceptance (Sono/Dubrovnik, 124). Through an inquiry or an invitation to submit an offer it may be communicated that one's own silence should be interpreted as acceptance (examples are given by Honnold, 182). The parties may also agree that for future contracts silence would amount to acceptance, e.g. in the case of continuous orders (Farnsworth/BB, 167). It is not clear, however, at which moment the contract is concluded in the event of agreed silence (Farnsworth/BB, 172), probably not when the offer is received but rather after a reasonable time. *Silence in answer to a commercial letter of confirmation* has taken on particular significance in the rather extensive (so Rehbinder/Freiburg, 167) jurisdiction of the Federal Republic of Germany. According to that state of affairs, a contract can be made through silence in answer to a letter of confirmation even if negotiations were not successful. While at the Hague Conference commercial letters of confirmation were considered as established practice, the Vienna Conference was against such treatment. Also in this regard the question will be decided in practical terms of whether or not the parties are familiar with this practice. (In its ruling A 9/78 of February 5, 1981 the Court of Arbitration to the Polish Chamber of Foreign Trade judged silence in answer to a letter of confirmation to be assent because this was established practice. See Z Orzecznictwa Kolegium Arbitrow Przy Polskiej Izbie Handlu Zagranicznego. Przeglad Wybranych Orzeczein za lata 1979-1983, Warsaw 1987, p. 53 fol).

If the parties were not familiar with this practice, the letter of confirmation could be regarded as a counter-offer (c. Article 19; Rehbinder/Freiburg, 170).

According to Farnsworth (BB, 172) it is not clear whether the reservation under Article 96 would affect a written agreement between the parties on future silence since Article 96 does not mention general agreements between the parties but only provisions of the Convention which should not apply. From the sense of that reservation, however, it becomes clear that not only oral contracts are to be excluded but even more so those concluded by silence.

4. Before an acceptance becomes effective, it can be withdrawn (Article 22). The *time of effect of the acceptance* and the date of the conclusion of the contract are identical (Article 23). This does not mean, however, that the contract itself is already effective, for its becoming effective may require approval by the State or other authorities. The contract may also become effective retroactively; in that case it will become effective upon approval (Schlechtriem, 45). Yet, pursuant to Article 4, questions relating to validity are excluded from the scope of the Convention.

5. This may be done through a statement of acceptance or conduct implying an intent (c. note 2). Compare also with note 12.

6. Even before it is received, the acceptance has a certain effect: its dispatch already excludes revoking an offer (c. Article 16).

The contract is made not when there is an intention to accept it or when the acceptance is dispatched, but only when it reaches the offeree (as to the moment of "reaching" compare Article 24). The *risk of transmission* is borne by the offeree. Should the acceptance be lost, there would be no contract. If there is a postal delay, the offeror has to react (c. Article 21, paragraph 2).

According to Farnsworth (BB, 172) it would be fairer if the dispatch of the acceptance were considered as decisive and the burden of the risk of transmission were placed on the offeror. The offeror, in the case of no reply to the offer, would likely be more concerned with the destiny of the contract than the offeree who would not know that his acceptance was lost.

An act to be regarded as acceptance, however, becomes effective immediately and not only when the offeror is informed accordingly (c. note 17).

If the offeror becomes aware of the act, e.g. because he is informed by the carrier or a bank that the goods or the money have arrived, no additional statement of acceptance will be required and the loss of such statement will have no negative effects (Farnsworth/BB, 168).

7. The statement of acceptance must be *received within the fixed period of time*; otherwise the acceptance will not become effective. There are, however, exceptions to this rule (c. Article 21).

8. The *period of time for acceptance* may be *fixed according to the calendar or in another way* (e. g. within four weeks). (As to the calculation of the time compare Article 20, paragraph 2 and the beginning of that period compare Article 20, paragraph 1).

9. What is reasonable always depends on the circumstances of each case. The offeree may, in any case, claim some *time for reflexion* which shall be the longer the more complex or complicated the contract offered is. In the case of perishable goods, where immediate delivery is taken for granted, such reasonable time would, for instance, be shorter than in the case of machinery. Account has to be taken also of the way in which the offeror transmits the offer. A simple letter calls for a longer time for reflexion than a telegram. Apart from the category and scope of the transaction, a reasonable time may be influenced by the practice that exists between the parties. Government regulations, which may require an examination as to whether the business transaction might be approved, have to be taken into consideration.

If the offeror is not sure whether the acceptance reached him within a reasonable time, he may give another confirmation. Such confirmation is, under Article 21, paragraph 1, considered as making a late acceptance effective. Farnsworth (BB, 173) is in contradiction to that view and believes that such a confirmation is the actual acceptance if no acceptance was received within a reasonable time.

10. The fact that *oral offers have to be accepted immediately* corresponds with the rules in many legal systems.

11. Also in oral negotiations it is up to the offeror to grant the offeree *time for reflexion* either at his own initiative or at the request of the latter. A period for examination (possible need to get information etc.) may be the outcome of negotiations. One has to expect from the offeree, however, that he will draw the attention of the offeror to unusual circumstances.

12. *Paragraph 3 constitutes an exception to paragraph 2.* Pursuant to paragraph 2 the offeror is informed of the acceptance within the time limit; however under paragraph 3 he is not, for conduct implying an intent would be sufficient already. The offeror who, after that time limit has expired, immediately concludes a contract with a third party, may thus end up in a difficult situation.

According to paragraph 3 a more unfavourable situation arises for the offeror compared to the provision in paragraph 2. Therefore, a conduct implying an intent is somewhat restricted. While paragraph 2 includes any such conduct, paragraph 3 limits a conduct implying an intent to such acts which the offeree undertakes on the basis of the offer, of existing usages or practices. The offeror himself may thus have suggested the conduct implying an intent. A specific action can, for instance, be stipulated in the offer ("Request immediate dispatch!"; c. Schlechtriem, 40).

According to Sono (Dubrovnik, 122), such an offer is only thinkable in the form of an order by the buyer. A seller may also pronounce an invitation in his offer to immediately open up a letter of credit.

13. Actually, *usages and practices do always apply* so that their mentioning here is superfluous. If this is done anyway, then it is done to preclude any doubts.

14. The two examples are, of course, the *main forms of conduct implying an intent*. For that reason a limitation to the supply of the goods and the payment of the price had been suggested in drafting the CISG (c. also note 2).

15. The formulation, "...an act...relating to..", expresses that it is sufficient to give an instruction to the carrier or the bank without actually having dispatched the goods or transferred the price (O. R., 24). Bydlinski (Doralt, 73) even believes that the instruction to an employee is enough. In our view, only those acts which go beyond the sphere of the offeree are relevant.

16. Since an acceptance is effective at the moment when the contract is made, even if the offeror knows nothing about it yet, an unsatisfactory situation may result, when, e. g., the goods are dispatched by ship and the ship is under way for a longer period of time. We, therefore, regard a solution in which the offeror has to be notified of the act within the period of time for acceptance as more favourable.

Depending on the circumstances of each specific case, from the general principles (Article 7) an *obligation* for the offeree *to inform the offeror* may be deduced. Rehbinder (Freiburg, 161) considers this as a supplementary obligation whose breach would entail liability for compensation. Honnold (186 fol) also includes the conditions under paragraph 2 and makes the need for the offeree to give notice dependent on whether or not, for instance, the goods are subject to constantly changing prices. In his view, the offeror also has to learn about the acceptance within a reasonable time.

17. Hence, the contract is concluded at that time. (This is put into doubt, however, by Rehbinder/Freiburg, 161.) Thus the possibility to withdraw or revoke the offer becomes inapplicable (c. note 4), and such prompt effect precludes a future revocation of the offer (Farnsworth/BB, 174).

Article 19

Additions or modifications to the offer)

(1) A reply to an offer which purports[2] to be an acceptance but contains additions, limitations, or other modifications[1] is a rejection[3] of the offer and constitutes a counter-offer[4].

(2) However, a reply to an offer which purports to be an acceptance but contains additional or different terms which do not materially[5] alter the terms of the offer constitutes an acceptance, unless the offeror, without undue delay, objects orally to the discrepancy or dispatches[6] a notice to that effect. If he does not so object, the terms of the contract are the terms of the offer[7] with the modifications contained in the acceptance.

(3) Additional or different terms[10] relating[9], among other things, to the price, payment, quality and quantity of the goods, place and time of delivery, extent of one party's liability to the other or the settlement of disputes are considered to alter the terms of the offer materially[8].

1. The CISG considers *modifications, including additions and restrictions, as detrimental to the conclusion of a contract.* This principle is, however, not made absolute. The main question is whether the modifications are material or immaterial (c. note 5).

There is a large gap here between theory and practice. In practice, most of the acceptances would actually be counter-offers, since it would suffice for the parties to have differing jurisdictional clauses in their business conditions; and the buyer and the seller regularly exchange their offers and acceptances on printed forms or together with their different business conditions. According to Honnold (188) businessmen do not read the backsides of those forms in their normal business relations because business would otherwise "come to a halt". Nevertheless, contracts are being fulfilled.

Since an acceptance including modifications constitutes a counter-offer and the fulfillment of the contract is conduct implying an intent, the conditions of the acceptance apply. These consequences are rejected in many instances. If a seller answers to an order by mailing his business conditions, which contain limited liability or an exemption therefrom, Hyland (Freiburg, 338 fol, giving rather impractical recommendations), for instance, wants the acceptance of the counter-offer by the buyer through an act implying an intent to be valid only if the seller has made a serious attempt to explain the different terms to the buyer.

Eörsi (Lausanne, 50) makes a distinction between whether the modifications are intentional or unintentional, the latter probably not being material in his view.

2. Not every answer to an offer is to be qualified as an acceptance. Inquiries or other remarks concerning the offer should not be promptly classified as a rejection. An answer to an offer can be rejected only when it has been accepted, i.e. the offeree wants it to be an acceptance.

Mere inquiries are neither acceptances nor rejections (Sono/Dubrovnik, 124). To save a contract, modifications are sometimes interpreted by the courts as being "mere suggestions" which the offeror might accept or reject. The acceptance is then divided into acceptance of the offer and a further offer to modify the contract (Farnsworth/BB, 178).

There is a dispute on whether a commercial letter of confirmation constitutes an acceptance (see Huber, 449 fol; Schlechtriem, 44; Rehbinder/Freiburg, 170).

3. An *acceptance including the modifications does not bring about a contract*, but is regarded as a rejection of the offer and, therefore, terminates the offer (c. Article 17).

4. While an *acceptance including the modifications* terminates the original offer, that same acceptance remains an independent act and *takes on the character of a counter-offer*. Now the provisions of Article 14 fol are applied to this counter-offer. To lead to the conclusion of a contract, this new offer needs to be unreservedly accepted. Such acceptance may be expressed through conduct implying an intent, (within the periods of time fixed under Article 18).

The counter-offer accepted through conduct implying an intent favours the party who, in the *"battle of the forms"* fires the last shot, i. e. sends the last printed confirmation. Farnsworth (BB, 179) believes this typically to be the seller when he sends his answer to the buyer's order. We doubt whether such a general statement can be made at all. In the case of technical goods the typical situation should rather be that the buyer calls for an offer and then, on his part, declares his acceptance.

5. Not every acceptance is limited to a simple "yes" as an answer to the offer. Often the terms of the offer are repeated in the offeree's own words. In so doing, modifications may be expressed verbally which are not based on differing intentions.

However, even actual *additions or modifications will not be considered if they do not materially alter the terms of the offer*. What is considered as material depends on the circumstances of each case. What is unimportant to one party may be important to the other, and vice versa (Sono/Dubrovnik, 126). The question will have to be asked, in particular, whether the modifications will cause the offeror additional efforts or difficulties or increase his risks. "Neutral" modifications will in general be regarded as immaterial. According to Rehbinder (Freiburg, 164), however, everything is material which is "not to the obvious advantage" of the offeror. *Immaterial modifications* could be, *for instance*, that a certain packaging of the goods was prescribed, but a more suitable packaging could be used to avoid additional costs or that global delivery dates are specified (Bydlinski/Doralt, 72).

6. The *offeror might*, however, insist on an unreserved acceptance of his offer and *reject any modification*, no matter how immaterial it may be. He should, therefore, carefully read the acceptance. Nevertheless, he must declare his rejection promptly. To do so, it suffices for him to dispatch a relevant communication. The risk of the loss of or a delay in transmitting the communication is borne by the offeree.

7. In the absence of an immediate objection by the offeror, a contract is created, the terms of which are drawn from the offer and the modifications made in the acceptance.

Basically, even an immaterial discrepancy constitutes a counter-offer, since the offeror retains the right to reject it. If he does not do so, he practically accepts the offer by silence. Rehbinder (Freiburg, 164) believes that in this connection a rule is missing concerning the moment the contract is concluded and wants to apply here the provisions of Article 21, paragraph 1 analogously. In our view such an analogy is superfluous for it can be seen clearly from Article 18 when a contract becomes effective, i.e. at the moment the unchallenged acceptance reaches the offeror.

8. *Material modifications of the offer* raised through acceptance *are obstacles to the conclusion of a contract*. This rule is supposed to protect the offeror. Farnsworth (BB, 178) therefore rightly raises the question of what happens if the modifications are such that they are to the advantage of the offeror. If changes in the price, the quality etc. were advantageous to the offeror, while other terms remained the same, they should not be in the way of a contract (Bydlinski/Doralt, 72).

Paragraph 3, in listing those terms whose modification should always be considered as materially altering the terms of the offer, strongly *limits* the *possibility*, as contained in paragraph 2, to *favourably interpret the offer and acceptance so as to come to the conclusion of a contract*. If certain changes are considered as material, then this is only an assumption which can be disproved, among other things, by invoking usages (Schlechtriem, 43). Rehbinder (Freiburg, 165) also advocates a refutable assumption, but claims at the same time that the irrefutability of an assumption ensues from genesis. Actually, at the Vienna Conference a relevant half sentence was deleted in the draft at the request of Bulgaria, which referred to whether or not the offeree, because of the offer or the particular circumstances of a specific case, had reason to assume that his modifications were acceptable to the offeror. There is no doubt that commercial practice does *not* consider *any alteration of the offer* relating to the above-mentioned factors as being an *obstacle to the conclusion of a contract*. Frequently, the offeror will commence with the realization of the contract in line with the terms of the acceptance, which will have to be regarded as an acceptance of the counter-offer through conduct implying an intent when acceptance, including the modifications, has led to the termination of the original offer.

9. What is unsatisfactory with regard to this solution is that only the object and *not the degree of discrepancy* should be *taken into account*. Though rather extensive, that listing is not even complete. Other material alterations could include prior negotiations which have no influence on a written contract, or oral alterations of the written contract which are not permitted. It is doubtful whether a *force majeure* clause which does not relate to the extent of liability but the liability itself, or a choice-of-law clause which does not relate to the settlement of disputes as such but rather to the rules for such settlement (e.g. the standard rules of the ECE or UNCITRAL) are considered as pertaining to the examples mentioned (Farnsworth/BB,

183). A restrictive interpretation should try here to save some of the intentions of paragraph 2.

10. Discrepancies between the offer and acceptance are, in particular, the result of the *transmission of contradictory general business conditions*, which is a problem that was solved under domestic law, e. g. in paragraph 33 of the ICCA. The inclusion of a relevant rule into the CISG was rejected both in the working group of UNCITRAL (proposal by the former GDR) and at the Vienna Conference (proposal by Belgium) (O.R., 289).

Under the rules of the CISG the party which is the last to transmit terms or to invoke them has the advantage (Schlechtriem, 44). Honnold (195) does not prefer the latest transmitted terms, but rather the concurring terms. He admits nevertheless that one always has to assume that a counter-offer is accepted by conduct implying an intent if the terms are contradictory, but the contract is fulfilled. According to Kramer (Doralt, 95) contradictory terms are a dissent and raise problems of validity, which pursuant to Article 4, are not covered by the CISG. In our view, however, a solution on the basis of Article 19 is preferable. It is recommendable for the offeror to always react to an acceptance irrespective of whether he wants the contract or not. If he wants the contract and says "yes", then this is either a superfluous confirmation, because the acceptance contained only immaterial alterations, or a necessary acceptance of the counter-offer if the alterations were material. If he does not want the contract and says "no", then this is either a superfluous clarification, because the acceptance contained material alterations, or a necessary step because there were only non-material alterations (Farnsworth/BB, 184).

Article 20

Time fixed for acceptance)

(1) A period of time for acceptance[1] fixed by the offeror in a telegram or a letter begins to run[2] from the moment the telegram is handed in for dispatch or from the date shown on the letter, or if no such date is shown, from the date shown on the envelope. A period of time for acceptance fixed by the offeror by telephone, telex or other means of instantaneous communication, begins to run from the moment that the offer reaches[3] the offeree.

(2) Official holidays or non-business days occurring during the period for acceptance are included in calculating[4] the period. However, if a notice of acceptance cannot be delivered at the address of the offeror on the last day of the period because that day falls on an official holiday or a non-business day at the place[5] of business of the offeror, the period is extended until the first business day[6] which follows.

1. Only if the period for acceptance is not calculated by the offeror according to the calendar (e.g. offer valid until April 30) but in days or weeks, in special cases also in hours, there is the question of when that period begins. The objective of this rule is for the two parties to find identical bases for the calculation of that period. Since the moment of dispatch is generally easier to prove than the moment of receipt, *the CISG chooses the moment of dispatch as the beginning of the period for acceptance* (Farnsworth/BB, 186).

2. There are *different provisions* in Article 20 regarding the *commencement of the period for acceptance depending on* which *way* was chosen *to communicate* the offer. The date contained in the letter and the date of the actual dispatch need not be identical. These dates provide, however, a basis for an identical calculation of the period because the sender has a copy and the addressee probably discards the envelope (Farnsworth/BB, 186). If the letter does not have a date, the date of the stamp will count; the handing in of the letter at the post office thus being decisive just as in the case of a telegram. Periods for acceptance fixed by telephone or telex begin to run with the moment of receipt (c. Article 24).

Article 20 is a rule of interpretation. The offeror might also prescribe something different, e.g. he may fix a time of ten days to begin upon receipt of the offer (Honnold, 197 fol; Farnsworth/BB, 187). In case the offeror has not set a time limit so that one can proceed on a reasonable time (c. Article 18); there will be no question as to when the period for acceptance begins to run but rather when it ends.

3. Insofar as the addressee himself has a telephone or telex, and the communication does not need to be transmitted through third persons, the moments of *receipt and dispatch* are practically *identical*.

4. In other words, when calculating the number of days of the period it is ignored whether they are *holidays*, non-business days or business days if the delivery of the acceptance is not impeded (c. note 6).

5. Only holidays or non-business days at the place of business of the offeror are being taken into consideration because those may not be known to the offeree. If, however, the last day of the period falls on a holiday at the place of business of the offeree and the offeree is prevented from dispatching an acceptance, he has to take this into account and hand in his acceptance for dispatch earlier.

6. The offeror will not be able to make different arrangements on the last business day of the period, but rather has to wait until the *next business day*. He has to consider that the offeree will fully exhaust the period (Schlechtriem, 42).

Article 21

(Late acceptance)

(1) A late acceptance[1] is nevertheless effective as an acceptance if without delay the offeror[2] orally so informs the offeree or dispatches[3] a notice to that effect.

(2) If a letter or other writing containing a late acceptance shows that it has been sent in such circumstances that if its transmission had been normal it would have reached the offeror in due time[4], the late acceptance is effective as an acceptance unless, without delay, the offeror orally informs the offeree that he considers[5] his offer as having lapsed or dispatches a notice to that effect.

1. The ruling under Article 21 covers *two cases of late acceptance*, i.e. an acceptance which has not reached the offeror in due time (c. Article 18, paragraph 2):

(a) The *acceptance was dispatched belatedly*, either after the period fixed by the offeror has expired and the offer has therefore already lapsed (Article 17) or still during that period but using a way of communication which has precluded the offeror from being reached in due time. The offeree has to be aware at all times that he is late in his acceptance. He thus knows that his acceptance is actually a counter-offer and needs to be confirmed through an acceptance. Silence by the offeror cannot be inferred by him to be an acceptance (Article 18, paragraph 1). The situation is more difficult if the offeror has not fixed a time, the acceptance having to be made nonetheless within a reasonable period (Article 18, paragraph 2). In that case, the offeror and the offeree may well consider different periods as being reasonable. Objectively, a reasonable time may have expired already, even though the offeree assumes that the acceptance was made in due time.

(b) The *acceptance was dispatched in time* but its delivery to the offeror was delayed because of unforeseen circumstances. In this case, the offeree believes to have concluded a contract since he does not know of the delay in delivering the communication.

Both cases of late acceptance can be remedied.

2. In both cases it *is up to the offeror whether* or not *he considers the acceptance to be valid*. If he wants a contract, in case (a) he must inform the offeree accordingly; in case (b) he may remain silent.

Should the offeror keep silent in case (a), there will be no contract. In the interest of clarity between the parties, a communication on the part of the offeror to the offeree is recommendable in any case. If the offeror wants the contract, the offeree may not invoke that he was late in accepting (Honnold, 210 fol, mentions examples which appear rather abstract because they disregard the date of delivery). This means that possibly changed circumstances, such as price developments, can only be to the advantage of the offeror, which may seem unjust because nothing is said about the causes for the delay. The acceptance, for instance, might have been dispatched only a little late and may in addition have been left at the post office for a long time. Such a case is not covered by paragraph 2.

3. *If* the *offeree is informed* accordingly, the *offer*, which actually should have *lapsed*, *remains in existence* and leads to the formation of a contract through late acceptance. In many legal systems there is a different solution for this case. Late acceptance is regarded as a new offer which can be accepted by the original offeror. If the latter remains silent there will, as under the CISG, be no contract. The practical difference lies in the date on which the contract is concluded; under the provisions of the CISG upon receipt of the late acceptance, otherwise when it is confirmed and/or the counter-offer is accepted.

The *risk of transmission is borne by the offeree*. The communication should indeed be received since it is the only way to bring about a contract and insofar constitutes the actual acceptance; otherwise, a contract might be created without the offeree knowing anything about it (Rehbinder/Freiburg, 163). In this context the wording "without delay" is not quite comprehensible since the offeror did not have to reckon with an acceptance and probably needs time for reflexion. He would have such time for reflexion if the late acceptance were treated as a counter-offer (Bydlinski/Doralt, 71). This rule is questionable, in particular when the acceptance is declared very late and the circumstances as a whole have changed in the meantime (Rehbinder/Freiburg, 162).

It is not clear whether the late acceptance becomes effective at the moment when the offeror informs the offeree or dispatches the relevant communication or whether it becomes effective retroactively from the moment it is received. (Since the offeror needs to inform the offeree without delay, there will only be a slight difference in time. Nonetheless the question might be important whether the offeree can withdraw his acceptance. (affirmative: Honnold, 200, doubting: Farnsworth/BB, 193)). It is doubtful whether oral information will be sufficient if a reservation was made pursuant to Article 96 (c. note 3 regarding Article 18).

4. In the case of *normal handling*, a contract would under Article 18 have been made with timely acceptance. But what is normal handling internationally? Is a two weeks' postal handling from Italy to Germany normal, not however four weeks? The offeree relies on the conclusion of the contract and such reliance shall be protected. Hence, the offeror may remain silent if he, too, still wants the contract. Here the rare case is involved where silence leads to the making of a contract (Farnsworth/BB, 192).

The same rule is contained in 30 (3) of the ICCA or 149 of the German BGB. The common law does not know such rules because according to the dispatch rule, that problem cannot arise (Honnold, 203).

5. On the other hand, the offeror could not foresee that an acceptance would arrive even after the period for acceptance had expired. Meanwhile he may have made other arrangements or have lost his interest in the transaction. He *is* therefore, *not obliged to be bound by* the *late communication*, but he can inform the offeree that he regards his offer as lapsed.

6. If the offeror no longer wants a contract, he has to *inform* the offeree *without delay* that after the expiration of the period for acceptance his *offer had* already *lapsed*. "Without delay" relates to the moment of receipt of the late acceptance and not to the expiration of the period for acceptance.

Article 22

(Withdrawal of acceptance)

An acceptance may be withdrawn[1] if the withdrawal reaches[3] the offeror before or at the same time as the acceptance would have become effective[2].

1. An acceptance can be withdrawn just as an offer (c. Article 15, paragraph 2) as long as it has not become effective.

The result is a situation where the *offeror* is *bound*, but *not yet* the *offeree*, for the offeror can no longer revoke his offer after the acceptance was dispatched (Article 16, paragraph 1). The offeree, however, can speculate during the time of postal handling. Farnsworth (BB, 196 fol) will prevent this by liberally applying the rule of good faith under Article 7, paragraph 1 or by way of invoking domestic law under Article 7, paragraph 2. It is not clear to us why the revoking of an acceptance which has not been received by the offeror constitutes a misuse which has to be fought with good faith. Unclear is also how such a misuse could be proved. Since our law is based on the assumption that an offer is generally binding, the unilateral binding of the offeror is not a problem.

2. As to the effectiveness of an acceptance, compare Article 18, paragraph 2. A late acceptance does not become effective under Article 18, but rather under Article 21, i.e. either by express information or silence.

3. Concerning receipt compare Article 24.

Article 23

(Time of conclusion of contract)

A contract is concluded at the moment[1] when an acceptance of an offer[2] becomes effective[3] in accordance with the provisions of this Convention.

1. Under the provisions of Article 18, paragraph 2 there should actually be no doubt as to the time when a contract is concluded. However, it was considered useful to expressly mention that time, namely for such cases where reference is made to the time of the conclusion, i.e. in Articles 33, (c); 35, paragraph 2 (b); 35, paragraph 3; 41, paragraphs 1 and 2; 42, paragraph 1; 55; 57, paragraph 2; 68;

71, paragraph 1; 73, paragraph 3, 74; 79, paragraph 1 and 100 paragraph 2.

The time of conclusion of a contract could also be of significance where questions not covered by the scope of application of the CISG are concerned.

What was *not settled* is the *location of the formation of the contract*. This may be important for several connecting factors. The proposal to include such a provision was rejected for varying reasons. We assume that the contract is concluded at the place where the acceptance reaches the offeror. Should the contract already be concluded by conduct implying an intent, then the place of performance of this act and/or the place of business of the offeree would probably be decisive.

2. The CISG provides for the conclusion of a contract through offer and acceptance. (Compare OR. 292 and note 1 of Article 14 as well as note 1 of Article 18.) In the case of negotiations where the outcome is a joint final document, both the time and the place of the conclusion of a contract are undisputed.

3. The parties may, however, make the effectiveness of the contract dependant on conditions (c. note 1, Article 15).

Article 24

(Definition: "reaches")

For the purposes of this Part[1] of the Convention, an offer, declaration of acceptance or any other indication of intention[2] "reaches" the addressee when it is made[6] orally[3] to him or delivered[4] by any other means to him personally, to his place of business or mailing address or, if he does not have a place of business or mailing address, to his habitual residence[5].

1. The *definition of "reaches"* according to the structure of the rule applies *only to Part II* of the CISG. The notion "reaches" is decisive where the effectiveness of the offer (Article 15, paragraph 1) and the acceptance (Article 18, paragraph 2) are concerned. That definition is of relevance for the commencement of the period allowed for acceptance under Article 20, paragraph 1. The rule of receipt itself does not automatically apply to the several statements which are governed by Part III of the Convention (c. also Articles 26 and 27). In that Part the rule of dispatch applies. Exceptions are made in Article 47, paragraph 2; Article 48, paragraph 4; Article 63, paragraph

2; Article 65, paragraphs 1 and 2 and Article 79, paragraph 4. The definition of "reaches" may be applied analogously in those cases.

2. *All declarations indicating the intent to conclude a contract need to reach the addressee* (Schlechtriem, 35). Other statements of intention are, in particular, the withdrawal or revocation of declarations (c. Article 15, paragraph 2; Article 16, paragraph 1, and Article 22) and the rejection of an offer (Article 17).

3. As to "him" or his agent, compare note 6. The authorization of an intermediary or intermediaries is determined by domestic law (Schlechtriem, 36). Regarding the written form of contracts, compare Article 11, note 1.

4. *Delivery does not mean* that the addressee has *taken cognizance* of the statement. The communication, however, needs to have reached his area of receipt or disposal, and it needs to have been "recognizable" (Schlechtriem, 36). It would not be sufficient if it were left in an unattended place or on the door steps (Honnold, 206; Farnsworth/BB, 203).

Delivery can be made on holidays. Only if this is not possible will the fixed period be extended (c. Article 20, paragraph 2). The risk of transmission is born by the sender.

5. Compare Article 10.

6. Delivery to the addressee and deliveries to his statutory representative or agent have equal status (c. also Article 13, note 18 concerning the Agency Convention).

Part III

Sale of goods

Chapter I

General Provisions

Introductory remarks

This Chapter incorporates very heterogenous provisions so that an *internal system* could *not* be *established*. Articles 25 and 26 (in part this refers also to Art. 27) supplement above all (more in detail note 2.2. of Art. 25) the provisions on the presuppositions regarding breach of contract, most of which can be found in Part III, Chapters II and III. They contain provisions applicable for both parties which out of theoretical considerations have been taken out of the brackets and are now left somewhat unrelated in this Chapter.

Article 27 in addition relates to communications on the substance of contracts and defines, in general terms, the principle of receipt. Article 28 refers to specific performance and the actual consequences of breaches of contract and should for reasons of systematology have been included in Chapter V. The Article best placed in this Chapter is Article 29 which covers specific aspects of avoidance and modifications of contracts.

Article 25

(Fundamental breach)

A breach of contract[1] committed by one of the parties is fundamental[2] if it results in such detriment to the other party as substantially to deprive him of what he is entitled to expect under the contract[3], unless the party in breach did not foresee and a reasonable person of the same kind in the same circumstances would not have foreseen[4] such a result.

1. Concerning the term *breach of contract* as part of the regulation regarding responsibility under the CISG, compare clause 5 of the introductory remarks to Article 79.

2.1. The CISG does not contain a specific term to complement "fundamental breach of contract" because "breach of contract" also functions as a generic term. We use the term *"simple breach of contract"* because the establishment of a complementary term by way of negation ("non-fundamental" - Huber, 461) is to be rejected for it could also serve to qualify a breach of contract which formally occurred but is so irrelevant that it would not entail any legal consequences.

2.2. A fundamental breach is a *condition for the immediate avoidance of the contract* in the case of non-fulfilment of an obligation (Art. 49, paragraph 1, subpara. (a); Art. 64, paragraph 1, subpara. (a) and/or of an anticipated non-performance of an obligation (Art. 72, paragraph 1) as well as of avoidance in the case of incomplete or partially conform delivery (Art. 51). The same applies to contracts on delivery by instalments where the contract is to be made void in regard to the affected partial delivery and possibly also in regard to other partial deliveries (Art. 73). It also holds true for the right to delivery of substitute goods in the event of non-conformity (Art. 46, paragraph 2). And, finally, it may cause certain rights to be retained which would otherwise be lost after the passing of risk (Art. 70).

2.3. The distinction between fundamental breach and simple breach of contract is the basic *criterion for the classification* of breaches of contract. This criterion offers a wide scope of interpretation, all the more since it is linked, to a large degree, to assessments. The outcome of this situation are uncertainties which have to be reduced in the discussion at the international level. In this endeavour, one should cooperate with those institutions which take the decisions in practice. A new step cannot be renounced just because not all of its implications can be foreseen. The fact that the fundamentality of a breach of contract in many cases is the condition for an avoidance of contract is expression of the trend of the CISG to preserve contracts, which we consider as essential in international trade.

2.4. The certain *awkwardness of the definition* of fundamentality is the result of a compromise (in detail see Eörsi, Convention, 336 fol). Basically, it refers to two essential criteria: to the party vis-a-vis to whom the breach was committed, the aggrieved party; (note 3) and, to the foreseeability of that breach (note 4). The elements which define a substantial detriment are extremely complex. In seeking a solution (as long as there is no experience) the legal consequence will not be deduced from the facts of the case, but rather will the facts be interpreted according to the legal consequence which is intuitively felt to be the just one. Article 10 ULIS also does not seem to be of great help considering the decisions given as examples by Schlechtriem/Magnus (171 fol).

3. The *detriment* itself is *characterized by three aspects*: In the end, and that is the decisive element in our view, there has to be a relevant detriment to the aggrieved party (3.1.); it has to be fundamental (3.2.); and proportionate to the expectations justified under the contract (3.3.). This shall be made clear by citing some important exam-

ples (3.4.). It will become obvious that the relevant detriment is not a static element, but in many instances occurs only when the breach of contract continues. Hence, one of the greatest difficulties in analyzing the fundamentality of a breach is to determine the time when the detriment has become so great that the prerequisites are met.

The parties may, from the outset, *characterize as fundamental*, certain categories of non-fulfilment of obligations; e.g. by determining that time is of the essence. This would correspond to the principle of contract autonomy. This can also be done by invoking established practices. The consequences will then follow from the Convention (not in agreement Huber/Dölle, 51).

The term "detriment" should be interpreted in a broad sense (accordingly Will/BB, 211 fol). Detriment basically means that the *purpose* the aggrieved party pursued with the contract *was foiled* and, therefore, led to his loosing interest in the performance of the contract (Schlechtriem, 48). From this follows his interest in avoiding the contract.

Though in commercial relations most things can be reduced to a damage, this is not the central issue here. On the contrary, when compensation for damages can serve as the adequate remedial action, this should be an indication of the fact that there is no detriment in the meaning of the Convention. It will be the case, however, when the aggrieved party in remaining bound to the contract is hindered in his commercial or manufacturing activities in such a way that he can no longer be expected to continue holding on to it. Hence, detriment can be a very complex phenomenon. But it must be in existence at the time of the avoidance of the contract. What matters most in commercial relations are economic results and not formal fulfilment of obligations.

3.2. As to the *substantiality*, there is, no doubt, a tautology between substantial and fundamental as characterizing a breach of contract. That repetition seems to have been unavoidable to ensure congruence of the *definiens* and the *definiendum*. Actually, we have taken account of the element of substantiality in discussing the term "detriment". It should be added that it is the circumstances of each individual case which are relevant.

3.3. Finally, the *expectations* of the aggrieved party have to be *discernible from the contract*. This element to which, in particular, the FRG had attached great importance (Huber, 464, and a relevant proposal, O. R., 99) is quite evident in itself and also contained in the element of foreseeability (note 4). It is to be stressed that a fundamental breach of contract must constitute also a non-fulfilment of a contractual obligation. Nothing can be said against this opinion. Sometimes, however, one gets the impression that when interpreting (Schlechtriem, 47) the main emphasis is shifted from the substantial detriment to the non-fulfilment of the obligation. Such approach, in our view, does not meet the intention of the provision insofar as it concerns the consequences of a contract violation which is then characterized more in detail. We thus consider reference to the contract more as a restriction of cases of fundamental breach rather than an extension (not every ambitious expectation is protected).

3.4. A *violation of the time for performance* constitutes a fundamental breach of contract when, for instance, the other party cannot use the late delivery for the purpose envisaged in the contract. When the contract stipulates that time is of the essence or uses such customary terms as "fixed", "absolutely", "precisely", "at the latest", it could be considered as an agreement, where non-fulfilment of this condition will have to be regarded as a fundamental breach of contract. Proof that the legal prerequisites of such breach are not fulfilled is then inadmissible (not in agreement Huber, 462 fol on the draft convention).

A *violation of the qualitative requirements* (non-conform delivery) is fundamental when the non-conformity considerably impedes the fitness for use of the goods and when it is irreparable. Whether or not a reparable lack of conformity is fundamental depends on the time element. Had the violation of the time for delivery been fundamental, much would speak in favour of considering a reparable fundamental lack of conformity as a fundamental breach of contract. If this is not the case, a non-conform delivery can then expand into a fundamental breach of contract when the lack is not removed.

We do not, however, consider the *delivery of an aliud* as a fundamental breach of contract. We hold that there are two approaches to this problem. Both proceed from the assumption that there is a fundamental breach from the very outset, of which notice is to be given (Art. 38 fol) and which entails the right to delivery of substitute goods (Art. 46, paragraph 2) or avoidance of contract (Art. 49, paragraph 1, subpara. (a)). The right to immediate avoidance in any case connected therewith cannot be justified. We, therefore, prefer an interpretation according to which there is non-delivery at first with the right of the other party to performance being retained, but the provisions governing the notice of a lack of conformity are applied by analogy. It would then have to be assessed whether a violation of the time for performance, which a further delivery (of now conform good) mostly entails, would have to be characterized as a fundamental breach of contract.

To what extent a *non-fulfilment of an obligation* is fundamental depends on its relevance for the achievement of the purpose of the contract. In regard to the most important obligations (delivery, payment, acceptance) the possibility of avoidance can be achieved by using the mechanism of the *Nachfrist* (Art. 49, paragraph 1, subpara. (b); Art. 64, paragraph 1, subpara. (b)). In the event of a non-fulfilment of another obligation, avoidance is possible only when it is to be regarded as fundamental. That there is indeed a non-fulfilment will practically become obvious only after a period of waiting for fulfilment. Cases where there is, or will be, fundamentality include the non-delivery of certificates of analysis of chemical substances; operating manuals of technical consumer goods; the lack of agreed labels or, on the part of the buyer, non-supply of agreed drawings or of part of materials.

And, finally, the case should be mentioned where the seller has delivered goods which, contrary to his obligations, are *not free from third party claims or rights* (Art. 42) based on industrial or other intellectual property. If this lack is not removed, e.g. by way of licences, payment of compensation, satisfaction of claims, and the use of the goods according to the contract is at least substantially impeded, there will be a fundamental breach of contract. If these lacks can be removed, the decisive factor will be time required as in the event of non-conform delivery.

4.1. It is assumed that a party who knows the far-reaching consequences of a breach of contract for the other party, if he is not sure of his possibility to fulfil, either does not conclude the contract at all or makes increased efforts to prevent its violation. Therefore, the fundamentality of a breach is made dependent not only on its consequences but also on its *foreseeability* by the other party. The same consideration can be found in Article 74 regarding the determination of the amount of damages. The rights of the aggrieved party are thus limited in the event that the other party did not foresee special consequences which make up the fundamentality of the breach of contract. It results that the parties should draw their respective attention to such consequences either in the contract itself or through additional information to be given in principle until the conclusion of the contract (but 3.3.), e.g. particularly serious consequences in the case of acceptance not in time because of lack of storage facilities, substantiality of proof of technical check-up for re-sale of the goods.

4.2. It cannot be inferred that one party indeed did not foresee the serious consequences of his breach of contract because this could be considered as professional competence below average. An *objectivization* is, therefore, made here (regarding the interpretation of the terms used here see Art. 8, note 5). If the party in question does, however, foresee more than average, this will be relevant (Will/BB, 220).

4.3. No *time* is fixed when this foreseeability or required foresight must exist. The interpretation is, therefore, different with the time of the conclusion of the contract or of the breach of contract playing a role (for a survey see Will/BB, 220 fol). While we hold that generally the time of the conclusion of the contract should be referred to, we consider it possible that in exceptional cases subsequent information should be taken into account as well. Such information could be given until the actual and/or required commencement of the preparation in view of performance so that the other party can still adapt itself to it. This seems justified to us because it can be doubted that the information available at the time of the conclusion of the contract has really made possible the foreseeability or required foresight of the consequences. This doubt may be removed when subsequent information is taken account of. When, for instance, in the case of a contract for delivery of consumer goods to be manufactured the buyer signals immediately after the conclusion of the contract that the imprint of agreed data on the packaging is of decisive importance because the goods otherwise could not be sold in the envisaged sales area, this will have to be regarded as sufficient for the violation of the respective obligation to be characterized as fundamental (agreeing Will/BB, 221).

Article 26

(Notice of avoidance)

A declaration[1] of avoidance of the contract[2] is effective only if made by notice to the other party[3].

1.1. Prescribing a *declaration of avoidance*, the CISG breaks with the *ipso facto* avoidance, i.e. avoidance by virtue of law, which has played a great role in ULIS, thus overcoming the uncertainty as to whether, and possibly when, the contract is made void. Avoidance constitutes a right. Since it is made dependent on a declaration, the entitled party can consciously decide to continue to claim performance of the contract even when there are grounds for avoidance. This being the case, the rule also has the effect of preserving the contract and its specific performance. The requirement of a declaration of avoidance is relevant because otherwise tradesmen, who are supposed to work on the basis of the CISG, would not always be aware that certain conduct could automatically entail the avoidance of the contract. The entitled party can, however, achieve partly similar effects when he, in cases where the right to make the contract void follows from the expiry of a Nachfrist without performance (Art. 49, subpara. (b); Art. 64, subpara. (b)), already in fixing such Nachfrist, declares the contract void if the other party does not perform within that additional period.

1.2. A specific *form is required for the one-sided avoidance* insofar as it has to be made in the form of a declaration, which can be oral or in writing (Secretariat's Commentary, O. R., 27; Date-Bah/BB, 224 referring to the legislative history of the provision). Avoidance of a contract by conduct implying an intent, e.g. the mere sending back of delivered and fundamentally non-conform goods, is not sufficient.

2. *Avoidance* of a contract is provided for by the Convention in Articles 49, 51, 64, 72 and 73. The rule applies to all those cases, but also for contractually agreed grounds for avoidance.

3.1. In a comparison with Article 27, it is sufficient for the declaration to be made with the means appropriate under the circumstances. An indirect, more accidental notice to the other party is, therefore, insufficient (example given by Date-Bah/BB, 224 fol). The *dispatch is decisive.* An oral notice could thus be given by phone to an answering machine. Written notices would have to be sent using the customary ways of communication. It is not necessary that the communication reaches the other party. The problem involved in the procedure envisaged in Article 27 becomes clearly evident in this case since it is possible for a party to continue performance of the avoided contract because he did not receive the notice.

3.2. The notice, of course, has the desired effect only when the *grounds for avoidance* were indeed *given.* But this can be doubtful. Since a fundamental breach of contract may become obvious only if it persists (note 3.4. of Article 25), it is possible, therefore, that this occurs only after the notice is given. In our view it should be considered as effective.

Article 27[1]

(Delay or error in communication)

Unless otherwise expressly provided[2] in this Part of the Convention, if any notice, request or other communication[3] is given or made by a party in accordance with this Part[4] and by means appropriate in the circumstances[5], a delay or error[6] in the transmission of the communication or its failure to arrive[7] does not deprive that party of the right to rely on the communication.

1.1. The CISG establishes the principle of the *theory of dispatch* even if it is formulated in a cautious way. This has been interpreted in such a way that a communication becomes effective with dispatch (Date-Bah/BB, 227 fol). But what is this to mean in detail? It becomes rather obvious from the text that one can relate to the communication beginning with the moment of dispatch, even if this expressed in the negative way. Hence, the risk of transport is covered. Decisive is also the date of dispatch where the punctuality of the communication is concerned. Leser (Freiburg, 237 fol) held the view that in regard to the legal consequences and the binding of the party dispatching the communication, *receipt* should be decisive. This, however, in the event of late or non-receipt of the communication requires an auxiliary construction providing for the coming into effect of those consequences after the expiry of the regular time of handling. For both cases there are hardly any clues in the text. As to the substance, the need for receipt would insofar be welcomed. Besides, an analysis of the individual provisions of the CISG, which provide for reference to the principle of dispatch, has clearly shown that invoking it in its rigorous form leads to inappropriate results (note 10 of Article 65).

1.2. *In favour of the principle of dispatch* it is argued, *inter alia*, that it offers a largely uniform rule (Secretariat's Commentary, O. R. 27), which is contradicted by the many exemptions provided for (note 2) and also by the fact that it only applies to Part III. If this were not so, a rule for receipt would have been required (ibid), which the CISG offer in Article 24 (for Part III). The theory of dispatch would be useful where a party fulfilled an obligation or required remedy for a loss; not, however, where it served to substantiate an obligation for the other party (O. R., 303). Such foundation, to which also other authors refer (Date-Bah/BB, 230, even though hesitatingly), is not quite true for he who asserts a claim because of a breach of contract thereby substantiates an obligation of the other party. This rule was also not strictly followed (according to Art. 65, paragraph

2, it is exactly the notice of the party keeping the contract which has to be received by the other party; see also note 3). Problems arise where the rule is applied to such contractually agreed communications like information on the possibility to use a right (to participate in carrying out a test). A proposal by the former GDR to restrict the scope of application of Article 27 to notices of a defect was rejected (compare O. R., 100).

2. *Exceptions* are contained in Article 47, paragraph 2, and Article 63, paragraph 2, in which receipt of a notice is actually already a condition for the activities of the other party caused by it; Article 48, paragraph 2, Article 65, paragraphs 1 and 2, and Article 79, paragraph 4.

3. This rule applies to *all kinds of communications* like notices of a defect (Art. 39, paragraph 1; Art. 43); claims (in particular Part III, Chapter II, Section III); information which entail legal consequences (Art. 32, paragraph 3); determining additional periods for delivery (Art. 47, paragraph 1) and warnings (Art. 72, paragraph 2; Art. 88, paragraph 1).

4.1. This, no doubt, refers to the *communications* mentioned in this Part, but also those which are *agreed in the contract* (e.g. notice of defects in guarantee, statement of readiness for dispatch, notice of dispatch). Part III generally relates to the substance of contracts. Furthermore, Article 27 formulates *expressis verbis* a general principle of the Convention and is, therefore, under Article 7, paragraph 2, to be applied to cases which are not expressly decided. Difficulties may appear, however, in the context of specific cases because the exceptions regulated by the Convention (compare note 2) cannot be reduced to a common denominator.

4.2. From the reference to this Part it is also deduced, and rightly so in regard to substance, as we believe, that the communication has to *meet the requirements* (Date-Bah/BB, 228) fixed in Part III (substantive, formal and according to schedule) in order to cause the expected effect (compare also note 6).

5. These have to be the *means* which correspond to the content of the communication in terms of rapidity and reliability. For instance, when choosing the means for communicating such an important decision, as it is the avoidance of a contract, particular care has to be exercised. However, sending a communication twice can only be requested when there is particular uncertainty in transmitting to the receiving party. Special circumstances can exclude specific means, e.g. sending by mail in the event of a strike of mailmen of

which the sender at least had to be aware. The party sending the communication may choose from among several possible means.

In the event that *contractually agreed requirements* in regard to the transmission are not met (e.g. telex with confirmation by certified letter), one cannot rely on the communication under Article 27, i.e. not on the telex not received if there was no confirmation, but very well on the latter if it was also not received.

Concerning the comprehensibility of the *language* compare Article 8, note 3.2. According to Date-Bah (BB, 230) it is irrelevant in this context.

6. The communication must be sent correctly, i.e. it can only be garbled or distorted in the *process of transmission*. In that case, the party having dispatched the communication, does not have to rescind but can rely on the actual content of the communication sent. When, for instance, a notice of non-conforming delivery of a replacement part having a specific number is requested, and that number is changed when communicated by telex, so that the other party, in response, sends the wrong replacement part, the latter retains the obligation to send the right one.

7. If, however, the sending party recognizes from the behaviour of the other party that the latter has *not received the communication*, it should be a matter of good faith (Art. 7) or of mitigating a loss (Art. 77) for the former to draw the attention of the latter to the content of the communication. Otherwise, he would, for instance, no longer have the right to assert accumulating claims for damages.

Article 28[1]

(Judgement for specific performance)

If, in accordance with the provisions of this Convention, one party is entitled to require performance[2] of any obligation by the other party, a court[4] is not bound[3] to enter a judgement for specific performance unless the court would do so under its own law[5] in respect of similar contracts of sale[6] not governed by this Convention.

1. This provision contains a *compromise* between the legal systems of the continental European countries and those countries which are influenced by their law, which generally provide for the right to performance, on the one hand, and the legal systems which are based on the common law, on the other (comparison of laws Reinhard/Dölle, 109 fol). The right to specific performance is granted in

the common law countries only under particular conditions (summarizing Honnold, 225 fol). The reasons given for that situation include the view that the well-being of the society requires that one party breaks a contract and makes other arrangements if this is more favourable to him, taking account of the damages payable to the aggrieved party. This would help to achieve the most effective allocation of resources (Farnsworth, 247 fol). For the scope covered by the CISG, this concept is questionable because the CISG limits claims for damages, in particular, to the damage foreseeable at the time of the conclusion of the contract (c. Art. 74). There is no differentiation between deliberate and negligent damage so that this limitation will become effective in any case. It seems problematic to refer to a more strict or even mandatory liability under national law in the event that a damage is caused deliberately. A situation where it becomes obvious retroactively that a different allocation of resources would have been more appropriate is, so to speak, *per definitionem* unforeseeable because it is exactly a re-distribution which is to overcome the consequences of an overly strict planning (Honnold, 226, referring to Farnsworth). Here the problems involved in the integration of concrete domestic rules into another context become clearly visible.

It has to be admitted, however, that the *right to specific performance of the contract* in international trade *in many instances* is *not practicable* because assertion of that right, even if it exists without any doubt, is much more complicated than in the case of financial claims and of the right to avoid the contract. But this depends on the state of performance. In general, the realization of a transaction cannot be halted until there is a decision on the right to specific performance. The enforcement of a relevant decision entails additional problems. The authors of this commentary, therefore, agree in that the right to performance is rarely asserted.

By contrast to many national laws, the CISG does *not provide for the possibility of exemption from specific performance*, even in the context of impediments (Art. 79, paragraph 5). Only in the case of a breach caused by the other party (Art. 80) may the result be an exemption from performance. Such exemption may, however, under this Article be granted in accordance with national law (Schlechtriem, 51; Lando/BB, 237; note 13.6. of Art. 79). This does not exclude that in regard to claims for damages, which may be based on the same facts, the reasons for exemption under Article 79 are invoked (unclear insofar Loewe, 50).

2.1. The CISG grants the obligee a *right to specific performance*. In the event of a breach of contract such right persists as long as there is no right to avoidance or it can be asserted alternatively instead of the latter (Art. 46, paragraph 1; Art. 62). The rights to delivery of substitute goods and to repair, respectively under certain restrictive conditions (Art. 46, paragraphs 2 and 3), constitute specific forms of the right to performance.

2.2. Publications (above all Honnold, 222 fol; similarly Lando/BB, 237 fol) rightly point to the fact that the CISG, apart from the restrictions indicated here, contains certain other, as we believe, *indirect restrictions of the right to specific performance*. This refers, in particular, to the obligation to sell the goods (Art. 88, paragraph 2), whose realization removes the right of acceptance and turns the right to a price into a right to claim damages for possible losses. Also the obligation to mitigate losses under Article 77 may entail substitute purchase or sale instead of insisting on performance (doubting insofar Farnsworth, 250, on the draft). The obligation to mitigate losses may, however, result in an obligation to cease preparation of the contract in the event of a notified breach of contract (cancellation of the contract), to avoid the contract (Art. 72, paragraph 1) and to claim damages.

3. This is not to limit rights to specific performance granted by the CISG. A court can grant a right to specific performance in such events where it would normally not do so (Honnold, 225; Lando/BB, 237).

4. At the diplomatic conference (O. R., 305) some speakers mentioned that these provisions would also have to apply to *arbitral tribunals*. Nothing should be said against, if arbitral tribunals would recognize the right to specific performance only in a limited way.

5. This rule positively determines the applicable national law. It does not refer to the norms of the international private law of the forum, as believed the Greek delegate at the conference (O. R., 305). The rule itself rather has the character of a conflict-of-law rule, to put it more concretely, of a *horizontal conflict-of-law rule*, (Introductory remarks 2.3.) even if only a very specific legal issue is connected. The law of the courts is to be invoked even when another law is the statute of the contract (in detail Honnold, 224). It is also not relevant whether what matters is material or procedural law.

6. In a Soviet-American compromise in the lobby, which referred, on the one hand, to the written form requirement and, on the other, to specific performance, "could" was changed into *"would"* at the conference following a British and an American proposal which, in regard to the substance, were identical (O. R., 100). Hence, American (Farnsworth, 250) and British (O. R., 304 fol) concerns were met, noting that their courts had a large scope of operation, but did not exhaust it. The projected rule, however, could force them to do so.

Article 29

(Modification or abrogation of contract by agreement)

(1) A contract may be modified or terminated by the mere agreement of the parties[1].

(2) A contract in writing which contains a provision requiring any modification or termination by agreement to be in writing[2] may not be otherwise modified or terminated by agreement[3]. However, a party may be precluded by his conduct[4] from asserting such a provision[5] to the extent that the other party has relied on that conduct[6].

1.1. This rule is, under many laws, a natural rule in itself and would also follow from the CISG system. Modifications or terminations of a contract include instances where one party gains unilateral advantages (e.g. price increase without modification of the volume of the delivery and vice versa). Their effectiveness can, however, be prevented under common law by *not granting consideration*. This rule was thus considered as necessary in order to preclude such an interpretation. Article 4, subpara. (a) does, therefore, not apply so that the contrary national law cannot apply either.

1.2. It is not expressly said in which way the agreement on modification or abrogation is made. We believe that the *provisions* of Part II *on the formation of a contract* should be applied here, provided that the States concerned have adopted also that Part. This also includes that the offer for modification or abrogation meets the requirements of Article 14, paragraph 1; hence it has to be recognizable as a proposal referring to the conclusion of a contract. This is generally not the case when modifications of the terms of contract appear without prior notice in declarations and documents which the parties send each other in the process of realizing the contract (the Secretariat's Commentary, O. R., 28, which does not emphasize this requirement is insofar at least misleading).

1.3. When a *reservation* is made *pursuant to Article 96*, freedom of form under Article 12 does not apply to the modification or abrogation of the contract. The form to use is to be deduced from the applicable national law (Art. 12, note 2.2).

2. This means that the agreement has to be *in writing and* must, therefore, be an *express* agreement. As became obvious in discussing an Italian suggestion (O. R., 101, 105 fol) a requirement of the written form is also decisive when it is contained in agreed general terms of business.

3.1. This can actually be inferred from the primary role which the CISG attributes to the agreements between the parties (Art. 6). Nevertheless, the provision is not superfluous irrespective of its role as an introduction to the following restriction, because some domestic laws allow that written form clauses are *cancelled orally* (Huber, 435 for the FRG; Hillman, 451 for the USA where they can hardly be enforced through the courts even though the UCC had wanted to give them effect) or that this is possible already in the case of doubt (Loewe, 50 for Austria). Insofar national law is superseded.

3.2. On various occasions the parties agree even *further-reaching form requirements*, for instance that modifications of the contract have to be marked as supplements and numbered continuously. Because of the priority of party agreements and/or, as Honnold (230) believes, *a forteriori*, a breach of such clauses will have to be attributed the same importance as a written form clause as such.

4. The majority of commentators (e.g. Secretariat's Commentary, O. R., 28; Honnold, 231; Date-Bah/BB, 243; Hillman, 459) obviously proceed on the assumption that such conduct is meant from which an agreement on modification or abrogation can be inferred, hence, a relevant oral offer or such arrangement. This presupposes, in our view, that persons who have shown such conduct had an authorization to modify and/or terminate the contract. We hold above all that the conduct has to be measured against a relatively demanding yardstick if the general rule contained in the first sentence is not to be ineffective. Thus apart from an oral arrangement, *further activities* should be required which on the part of the other party would have caused the impression that the agreement lacking form were of a binding nature, e.g. reference to their substance in correspondence and/or further negotiations, performance and/or acceptance without contradiction according to the content of the modified agreement. An established practice of exchanging oral modifications may also have developed between the parties after the conclusion of the contract (Art. 9, paragraph 1).

5.1. Here, too, reference is made to a specific manifestation of the prohibition of the *venire contra factum proprium*. This rule is directed against the *misuse of agreed requirements as to form*. It is to prevent the strict application of the principle pursuant to paragraph 1 from infringing upon the necessary adaptation of the contract.

5.2. Sentence 2 is not invoked within the *scope of application of Article 12* when the agreement of the written form only serves to reaffirm a written form requirement which is prescribed by the applicable material law determined by way of a reservation. It has to be deduced, in this case from national law, which are the possible limitations on the consequences of a lack of form. If, however, a national law, which does not prescribe any form, is applied to a contract as a consequence of a reservation, the form requirement may be substantiated only by the agreement, thus meeting a requirement of the CISG. Here it should be considered to invoke Article 29, paragraph 2, sentence 2.

6.1. Hence, it matters here to what extent the *other party* showed a *conduct* in accordance with the agreement that was lacking in form. His conduct may become manifest in an oral statement, but then it should be complemented, in our view, by further activities, like an organization of the future economic activities that would be in line with the modification or termination. In this context, it does not matter solely whether a party has already started performance, but it has to be taken into account which preparations he has made for it. Mere conduct implying an intent will be considered as sufficient, however, even it is not manifest vis-a-vis the other party (Date-Bah/BB, 243). In both these cases it has to be taken into consideration whether such conduct was reasonable (analogy to Art. 16, paragraph 2, subpara. (b)), which on its part depends on the first party.

6.2. The solution given to a number of examples discussed in publications is not convincing to us. Instead of entering into polemics we mention here an *example* where the party, which asserts a claim, cannot rely on the written form clause. Buyer and seller, in spite of the existence of such a written form clause, orally agree to postpone the three months' date of delivery. The seller delivers accordingly, and the buyer accepts delivery and pays for it. Later, as differences of opinion emerge because of other things, the buyer refers to the written form clause, declares the modification of the date of delivery void and asserts a claim for liquidated damages in the context of late delivery. The buyer through his statement, acceptance and payment has displayed such a conduct as to bring about a modification. The seller, by way of a statement and the respective delivery, has relied on it. The claim for liquidated damages is thus not justified.

6.3. We believe that the parties can *exclude sentence 2*, whereas Hillmann (462), who is opposed to written form clauses, prefers the opposite interpretation. However, the exclusion cannot be achieved merely by a simple clause because it is under sentence 2 that such a clause is to be interpreted; rather sentence 2 must expressly be excluded. This will be possible in practical terms and provable only by way of express exclusion.

Chapter II

Obligations of the seller

Article 30

(General obligations)

The seller must[2] deliver[3] the goods, hand over[4] any documents relating to them and transfer[5] the property in the goods, as required by the contract[1] and this Convention.

1. Like in other parts, it is stressed here that the *parties decide themselves on their mutual rights and obligations,* and that their contractual arrangements have priority and shall only be supplemented by the provisions of the Convention. The Convention, therefore, plays a supporting role, gives answers to those questions which the parties in their contract forgot to provide an answer for, and helps to solve problems (Honnold, 48). Compare also the importance of the parties' intentions (Article 8), their usages and practices (Article 9), their possibilities to exclude the Convention and/or deviate from its provisions (Article 6). Should there be a contradiction between a contract and the Convention, the former shall be considered as decisive.

2. The *main obligations* of the seller *correspond largely with general legal opinions* and are settled accordingly in most legal systems. This refers definitely to the obligation to deliver the goods and to transfer title in the goods. Part of these general obligations of the seller are explained in greater detail in the following provisions.

According to Lüderitz (Freiburg, 195) this section actually contains only minimum rules. What is dealt with here is more like a cover or wrapping than the content. Only in the case of guarantee for defects and third party rights and claims genuine obligations are substantiated, and the beginnings of an obligation to cooperate are basically settled.

3. Compare the provisions concerning the place of delivery (Article 31), transport of the goods (Article 32) and time for delivery (Article 33). In this context, the *decisive factor is what the parties have themselves agreed in the contract.*

From this state of affairs it may even result that the seller does not have to deliver the goods because they are already in the possession of the buyer.

Also non-conformity of the goods or the delivery of an *aliud* generally constitute a delivery, only in this case they would not be a delivery in conformity with the contract (see the extensive note 5 under Article 35). Such instances are cured by not giving notice (Welser/Doralt, 106). It is disputed whether delivery of completely different goods should be considered as delivery, e.g. corn instead of potatoes.

4. Compare the rule given under Article 34.

5. Although the *transfer of property* constitutes a *main obligation of the seller* under the CISG, it is not explained here in greater detail because in Article 4 questions relating to the transfer of property are expressly excluded from the scope of the Convention. It may occur that the obligation to transfer title of the goods lasts longer than the obligation to deliver them, if under the legal provisions to be applied the property transferred only later (Lüderitz/Freiburg, 186). The *transfer of property* in most legal systems is done *as agreed between the parties*. The legal basis for the transfer of property sometimes greatly differs from country to country. In many countries (as in the Anglo-American and Roman legal families) the property in *specific goods* is transferred at the moment of the conclusion of the contract. In the case of *generic goods*, that transfer is done when the goods are specified, i.e. not later than with their handing over to the carrier. In some countries the property in the goods is passed to the buyer only when he receives the goods from the carrier. This distinction is important when a creditor of the seller or the buyer wants to take possession of the goods in transport (Lando/BB, 248).

The conflict-of-law rules relating to the passing of property differ from country to country as well. A widely adopted principle is that of the *lex rei sitae*, which means that a transfer of property effected in the seller's country remains valid even if not all conditions for the transfer of property are fulfilled in the buyer's country. Conversely, title may immediately be transferred in the buyer's country while the goods are being transported there, even if conditions for it are still lacking in the seller's country (Lando/BB, 248).

Section I

Delivery of the goods and handing over of documents

Article 31

(Absence of specified place for delivery)

If the seller is not bound to deliver the goods at any other particular place[1], his obligation to deliver[2] consists:

(a) if the contract of sale involves carriage[3] of the goods - in handing the goods over[5] to the first carrier[4] for transmission to the buyer;

(b) if, in cases not within[6] the preceding subparagraph, the contract relates to specific goods, or unidentified goods to be drawn from a specific stock or to be manufactured or produced, and at the time of the conclusion of the contract the parties[7] knew that the goods were at, or were to be manufactured or produced at, a particular place - in placing the goods at the buyer's disposal[9] at that place[8];

(c) in other cases - in placing the goods at the buyer's disposal[9] at the place where the seller had his place of business[10] at the time of the conclusion of the contract.

1. The place of delivery is the place where delivery has to be made. If the seller at the time of delivery delivers at the place of delivery, he fulfills his obligation. *Of importance is the place of delivery where the passing of the risk is concerned* (Article 67 fol), but also in regard to other questions. Generally, the parties reach agreement in their contract on where delivery shall take place. Therefore, the provisions under Article 31 will relatively seldom apply.

Rather often the parties refer to customary delivery clauses, in particular to the INCOTERMS. As to whether the INCOTERMS may be invoked to interpret basic delivery clauses without such reference being made, compare Handbuch 1, 99 fol.

In accordance with the INCOTERMS the place of delivery is determined as follows:

* *EXW* (Ex Works) - the seller's premises;
* *FCA* (Free Carrier) - the named departure point;
* *FAS* (Free Alongside Ship) - the named port of shipment, the buyer may name the loading area;
* *FOB* (Free on board) - the named port of shipment;
* *CIF and CFR* (Cost, insurance and freight; Cost and freight) - the named port of destination;
* DES (Delivered Ex Ship) - the named port of destination;
* *DEQ* (Delivered Ex Quay) - the usual quay at the named port of destination;
* *DAF* (Delivered at frontier) - the named point at the frontier in the seller's country;
* *DDP* and DDU(Delivered Duty Paid/Delivered Duty Unpaid); - the named place in the country of importation;
* *FRC* (Free Carrier) - the named place or point (mostly in the seller's country);
* *CPT and CIP* (Carriage paid to; Carriage and insurance paid to) - the named point of destination (mostly in the buyer's country).

(Concerning the INCOTERMS compare also Handbuch 1, 99 fol; Handbuch 3, 393 fol).

As can be seen, the place of delivery and the place of dispatch or destination need not be identical. The place of destination is the place where the goods are transported to; it is the final destination of a dispatch. But the place of delivery is that place where the seller has to fulfil his obligation to deliver; the place where the obligations of the seller finally end (Lüderitz/Freiburg, 182). Therefore, there is no difference between the place of destination and the address to which the goods are sent (c. note 11).

The place of destination is of importance for the examination of the goods (Article 38, paragraphs 2 and 3). The place of destination may also be the result of usages and practices (Honnold, 235).

The delivery clauses, in most cases, settle further questions which could not be considered in the CISG, e.g. who should be responsible for providing the export or import licenses, who should pay export taxes etc.

Under the INCOTERMS the seller is not generally responsible for providing the export license, i.e. he is not responsible where the clauses "EXW" and "FAS" apply. In those instances he has to grant assistance only at the request and the cost of the buyer. Conversely, the seller sometimes is responsible for providing an import license in the country of import, i.e. where the clauses "DEQ" and "DDP" apply.

It is to be taken into consideration also that the providing of an export license, e.g. where "FOB" applies, is considered as a kind of guarantee; and in the event of denial of such license it is not permitted to invoke *force majeure* (F. Eisemann/W. Melis, INCOTERMS, 1980 edition. Commentary, Vienna, 1982, p. 194).

2. Further obligations of the seller in the context of transporting the goods are contained in Article 32.

The supplier has fulfilled his obligation to deliver even when the goods delivered do not conform with the contract. According to ULIS the term delivery comprises the handing over of goods which are in conformity with the contract. The handing over of goods which fail to conform with the contract does, therefore, not constitute a delivery (Bianca/BB, 269; Honnold, 238); and even less so the performance of an *aliud*.

3. This happens regularly in the international sale of goods, unless the goods are already in the possession of the buyer (e.g. in the event of a sale of an object that had originally been leased or goods that were available for inspection) or the buyer himself collects the goods from the seller (e.g. in the event of the clause ex works). Here *carriage is always transport by* one or several *independent carriers*. In so far as the parties have their own vehicles and therewith transport the goods, this does not fall under carriage (Honnold, 236). This is of significance in cases where the seller may be discharged, hence whether the risk is passed or not (Article 66 fol). Schlechtriem (Doralt, 195) is against making the passing of risk dependent on whether the seller hires a dependent division of a company or an independent subsidiary for the transport of the goods.

4. A carrier is the collective term used for the different means of transportation (see, for instance, multimodal carrier). The place of delivery where the clauses "FCA", "CPT" and "CIP" are applied is the first carrier, whereas the named port of shipment and/or destination is the place of delivery (even if transportation by ship is not the first means of transportation, where the clauses "FOB", "CIF" and "CFR" are concerned). It is, therefore, not sufficient for the seller, in the case of FOB, to hand over the goods to the railway

company as the first carrier. To what extent a forwarding agent can be considered as the carrier depends on whether he himself undertakes to transport the goods (see also Loewe, 52).

5. Most of the time the *seller has an obligation to dispatch the goods. Distance sales* and *sales by delivery to a place other than the place of performance* are, in most instances, treated equally (critical remarks - with reference to Schlechtriem and Enderlein - by Lüderitz/Freiburg, 191, who doubts the conclusion that also where carriage is performed by independent carriers the seller has to arrange for carriage if there is doubt).

As to the *obligation to be performed at the debtor's place of business where the debtor must, however, dispatch the goods or remit the money,* compare Article 32, paragraph 2.

The goods may, however, also be handed over to a carrier which was hired by the buyer, if the clause "FOB" was agreed, in which case the buyer will have to provide a means of transportation. International sales contracts usually involve several carriers. (Concerning the possibilities of multimodal carriage compare Handbuch 3, section 5.6, 306 fol).

6. This means that there is neither an arrangement under the contract as to the place of delivery nor is carriage an obligation of the seller.

7. It should suffice that the buyer had knowledge of it. It is self-evident that the seller is aware of it.

8. That place may be a *warehouse or a production facility*. Where a warehouse is used, but also in other cases, there might be a need to hand over documents in the form of a claim or directive for delivery. (Schlechtriem, 54). The INCOTERMS, too, contain for instance the clause "ex works" (ex factory, ex mill, ex plantation, ex warehouse etc.). If there is agreement to apply the INCOTERMS, then delivery has to be made at a specific place because of this agreement (c. note 1), and subpara. (b) need not be invoked.

9. To place at the disposal means that the *seller must have the goods available at that place* (Schlechtriem, 54; Welser/Doralt, 107).

Having them ready at that place, the seller has done his share. The initiative to take possession of the goods now rests with the buyer (Lando/BB, 254). Lando (BB, 254) holds that subpara. (b) of Article 31 also refers to the trade terms "FAS", "Ex Ship" and "Ex Quay". Subpara. (b), however, only applies if no specific place was agreed on (c. note 8). When the seller places the goods at the disposal of the buyer, he has to inform him accordingly so that the latter can take possession of the goods. For this to come true, the goods have, if necessary, to be clearly identified to the contract and appropriately wrapped.

10. Here reference is made to the *obligation to be performed at the debtor's place of business*. When the seller changes his place of business after the conclusion of a contract, he nonetheless has the obligation to place the goods at the disposal of the buyer at the agreed place and/or to bear the additional costs or the risks that are likely to be incurred. (As to the bearing of the risk in this case see Article 69, paragraph 1)

Article 32

(Obligations in respect of carriage of goods)

(1) If the seller, in accordance with the contract or this Convention, hands the goods over to a carrier[1] and if the goods are not clearly identified[3] to the contract by markings[2] on the goods, by shipping documents or otherwise, the seller must give the buyer notice[4] of the consignment specifying the goods.

(2) If the seller is bound to arrange[5] for carriage of the goods, he must make such contracts as are necessary[8] for carriage to the place fixed by means of transportation[6] appropriate[7] in the circumstances and according to the usual terms[7] for such transportation.

(3) If the seller is not bound[9] to effect insurance in respect of the carriage of the goods, he must, at the buyer's request[10], provide[11] him with all available information necessary to enable him to effect such insurance.

1. As to the carrier compare note 4, Article 31.

2. Under the CISG there is *no general obligation to identify* or mark the *goods*. Whenever markings are possible, the seller should, in his own interest, use them to identify the goods (see also Article 67, paragraph 2).

3. The *need for a notice of dispatch* is made dependent on whether the goods are clearly marked or in any other way identified to the contract. Only if this is not the case, has the seller an obligation to give notice of dispatch.

4. The CISG does not provide rules for when such notice has to be given. In so far as *delivery clauses* are agreed, the latter *frequently contain* relevant rules (e.g. FOB A.7. - The seller has to "inform the buyer without delay that the goods were brought on board the vessel"). Even without agreeing to invoke the INCOTERMS, it would seem to follow from the general principles of the CISG (Article 7) that notice must be given within a reasonable, possibly very short time (Lando/BB, 259).

Paragraph 1 is applied irrespective of whether the seller or the buyer contracts a carrier. This is sufficiently provided for by the condition that the goods have to be handed over to a carrier. The CISG does not provide for a notice to the buyer in any other case (Lando/BB, 259).

If the CISG is invoked the buyer should not forget to commit the seller in the contract to *send a notice of dispatch* if it is necessary for him to make the required arrangements for taking over the goods, in view of their nature, and the means of transportation.

The *obligation to give notice* is a supplementary obligation of the seller (Lüderitz/Freiburg, 191), its breach having the possible consequence that the risk is not passed (Article 67, paragraph 2), that additional costs arise for the buyer, and the seller is rendered liable in this respect. A breach of the obligation to notify dispatch may, as an exception, be a fundamental breach of the contract which gives the buyer the right to make the contract void (O. R., 30). Therefore, the obligation to notify dispatch can in no way be construed as being merely an obligation of the seller in his own interest (as believes Stoll/Freiburg, 260).

5. Whether the seller has to take charge of the goods' carriage follows from either the contract or commercial practice. (Compare also Article 31, notes 1 and 4.)

6. As to the circumstances, which have to be taken into account, they include the *category and quantity of the goods*, their *packaging*, the *distance which will have to be covered by transport*, the *available means of transportation and existing transport routes*.

In the case of perishable goods, cold storage waggons could be appropriate means of transportation or, depending on the nature of the goods, fast means of transportation like an aircraft or express train.

7. Here the seller must choose the *usual transport routes* and avoid unnecessary transshipment or unnecessary unloading (Lando/BB, 259). Some of the trade terms, e.g. CIF, contain duties pertaining to the seller and, if applicable, will supersede the CISG.

The conditions which are considered as customary for transport follow quite often from the binding prescriptions by international conventions (Handbuch, chapter 5, 115 fol).

8. The seller does not himself have to conclude contracts with the carrier; he can so instruct a forwarding agent.

9. A relevant binding clause may directly be deduced from the contract and/or the delivery clause chosen (e.g. CIF). There is no general obligation for the seller to *insure the goods during carriage*.

10. The seller may, because of commercial practices, have to transmit relevant information to the buyer at his own initiative (O. R., 30; approving Schlechtriem, 54; also Honnold, 244, who wants the obligation of the seller to be largely deduced from general principles). Lüderitz believes that these are the beginnings of an obligation to cooperate.

11. A breach of this obligation entails liability (Stoll/Freiburg, 260).

Article 33

(Time of delivery)

The seller must deliver[7] the goods:

(a) if a date is fixed by or determinable[1] from the contract, on that date[6];

(b) if a period of time is fixed by or determinable[1] from the contract, at any time within that period[2] unless circumstances indicate that the buyer is to choose[3] a date; or

(c) in any other case, within a reasonable time[4] after the conclusion of the contract[5].

1. *Usually* the parties will *agree on a time of delivery* in the contract. The time of delivery may, however, be deduced from usages or established practices (c. Article 9). The time can be determined by choosing a date or in any other way by the calendar (two weeks after Easter), or by referring to a definite event (one week after first open water) (Lando/BB, 263). The time of delivery can also be fixed in relation to the latest of several events, e.g. as in clause 7.1. of the General Conditions for the Supply of Plant and Machinery for Export No. 188/574 of the Economic Commission for Europe (concerning the character of the ECE conditions compare Handbuch 2, 90 fol) which list: the date of the formation of the contract as defined in clause 2, the date on which the seller receives notice of the issue of a valid import license where such is necessary for the execution of the contract, and the date of the receipt by the seller of such payment in advance of manufacture as is stipulated in the contract (c. Handbuch 2, first edition, Berlin 1974, p. 422).

2. If July is the agreed time of delivery, the seller may deliver on the first but also on the thirty-first of July. *Agreement on a period of time for delivery* often gives the seller the required flexibility to prepare the goods for delivery and arrange for their transport. Should the parties have agreed a period of first to fourth quarter of a year, it should be assumed that the same quantity of the goods is to be delivered in every quarter.

3. This will be the case, in particular, when the buyer himself arranges for the transport or when he, for other reasons, e.g. limited capacity of his warehouse, has to be interested in *fixing an exact date for receipt of the goods*. The buyer will have to choose the date if, for instance, the delivery clause "FOB" is agreed. Also in the cases mentioned under Article 31, (b) and (c), where the buyer has to receive the goods, he himself chooses the date. The seller can, in those instances, not place the goods at the disposal of the buyer only on the last day of the period for delivery (Lando/BB, 263).

In these instances the buyer has to provide the seller in time with the necessary shipping instructions for dispatch and/or calls. It would, however, be thinkable that the seller in such events had the right to choose the date when he provides the goods within the period agreed, that he must inform the buyer accordingly, and that then the latter must receive the goods within a reasonable period.

4. Subpara. (c) is applied if "as soon as possible" has been agreed or if the delivery is tied to the occurrence of an unspecified event (c. Lando/BB, 263). *What is* in each individual case considered as *appropriate depends on the circumstances.*

5. The date of the conclusion of the contract is provided for under Article 23.

6. The *date of delivery* may be so essential to the buyer that non-compliance with it may constitute a fundamental breach of contract. This is so in the case of fixed-time contracts. If the seller delivers before the date fixed, the rights of the buyer follow from Article 52, paragraph 1.

7. This does not apply where the seller, in exceptional cases, has the right to retain the goods (c. Article 71).

Article 34

(Handing over of documents)

If the seller is bound to hand over documents relating to the goods[2], he must hand them over at the time and place[3] and in the form[4] required[1] by the contract. If the seller has handed over documents before that time, he may, up to that time, cure any lack of conformity[5] in the documents[6], if the exercise of this right does not cause the buyer unreasonable inconvenience[7] or unreasonable expense[8]. However, the buyer retains any right to claim[9] damages as provided for in this Convention.

1. It has to follow from the *contract* (or from *usages or practices,* Article 9), which documents the seller has to hand over to the buyer. The same applies to the kind of documents and the modalities of the transfer. Lando (BB, 267) refers in this context to the requirements of good faith.

2. Such documents are in the first place *documents of title* (bills of lading, warehouse receipts etc.) which are handed over in the place of the goods and allow the buyer to have disposal over the goods (Honnold, 246). Which documents are to be handed over can mostly be seen from the trade terms agreed (c. Article 31, note 1).

In fulfilling the contract the goods, in most cases, are not handed over to the buyer directly, but the seller transfers the goods to a carrier who, after having carried them, hands them over to the buyer. Regularly, the carrier takes charge of the goods against receipt, i. e. an *acknowledgement of receipt* which has a different form and a different content depending on the means of transportation. While simple documents of transport - a duplicate of the waybill in the case of railways (Handbuch 3, 235 fol), the dispatch copy of the waybill in international air traffic (Handbuch 3, 284 fol) and in freight traffic by land (Handbuch 3, 265 fol) - only confirm that the goods were taken over for transport purposes and the seller has fulfilled his obligation of delivery, other documents are issued as *documents of title* which take the place of the goods in relation to the transfer of title, e.g. the bills of lading in transport by sea (Handbuch 3, 178 fol) and the bills of lading in inland navigation (Handbuch 3, 297 fol). The goods are handed over to the addressee only against return of the documents of title. (Concerning the documents of title compare also R. Richter.) The INCOTERMS contain detailed provisions with respect to the procurement, tender and transfer of the required documents.

In the case of the trade term "Free Carrier" it is for instance a railway consignment note; in that of "FAS" it is a quay receipt or receipt for the bill of lading; of "FOB" it is the mate's receipt; of "CFR" and "CIF" the on-board bill of lading; of "ex ship" a bill of lading or a delivery order; of "DEQ" a delivery order, and of "DAF" the usual transport document and/or a docking or warehouse certificate (Handbuch 3, 366) or a delivery note etc. As to the bills of lading the INCOTERMS demand that they be "clean". This means that the documents of title in the goods must not contain any additional remarks which indicate that the status of the goods or their wrapping are insufficient.

The documents to be handed over may, however, be *insurance certificates, invoices, certificates of origin, certificates of control* etc. And finally, *technical documentation* may be required, if it is not the object of the contract itself, which refers to the goods. Loewe (55) mentions as examples the model certificate of a vehicle or a mere manual for operation.

3. This can be the *place of delivery*, but *also any place that deviates from the former*. As far as documents relating to the goods are concerned, a transfer may be envisaged through the banks involved, depending on the terms of payment. If the contract mentions nothing about date and place, the principle of good faith will probably require the seller to hand over the documents to the buyer in such a way that

the latter can take over the goods from the carrier when they arrive and bring them through customs (Lando/BB, 266).

4. That form includes the *number of copies*, the *language* and probably the *kind of duplication* used (e.g. printed, written, photocopied).

5. The *lack of conformity* may relate to both the contents of the documents and their form. It may, for instance, refer to a situation where the buyer is not in a position to receive the goods. There may, however, also be an insufficient number of copies, copies in the wrong language, or illegible copies.

The rule concerning the curing of such a lack of conformity of the documents was adopted according to a Canadian proposal (O. R., 106) and corresponds with Article 37 relating to material defects.

The right to remedy a lack of conformity exists only until the moment the documents should be delivered, hence requires their early delivery. Once the period of delivery is over, the seller can no longer remedy defects under Article 34 but only pursuant to Article 48.

6. It will be up to the seller to remedy a lack of conformity of the goods. He may do so, for instance, through *exchanging, correcting, or amending the documents.*

7. Such inconvenience may occur when, e.g., the buyer has already passed on the documents and cannot obtain them again.

8. The buyer does in no way need to bear those costs; on the contrary, he may demand to *be refunded* by the seller. Since a reimbursement may entail a risk, the buyer has the possibility to refuse a curing of deficient documents when the costs to be incurred are unproportionately high.

9. Compare Article 45, paragraph 1 and Article 74 fol.

Section II

Conformity of the goods and third party claims

Article 35

(Conformity of the goods)

(1) The seller must deliver goods which are of the quantity[3], quality[4] and description[5] required by the contract and which are contained or packaged[6] in the manner required by the contract[1].

(2) Except where the parties have agreed[2] otherwise, the goods do not conform[7] with the contract unless they:

(a) are fit for the purposes for which goods of the same description would ordinarily be used[8];

(b) are fit for any particular purpose[9] expressly or impliedly made known[11] to the seller at the time of the conclusion of the contract[10], except[12] where the circumstances show that the buyer did not rely[13], or that it was unreasonable for him to rely[14], on the seller's skill and judgement;

(c) possess the qualities of goods, which the seller[15] has held out to the buyer as a sample or model[16];

(d) are contained or packaged[17] in the manner usual for such goods or, where there is no such manner[18], in a manner adequate to preserve and protect the goods.

(3) The seller is not liable under subparagraphs (a) to (d)[19] of the preceding paragraph for any lack of conformity of the goods if at the time of the conclusion of the contract the buyer knew or could[20] not have been unaware of such lack of conformity.

1. With regard to the quantity, the quality and the description of the goods, as well as their packaging or container, *the provisions of the contract are to be referred to.* The general provisions of the Convention can only be used as a supplement. Specific requirements may be deduced, however, from the purpose and the circumstances of the contract, and from usage even if there is no direct agreement. The parties' agreement is complemented by a number of objective standards by which the fulfilment of the contract is judged (Bianca/BB, 272).

Where do the requirements of the contract ensue from? Do presentations by the seller concerning the quality of the goods become terms of the contract? In many legal systems a distinction is made between *descriptions of the quality and promised characteristics*, e.g. under American law between representations and promises. According to Honnold (251) such a distinction was, however, not included in the CISG because Article 8 does not provide for a distinction between different types of statements. Thus, the requirements of the contract are not only express assurances (see Welser/Doralt, 109). Posch (Doralt, 151), in contrast, believes the English text indicates that an express assurance is referred to.

2. Subparagraphs (a) to (d) apply whenever the parties have not agreed otherwise. They contain such provisions which the parties agree by reason or usage. If they are not to apply they must be disclaimed (Hyland/Freiburg, 338). What we are talking here about are the so-called disclaimers. Under some legal systems the *exclusion of qualitative standards as are required by law* is invalid. But questions of validity are not covered by the scope of application of the Convention (Article 4). Honnold (257 fol), therefore, warns that domestic law should be brought in through the backdoor. Where clauses regarding the limitation of liability are invoked, domestic law will probably have to be called in (Hyland/Freiburg, 313). In this context, attention should be drawn again to the problem of contradictory business conditions (Article 19, note 10).

3. The CISG treats *differing quantities* (partial deliveries, lesser than agreed quantities) as a *lack of conformity* (and not as partial late delivery) having the consequence that differing quantities under Article 39 generally must be notified. A difference has to be made, however, whether or not the documents allow for a minimum quantity. Notice has to be given only when the seller really delivers less than indicated in the documents. If the documents correspond with the actually delivered quantity, the result is an incomplete performance or probably partial late delivery. The seller may not invoke that notice has not been given if he was aware of the lack of conformity, e.g. if he himself made out the documents in accord-

ance with the actually delivered quantity. (Analogous to Article 40, even though it is a condition for that Article to be invoked that the seller has not disclosed the non-conformity to the buyer.)

If parts are missing in a delivery it is not important under the CISG, if the same legal consequences follow, whether there is a lack in quality or in quantity. (Compare Article 51 which makes reference to Articles 46 to 50. As to a quantity greater than provided for in the contract, compare Article 52.)

4. The question of whether *insignificant differences in quality* have to be considered remains open. A relevant Australian proposal (O. R., 77) was not successful. (Concerning the possibility of an additional period of time for delivery in this case compare Article 47, note 3).

5. As regards the description of the goods, the parties in general determine the content of their obligations in describing the goods. The *description of the goods as in the offer*, is *binding* for the seller without the need of a specific promise. Even if the offer relates to an advertisement illustrating the goods and their quality, this illustration constitutes part of the offer and becomes binding when the offer is accepted.

The description of the goods may also be part of an offer made by the buyer. If the seller raises no objection, he is bound in the contract by this description (Bianca/BB, 273).

Views differ when it comes to the *delivery of an aliud*. While Article 33, subparagraphs (a) and (b) of ULIS describes non-conformity and false deliveries as being lack of conformity, thus treating a false delivery expressly as a delivery of defective goods, this was not included in the CISG. We believe, however, that the legal situation is still the same, no matter how significant the deviation may be (see also Schlechtriem, 54 fol referring to Huber, 483 fol). The same opinion is represented by Welser (Doralt, 111); undecided Bydlinski (Doralt, 133); c. Bianca/BB, 273 fol).

Hyland (Freiburg, 305 fol) gives an extensive statement on the scope of the deficiency and on the difference between *aliud* and *peius*.

The solution according to which the delivery of an *aliud* constitutes non-conformity under the CISG, is supported by the fact that any deviation from the description of the goods as given under the contract can be remedied by not giving notice (Schlechtriem, 54). The Secretariat's commentary, which draws a distinction between bad delivery and false delivery (O. R., 29), is therefore inconsistent.

As far as the delivery of an *aliud* is concerned, the Secretariat's commentary (O. R., 32) points out that at least the general description must be met for an *aliud* to be a non-conformity. The obligation to deliver would not be fulfilled, if the seller delivered, e.g. potatoes instead of corn. (Agreeing Bianca/BB, 273; likewise Binder/Doralt, 146.) Such commentary by the Secretariat does not refer to the difference between the delivery of non-conform goods and an *aliud* but rather to a limitation of the notion *aliud*. According to Lüderitz (Freiburg, 185) the distinction between "*aliud*" and "defective delivery" is back to its origins. How can the tendering of goods that are "completely different" from those described in the contract constitute a delivery?

Should the seller deliver goods which have absolutely nothing to do with the goods desired by the buyer, then under the legal systems of many countries this does not constitute a delivery. The German BGB/Commercial Code considers the delivery of an *aliud* as no delivery (see R. Knoepfle, "Aliud-Lieferung beim Gattungskauf: Nichterfüllungs- oder Gewährleistungsrecht?", NJW, 1989/14, p. 871 fol) while 378 of the German Commercial Code makes a distinction between *aliuds* that may or may not be approved.

Some authors hold the same to apply to the CISG. A gross *aliud* would, therefore, be no delivery but would have to be treated as a delivery of unordered goods (see Neumayer/Doralt, 136; agreeing Loewe, 51). Though there is something to be said for this opinion, there are several factors that speak against it. For one, the need to give notice (since the seller does not have to be aware of the false delivery) and the possibility of curing it through not giving notice. But also, the theoretical and practical difficulty to differentiate between lacking quality and *aliud*, on the one hand, and a "simple" and a "gross" *aliud*, on the other.

The fact that no notice was given over a period of one year was reason for the Court of Arbitration to the Polish Chamber of Foreign Trade in the proceedings A. 737/70 (ruling of May 10, 1971) to reject any claims by the buyer because of the delivery of an *aliud* (Collection of Awards 1960-1978, p. 75 fol).

6. Requirements in respect to the *packing* partly follow from agreed delivery clauses. For further comments compare note 17.

7. The wording "conform with the contract" and conformity of the goods are identical.

8. The goods must be fit for ordinary use. Goods as detrimental to an ordinary use when they *lack specific ordinary characteristics* or when they *have defects* which impede their material use. Goods are also unfit for ordinary use when the defects, though not affecting the material use of the goods, *considerably lessen their trade value* (Bianca/BB, 274).

The goods can be more or less fit for ordinary use. The seller must on the whole deliver goods of average fitness. The fitness of the goods is measured against the standards of the seller's country (Bianca/BB, 274). Average fitness does not necessarily mean that the goods have to be of average quality. In some legal systems the seller has the right to deliver goods whose quality is below average. Under common law the goods must be merchantable. However, any goods are merchantable whether they are of high or low quality (Bianca/BB, 281). (Article 33, paragraph 1, subpara. (d) of ULIS requires the goods to have the *characteristics needed for their commercial use*, which includes their resale; c. Lüderitz/Freiburg, 185).

Hence the quality may be more or less good, but at least it must not be much below the standard that can reasonably be expected according to the price and other circumstances (Bianca/BB, 281). Since the requirement of ordinary use of the goods can be met in quite varying quality, one may safely assume that the buyer can only insist on a certain minimum (dti, 32).

The CISG does not prescribe any quality standards; e.g. cars can be traded for resale, but also for scrapping (Honnold, 252).

If the goods in question are only from time to time used for other purposes (e.g. after converting a printing machine) the buyer has no rights if he has not indicated a specific use. If the goods in the buyer's country or another country of destination have to meet special conditions, for instance with regard to the fulfilment of specific *test or security regulations*, the seller has to take these into account only if the buyer informs him accordingly in advance (c. note 11). The CISG stipulates nothing with respect to *qualitative prerequisites* which may be *mandatory* in the buyer's country or *in the country of destination*. An obligation of the seller to fulfil those requirements would have to be expressly agreed in the contract (Bianca/BB, 282). (Such requirements could also be as under subpara. (b) fitness for a particular purpose].

It should, however, not be sufficient if the buyer informed the seller of the country where the goods are to be used, in order to bind the seller, to meet the requirements under that country's law (Bianca/BB, 283).

After all, fitness for ordinary purpose includes that the goods remain fit for a reasonable period of time even if no express guarantee was granted for them (Bianca/BB, 289). Such an interpretation can be expected at least in the Common Law countries (dti., 33).

A specific problem relates to the *period of durability or fitness* which plays a role in the foodstuffs and the pharmaceutical industries. Since no general standards have emerged yet in this respect, a relevant agreement in the contract should be recommended.

9. The seller can take account of the purpose of the goods only if he is aware of it at the time of concluding the contract. It is, therefore, recommendable that the *buyer makes this purpose known to the seller* to secure probable claims. If the seller wants to avoid the agreement in regard of the quality of the goods, he must contradict it (Lüderitz/Freiburg, 186). If the seller is aware of the purpose of the goods, the principle of fairness requires him to conform to it (Bianca/BB, 275).

10. It is insufficient for the buyer to make the purpose of the goods known to the seller at a later date.

11. If the buyer has named the purpose of the goods in the offered contract and the seller has agreed, the result would be an agreement to which paragraph 1 of Article 35 applies. *Make known is less than contractually agreed* (see Huber, 480 fol). Welser (Doralt, 109) sees a problem in such interpretation "because hardly can something not conform with a contract that had not become a term of the contract". What matters here is that the purpose which is made known becomes a term of the contract by invoking the Convention. Hyland believes there will be difficulties when the seller is supposed to know the particular purpose intended by the buyer, but actually is not aware of it. We would, however, interpret "make known" in such a way that the seller was able to take note of it. While "expressly ... made known" does not cause any problem, disputes can be foreseen when it comes to interpreting "impliedly made known". In the proceedings SG 373/84 at the Court of Arbitration to the Chamber of Foreign Trade of the former GDR, the question was dealt with whether the seller by inspecting the production facilities became aware of their cleaning regime and thus of the conditions required to ensure anti-rust protection (see RiA, 111; Supplement to AdW-Dokumentationen, 1989/22, p. XIV).

12. The buyer may, for instance, have greater *knowledge* with regard to the goods he wants to buy than the seller.

13. Whether or not the seller gave a judgement in the process is ir-relevant. The buyer may, e.g. indicate the purpose for which the goods must be fit, and at the same time have ordered them accord-ing to particular technical specifications. The seller may have an *ob-ligation to advise the buyer* in this context. If the buyer, contrary to the advice of the seller, insists on his order, it is obvious that he does not rely on the judgement of the seller.

If the buyer participates in choosing the goods, inspects the goods before he buys them, selects the manufacturing process, hands over the specifications or insists on a particular brand, he does (c. the ex-amples mentioned from the British Sale of Goods Act) not rely on the skill of the seller (Hyland/Freiburg, 321).

Honnold (253 fol) believes that the buyer has to prove that the seller was aware of the particular purpose, and then the seller has to prove that the buyer did not rely on the skill of the seller (agreeing Hyland/Freiburg, 322).

14. This refers to when the seller is not the manufacturer of the goods but only a trading agent who indicates that he has no special knowledge, or when the required judgement capacity in the seller's trade branch is not common under normal circumstances (Bi-anca/BB, 276).

15. Whether, as in this case, the seller has held out to the buyer, or whether the buyer has held out to the seller a sample or model, both events constitute contractual agreements having the approval of the other party, to which Article 35, paragraph 1 should apply. Under American law this is *express* and not *implied warranty* (Hon-nold, 254). (As to the differences between express and implied war-ranty see in extenso A. Henselmann, Zum Kaufrecht der USA, Aktuelle Beitrage der Staats- und Rechtswissenschaft, Heft 178, Potsdam-Babelsberg 1978.)

16. A *sample* is normally taken from an existing quantity while a *model* serves as a model for manufacturing goods (see Honnold, 255). The submission of a model or sample is a factual description of the goods and, therefore, excludes the application of subpara-graphs 1 and 2 (ordinary purpose, particular purpose) (Bianca/BB, 276). Since goods possess numerous characteristics it is sometimes difficult to decide which are the characteristics intended to be shown by a sample or model (Hyland/Freiburg, 324).

The seller is bound only if he has not pointed out in which way the goods will deviate from the submitted model. If the description of the goods in the contract and the model do not conform with each other, it may not be deduced, from the fact that without a description in the contract the model replaces an agreement; that the model shall have priority over contractual agreements.

17. These provisions regarding packaging are *minimum requirements*. The seller is free to provide better protection for the goods at his own cost. This is influenced not only by the category of the goods themselves, but also the means and duration of transport, the route, and the country of destination (climatic conditions etc.). Whether or not interior packaging is required apart from exterior packaging, or vice-versa, or whether the goods are contained instead of packaged also depends on the means of transportation used and the category of goods involved.

An adequate manner also includes that the seller reckoned with a foreseeable delay in transport and the possibility of a redirection in transit or a redispatch (Article 38) in case where he became aware of it at the time of concluding the contract (Bianca/BB, 278).

It does not matter whether the packaging is part of the goods, but the *obligation to package the goods depends on what is customary*. The seller has an obligation to package the goods not only when the goods are dispatched, but also under Article 31, subparagraphs (b) and (c) if the seller only has to place the goods at the disposal of the buyer. Also in these cases, the goods have to be packaged so as to allow the buyer to load and transport them. If the buyer himself is to provide for packaging, a clear relevant clause has to be agreed in the contract (Bianca/BB, 277).

18. This may relate in particular to new goods, but also to such which have to be manufactured in a special way.

19. The *exclusion of liability* of the seller *refers exclusively to the qualitative requirements under paragraph 2*. Qualitative requirements agreed upon under paragraph 1 as well as differing quantities and false deliveries, which under paragraph 1 also do not conform to the contract, have not been included here. It is hardly imaginable that the buyer should be aware of false deliveries when the contract is concluded.

We could imagine that paragraph 3 be applied analogously to the requirements under the contract pursuant to paragraph 1. Norway at the Diplomatic Conference spoke out in favour of an inclusion of paragraph 1 into paragraph 3, but without success (O. R., 426 fol).

Bianca (BB, 280) is against the analogy suggested by us for he believes that the distinction has to be kept clear between contractual clauses (Article 35, paragraph 1) and the criteria of the CISG and/or usages (Article 35, paragraph 2). Hyland (Freiburg, 326), however, agrees that similar principles can be effective also vis-a-vis express guarantee. Welser (Doralt, 109 fol), too, is in favour of adopting the same yardstick. According to Loewe (56) it is not detrimental to the buyer if he was not, and need not be, aware of the deficiency, provided the seller committed himself to deliver according to the characteristics required.

20. Here the CISG proceeds on the assumption that the offer of the seller relates to specific goods with a specific quality and that the buyer purchases the goods as they are, provided that he had reasonable opportunity to examine them at the time of the conclusion of the contract (Bianca/BB, 278).

Such examination does in no way include complex or detailed methods. The seller remains responsible for latent defects. He even remains responsible for apparent defects which are not detected during spot checks (Bianca/BB, 279).

The *buyer* has, however, *no obligation to inspect the goods before the conclusion of the contract.* There is no solution offered in the CISG for the eventuality that the seller invites him to inspect the goods and he fails to do so. Under domestic law there would be different results in such an event (see Hyland/Freiburg, 325).

The CISG provides no information on the yardstick against which *"have to be aware"* should be measured. There are several formulations in regard to it. Apart from "knew/has become aware" (see Article 43, paragraph 2; Article 49, paragraph 2; Article 64, paragraph 2, subpara. (a)) there is "could not have been unaware" (like in Article 35, paragraph 3 and further in Articles 40; 42, paragraphs 1 and 2) as well as "knew or ought to have known" (see Article 38, paragraph 3; Article 39, paragraph 1; Article 43, paragraph 1; Article 49, paragraph 2, subpara. (b); Article 64, paragraph 2; Article 68 and Article 79, paragraph 4).

The wording "could not have been aware" is often qualified as gross negligence (so Herber/Doralt, 141). According to Huber (479) this should not suffice. Welser (Doralt, 109) holds that there should be an objective and clearly recognizable deficiency of the goods, which must be obvious to the average buyer.

Circumstances which suggest that the buyer could not have been unaware would be given, for instance, if the seller had sold in the past to the buyer poor quality goods without complaints from the buyer; or if the price corresponds to the price generally paid for poor quality goods (Bianca/BB, 279).

It *is, however, not absolutely excluded for the seller to bear responsibility.* If the buyer is aware of the non-conformity of the goods at the time of the conclusion of the contract, but insists on faultless quality, the responsibility will remain with the seller for he must be expected to remedy the deficiency.

Article 36

(Seller's liability for lack of conformity)

(1) The seller is liable[1] in accordance with the contract and this Convention for any lack of conformity which exists at the time when the risk passes[2] to the buyer, even though the lack of conformity becomes apparent[3] only after that time.

(2) The seller is also liable for any lack of conformity which occurs[4] after the time indicated in the preceding paragraph and which is due[5] to a breach of any of his obligations, including a breach of any guarantee[6] that for a period of time[9] the goods will remain fit for their ordinary purpose[7] or for some particular purpose[8], or will retain specified qualities or characteristics.

1. What is dealt with here is *lack of conformity* of the goods and not necessarily a lack of conformity in the conduct of the seller (Bydlinski/Doralt, 140, would prefer the latter). The responsibility of the seller for such lack of conformity *comprises quality, quantity and description of the goods as well as the manner in which they are packed* (Article 35).

2. The *seller's responsibility* traditionally *begins* the moment *when the risk is passed* (Article 66 fol). This rule is clearly intended to distinguish between buyer's risk and lack of conformity in the quality of goods (Bianca/BB, 285). In the practice of international economic relations, however, the moment when the risk passes is frequently *difficult to prove.* The CISG does not answer the question of who bears the burden of proof. Does the seller have to prove that the goods, at the time of the passing of risk, conformed with the contract (as believes Huber, 479 fol) or does the buyerhave to prove

that the goods, already at that time, did not conform with the contract (as holds Welser/Doralt, 110). In the international trade practice it is always the party that claims non-conformity of the other party with the contract who has to furnish proof (Bianca/BB, 288).

3. It is only in rare cases that the lack of conformity becomes obvious at the time of risk passing and may, for instance, be taken note of by the carrier in the documents relating to the goods. Mostly the buyer *will detect deficiencies in the quantity, damages to the packing, and apparent defects when he receives the goods*. Latent defects will become evident only after careful examination of the goods or their being put to use (c. Article 38).

An obvious breach of contract is given when the lack of conformity in quality is the result of a natural process which requires more time than the time that elapsed between the moment the risk passed and the goods were received by the buyer, hence a process which must have started even before the risk was passed (Bianca/BB, 288).

4. Here we are dealing not only with *defects* which *become evident after risk passing* but also with those which become obvious later, provided that the seller has breached his obligations (note 5) or given a guarantee (note 6). Welser (Doralt, 110) obviously believes that in delivering goods which do not conform with a contract, one party has always committed a breach and conversely, the judging of goods to be non-conform to a contract implicates a breach of an obligation.

5. A *defect* may have been *caused* by the seller *before the risk was passed*, e.g. using inappropriate containers or insufficient packing which damage the goods during transportation. It may also occur that additional requirements were not fulfilled, e.g. the wrong ship was chosen or containers were badly piled (Herber/Doralt, 142). The passing of the risk does not free the seller from the consequences of his breach of contract (c. Articles 66 and 70 as well as the relevant comments).

Under specific circumstances the defect may also have been the result of acts which the seller commits after the risk has passed (Article 69, paragraph 1).

6. *Guarantee* is not a given right, but *requires an agreement between the parties* or a unilateral promise by the seller. It is hardly imaginable that guarantee is given impliedly (as believes Schlechtriem, 58); compare Article 35, note 8.

It is not a *breach of guarantee* when goods become unusable, but only when the guarantee is not fulfilled (Bydlinski/Doralt, 141).

7. Compare Article 35, note 8.

8. Compare Article 35, note 9.

9. Also, if no guarantee is given, the goods have to remain fit for use for a reasonable time; otherwise they are not fit for ordinary use. *Ordinary use includes a certain durability* (Bianca/BB, 288 fol; doubting Welser/Doralt, 111; Article 35, note 8). The developing countries generally advocate a certain durability, a fixed time limit during which the goods have to retain their fitness. Such time may be relatively short and is expressly agreed, for instance for parts subject to wear and tear, and/or such parts are excluded from the guarantee. As to Welser, the wording "for a certain time" indicates a time that is fixed in the contract; but this relates to the German translation and the English version only mentions "a period of time".

This would leave open the question of who would fix such a time, the contract or the court (Welser/Doralt, 111, following Schlechtriem, 58, who does not exclude a different interpretation, but rather tends to a contractual stipulation).

In so far as a guarantee was given, no breach of obligation at the moment of risk passing *has to be proved*. The giving of a guarantee does not preclude the seller from proving that *lesser quality is the result of improper handling* of the goods by the buyer or a third party and the seller is not responsible. An improper handling involves, e.g., not following the instructions given by the seller or use of the goods without the normal or specific skills that are required (Bianca/BB, 287).

Article 37

(Cure of lack of conformity prior to date for delivery)

If the seller has delivered goods before the date[1] for delivery, he may[2], up to that date, deliver any missing part or make up[3] any deficiency in the quantity of the goods delivered, or deliver[4] goods in replacement of any non-conforming goods delivered or remedy[5] any lack of conformity in the goods delivered, provided that the exercise of this right does not cause[6] the buyer unreasonable inconvenience or unreasonable expense.

However, the buyer retains any right to claim[7] damages as provided for in this Convention.

1. Early delivery is either *delivery before the date for delivery* (c. Article 33, subpara. (a)) or *delivery before the period for delivery* (c. Article 33, subpara. (b)). The buyer has no obligation to accept a delivery before the date for delivery (c. Article 52, paragraph 1). Therefore, Article 37 presupposes that the buyer has accepted an early delivery without objection or that it was up to the seller to deliver within a period of time which had not yet elapsed.

The *seller* may *remedy any lack of conformity up to the moment fixed* (where a period was fixed up to the end of that period). (This was the case under Article 37, ULIS; c. Stumpf/Dölle, 281.) After this time, and/or after a period of time, he may do so under specific circumstances (Article 48). Even if an early delivery was agreed between the parties, i.e. the buyer's agreement with an early delivery constitutes an amendment of the contract, the seller could remedy a lack of conformity only under the provisions of Article 48 (Bianca/BB, 293).

2. Article 37 provides for *four possibilities to remedy a lack of conformity*, which can occur individually or combined. To exercise this right the *seller has to be aware of the lack of conformity with the contract*. As far as he does not know of the lack of conformity with the contract, e.g. in the case of deficiencies in the quantity, or was informed accordingly by the carrier, he should receive the relevant information from the buyer. The buyer has the obligation to examine the goods when he receives them (Article 38; compare note 2) and to give notice of it (Article 39). A delivery before the date for delivery will, however, not result in a change of the date of delivery so that the buyer must wait to invoke legal remedies under Article 45 fol (see note 7). If the seller, however, does not exercise his right and if it becomes clear that he will not cure the lack of conformity, Article 72, paragraph 1 may be applied (Honnold, 271). The *right of the seller* is only *restricted* by inconveniences and expenses that may be caused to the buyer. It refers even to such serious defects which otherwise would constitute a fundamental breach of contract (Honnold, 271). Problems arise in connection with this right if it can be exercised to the detriment of the buyer. If the buyer has already paid the price and if the goods have to be sent back to the seller to be remedied, the buyer is left with no security. The buyer should, therefore, only have to return the goods for which he already paid if the seller gives a proper guarantee for their restitution (Bianca/BB, 294).

Article 37 does not provide for a *refusal of the buyer* to allow the seller to remedy the lack of conformity. In such case the buyer should lose the right to claim a lack of conformity (Bianca/BB, 294).

3. Missing parts (of a larger unit) or a missing quantity (of the same goods) can be delivered until the date for delivery, if need be up to the end of the period for delivery. The right of the seller to deliver any missing part or make up any deficiency in the quantity of the goods may be self-evident and not need special mention. Since *fractionated delivery*, definitely entails *inconveniences* for the buyer, for a fractionated delivery generally needs approval, it was recommendable to expressly provide for the right of the seller to complete delivery of missing goods.

4. Goods which do not conform with the contract may have defects in the quality, legal defects, or they could constitute an *aliud* (c. Article 35, note 5). (Concerning the subsumption of legal defects in the context of lack of conformity with the contract compare Article 46, note 3.)

If goods are delivered in replacement, the seller, at his own expense, may have the goods he originally delivered returned.

5. To remedy a lack of conformity relates to *touching up (repairing)* the goods either after they have been returned to the seller or at the buyer's place (c. note 6). According to Honnold (271 fol) such repair may be imperfect. Repair of goods which are already in the possession and/or are property of the buyer requires extra cooperation by the buyer (Bianca/BB, 292), either sending the goods back to the seller or grant the mechanics of the seller access to the buyer's facilities.

6. It does not matter whether there are *inconveniences* or not; what counts here is whether they are *reasonable*. This can only be ascertained in individual cases. An inconvenience that may not be considered as reasonable could, for instance, be caused if a relatively long time were required to repair a machine that is part of an assembly line. Other inconveniences that would not be considered reasonable might occur if the seller wanted to cure a lack of conformity without telling the buyer in advance. While the CISG does not require the seller to notify the buyer of the intention to cure such lack, it may become necessary in order to avoid inconveniences to the buyer (see Honnold, 273).

(In this context and regarding expenses compare Article 34, notes 7 and 8.)

7. The right to claim damages is deduced from Article 45 fol. As to the calculation compare Article 74 fol.

Article 38

(Examination of the goods)

(1) The buyer must examine the goods, or cause them to be examined[1], within as short a period[2] as is practicable in the circumstances[3].

(2) If the contract involves carriage of the goods[4], examination may be deferred[5] until after the goods have arrived at their destination.

(3) If the goods are redirected in transit or redispatched[6] by the buyer without a reasonable opportunity for examination by him and at the time of the conclusion of the contract[7] the seller knew or ought to have known[8] of the possibility of such redirection or redispatch, examination may be deferred[9] until after the goods have arrived at the new destination.

1. This article stipulates an *obligation of the buyer* to examine the goods and, therefore, *de facto* does not belong under the chapter Obligations of the seller.

From the context of Articles 38 and 39 it can be seen that it is *not* really *an "obligation"* of the buyer, *but* rather a *burden* to examine the goods within a short time. If the buyer fails to do so, he does not commit a breach of contract (Bianca/BB, 297). If he does not comply with his obligation to examine the goods the buyer may lose (c. Articles 39 and 44) his rights vis-a-vis the seller that would devolve from a lack of conformity. It is, however, decisive for retaining his rights that he gives notice of a lack of conformity; the examination only serves to prepare such a notice. The duty to examine the goods also applies to an *aliud* (Huber, 483 fol; Herber, 28; Schlechtriem, 54, 59; Welser/Doralt, 111).

The purpose of the examination of the goods is to determine whether or not the goods are in conformity with the contract. The goods must be examined with care and skill.

The *way in which the examination is performed* is frequently agreed between the parties, in particular in the case of machines and equipment, e.g. operation and performance tests, and depends primarily on the category of goods. The parties may, for instance, agree on a mathematical and statistical quality check and prescribe the use of specific examination or analysis proceedings. There may already exist specific usages between them. In general, customary methods of examination have emerged for certain branches of trade, which have to be observed (individual examination, spot checks; c. Article 9).

The buyer must examine the goods in a way that is reasonable according to the nature of the goods, their quantity, their packing and all other relevant circumstances. The buyer, therefore, is not bound to undertake an examination involving a complex technological analysis. When the goods are too complex or too numerous, the buyer is neither bound to undertake a thorough examination of every single good nor of every single part (Bianca/BB, 298). An *examination* in general *only uncovers apparent defects*. While the CISG does not use the terms "apparent" and "latent" defects, it can be deduced from the rule under Article 39 that a distinction is made between them.

Pursuant to Article 38, paragraph 4, ULIS, the methods and modalities of examination follow from the laws that govern and *usages* that are customary *at the place of examination*. Even though the CISG does not provide for that, one can often assume that this has impliedly been agreed (see Schlechtriem, 59).

The buyer does not have to undertake the examination himself; he may instruct a third party to do so. *Impartial controlling organizations* are frequently used (compare Handbuch 3, paragraph 8.3., 375 fol).

2. The *length of the period* within which the goods must be examined *depends on the circumstances of each case*. For this reason, that period was not determined in days. This short period of time is based on the principle of reasonableness. The buyer must examine the goods as soon as this is reasonably possible. The buyer has to act with reasonable speed. Generally, it can be said that goods of sophisticated technology or of complex composition require a longer time to be examined. Impediments relating personally to the buyer or to his employees are not relevant. A delay in examining the goods may be justified only when it is due to general and objective impediments, e.g. a general strike (Bianca/BB, 298).

The examination within a reasonably short time is *decisive for determining when the period begins* during which *notice* of a lack of conformity *is to be given* (for Article 39, paragraph 1 refers to the moment when the buyer has discovered or ought to have discovered it).

In the case of early delivery, that period only commences with the date set for delivery and/or not before the beginning of a period for delivery (Article 33), except when there was agreement on such early delivery (c. Article 37, note 2, and Article 52).

3. The provision refers to *objective situations and factors* influencing the examination's length (Bianca/BB, 299). Circumstances that have to be taken account of include the place where the goods are at the moment the risk passes (c. Article 36, paragraph 1, and Article 66 fol) and the nature of the goods, i. e. single pieces, mass-produced articles, perishable goods, consumer goods. An example given by Honnold (276) relates to gas canisters, the content of which can be examined only when using the gas. Those circumstances further include how the goods are packed, e.g. whether the interior packaging remains closed until it reaches the final user; whether the goods are used by the buyer himself or are resold by him; the technical facilities of the buyer to examine them (O. R. 34); and finally, the practices and usages that have emerged (c. Article 9).

If the goods are resold (c. note 3) they can be examined by the repurchaser, who, however, has to do so equally within a reasonably short time. If the new buyer fails to examine the goods promptly, he and the original buyer lose the right to claim a lack of conformity (Bianca/BB, 297).

4. Paragraph 2 also applies when the buyer arranges for carriage but does not carry the goods himself. In this case, the carrier acts only as the agent who has the goods transported from the seller to the buyer. The situation is different when the handing over of the goods to the carrier constitutes delivery to the buyer and the carrier receives the goods as agent of the latter (Bianca/BB, 299). Then it is his duty to examine them.

5. This is generally the *standard case in the international sale of goods*, which was not considered in ULIS. Hence the CISG better meets the requirements of commercial practice (Honnold, 275). An examination of the goods when passing a border, or when transferred over the deck rail of a ship, in general is not possible and not necessary. However, should disputes arise often over whether defects that are discovered when the goods are received occurred during transportation and before or after the risk had passed, it is recom-

mendable to call in a controlling organization which should examine the goods at the place and the date of risk passing.

6. This provision covers *two different situations*: on the one hand, the buyer himself, at the place of performance, is responsible for *redispatch* to the place of destination, and, on the other, the buyer *resells* the goods without receiving them first. But even if he receives the goods, e.g. 1,000 TV sets, and resells them from his stocks he is not obligated to open each wrapping and to examine each individual TV set. In this case it is customary that the buyer undertakes only *spot checks* (c. note 1).

7. A redirection in transit or a redispatch must be taken into consideration *when the contract is concluded*. It is not up to the buyer to postpone at his discretion the examination of the goods and to give notice to the seller of an unexpected change in their original destination (Bianca/BB, 301). The possibility that goods are redirected or redispatched is not related to what abstractly could happen but rather to a foreseeable event. The seller must face this possibility when the buyer has expressly mentioned it or when it results from the circumstances. The seller, however, does not have to consider the possibility of a further redirection or redispatch if it was not expressly mentioned to him (Bianca/BB, 301). (It must be seen from the contract whether a redispatch to third countries is admissible. Compare also Article 42, paragraph 1, subpara. (a).)

Redirection or redispatch and resale are *not identical*. Except for retail trade a resale normally involves a redispatch of the goods (Bianca/BB, 302).

8. That the seller *knew* or *ought to have known* is required because by deferring the examination he might be confronted with a notice of non-conformity at a much later date. The seller has to reckon with the possibility of a resale of the goods whenever the buyer is a trading company.

9. *Two conditions are required for a deferral of an examination*:

(a) the buyer had previously no reasonable opportunity to examine the goods; and

(b) the seller knew or ought to have known of the possibility of such redirection or redispatch (Bianca/BB, 300).

Whether or not the buyer has a reasonable opportunity to examine the goods depends on how long the goods stay with him before their redispatch. Generally a quick redispatch of the goods does not allow the buyer to examine the goods. Another relevant circumstance is the way the goods are contained or packaged. If the examination is not possible without removing or breaking the vessels, boxes, wrappers, etc., necessary to protect and transport the goods, it is normally assumed that the examination will be effected at the place of their new destination. The same is understood when the examination of the goods requires the removing of the trade mark attesting the authenticity of the product (Bianca/BB, 300).

Article 39

(Notice of lack of conformity)

(1) The buyer loses the right[1] to rely on a lack of conformity of the goods[2] if he does not give notice[9] to the seller specifying[5] the nature of the lack of conformity within a reasonable time[3] after he has discovered it or ought to have discovered[4] it.

(2) In any event, the buyer loses the right[1] to rely on a lack of conformity of the goods if he does not give the seller notice[9] thereof at the latest within a period of two years[6] from the date on which the goods were actually handed over[7] to the buyer, unless this time-limit is inconsistent with a contractual period of guarantee[8].

1. The right of a buyer to rely on a lack of conformity of the goods lapses if he *does not give notice of* such *lack of conformity within a reasonable time*. A lack of conformity refers here only to quality, quantity (deficiencies in quantity, missing parts) and false deliveries (c. Article 35, note 5; Loewe, 58, believes differently). Notification of third party rights and claims is dealt with elsewhere (c. Article 43, paragraph 1).

The *rights which the buyer loses in case of omission of notice* include the right:

(i) to *claim damages* (Article 45, paragraph 1, subpara.(b)),

(ii) to require *delivery of substitute goods or repair* (Article 46, paragraphs 2 and 3,

(iii) the right to *declare the contract avoided* (Article 49) and,

(iv) the right to *reduce the price* (Article 50).

Finally, the buyer loses the right to set off with his claims in regard to defects (Honnold, 282).

Hence, after failing to give notice, the buyer has to retain the non-conforming goods and pay the price in spite of the non-conformity, provided that Articles 40 or 44 do not apply.

At the diplomatic conference, many delegations from developing countries spoke against the loss of the buyer's rights in the case of not giving notice within a reasonable time.

According to their views, such a consequence would be unknown in many countries; moreover, it would be too harsh a penalty for the buyer and would unjustifiably favour the seller (O. R. 320 fol). Conversely, other delegations stressed that the practice of short-time notice of a lack of conformity had stood the test in their countries and that there was no reason why a buyer should not be interested in notifying non-conformities to the seller once he has discovered them. The seller's possibilities to remedy such non-conformities, and to establish their cause would depend on whether he is aware of them or not (O. R., 321). This discussion resulted in a new Article 44 which was not contained in the draft at that time (Article 44).

2. The *duty* under Article 39 *to give notice* is analogously applied *also* to a *lack of conformity of documents*. The seller cannot exercise his right to cure any lack of conformity under Articles 34 and 48, unless such lack is made known to him. As far as non-conformity of documents is concerned, there will, however, be no more problems after the goods are handed over (Honnold, 280). This concerns, however, only documents transferring title in the goods.

3. The *reasonable time* is in any case a *short period* (just like in Article 39, paragraph 1 ULIS). Such time is a relative time (unlike the absolute time of paragraph 2, see Welser/Doralt, 112). It is in the interest of the buyer himself to inform the seller because the latter can do nothing to cure the lack before he becomes aware of it. In the event that a lack cannot be remedied, like in the case of perishable goods, there would be need for speed so that impartial control would be possible (Honnold, 281). Reasonable, in many cases, will mean *giving notice immediately*.

According to Sono (309) there is actually no reason for a short time if the buyer wants to retain the goods and content himself with claiming damages. The wording of this paragraph, however, requires the giving of notice within a reasonable time also in this case. Furthermore, this view underestimates the difficulties to prove a non-conformity which grow as time goes by.

The *reasonable time commences* at the time of discovery of the non-conformity. In the case of apparent defects this will usually be the time of the taking over and examination of the goods. In regard to latent defects, the time of discovery of the non-conformity will be the time of commencement of the use of the goods, the time of putting them into operation or even later. If the buyer already discovers defects before taking over the goods, the reasonable time also commences at the time of discovery, i.e. before taking delivery (c. Article 60).

4. It should be taken into consideration that it is *not only* the *factual discovery* of non-conformity which is decisive, but as the Convention proceeds, the time when the non-conformity ought to have been discovered. In the case of apparent defects this will be the time when the buyer has the obligation to examine the goods (c. Article 38).

5. Notice of non-conformity serves several purposes: It allows the seller to examine the goods himself, to substitute or repair them, and to collect or obtain evidence which he might need in a probable dispute with the buyer (Sono, 309). The buyer's *notice should enable the seller to take the necessary steps to remedy the non-conformity*. For this reason, an exact description of the non-conformity is required. The notice should relate the essential result of the examination of the goods.

The parties may agree whether and which means of evidence have to be attached to the notice.

It is recommended that the buyer *specify his claims* at the time of giving notice. Whether he requests substitute goods or repair, he has to do so in conjunction with his notice or within a reasonable time thereafter (Article 46, paragraphs 2 and 3).

6. *Latent defects*, which in spite of an examination at the time of the taking over of the goods could not be discovered, can become visible while the goods are being used. The later the defects are discovered, the more difficult it is to decide whether they were caused by a breach of an obligation of the seller or by outside influence after the passing of the risk, e.g. wrong use by the buyer or normal

wear and tear. Therefore, a *maximum period* of two years after the taking over of the goods is laid down in the Convention. This is not a limitation period but rather a *period of exclusion*. It may neither be checked nor interrupted, e.g. through repair.

This exclusive period was greatly disputed during preparation of the Convention since the relevant period is much shorter in many domestic laws. (In Mexico, for instance, the period is extremely short: five days from receipt for curing a deficiency in the quantity and apparent defects, 30 days after receipt for inherent defects. C. Honnold, 281). However, under the conditions of international trade, the *two-year period* has been considered justifiable. Moreover, it may be modified by the parties (c. note 8.) This two-year period causes difficulties to countries which have a *shorter limitation period*, like Germany, Switzerland and Austria, because claims to remedy non-conformity are in lapse already before the period for giving notice has expired (Krapp/Lausanne, 105). On the other hand, the Limitation Convention prescribes a limitation period of *four years*, counted from the day the goods are handed over to the buyer, during which the buyer may take action against the seller because of a lack of conformity with a contract (Article 8, Article 10, paragraph 2, Limitation Convention). The above-mentioned difficulties should thus not arise if all States Parties to the CISG also acceded to the Limitation Convention. Otherwise, problems will have to be solved in the respective countries invoking domestic legislation or judicature (Loewe/Lausanne, 106).

After long discussions, a two-year exclusive period was stipulated in the CISG because at a later date *difficulties* would almost *inevitably arise with regard to evidence* on the status of the goods at the time of delivery, and the seller would no longer be in a position to take action against his suppliers (of the goods themselves or of the material needed for their manufacture) (Sono, 307).

A period that would be equally suitable for all goods cannot be established. Whether or not the two-year period is too short or too long depends on the goods in question (see Farnsworth/Lausanne, 106).

7. A factual handing over means *physically handing over* the goods and not just a transfer of title through handing over the respective documents. The maximum period does not commence when the risk passes or when the goods are handed over to the first carrier. If the goods are redispatched to a new buyer then it is the actual handing over of the goods to the latter that is decisive (see Schlechtriem, 62, relating to discussions at the diplomatic conference). If the buyer has taken over the goods himself, but has no suf-

ficient time to examine them (c. Article 38, notes 6 and 9), the two-year period nevertheless commences with the handing over of the goods to him. The beginning of the two-year exclusive period may hence be much earlier than the time of examination required under Article 38, paragraph 3 (Sono, 311).

8. If a *contractual guarantee* is given the question has to be asked whether this guarantee as agreed between the parties is given in addition to the remedies of the CISG or whether the guarantee shall replace the Convention's remedies. There are several kinds of "guarantees". A seller could, for instance, guarantee that he will substitute defective parts if the buyer gives notice within 30 days after having taken over the goods. Where perishable goods are concerned such a short period would certainly be justifiable (Sono, 311).

If the *guarantee* clearly is granted *in addition to the remedial rights* under the Convention, and if the period of guarantee is shorter than two years, the buyer's rights to notify latent defects within a period of two year is not affected.

Sono (313) makes a distinction between guarantees which refer to the original status of the goods (practically in the sense of promised characteristics and qualities) and such which assure that the goods will retain their specific characteristics or their fitness for an ordinary or particular purpose over a certain period. If the contractual period of guarantee does not cover two years the buyer may nonetheless take action against the seller within two years if he can prove that in their original status the goods were not in conformity with the contract. If the *guarantee* is *to replace the remedies* under the Convention, which is absolutely possible under Article 6 and is what many sellers aim to, the period under Article 39 may also be extended or shortened. See here Welser (Doralt, 113); Loewe, 60. Other authors only mention the possibility of extending the exclusive period of two years by a contractual period of guarantee (see Schlechtriem, 62; Honnold, 282).

In the event that a guarantee was granted, the seller will have the duty to examine the goods immediately and to give notice, without delay, of a non-conformity at its discovery. Apparent defects may not be notified at the end of a guarantee period. If the period of guarantee covers more than two years the seller may give notice of non-conformity till the end of that period. In the case of a contractual guarantee period notice should be possible within a reasonable time even after that period itself has elapsed, provided that the defect was discovered only a short time before the guarantee expired (Sono, 312).

9. A seller does *not have to acknowledge the receipt of a notice*. The buyer retains his rights even if there is a delay in the transmission of the notice or if the notice gets lost on its way to the seller. The buyer, however, must give notice of non-conformity using the means that are appropriate in the circumstances (c. Article 27).

Article 40

(Seller's knowledge of lack of conformity)

The seller is not entitled to rely[4] on the provisions of articles 38 and 39 if the lack of conformity relates to facts of which he knew[2] or could not have been unaware[3] and which he did not disclose[1] to the buyer.

1. If the seller has not disclosed to the buyer non-conformity of the goods, he can neither require the latter to examine the goods within a reasonably short time (Article 38) nor can he demand from him to give notice of such defects (Article 39). In this case the buyer retains his rights devolving from a lack of conformity of the goods, even if he fails to examine the goods and to give notice. This also applies to the maximum period mentioned under Article 39, paragraph 2 (it being unlikely, however, that the seller knows of latent defects which become apparent only after two years).

The seller has thus an *obligation to disclose defects,* which is based *on the principle of good faith* (Article 7, paragraph 1). (Irrespective of this situation, domestic rules governing fraud may apply here, see Honnold, 283.)

The facts to be communicated not only include the qualities of the goods sold, but also the conditions which could influence or alter the goods once they have left the seller's area of competence (Schlechtriem, 60).

By contrast to many domestic legal systems the CISG favours the buyer; it already suffices that the seller could not have ignored the lack of conformity. Under Swiss law, however, the buyer has to prove that the seller has cunningly mislead him (Widmer/Lausanne, 106). Also under 377, section 5 of the German Commercial Code the seller must have cunningly hidden the defect from the buyer.

2. What is referred to here is not only the knowledge of the seller personally, but also of his employees. Not, however, that of independent companies which he employs to fulfil his contract (Bydlinski/Doralt, 138), like subsuppliers and carriers (Binder/Doralt, 146 fol, leaves open whether he would include their knowledge). Nothing is said about the *time when the seller should have known or should not have been unaware* of the lack of conformity (in contrast to Article 42, paragraph 1 where reference is made to the date of the conclusion of the contract). From the context of Articles 38 and 39 it can be concluded, however, that like in the case of the Articles mentioned above, the time of the handing over of the goods to the buyer is decisive (see also Article 40 ULIS, Stumpf/Dölle, 291).

3. Compare Article 35, note 20.

The wording "could not have been unaware" is defined by Huber (482) as being a little bit less than cunning and a little bit more than gross negligence; others treat it as being equivalent to gross negligence (Schlechtriem, 60; Welser/Doralt, 113). In this context it is felt that efforts are made to protect the seller following domestic law. The wording of the CISG itself would, in our view, include simple negligence, which could also be described as a violation of customary care in trade.

4. The consequence of the seller being aware of the rights and claims of third parties is contained in Article 43, paragraph 2 where, in contrast to Article 40, it is assumed that the seller has positive knowledge of the non-conformity.

Article 41

(Third party claims in general)

The seller must deliver goods which are free from any right[2] or claim[4] of a third party[1], unless the buyer agreed[3] to take the goods subject[5] to that right or claim. However, if such right or claim is based on industrial property or other intellectual property, the seller's obligation is governed by article 42[6].

1. The buyer has the right to claim that the goods be *free from third party rights or claims*. This regards above all rights relating to title (c. note 2) because separate provisions are laid down for intellectual and industrial property (c. Article 42).

The *decisive* time for the existence of third party rights or claims is the *time of the delivery of the goods*. This follows indirectly from the fact that the seller must deliver goods that are free from such rights or claims and that the *buyer may agree to take goods that are not free from such rights or claims* (c. also note 5). If the seller delivers goods in regard to which third party claims exist, the buyer can invoke all the rights under Article 45 fol concerning fundamental breach of contract and also the right to avoid the contract pursuant to Article 49.

2. The rights and claims under Article 41 include *rights of title* (reservation of title), *rights to possession* and *possessory and non-possessory pledges*. To what extent a third party can exercise its right in title is not regulated by the CISG but by domestic law to be applied according to the *Lex rei sitae*. It is also domestic law which stipulates whether a buyer may purchase property in good faith because Article 4 excludes property issues from the scope of the Convention. (See also the draft Convention on the Protection of the *Bona Fide* Purchaser, UNIDROIT 1974, Study XLV - Doc. 55, and the Hague Convention of 15 April 1958.)

The *rights of a third party* must be able to *affect the buyer* and infringe upon his property in the goods. Therefore, the rights and claims of a third party *may also extend to obligatory claims* which procure a third party possession of goods, e.g. rent or lease.

Third party rights and claims often include public law restrictions on the use of the goods (see Huber, 501; Welser/Doralt, 114). Honnold (241) counts exports duties and taxes, which must be born by the seller, among such rights and claims. Schlechtriem (63), who attributes legal restrictions, e.g. environmental protection, to Article 35, believes otherwise.

3. The agreement need not be given expressly by the buyer, but it could also be construed if the *buyer knows of the rights or claims of the third party, and nevertheless takes the goods without reserving his rights*. In this case and in contrast to the buyer's awareness of a lack of conformity relating to quality (Article 35, note 20) and to intellectual property rights of a third party (Article 42, note 9), the buyer must have positive knowledge of such claims.

The *buyer may express his consent* already at the conclusion of the contract, but he may do so also *retroactively*, in particular when third party claims on goods become effective only after the conclusion of the contract. Acceptance with knowledge of the defects in title requires an implied agreement (Schlechtriem, 62 fol). Also a notice by the seller of the third party claims and a failure to protest by the buyer are to be considered as implied acceptance (Lüderitz/Freiburg, 187). (Silence is regarded here as agreement.)

The buyer will agree to take goods which are subject to third party rights of title whenever he can foresee that those rights will soon disappear or lapse (e.g. a pledge of the carrier which disappears when the cost of freight is paid).

4. While usually only third parties rights are referred to, i.e. existing rights, the CISG *also* includes *claims* by third parties, and supposed claims for which there is no legal basis in reality. (Frivolous or vexatious claims would not be sufficient in the view of Schlechtriem, 63 fol). Unjustified claims may hinder the buyer in exercising his rights, and even *unjustified* third party *claims* can be asserted before a court (even if the third party claimant has no chance of winning); which may cost the buyer time and cause him expenses. Therefore, the seller has the duty to refuse and contest such claims and/or, if the buyer had to incur expenses, reimburse the latter (see Honnold, 287 fol; disagreeing Prager, 150).

5. *Third party rights or claims* need not exist at the time when the contract is concluded, but definitely *at the time of the delivery of the goods.* The seller will not be responsible for claims that arise only later. (As to the obligation to give notice compare Article 43.)

6. The differences between Articles 41 and 42 are the following:

	Article 41	Article 42
(a) *Existence of* **a third party** *right* **required at the conclusion of the contract**	no	yes
(b) *Knowledge of the seller required at the conclusion of the contract*	no	yes
(c) Third party rights	no territorial limits	in the country of destination
(d) *Existence or non-existence of third party rights*	seller's responsibility even though rights do not exist (in the case of unjustified claims)	no responsibility of the seller even though rights exist (if the seller has no knowledge or the buyer is aware)

	Article 41	Article 42
(e) *Exclusion of seller's responsibility*	**if buyer agrees**	**if buyer knows or could not have been unaware**

Article 42

(Third party claims based on industrial or intellectual property)

(1) The seller must deliver goods which are free from any right[1] or claim[2] of a third party based on industrial property or intellectual property[3], of which at the time of the conclusion of the contract[5] the seller knew or could not have been unaware[4], provided that the right or claim is based on industrial property or intellectual property:

(a) under the law of the State where the goods will be resold or otherwise used, if it was contemplated[7] by the parties at the time of the conclusion of the contract that the goods would be resold or otherwise used in that State; or[6]

(b) in any other case, under the law of the State where the buyer has his place of business8.

(2) The obligation of the seller under the preceding paragraph does not extend to cases where:

(a) at the time of the conclusion of the contract the buyer knew or could not have been unaware[9] of the right or claim; or

(b) the right or claim results from the seller's compliance with technical drawings, designs, formulae or other such specifications furnished[10] by the buyer.

1. It is a generally recognized obligation of the seller to deliver goods that are free from third party rights or claims. Since *industrial property rights* only have a *limited scope of application in accordance with the principle of territoriality*, it is justified to restrict this obligation in the case of international sales contracts. Such *restriction* is made here in respect to the *time* (note 5) and the *place* (note 6) as

well as with regard to the knowledge of the seller (note 9) and to specific demands of the buyer (note 10).

2. Concerning claims and their relationship to rights compare note 4 of Article 41. Also under Article 52 of ULIS it was sufficient for a third party to make a claim, irrespective of whether that party actually had the right to do so. (Compare the respective decisions in Schlechtriem/Magnus, 332 and 402.) The seller's responsibility is restricted in dealing with those third party claims based on industrial or other intellectual property of which the seller knew or of which he could not have been unaware when the contract was concluded.

3. While one used to talk mostly of industrial property rights, today the term *intellectual property* is gaining ever more acceptance. It is used to denote patents, registered designs, trade marks, models, denomination of origin, copyrights, equipment and company names. Hence the notion "intellectual property" is more extensive than the notion "industrial property".

Schlechtriem (64) believes that the existence of intellectual property rights of third parties constitutes a special category of breach of contract that is closer to a lack of conformity than to a genuine defect in title. As in the seller's obligation with regard to the quality of the goods, it generally depends here on where and how the goods are to be used according to the contract.

4. The *seller is obligated to conduct research* (e.g. regarding the patent situation). Schlechtriem (65) agrees referring to the Secretariat's commentary according to which the seller would be responsible whenever the property rights in question were made public. According to Honnold (290), it would be in the seller's very interest to conduct research. Prager (166 fol), however, holds that there is no such obligation of the seller. This would mean that the seller could restrict his responsibility following the motto, "What the eye does not see the heart cannot grieve over."

Huber (502 fol) interprets the wording "knew or could not have been unaware" in such a way that the seller's responsibility would reduce itself to his maliciously keeping silence with regard to third party rights (critical remarks by Welser/Doralt, 115, and Schlechtriem, 65).

Subparas. (a) and (b) of para. 1 stipulate that the seller does not have to conduct research worldwide (which he could not do anyway). In conducting such research the seller will establish rights but hardly any unfounded claims.

5. The seller's responsibility requires that he *knew* of the rights or claims of third parties *when the contract was concluded*. Between the time of the conclusion of the contract and the date of delivery third parties could acquire rights that the seller could not have taken into consideration.   Prager (151) construes here a knowledge of the seller at the time of delivery, which is contrary to the exact wording of the CISG.

6. The seller's responsibility to deliver goods which are free from third party rights or claims based on industrial property or other intellectual property rights *always applies to only one country*, either the country for which the goods were destined the conclusion of the contract or the country of the buyer.

Honnold (289) considers it possible, mistakenly, we believe, that for specific goods a patent may be registered in the seller's country or in a third country, and claims may be asserted in the buyer's country where those goods are used, but where there is no such patent. And the claims may be recognized by the courts of the buyer's country "based on rules of private international law or on a treaty providing for the international recognition of patent rights". This, however, would contradict the exclusively territorial effect of a patent.

(If, by contrast, a trademark is registered with WIPO it will consequently be protected in all Member States of the Organization, compare Handbuch 1, 123.)

Lüderitz (Freiburg, 187) doubts whether, given the international agreements dominating the scene, the territorial restriction of Article 42 will have the practical effect of freeing from liability in individual cases.

7. In this event, no direct contractual agreement is called for. *Contemplation by the parties* means, however, that not only the buyer but also the seller has taken that possibility into account.

8. In most cases this will be the *country where the goods were a priori intended to be used*. Here account will have to be taken of the fact that international sales contracts frequently contain clauses *prohibiting re-export* of the goods by which the seller can protect himself against claims from non-contemplated countries.

9. In contrast to third party rights relating to title, which need the agreement of the buyer (compare Article 41, note 3) in order to free the seller from liability, it is *sufficient* here *that* the *buyer knows or has to be aware of third party rights or claims*. It is unclear what care should be demanded from the buyer. It may be asking too much that he inform himself of the *property rights situation in the country of destination*. Honnold (292), therefore, attaches little importance to that restriction. (Since it is the seller, and not the buyer, who under the wording in para. 1 is obligated to carry out research, it is inferred here that generally the seller and not the buyer is responsible for the delivery of goods that are free from third party rights or claims).

There are, however, some contracts in which it is agreed that the buyer has to conduct the required research and to inform the seller thereof.

10. If the buyer himself has provided the *technical specifications for the manufacture* of the goods it is assumed that he has sufficient knowledge to correctly judge the intellectual property rights situation in his country. If the seller, however, knows that following the buyer's instructions he will infringe upon third party rights or claims he has to notify the buyer (this is deduced from the general *rules of good faith*, compare Article 7, para. 1). He does not, however, have an express obligation to conduct relevant research.

Article 43

(Failure to give notice)

(1) The buyer loses the right to rely on the provisions of article 41 or article 42 if he does not give notice[1] to the seller specifying[4] the nature of the right or claim of the third party within a reasonable time[2] after he has become aware[3] or ought to have become aware of the right or claim.

(2) The seller is not entitled to rely on the provisions of the preceding paragraph if he knew[5] of the right or claim of the third party and the nature of it.

1. Just as in the case of non-conformity in quality (Article 39) the *buyer has the duty to give notice in the case of defective title*. If he does not give notice, he loses his rights under Articles 41 and 42, i.e. his rights pursuant to Article 45 fol.

The buyer does not have to communicate his demands immediately when he gives notice; though this is recommendable. But if replacement of the goods is demanded, he must request it within a reasonable time (c. Article 46, para. 2; c. also Article 39, note 5).

2. Here, too, a *reasonable time means as early as possible* (c. Article 39, note 3). Such reasonable time may include a certain *period for contemplation by the buyer*, including time for an inquiry into the legal situation by consulting a lawyer (so for ULIS Neumayer/Dölle). Unlike Article 39 (c. note 6) there is no *time limit* here. A motion by the former GDR suggesting a two-year time limit was not adopted (O. R., 327 fol), which Schlechtriem (65) regrets. It is, therefore, recommended that the seller proposes a contractual time limit for the notice.

The buyer thus has the right to give notice of third parties' intellectual property rights during the entire period of validity of those rights, provided, of course, all other conditions of Article 42 are fulfilled. It has to also be taken into account that the claims under Article 42 fall under the *statute of limitations* with the limitation period beginning the day the goods are handed over to the buyer (c. Article 10, para. 2 Limitation Convention). According to Schlechtriem, there are only a few practical cases left so that there is no need for a time limit.

3. *When the buyer receives knowledge of third party rights or claims he has to give notice* within a reasonable time. He must not wait. The reasonable time commences when the buyer ought to have become aware of the third party right or claim. The buyer must not carelessly neglect rights or claims of third parties of which he becomes aware. But *he does not need to carry out research* into whether a third party might intend to assert a claim.

4. *The buyer* not only has an obligation to give notice, he also *has to specify the nature of the right or claim*, the steps that the third party has undertaken etc., so as to enable the seller to *take immediate measures defending his rights*. (Compare here also the obligation to mitigate losses under Article 77.)

5. It is logical that *no notice is required if the seller knows of the right or claim of the third party*. In that case, the buyer retains his rights in spite of his failure to give notice. Here we see a parallel to Article 40, although there are certain differences. Definite knowledge of third party rights is required on the part of the seller, whereas, in regard to non-conformity of the goods, it was sufficient that the seller could not have been unaware. In the case of non-conformity,

there is the additional requirement that the seller did not disclose the non-conformity to the buyer.

In Articles 41 and 42 the seller has to know at a different time: In Article 41 it is the time of delivery, which is mostly identical with the time of the passing of risk; in Article 42, however, it is the time of the conclusion of the contract.

Article 44

(Excuse for failure to give notice)

Notwithstanding the provisions of paragraph (1) of article 39 and paragraph (1) of article 43, the buyer[2] may reduce the price in accordance with article 50 or claim damages, except for loss of profit, if he has a reasonable excuse[1] for his failure[4] to give the required notice[3].

1. In discussing Article 39 (see note 1) it was pointed out that it would *not always* be *possible to give notice* of a lack of conformity within a reasonable time. The loss of all rights by the buyer as a consequence of the failure to give notice seemed to some to be too harsh a punishment because it was the seller who committed the breach of contract. It was expressed at the diplomatic conference that in many developing countries illiterate traders will learn of the notice requirement only after they consult their lawyer because of a non-conformity, and also that under the law of some developing countries there is no obligation to give a written notice of such non-conformity. To permit the seller to collect the full price nonetheless is considered as unfair (see also Date-Bah, Standpoint, 39, 48).

It was, therefore, decided to add Article 44 which is to *ease, to some extent, the buyer's burden in regard to the harsh consequences of a failure to give notice* (c. note 2), if he has a reasonable excuse for such failure. No examples were given at the conference of what could be a reasonable excuse. Sono (326), citing Date-Bah, leaves open whether he would consider insufficient knowledge as a reasonable excuse. One would imagine that *impediments like force majeure* could have prevented the buyer from giving notice. It is difficult to justify a failure to give notice within a reasonable time if the buyer knew of the non-conformity. One could assume that the buyer, at first, might have believed the defect to be unimportant and have learnt of its significance only later. Article 44 could apply if the buyer has given notice without specifying the nature of the non-conformity (Article 39) or the nature of the right or claim of a third party (Article 43). (Compare Honnold, 284.) Article 44 could, as Honnold (284) sees it, also be applied when, for justifiable reasons, the buyer's inspection is not made as called for under Article 38 (not so Schlechtriem, 61). It remains to be seen how the courts interpret the requirement of a reasonable excuse. It cannot be excluded that remaining payments are withheld or recourse is taken against securities (Schlechtriem, 60 fol).

But summed up, only in exceptional cases will the buyer have a chance to successfully invoke Article 44 (Sono, 328).

2. Failure to give notice will entail some consequences for the buyer. He will be *deprived of some of the rights* which he would have had, if he had given notice within a reasonable time. He will then no longer have the right to delivery of substitute goods or to repair of the goods (Article 46); neither will he have the right to make the contract void (Article 49). As far as his right to claim damages is concerned, this will remain limited to the direct damage, excluding restitution of lost profit, and the buyer will retain the obligation to mitigate losses (Article 77).

3. The required notice relates here to the reasonable time; *upon the expiration of the time limit* under Article 39, para. 2 there will *no longer be a possibility for excuse.*

4. A *failure to notify may cause damage to the seller*, e.g. if he is no longer in a position to claim compensation from the supplier. The damage to the seller could also be higher expenses for the examination of the goods or for procuring evidence; such evidence by witnesses may have been lost in the meantime (Sono, 327).

According to a proposal made originally to the conference by Finland, Ghana, Nigeria, Pakistan and Sweden, the seller could set off the demands of the buyer with the damages that are caused to him by, or can be foreseen by him as a consequence of, the failure to give notice (O.R., 108). This consequence may also be inferred from Article 77. (As to the relationship between Articles 44, 77 and 80 see also Schlechtriem, 61).

Section III

Remedies for breach of contract by the seller

Article 45

(Buyer's remedies in general; claim for damages;no period of grace)

(1) If the seller fails[1] to perform any of his obligations[2] under the contract or this Convention[3], the buyer[4] may:

(a) exercise the rights provided in articles 46 to 52;

(b) claim damages[5] as provided in articles 74 to 77;

(2) The buyer is not deprived of any right he may have to claim damages by exercising his right to other remedies[6].

(3) No period of grace may be granted[7] to the seller by a court or arbitral tribunal when the buyer resorts[8] to a remedy for breach of contract.

1. The *notion of breach of contract* under the CISG comprises *any non-fulfilment of contractual obligations*. Those obligations may have their origin not only in the contract between the parties, but also in the Convention, established practices and usages (Article 9). This refers to non-fulfilment of obligations by the seller and to non-performance of obligations by the buyer. The rights of the other party are provided for in parallel; compare Article 45 fol with Article 61 fol. In addition the CISG contains some provisions which relate both to the seller and the buyer (Article 71 fol). There is no distinction between breaches of main or breaches of auxiliary obligations, rather, a *distinction is made between fundamental and other breaches of contract* (c. Article 25). The consequences which a fundamental breach of contract entails are more severe than those of ordinary breaches of contract. Some of the remedies are available only for fundamental breaches (e.g. avoidance of contract - Article 49; delivery of substitute goods - Article 46). A breach of contract constitutes an objective fact; no matter whether the party who commits the breach is at fault or not. Insofar as that party has not been able to prevent the breach and/or the breach is caused by the conduct of the other party, the former *may be exempted from certain consequences of the failure to perform his obligations* (compare Articles 79 and 80, exemption from liability).

Using the uniform term of breach of contract the CISG relinquishes such categories as initial impossibility to perform, delay, positive breach of contract, guarantee etc. (Welser/Doralt, 116). But that concept did not fully succeed in regard to the remedies (Schlechtriem, 65; agreeing Welser/Doralt, 116).

Under ULIS each individual type of breach was followed by the proper remedy. Performance by the seller was divided into five categories and a separate remedial system was provided for each (e.g. non-fulfilment in regard to the place of delivery, time of delivery, quality etc.). This approach was intended to make the remedial system clear, but produced ambiguity, complexity and unnecessary length (as Honnold judges it, 295). Farnsworth (Lausanne, 83 fol) believes that the change in the structure of the legal consequences, which he calls consolidation, is an important achievement of the CISG. (Other specific characteristics are in his view contractualism, i.e. priority of the contractual agreements of the parties; and stabilization, i.e. the tendency to maintain the contract.)

2. The *CISG does not differentiate between main, auxiliary and participatory obligations.* On the other hand, not everything that is considered an obligation under the CISG in the case of breach will entail the consequences of Articles 45 fol and/or 61 fol (see the "obligation" to examine the goods, Article 38). There is a certain differentiation in the CISG insofar as specific consequences (Article 46, paras. 2 and 3, and Article 50) are defined in the case of non-conformity of the goods (Article 35).

3. The obligations under this Convention (as in Article 30 fol) *also relate to obligations that are inferred from established practices and usages* (c. Article 9). On the other hand, *all obligations* deriving from the Convention *are capable of alteration subject to mutual agreement* (c. Article 6).

4. Here an *overview is offered of all remedies* available to the buyer in the event of a breach of contract by the seller (see also Articles 71 to 73). While subpara. (a) only draws attention to the remedies for breach by the seller and constitutes an introduction to the following; subpara. (b) constitutes the actual basis for claiming damages (Honnold, 296). Therefore, Article 78 should, in our view, refer to Article 45, para. 1, subpara. (b) and Article 61, para. 1, subpara. (b) instead of Article 74. Articles 74 to 77 do not state that damages are to be awarded; they merely explain the damages.

The buyer has the rights described under (a) *and* (b) (Schlechtriem, 66) and not only (a) *or* (b) (as believes Welser/Doralt, 116). In the event of a delivery of defective goods the buyer always has the right to claim damages (c. Hoffmann/Freiburg, 293) (and not only in exceptional cases like under BGB 463).

Compensation for damages because of non-performance and avoidance of a contract will be combined on a regular basis (Leser/Freiburg, 229). Before the CISG was in existence, a choice between the two always entailed difficult decisions on the part of the buyer (Honnold, 297).

According to Huber (Freiburg, 220) the remedies of the parties are now in a polished, mature and systematically closed final form.

5. The *right to claim damages is stipulated here in principle* - for Articles 74 to 77 merely contain a definition, describe the calculation of such claims for damages and state its limits and means to mitigate losses. Whereas paragraph 2 offers clarity in regard to the relationship between the right to claim damages and the other rights of the buyer.

The *right* of the buyer *to claim damages does not presuppose a failure* by the seller as it is stipulated in many domestic legal systems (Honnold, 297). There is, however, no such right in the case of *force majeure* under Article 79.

A *breach of contract alone is not a sufficient basis* for the right to claim damages. The actual damage suffered and, in the event of non-conformity with the contract or the existence of third party rights or claims, notice of such non-conformity or third party rights or claims, have to also be taken into account (c. Articles 39 and 43).

6. The *right to claim damages* exists either *as a right by itself or in addition* to the right to performance of the contract, mitigating losses or avoidance of the contract. (The buyer can, however, not doubly liquidate a disadvantage, Welser/Doralt, 116). This corresponds to the legal situation in many countries, but deviates from the rule existing under German, Swiss or English law (Will/BB, 331).

7. This stipulation was considered necessary because in some countries under the influence of the French Code Civil, *avoidance of a contract can only be forced with the help of a court* and the court can grant the seller an additional period (delai de grace) against the interests of the buyer. The situation is completely different when the buyer himself grants the seller a reasonable additional period (s. Article 47).

8. Here reference is not made to each and every remedy to which a buyer will resort in the event of a breach of contract by the seller, but only to the right to make a contract void (Article 49). This stipulation could be found, therefore, in ULIS in connection with the right to avoid a contract (c. Will/BB, 332).

Article 46

(Buyer's right to require performance)

(1) The buyer may require[1] performance by the seller of his obligations unless the buyer has resorted to a remedy which is inconsistent[2] with this requirement.

(2) If the goods do not conform[3] with the contract, the buyer may require delivery of substitute goods[4] only if the lack of conformity constitutes a fundamental breach of contract[5] and a request for substitute goods is made either in conjunction with notice given under article 39 or within a reasonable time thereafter[6].

(3) If the goods do not conform with the contract, the buyer may require the seller to remedy the lack of conformity by repair[7], unless this is unreasonable[8] having regard to all the circumstances. A request for repair must be made either in conjunction with notice given under article 39 or within a reasonable time thereafter[6].

1. This Article stipulates the right of the buyer to performance of a contract, i.e. is an expression of the *maxim pacta sunt servanda*. The right to require performance is laid down in many legal systems; but under the common law the primary remedy in the case of a breach of contract is not performance but the claim for damages. In practical terms, however, there is only a small difference between civil-law countries and common-law countries. While the United States Uniform Commercial Code in sec. 2-716 grants the right to performance (so that there is a right to specific performance if the compensation for damages offered to the damaged party provides no adequate protection, Honnold, 300), claims for performance are rare in civil-law countries.

The *buyer's right to performance* by the seller is, however, *restricted* by Article 28 (and, therefore, may be unenforceable by the courts, Schlechtriem, 66) and will remain without much practical effect in large parts of the world (Will/BB, 334). The right for performance will not hinder the buyer from resorting to other claims later.

Pursuant to Article 46 of the CISG the buyer can insist on performance as long as the seller has not delivered. The right to performance also covers the event in which the seller has delivered only part of the goods or delivered goods to the wrong place (c. Article 31) or in which documents are lacking (Article 34). If he has delivered, but the goods do not conform with the contract, paras. 2 and 3 provide *remedies for specific claims for performance*. The requirement of performance also relates to such cases where goods are not free from third party rights or claims (c. Articles 41 and 42). According to Honnold (302), the right to require performance under Article 46, paragraph 1, is completely impractical and meaningless, whereas the rights under paras. 2 and 3 are in the interest of the seller.

2. The buyer may not demand performance and at the same time avoid the contract under Article 49. This appears to be a matter of course. *Avoidance of contract frees* both parties *from the requirement to fulfil their obligations* (c. Article 81, paragraph 1). Equally incompatible are the claims for performance and price reduction pursuant to Article 50 which would re-establish equivalence. But claims for damages remain untouched. Therefore, compensation for damages suffered through delay is frequently asked for apart from the claim for performance.

3. *Non-conformity of goods* not only *comprises defective quality and deficiencies in quantity* but also *wrong deliveries* (c. Article 35). Goods do not conform with the contract when they are not free from third party rights or claims (c. Articles 41 and 42; Schlechtriem, 56 fol; v. Hoffmann/Freiburg, 294; Moeckc/Doralt, 150). However, the buyer may require performance of the contract only under the condition that he has given notice within the required periods (c. Articles 39 and 43).

According to Will (BB, 336), delivery of an *aliud* comes under paragraph 2, non-conformity of the goods, and always constitutes a fundamental breach of contract (337) so that the buyer may invoke his right to declare the contract avoided in accordance with Article 49. If an *aliud* were not to be considered a fundamental breach the buyer would only have the right to repair; which would seem a rather senseless demand in the case of an *aliud*.

4. The buyer may request *delivery of substitute goods*. Also, in the case of a fundamental breach of contract, he can decide in favour of *repair* (Welser/Doralt, 119). The right to delivery of substitute goods may be excluded because the buyer cannot restitute the goods in their original condition (c. Article 82).

Even if the buyer is not allowed to require delivery of substitute goods, the seller may deliver such goods if this is more favourable to him (unless such substitution of goods is an unreasonable inconvenience to the buyer, Welser/Doralt, 119).

Substitute goods only serve the interest of the buyer if they are *delivered within a reasonable time*. Hence the seller does not have unlimited time to deliver such substitute goods. On the other hand, in the event that the buyer has required delivery of substitute goods, for which he may set the seller a reasonable time limit, the former is bound to his decision during this time and cannot declare avoidance of the contract. We believe that this follows from paragraph 1, whereas Will (BB, 338) wants to deduce this from the application of Article 47. During this time the buyer may, however, agree to accept a repair of the goods.

5. Under the CISG *substitute goods* can be requested by the buyer only *when* the non-conformity of the goods constitutes a *fundamental breach of contract*; hence not in the case of minor defects as was the case under ULIS. This is in line with Article 49 according to which avoidance of a contract (at first) can only be requested if a fundamental breach of contract is committed for the economic consequences of a delivery of substitute goods may be the same for the seller as in the case of an avoided contract (O. R. 337). The Federal Republic of Germany had intended to facilitate claims for substitute goods, but for the above-mentioned economic reasons, the relevant proposal was not successful (Schlechtriem, 67).

The economic consequences could even surpass those of an avoidance of contract because the additional expenses incurred and the risks involved in transporting substitute goods are to be born by the seller (Honnold, 296).

There might be a dispute over whether or not the breach of contract is fundamental. A machine may be operational, for instance, but its performance may reach only 90 per cent of its specified capacity (v. Hoffmann/Freiburg, 295).

It was suggested at the diplomatic conference to stipulate a choice between the delivery of substitute goods and repair following other criteria (O. R., 335, 337). A solution which leaves the seller the choice between the delivery of substitute goods and repair also seems to us to be more appropriate.

Even when the buyer is not allowed to claim substitute goods, it is not excluded that in the event of non-conformity, the seller decides to deliver substitute goods if this is more favourable to him.

If the delivery of non-conform goods is not a fundamental breach of contract, no delivery of substitute goods can be requested but, rather, only repair. Even *if repair is not possible*, the defect does not automatically turn into a fundamental breach of contract. The buyer is left only with the *right to claim a reduction of the price and/or compensation for damages*. This solution has been justly criticized, as believes Welser (Doralt, 119). On the other hand, the buyer can avoid any discussion on whether a breach of contract is fundamental when he confines himself from the very beginning to requiring compensation for damages.

6. If the buyer does not through immediate notice request a delivery of substitute goods or repair, he has to do so *within a reasonable time*. The CISG is based on the assumption that this rule serves the interests of both parties. Usually the buyer is interested in receiving conform goods as quickly as possible, and the seller wants to know the claims of the buyer. It should be avoided in any case that the buyer can speculate on rising market prices. What is appropriate here is therefore to fix a short time and by no means another two-year period as allowed for under Article 39, paragraph 2 (Will/BB, 337).

7. *Cure includes delivery of spare parts* (O. R., 336), and *substitution of parts as well as repair itself.* This can be done at the buyer's place, but may also require sending the goods back to the place of manufacture. According to ULIS, repair could be claimed only if the seller was also the manufacturer of the goods. Under the CISG such right exists, no matter whether the seller is in a position to repair the goods by his own means (v. Hoffmann/Freiburg, 296). If he is not in a position to do so, this could indeed amount to unreasonableness. The right to require repair must not be rejected under the circumstances of Article 29 (Schlechtriem, 66). Not only has the seller an obligation to repair defective goods, but he has to bear all costs involved in such repair.

If there is a third party right or claim in respect of the goods, the cure may be such that the seller buys a patent or a license, or redeems a pledge or other right in title.

8. A claim for repair may be unreasonable if there is no reasonable *ratio between the costs* involved *and the price* of the goods or if the seller is a dealer who does not have the means for repair (Article 42 ULIS made a difference between producer and manufacturer, on the one hand, and distributor and dealer, on the other), or if the buyer himself can repair the goods at lesser cost (Honnold, 301).

Repair may not only be unreasonable; it may be *technically impossible* (this could, however, constitute a fundamental breach of contract). The nature of some goods is such as to exclude repair at all, e.g. in the case of agricultural products. A repair can also be impractical, e.g. as with throw-away goods.

In such cases the buyer nevertheless retains the right to a reduction in price and compensation for damages (c. Article 50).

When *judging what is unreasonable*, all circumstances have to be taken into account. According to v. Hoffmann (Freiburg, 297) it is doubtful whether the (little) interest of the buyer in performance in conformity with the contract must be considered. As a matter of fact, there can be no doubt. The requirement of repair is a right and not an obligation of the buyer. When the buyer is not interested in having goods repaired, he will not require it. The little interest of the buyer could, however, constitute a problem of Article 48 when the seller of his own accord offers repair.

Article 47

(Fixing of additional period for performance)

(1) The buyer may fix[4] an additional period of time[1] of reasonable length[2] for performance by the seller of his obligations[3].

(2) Unless the buyer has received notice from the seller that he will not perform within the period so·fixed[6], the buyer may not, during that period[5], resort to any remedy for breach of contract. However, the buyer is not deprived thereby of any right he may have to claim damages for delay in performance[7].

1. Unlike in the case of fixed-term contracts (c. Article 33, note 6), a *delay in performance is not automatically a fundamental breach of contract* (c. also Will/BB, 343). The buyer would in the case of a fundamental breach be entitled to avoid the contract immediately (c. Article 49, paragraph 1, subpara. (a)), but for him this is not necessarily the best solution. Hence, the buyer has the right to give the seller an additional period of time, irrespective of whether or not the lack of conformity constitutes a fundamental breach of contract.

In setting an additional period of time, the buyer expresses his continuing interest in contract performance and offers the seller a chance to fulfil the contract nonetheless. If the seller does not perform within the additional period, the buyer may set another (or more) additional period(s) of time, or avoid the contract. Neither does the contract end automatically upon the expiration of the additional period nor has the buyer an obligation to avoid the contract.

Under ULIS an additional period of time had a different function: its expiration automatically lead to avoidance (Farnsworth/Lausanne, 105).

The legal institute of *Nachfrist* is considered as an essential contribution of the German sales law to the uniform sales laws (Huber/Freiburg, 201 fol). It is not translated into English. Under 326 BGB the setting of a *Nachfrist* was meant to announce that upon its expiration, performance would be rejected. Farnsworth (Lausanne, 105) referring to the *Nachfrist* said: "We don't understand it, we never heard of it, but we like it." That the Common Law never heard of it is not true. The commentary on sec. 2-309 of the United States Uniform Commercial Code recommends use of the *Nachfrist* to bring certainty into the relations between the parties (Honnold, 307). The *setting of a Nachfrist* not only brings *certainty* with regard to the buyer's interest in fulfilment of the contract, but also in respect of the possibility to avoid the contract. (It may be risky for the buyer to avoid the contract if there is a dispute whether the non-performance constitutes a fundamental breach of contract.)

Nachfrist must be determined by indicating a given date or a period of time (c. Article 33); vague terms like "soon" or "promptly" do not suffice (O. R., 39; also Honnold, 306).

2. What is reasonable can only be decided with regard to specific cases. The *Nachfrist* must not be too short and must not serve the buyer as a pretext upon its expiration to declare the contract avoided under Article 49, paragraph 1, subpara. (b). In *determining an additional period of reasonable length*, such elements as the extent and the consequences of the delay have to be taken into account just like the possibilities of the seller and the interest of the buyer (Will/BB, 345).

Referring to Article 27 ULIS Huber (Dölle, 235), among others, included the following elements in calculating what is a reasonable length of a *Nachfrist*: the length of the contractual period for delivery; nature of the seller's performance, e.g. delivery of complicated equipment out of his own production; and nature of the obstacle in the way of delivery.

3. What *matters most* in setting a *Nachfrist* is the *obligation to deliver*. Honnold (304 fol) exclusively speaks of delivery. This would follow from Article 49, paragraph 1, subpara. (b). The possibility to fix a *Nachfrist* was rejected in the case of defects so as to avoid that by way of the additional period, trivial defects could be converted into fundamental breaches (also Schlechtriem, 67). A *Nachfrist* can, however, be set if parts are missing in a delivery (c. Article 51, paragraph 2).

The *buyer may set additional periods in regard to the fulfilment of other obligations,* such as delivery of substitute goods or repair under Article 46. But in such cases the expiration of the additional periods does not give the buyer the right to avoid the contract. In contrast to ULIS there is no longer a possibility for a *Nachfrist* if the goods are defective. This situation has created uncertainties (see Schlechtriem/Doralt, 139).

Persistent refusal to repair defective goods may, however, turn out to be a fundamental breach of contract and thus entail the right to declare the contract avoided (Will/BB, 346).

4. The buyer must *set an additional period, i.e. inform the seller accordingly either orally or in writing.* No form is prescribed for that. It must be clear from the communication that it is an additional period of time for performance, i.e. fulfilment after expiration of that period is rejected. The seller should be well aware of his situation (Honnold, 306). As to the communication to the seller, Article 27 (O. R., 338) applies, and the risk of transmission lies with the seller. The buyer may draw his conclusions when the *Nachfrist* has expired, even when the seller has not perceived the communication.

5. Even if the non-fulfilment was *a priori* a fundamental breach of contract, the buyer is not in a position to declare the contract avoided; he has to wait *until the period of time has expired.* He cannot require performance and at the same time avoid the contract. This does not have to be expressly laid down here; it would follow from the general principles, like waiver or estoppel (Honnold, 308). The wording of the rule, on the other hand, is not completely exact. If the seller delivers within the *Nachfrist* and a lack in quality becomes

apparent the buyer may well invoke his rights under non-conform delivery before the period set has expired (Leser/Freiburg, 236).

If the buyer has required repair within a fixed period of time, he cannot request delivery of substitute goods before that period has expired, even if there was originally the possibility to do so. The *setting of an additional period of time for performance* at first has a *disadvantageous effect on the buyer* (Welser/Doralt, 119). On the other hand, the buyer has the right to declare the contract avoided in the case of a delay in delivery upon the expiration of the additional period, even if the delay did not constitute a fundamental breach of contract (Welser/Doralt, 120).

6. The buyer does not need to wait until the *Nachfrist* has expired, only when the seller has declared that he will not perform within the additional period of time because such a declaration on the seller's part will mean an early end of the existing uncertainty (Welser/Doralt, 119).

7. The buyer will in any event, even when the seller has performed within the *Nachfrist*, retain the right to claim compensation for damages sustained because of the delay. If the seller does not perform, the buyer has the right to claim damages because of non-performance (c. Article 45).

Article 48

(Seller's right to remedy failure to perform)

(1) Subject to article 49, the seller[1] may, even after the date for delivery[3], remedy[4] at his own expense any failure to perform his obligations[2], if he can do so without unreasonable delay[5] and without causing[8] the buyer unreasonable inconvenience[6] or uncertainty of reimbursement by the seller[7] of expenses advanced by the buyer. However, the buyer retains any right to claim damages[9] as provided for in this Convention.

(2) If the seller requests the buyer to make known[10] whether he will accept performance and the buyer does not comply with the request within a reasonable time[11], the seller may perform[13] within the time[12] indicated in his request. The buyer may not, during that period of time[14], resort to any remedy which is inconsistent with performance by the seller.

(3) A notice by the seller that he will perform within a specified period of time is assumed[15] to include a request, under the preceding paragraph, that the buyer make known his decision.

(4) A request or notice by the seller under paragraph (2) or (3) of this article is not effective unless received by the buyer[16].

1. The *seller's right to remedy failure to perform is limited by avoidance of the contract* by the buyer. If the buyer has already declared the contract avoided under Article 49, the seller can no longer remedy a defect in performing his duties. Bulgaria and the FRG suggested that the seller should always have the right to remedy a failure to perform, hence to exclude the reservation made in Article 49 (O. R. 351 fol). This was rejected because Article 49 presupposes a fundamental breach of contract and the seller's right to cure exists practically at all times (c. also Schlechtriem, 69).

The relationship between the seller's right to cure and the buyer's right to avoid the contract was often discussed (e.g. Honnold, 311 fol). This would be of interest in a situation where the buyer could avoid the contract under Article 49 but has not done so yet, and the seller has offered to cure the defect. Honnold (312) believes that the right to remedy failure to perform should have priority. It was, in his view, more specific than the buyer's right to avoidance; and the more specific right would always prevail over a more general one. Furthermore, the offer to cure would prevent a non-conformity becoming fundamental. See here also note 10.

According to Will (BB, 349 fol), the seller's right to cure is ever more suppressing the buyer's right to avoidance. When the buyer, because of prior experience with the seller, is aware that the latter can cure a defect, even if a fundamental breach of contract is involved, he is not allowed to avoid the contract.

Will's (BB, 351) reference to general conditions of the contract seems to us out of place because there is a contractual agreement in existence which prevails over the provisions of the CISG.

The right to cure is often called second tender (see Schlechtriem, 68; v. Hoffmann/Freiburg, 298). This term is actually justified only in the case of non-conformity since there was no first tender where a delay in delivering goods is concerned.

The right of the seller to cure, limits the rights of the buyer insofar as he may not draw all consequences from the breach of contract as long as the seller has the right to remedy a failure (according to Welser/Doralt, 124).

2. The seller's *right to cure relates to all his obligations.* Thus he can deliver missing parts or documents, compensate for a deficiency in quantity, deliver substitute goods to replace non-conforming goods or repair the latter.

The seller can cure the lack of conformity after the time of delivery has elapsed. In doing so, he may choose whether he repairs the defective goods or delivers substitute goods (v. Hoffmann/Freiburg, 298), and he can make up the delivery as a whole.

According to Honnold (310) the wording "any failure to perform" is broad enough to include a delay. There is, however, hardly any incentive because either the buyer has already declared the contract avoided or the seller has had to suppose so; hence there is no need for "cure". He holds that time which has passed cannot be recalled and therefore a delay cannot be remedied. Will (BB, 353) rightly turns against this because the question is not to cure a delay but a non-performance.

3. As to the *curing of non-conformity* before the time of delivery, compare Articles 34 and 37.

4. The *conditions to be fulfilled for the seller to remedy a failure to perform* are:

(a) the contract must be in existence, i.e. the buyer must not have exercised his right to avoid the contract; and

(b) the cure must not cause unreasonable inconvenience to the buyer.

According to the Secretariat's commentary (O. R., 40) there is another condition still: The seller must be able to perform without such delay as will amount to a fundamental breach of contract. We believe that this third condition is included under (b).

5. It is generally assumed that a *delay* is *unreasonable* when it amounts to a fundamental breach of contract (as states the Secretariat's commentary, O. R., 40). In this case the seller cannot assert his *right* to cure against the will of the buyer; he needs the buyer's agreement.

6. It cannot generally be said what *unreasonable inconvenience* means; this can only be decided on a case-by-case basis. The Secretariat's commentary (O. R., 40) mentions the case of resold goods of which the buyer has declared a price reduction (but see Article 50, note 6) or the need to have broad access to the buyer's production facilities.

7. At first it seems quite natural that the *seller must bear the costs* involved in remedying a failure to perform. However, the buyer may incur expenses, for instance when he has to send back exchanged goods. What matters is not the amount of the expenses, but irrespective of that, the uncertainty of reimbursement, e.g. the risk that the seller is insolvent or not willing to reimburse expenses incurred by the buyer (Will/BB, 353).

8. The seller has the right to cure only if there are no circumstances which could be summed up under the notion unreasonable inconvenience. Will (BB, 352), too, considers the conditions to be mentioned below as examples of inconvenience.

9. The right to claim damages, e.g. as a result of delay, does not lapse on the ground that the seller has performed in the end. But the *curing of a failure* to perform may have an *influence on the amount of the damage claimed*. Also in the case of a cure, damage may be claimed to compensate for a possible stoppage in production (v. Hoffmann/Freiburg, 298).

10. *Insofar as* the seller has the *right to cure* there should be no need to request information as to whether the buyer will accept performance. The *buyer* is in that case *obliged to accept the cure*. If he refuses to do so, he loses the right to reduction in price (c. Article 50, 2nd sentence) in the case of non-conformity of the goods. The right to cure may well be doubtful and, in particular, the period of time which the seller offers for performance may reinforce that doubt (c. note 5).

In the event of a fundamental breach of contract that request also refers to whether or not the buyer will assert his right to declare the contract avoided. The *right to avoidance prevails* (c. note 1 and Article 49). When the buyer has the right to avoid a contract but does not exercise it, the seller is left with uncertainty. He may end this uncertainty, requesting the buyer to communicate whether he accepts performance.

The *buyer may* temporarily *renounce his right to avoidance* and declare his agreement with performance. If the seller does not perform nonetheless, the right to avoid the contract will, of course, persist. The buyer may lose his right to avoidance also when he does not answer to the request of the seller (c. note 11) or when he does not declare the contract avoided within a reasonable time in case he rejects performance (Article 49, note 13).

Should the buyer in the event of a fundamental breach of contract require *delivery of substitute goods* under Article 46, paragraph 2, the seller may nevertheless offer him *repair*. The buyer may request *repair* and the seller offer substitute goods. It depends on the circumstances of each and every case which right will prevail; but the buyer's obligation to mitigate losses under Article 77 has to be taken into account (O. R., 334).

According to Will (BB, 354) paragraphs 2 - 4 do not describe the way in which to exercise the right to cure under paragraph 1; rather they offer an independent second way of curing to the seller. Also according to Honnold (313) paragraph 2, does not duplicate para. 1. In para. 2 the seller is not confined to the circumstances under paragraph 1. He can offer a period for late performance which may well result in an unreasonable delay. If the buyer keeps silent, he may later not invoke paragraph 1.

The *buyer may reject cure.* Welser (Doralt, 125) holds, however, that the buyer, in refusing the offer of cure, may not thwart the right of the seller to remedy his failure. If the buyer refuses to accept and the seller insists on performance it will have to be decided in a legal dispute whether the conditions were given for a second tender (ibid). This does not seem conclusive to us. The right of the seller to cure is given under the conditions of paragraph 1. This right cannot be thwarted by the buyer in the case of a non-fundamental breach of contract. But under paragraph 2 the seller has the right to cure only when the buyer agrees or remains silent.

11. This time can be very short. The buyer must be in a position to decide promptly. *This time* must be *shorter than the period of time offered for cure.* Article 27 applies where the communication of the buyer is concerned, i.e. in contrast to the request or notice by the seller (c. paragraph 4) dispatch will be sufficient.

12. It does not suffice that the seller states his readiness to deliver or to cure only in general terms. He has to *indicate* an envisaged *period of time*, which is a *condition* for the buyer to take his decision or to be obligated to accept performance if he keeps silence.

13. In this way the buyer is, at least temporarily, *deprived of his right to avoid the contract*. He cannot declare the contract avoided during the period of time offered by the seller.

14. The *buyer* is thus *bound to the contract* for this period of time (c. Article 47, note 5). During the said period he can neither avoid the contract nor declare a reduction in price. This rule clearly shows the underlying concept of the CISG, i.e. to keep to the contract, if possible.

15. This *assumed interest of the seller* also serves to retain the contract. The buyer has to respond to the communication of the seller, even if no request in accordance with paragraph 2 was added to it.

16. In contrast to Article 47, paragraph 4, the *buyer must receive the request or notice by the seller*. Hence, unlike in the event of the buyer's notice (note 11), it is not Article 27 which applies here, but Article 24 which, even if expressly conceived for part II of the CISG, is applied analogously.

Here the *general principle* obviously is *to place the risk* of transmission always *on the party which has committed a breach of contract* (Honnold, 314).

Article 49

(Buyer's right to avoid contract)

(1) The buyer may declare[2] the contract avoided[1]:

(a) if the failure by the seller to perform any of his obligations under the contract or this Convention amounts to a fundamental breach of contract[3]; or

(b) in case of non-delivery[4], if the seller does not deliver the goods within the additional period of time fixed by the buyer in accordance with paragraph (1) of article 47 or declares that he will not deliver[5] within the period so fixed.

(2) However, in cases where the seller has delivered the goods, the buyer loses the right to declare the contract avoided[6] unless he does so:

(a) in respect of late delivery[8], within a reasonable time[7] after he has become aware that delivery has been made;

(b) in respect of any breach other than late delivery[9], within a reasonable time[7]:

(i) after he knew or ought to have known of the breach[10];

(ii) after the expiration of any additional period of time[11] fixed by the buyer in accordance with paragraph (1) of article 47, or after the seller has declared that he will not perform his obligations[12] within such an additional period; or

(iii)after the expiration of any additional period of time indicated by the seller in accordance with paragraph (2) of article 48, or after the buyer has declared[13] that he will not accept performance.

1. The effects of avoidance are regulated under Article 81. The buyer has the *right to avoid a contract only under specific conditions.* If these conditions are given, he can, but does not have to, declare a contract avoided. He can also insist on performance (Article 46). There is the possibility to avoid parts of a contract (Article 51), and a contract can be avoided prior to the date of performance (Article 72). The specific case of avoiding a contract for delivery by instalments is provided for in Article 73. (Here the avoidance of a contract has the effect of a denunciation of contract. The contract can be avoided in respect of deliveries already made or of future deliveries.)

The buyer has the right to avoid a contract provided *two conditions* are fulfilled: (a) the seller must have committed a *fundamental breach of contract,* or (b) the *additional period for performance* set by the buyer in the case of non-delivery must have *expired.*

The buyer has no right to avoid the contract if he is not able to make restitution of the goods (c. Article 82), or if he has lost that right under Article 48, paras. 2 and 3, or if he fails to give notice in the case of non-conformity or of third party rights or claims (c. Articles 39 and 43).

The buyer may lose his right to avoidance also under the conditions of paragraph 2.

2. A *contract is not avoided automatically*; the buyer must declare avoidance. We are dealing here with a *right which the buyer may shape as he wishes*. The buyer himself brings about the success without a court having to become active, as is required under Article 1184 Code civil (Leser/Freiburg, 232).

ULIS, however, provided for two forms of avoiding the contract, an avoidance wanted and declared by the buyer and the so-called *ipso facto* avoidance under Articles 25 and 26, i.e. automatic avoidance as of law. This structure entailed some uncertainty over the fate of the contract and was, therefore, frequently criticized and not included in the CISG. (With regard to criticism of the *ipso facto* avoidance and the question to what extent such criticism is justified see J. Hellner, "*Ipso facto* avoidance", in: Privatautonomie, Eigentum und Verantwortung, Festschrift fur Hermann Weitnauer zum 70. Geburtstag, Berlin (West), 1980, p. 85 fol).

The declaration of avoidance must be forwarded to the seller (c. Article 26); *dispatch* is sufficient (c. Article 27). Also in this case, the risk of transmission is born by the party which committed the breach of contract.

There are three problems involved in contractual declarations, notices and avoidance of contract: effectiveness in respect to the decisive moment, including keeping to the time; the moment when the sender is bound; and the distribution of the risk of transportation. If a communication has to reach the addressee, these three aspects fall together. It is questionable, however, whether these three aspects also fall together in the case of dispatch (Article 27). The wording of the Article only points to the risk of transportation. It seems that receipt is necessary as to the timeliness and the binding effect (so Leser/Freiburg, 237). The *declaration is unilateral, does not permit conditions and cannot be revoked*. It becomes effective ex nunc (Leser/Freiburg, 233).

There is *no time limit* for the declaration (but c. note 6). However, the seller may put an end to uncertainty by making an offer under Article 48 (Welser/Doralt, 121).

3. As to a fundamental breach of contract compare Article 25. *Delivery of an aliud regularly constitutes a fundamental breach of contract* and also the failure to hand over negotiable, traditional, documents (Schlechtriem, 69; differently Huber, 509). Non-observance of fixed dates are also fundamental breaches (Welser/Doralt, 120). A deci-

sion is more difficult to take in the case of a delay where there is no fixed-term contract. To clarify the situation the buyer may set a *Nachfrist* (Farnsworth/Lausanne, 86). In the case of goods which have a stock market or market price, non-timely delivery certainly constitutes a fundamental breach of contract (Huber, 413; in agreement Schlechtriem, 48). Later, however, his own view seems to Huber (Freiburg, 202) "increasingly doubtful". No *Nachfrist* is required according to Honnold (319), when the prices for goods are subject to sharp fluctuations.

When there is a fundamental breach of contract - of any obligation, not only the obligation to deliver- the buyer can immediately declare the contract avoided. He is not obligated to grant to seller a *Nachfrist* pursuant to Article 47 nor must this be done by a court or arbitral tribunal (Article 45, paragraph 3).

Since every *avoidance of contract* can entail *additional expenses and risks*, the ceiling for exercising this right should be raised high (Schlechtriem/Doralt, 139). Concerning the right to avoid a contract in the case of performance offered by the seller, compare Article 48, note 10.

Where the failure to meet a deadline in itself does not constitute a fundamental breach, in other words, when time is not of the essence, the seller's cure within a reasonable time after the due date, in the view of Schlechtriem (69), will normally prevent the delay from constituting a "fundamental breach of contract". Welser (Doralt, 125) believes here that the term "non-conformity" would be overstretched if the ways and means of the debtor to remedy such non-conformity were taken into consideration to qualify it. According to the Convention, however, it should obviously matter in this context how grave a disturbance it is in itself and not what could be done to remedy it. Critical remarks also on the part of v. Hoffmann (Freiburg, 299): a right to delivery of substitute goods is given when grossly non-conform goods are delivered and does not depend on whether or not there is a second tender.

Honnold (312) believes, however, that an offer to cure defects prevents the breach from being fundamental. Hence it is not the time of delivery that is regarded as decisive in judging whether or not a breach is fundamental; and/or the seller's declaration retroactively removes a fundamental breach.

4. Pursuant to Article 47, paragraph 1 the buyer can set the seller a reasonable *Nachfrist* in regard to any obligation the latter may have. Here the rule is limited to the event of non-delivery. *Only in the event of non-delivery does the expiry without performance of the Nachfrist entail the right of the buyer to avoid the contract.* A delay during the *Nachfrist* can turn the original delay into a fundamental breach; but this is a consequence of the expiry of time limits and not of the setting of a *Nachfrist* (Schlechtriem, 68; differently Beinert, 89). We believe that it is an academic dispute to find out whether it is the setting of a *Nachfrist* in itself during which there is no performance of obligations, or the expiry of the time limit which turns the breach of contract into a fundamental one. It would seem reasonable to apply this rule analogously to the expiry of a *Nachfrist* where there was no performance, in the case of curing a non-conformity. But this was rejected repeatedly and for good reasons at the diplomatic conference (O.R. 116, 335; Article 46, note 5).

5. In the case of such a declaration there will be no need for the buyer to wait until the additional period of time he has fixed has expired (c. also Article 72).

6. Paragraph 2 of Article 49 should contain the most complicated rule of the entire Convention.

There is in general no time limit for the buyer to declare the contract avoided. This creates a *phase of uncertainty* for the seller which he cannot shorten, not even by refusing to perform prior to (Article 72) or after the expiry of the time for performance (Article 47, paragraph 2) (Leser/Freiburg, 235). The situation changes once delivery is made before the buyer has declared the contract avoided as he had the right to do. Now he must promptly exercise his right to avoidance, if not it will be forfeited.

The buyer's right to avoid the contract is lost "if the buyer waits too long after delivery to declare his intent to avoid" (Schlechtriem, 70).

7. A *reasonable time* in this case more or less means *immediately*. The time limit for clarifying always has to be a short one because otherwise additional costs and risks would be incurred (so Honnold, 319 fol, referring to the UCC and the Sale of Goods Act).

For the declaration of avoidance there will always be a *period of exclusion* because of the risk of speculation involved. This is, according to Leser (Freiburg, 234), a necessary correlative to the unilateral power of the formal right. This period, however, presupposes a delivery. In the case of paragraph 2, subpara. (a) the time begins to run when the buyer has learned that delivery has been performed.

(Honnold, 320, contrary to the wording of the rule, considers delivery as the beginning of that time.) In the case of paragraph 2, subpara. (b) it is stipulated in detail and subtly differentiated under (i), (ii) and (iii) when this time commences. A comparison with Articles 38 and 39 is recommended with regard to case (i).

8. In the event of late delivery there must be a fundamental breach of contract, as in the case of a fixed-term contract, or a delivery after the *Nachfrist* set by the buyer has expired. Concerning late delivery in regard to instalment contracts compare Article 73.

9. Other breaches could be for instance a breach of third party rights under Article 41 and 42 or the delivery of non-conforming goods under Article 35.

Any other breach *always needs to be a fundamental breach of contract* if the buyer is to have the right to avoid the contract.

10. Hence, failure to examine the goods is detrimental to the buyer. The *period of avoidance does not begin to run* as long as the buyer requires performance, e.g. requests delivery of substitute goods under Article 46, paragraph 2.

11. This refers to when the buyer, for instance, has set a time limit for the delivery of substitute goods. This applies also to a *Nachfrist* in the case of repair if there was a fundamental breach of contract and the buyer did not decide in favour of substitute goods but rather preferred repair. If *no fundamental breach was committed* and the buyer has set a *Nachfrist* for repair, he has no right, neither before nor after the expiration of that period, to avoid the contract.

According to Leser (Freiburg, 236), notice can turn into a dangerous instrument because the buyer is still bound to the additional period of time he has set. To begin with, the setting of an additional period of time obstructs the rights of the buyer (c. Article 47, note 5), and furthermore it restricts the period for avoidance later.

Instead of declaring the contract avoided upon the expiration of the first *Nachfrist*, the buyer could set a second *Nachfrist* without losing the right to avoidance (c. also Will/BB, 365).

According to Will (ibid) the cases given under (ii) and (iii) are superfluous since they are contained already in Articles 47 and 48.

12. Here it is of no importance whether the seller does not want to perform his obligations or whether he cannot do so (c. also note 5).

13. When the buyer has declared that he will not accept performance it hardly seems understandable why he would need an additional reasonable period of time to declare the contract avoided. If
he fails to set that period he loses the right to avoidance, and performance by the seller is excluded. Whether this stalemate was intended is not quite clear. But the structure of the Article shows that
rule (iii) does not follow from Article 48, as Will (BB, 365) concludes.

It was, therefore, assumed in the 1985 CISG Commentary that the
buyer's declaration of *non-acceptance of performance* by the seller was
to be treated as *equivalent to* a declaration of *avoidance of a contract*.

Article 50

(Reduction of the price)

**If the goods do not conform[1] with the contract and whether
or not the price has already been paid[3], the buyer may
reduce[2] the price in the same proportion[4] as the value that
the goods actually delivered had at the time of the
delivery[5] bears to the value that conforming goods would
have had at that time. However, if the seller remedies any
failure to perform his obligations in accordance with
article 37 or article 48 or if the buyer refuses to accept
performance by the seller in accordance with those articles,
the buyer may not reduce[6] the price.**

1. Pursuant to Article 35 the goods do not conform with the contract if they are not of the quantity, quality and description required
by the contract, and if they are not contained or packaged in the
manner required by the contract. It was discussed at the diplomatic
conference whether price reduction under Article 50 should also be
applied to cases where goods are not free from rights or claims by
third parties. A relevant motion by Norway was withdrawn after
discussion in favour and against, and the problem was left to the
courts to decide (O. R., 360 fol). Thus the *dogmatic gap between non-
conformity of goods, and third party rights or claims* was not closed
completely, and the right to reduction of the price was practically
restricted to non-conformity (Schlechtriem, 56).

It would indeed be justifiable to grant a right to price reduction in
the case of third party rights or claims (Schlechtriem, 70). It cannot
be overlooked that Article 44 expressly refers to Article 50: A buyer
who failed to give notice of the existence of third party rights or
claims, but has a reasonable excuse, may nevertheless claim a price
reduction. It is hardly understandable that a buyer should have the

right to a reduction of the price only if he fails to give notice, but not if he gives notice in time (c. also Will/BB, 376). Another interpretation would, according to Welser (Doralt, 123), presuppose the existence of schizophrenic legislators and would, therefore, have to be rejected. In contrast to this view, Schlechtriem (63) obviously believes that the reference made in Article 44 to Article 50 only relates to the case described under Article 39, paragraph 1, but not to Article 43, para. 1.

2. The *price is reduced by a simple declaration of the buyer*. There is no need for the seller's agreement (unlike in the case of Austria, see Welser/Doralt, 117). It is surely always more appropriate that the parties agree on the amount of the reduction.

Compared to cure and avoidance, a reduction of the price of goods is the simplest remedy where the least additional expenses occur and should, therefore, be facilitated (v. Hoffmann/Freiburg, 301). *Irrespective of the right to reduction* the buyer *also* has the *right to claim* compensation for *damages* he may have sustained. He thus can decide whether he wants to claim a reduction of the price and/or damages. While he can unilaterally declare a reduction and, provided he has not paid yet, force the seller to file suit if he does not agree, the buyer himself must, if need be, sue for compensation of damages.

Unlike in the case of a claim for damages, *in regard to reduction* there can be *no exemption from liability* (c. Article 79, note 5) because the reduction, irrespective of the seller's responsibility, serves to re-establish equivalence between performance and counter-performance.

Legal experts in common law countries have a special relationship to reduction because it is unknown in Common Law. Farnsworth (Lausanne, 105) said regarding reduction, that he did not know it and also did not like it. Also in UNCITRAL discussions the problem of reduction was quite often not understood (see the self-critical remarks by Honnold, 327). A claim concerning price reduction, *actio quanti minoris*, will under Common Law be treated as any other claim for damages (Honnold, 326).

If the seller is responsible for the non-conforming goods, the buyer has, according to Honnold (325), the choice between price reduction and a claim for damage. When prices are rising a claim for damages is more favourable than a price reduction, in the case of falling prices price reduction is more favourable than a claim for damages. The buyer will, however, prefer in such cases to avoid the contract and to look for new purchases (Honnold, 324, giving examples). Honnold (ibid) holds that a reduction of the price rarely plays a role, namely only if the buyer keeps the defective goods and the seller can keep himself free from claims for damages under Article 79.

The *declaration by the buyer* is governed by Article 27, i.e. it is *directly effective*, even if it does not reach the seller. It follows therefrom that the buyer, having declared a reduction, no longer has the right to performance by the seller (Article 46).

The CISG provides *no time limit for the buyer to exercise his right to reduction of the price*; provided that notice under Article 39 (and 43) is given in time this right is subject to the general limitation rules only.

3. If the buyer has not paid the price, he may immediately reduce the amount to be paid. If he has paid already, he has a right to be reimbursed in the amount of the reduction.

4. The reduction is a proportional reduction of the price of goods: the *proportion of conforming goods to the goods actually delivered*. In calculating that proportional reduction the value of the conforming goods is not just treated as equal to the price under the contract, the latter may well be below or above the former. If the conforming goods had a value of 100, the actually delivered goods only 80, the price would be reduced by 20 per cent.

According to the Secretariat's Commentary (O. R., 42 fol) there might even be cases where there can be no price reduction in spite of the non-conformity of goods. (See also the commentary by Will/BB, 370.) A reduction, therefore, is not merely a facilitated claim for damages as it may sound from Bergsten/Miller. (Critical remarks by v. Hoffmann/Freiburg, 300.)

The CISG leaves open where the value of the conforming and/or non-conforming goods will be assessed (c. O. R., 358 fol). According to the sense and purpose of the price-reduction provision, the *decisive place* must be the place *where the seller has to perform*; in the case of sales involving carriage it should be the place of destination (so Schlechtriem, 70). Will (BB, 375) suggests a three-step solution: the place of destination, then the place of delivery and finally the place of business of either the buyer or the seller, depending on where a market price can best be assessed. V. Hoffmann (Freiburg, 301) also would like to take into account the current value in the buyer's country.

5. What is *decisive is the time of delivery* and not the time of the conclusion of the contract (as is laid down in Article 46 ULIS and also in 472 (1) German BGB). Consequently, the buyer may lose "the advantages of a profitable purchase if, between the conclusion of the contract and the date of delivery, the price of the delivered but non-conforming goods increases more than the price of the conforming goods" (Schlechtriem, 70).

The choice in regard to the time of delivery can, as Welser (Doralt, 123) believes, lead to strange distortions in the case of the delivery of an *aliud*. In the event of an *aliud* the buyer, in our view, will in most cases prefer substitute goods and only refer to a price reduction when it is more profitable for him. Whether or not a seller in such a case will be content with a reduction that is detrimental to him, or will have to be content in the case of a legal dispute, will *inter alia* depend on whether the *aliud* was delivered intentionally or by accident.

Concerning the reasons for the change in comparison to ULIS see Will/BB, 370 fol. In general, the *current value at the time of delivery is easier to establish*, whereas the current value at the conclusion of the contract (except for stock market goods) always tends to be somewhat hypothetical (Honnold, 327; agreeing v. Hoffmann/Freiburg, 301).

Posch (Doralt, 151) obviously attaches no importance to the date. He believes that a profitable contract will always remain a profitable contract whereas an unprofitable contract will remain unprofitable. Believing so he ignores the possibility of differing price developments.

6. The buyer has no right to reduction if the seller cures the defective goods. Insofar as this is done according to Article 37, before the time of delivery, this should be quite natural. And also if the seller remedies a defect under Article 48 there will be no need for a price reduction because equivalence will be re-established. What is of significance here is that the *right to price reduction will be lost when the buyer refuses to have the defect cured by the seller*. The reason for this rule lies, as Honnold (327) believes, in the obligation to mitigate losses. It is of no importance here why the buyer refuses the cure, e.g. because of unreasonable inconvenience (c. Article 48, note 6). In this case the buyer might retain the right to claim damages taking account of the probable mitigation of losses under Article 77.

Article 51

(Partial non-performance)

(1) If the seller delivers only a part of the goods[1] or if only a part of the goods delivered is in conformity with the contract[2], articles 46 to 50[3] apply in respect of the part which is missing or which does not conform.

(2) The buyer may declare the contract avoided in its entirety[4] only if the failure to make delivery completely or in conformity with the contract amounts to a fundamental breach of the contract[5].

1. If the seller delivers only part of the goods, the result may be a *partial delay or non-conformity*. In the latter case the documents indicate a higher than delivered quantity, and a notice under Article 39 need only to be given (c. also Article 35, note 3).

2. As to conformity compare Article 35.

3. It seems logical that the right to performance (Article 46) and the setting of a *Nachfrist* (Article 47), and a cure of a failure (Article 48) or a reduction of the price (Article 50) can only refer to the missing or non-conforming part of the goods. It is significant, however, that the *right to avoid a contract* (Article 49) as a matter of principle *only relates to that part* and not, as might be deduced from the wording of Article 49, to the contract in its entirety (Honnold, 329).

4. Even if the seller has not performed within the *Nachfrist* set by the buyer, the latter may *declare the contract avoided only in regard to the missing or non-conforming part* (O. R., 44). Only if the partial non-delivery or the non-conforming performance constitutes a fundamental breach of contract (c. Article 25) can the buyer avoid the entire contract. Should the partial non-delivery refer to an instalment contract, the contract may be avoided as prescribed under Article 73.

5. Concerning a fundamental breach of contract compare Article 25. The buyer is not forced to sort out the non-conforming goods. The question is whether the non-conformity of part of the goods interferes with the use or salability of the remainder (Honnold, 330).

Article 52

(Early delivery; delivery of excess quantity)

(1) If the seller delivers the goods before the date fixed[1], the buyer may take delivery or refuse[2] to take delivery.

(2) If the seller delivers a quantity of goods greater than that provided for in the contract[3], the buyer may take delivery or refuse[4] to take delivery of the excess quantity. If the buyer takes delivery of all or part of the excess quantity[5], he must pay for it at the contract rate[6].

1. The date fixed follows from Article 33. An interpretation of the contract is needed if, for instance, "not later than..." is stipulated in the contract (Honnold, 331).

2. The buyer has *no obligation to take* early *delivery*. If he refuses to take delivery he may, however, have to assume an *obligation* under Article 86 *to preserve the goods*.

The buyer does not have to indicate any reason when refusing the goods, but he could gain little through a refusal if he has to take the goods later anyway (Honnold, 331).

The option to refuse to take delivery may be restricted by Article 7 (observance of good faith), or Article 9 (practices and usages).

If the buyer takes possession of the goods for the seller under Article 86, but intends to return them, he has to inform the seller accordingly (c. Article 27) in order to avoid that his conduct might be interpreted as implied acceptance.

If the buyer takes early delivery, this may constitute a *modification of the contract in regard to the period for performance* (c. Article 29). In such a case the buyer will also have to perform his obligations at an earlier date (O. R. 44). If he is not ready yet to receive the goods, e.g. in regard to the examination of the goods as required pursuant to Article 38, he should declare a relevant reservation when taking delivery. According to Schlechtriem (71) the buyer is not obligated to examine the goods prior to the contractual date for delivery.

Whether or not the taking of an early delivery constitutes a *modification of the contract* is *of importance where* the *possibility to claim damages* for breach of contract is *concerned.* Will (BB, 381) holds that the claiming of damages does not require making a reservation when taking the goods. We believe, however, that a buyer should never renounce a reservation if he wants to avoid the impression that the contract has been modified.

3. The seller may be tempted to do so when prices fall (Honnold, 332). The buyer is not obligated to take delivery of the excess quantity, but he has the right to make a choice in this case. This right may, however, be restricted by the above-mentioned Articles 7 and 9. *If the excess in quantity is trivial* the *buyer must not refuse to take delivery* (Honnold, 332). Several delivery clauses also allow tolerances in quantities.

4. In the event of a refusal to take delivery, the obligation to preserve the goods (Article 86) is to be taken account of. There is *no time limit for refusing to take delivery*, but the goods are considered received when no notice is given pursuant to Article 39 (Will/BB, 381). Also when he has given notice and refused to take delivery of the excess quantity, the buyer must accept the quantity agreed in the contract. Only when it is impossible to take delivery of the agreed quantity, e.g. because a bill of lading has been made out for the entire quantity, and if there is a fundamental breach of contract, can the buyer refuse to take delivery of the goods in their entirety (Honnold, 332; Schlechtriem, 71; Will/BB, 381).

If the buyer accepts the excess quantity, or if he fails to give the relevant notice, he has to pay for the goods delivered in excess.

5. Insofar as the acceptance does not constitute a contractual modification there is a *breach of contract* which entails the *right to claim damages* (c. Article 45, paragraph 1, subpara. (b)). The damage caused may be in the form of additional costs for storage, as in the case of an intended later resale (O. R., 44).

6. The goods delivered and accepted are to be paid at the *contractual rate*, and not at the *market rate* at the time of delivery (as under the rule of reduction, Article 50).

Therefore, the buyer will probably take delivery if the price of the goods has risen in the meantime and refuse to take delivery, and/or negotiate a lower price with the seller, if the price has fallen.

Chapter III

Obligations of the buyer

Introductory remarks

1. The structure of this Chapter is the same as of the preceding one on the obligations of the seller. Hence, it describes the obligations of the buyer in general (Article 53); then prescribes detailed rules for those (Sections I and II); and finally, it deals with the rights of the other party, here the seller, in cases where there is a breach of contract by the buyer (Section III).

This *mirror-like construction* does not preclude problems, which Sevon (Dubrovnik, 205) rightly pointed to, because the parallel rules could also be understood to have the same substance. This, however, is not true insofar as the factual conditions are different.

2. This Chapter regulates those obligations which are imposed *solely on the buyer*, whereas those which apply to both, are the substance of Chapter V.

Article 53[1]

(General obligations)

The buyer must pay the price for the goods[2] and take delivery[3,4] of them as required by the contract and this Convention.

1.1. This article is to be seen in connection with Article 30 and is to complete the *definition of a contract of sale* whose existence is an essential condition for invoking the Convention. The obligation to deliver under Article 30 meets its counterpart in Article 53 in the form of the obligation to take delivery. An obligation to hand over documents, as in Article 30, is not included in Article 53. Insofar as documents are concerned which are necessary for taking delivery of the goods, e.g. documents of title, the obligation to take delivery of the goods regularly comprises an obligation to take those documents.

2. This Chapter regulates those obligations which are imposed *solely on the buyer*, whereas those which apply to both, are the substance of Chapter V.

2.1. Compare here Articles 54 - 59.

2.2. Since the payment of the price for the goods is expressly mentioned and, as the detailed explanation in Articles 54 fol shows, such payment obviously constitutes an obligation to *pay a sum of money*. There may be doubt as to whether genuine barter contracts fall under the CISG (Article 1, note 1).

2.3. *In paying the price for the goods* the *buyer* generally *fulfills all his obligations* under the contract, including payment for packaging, dispatch, insurance, insofar as these performances are due to him (Kahn, 980 fol), provided there are no practices to the contrary.

3. Compare here Article 60.

4.1. The *payment of the price and the taking delivery of the goods* are *the most important obligations of the buyer* and are, therefore, considered by some legal systems as being the main obligations. The CISG does not make a distinction between main obligations and auxiliary obligations. Also the legal consequences of a breach of contract do not primarily depend on the role and type of the violated obligation (but see Article 64, paragraph 1, subpara. (b)), but rather on the effects of a breach on another party (Article 25). After all, the latter are often influenced by the weight of the violated obligation, so that a particular stress on these obligations might be an indication of the fact that their breach would be fundamentally to the detriment of the other party.

4.2. *The obligation to pay the price and the obligation to take delivery of the goods are of a complex nature.* They may include a host of individual acts whose specific features are the result of the contract, the Convention, practices and usages together with the concrete circumstances of the contract. Of special importance in this context are codified practices and/or rules for international trade, e.g. INCOTERMS, the Uniform Rules for Letters of Credit and the Uniform Rules for Collections.

4.3. Apart from those mentioned under Article 53, the *buyer* generally *has other obligations*. Insofar as they are primary obligations, hence such which in the normal, undisturbed course of a contractual relationship will have to be fulfilled in any case, they are dealt with under the CISG only to a very limited extent. The Convention provides for the other obligations of the buyer only in the event of disturbances of the contract performance. Insofar it views them as *reasons for exemption* for the seller (generally Article 80, for a specific case Article 42, paragraph 2, subpara. (b) which presupposes that the buyer fulfills his other obligation to provide technical drawings etc.).

The CISG also regulates the *legal consequences* in the case of breach of the other obligations of the buyer, in a general form in Article 61 which refers to all obligations of the buyer and thus forms the basis of all following provisions governing the rights of the seller. Article 62 makes express mention of the other obligations. Article 65 provides for a specific sanction in the case of a specific breach of contract by the buyer.

In the event that the seller commits a breach of his obligations, the CISG provides for the obligation of the buyer under certain conditions to permit a similar, hence late performance and/or late cure of defects as a *modification of the original obligation to take delivery* (Article 48 - after the date for delivery, under different conditions also Article 34 and Article 37 - curing of a lack of conformity up to the date for performance).

Furthermore, *obligations and/or responsibilities* arise for the buyer, like the obligation to examine the goods and to give notice, if he wants to ascertain his rights from non-conform delivery (Article 38 fol; Article 43). Of a similar character is the obligation to mitigate losses under Article 77. Finally, special circumstances may give rise to further obligations, a specific category of *secondary obligations* of both parties and thus also of the buyer. These include obligations to inform the other party (Article 71, paragraph 3; Article 72, paragraph 2; Article 79, paragraph 4) and, in particular circumstances, the obligation to provide assurance of performance of one's own obligations (Article 71, paragraph 3; Article 72, paragraph 2).

Section I

Payment of the price

Article 54[1]

(Obligation to pay the price)

The buyer's obligation[7] to pay the price includes[2] taking such steps[3] and complying with such formalities[4] as may be required under the contract or any laws and regulations[5] to enable payment to be made[6].

1. This article generally determines the specific *activities which make up the obligation to pay the price*. The parties, however, usually make detailed arrangements in the contract. Articles 55 and 56 stipulate how the price is calculated; place of payment is determined in Article 57 and date of payment in Articles 58 and 59.

2. This means that *further activities* may be necessary and are not excluded (Article 53, note 4.2.).

3. If nothing is agreed to the contrary, the *measures* which the buyer has to take *on a commercial basis* include, above all, the transfer of a sum through the customary way, e.g. bank transfer order, and handing over of a cheque or payment in cash. Where the provision of payment guarantees is planned, those measures comprise the provision of such guarantees, above all from which payment is to be made directly (letter of credit, indemnity). We believe that the buyer should generally have the obligation to ensure the success of such activities, i.e. to actually provide a letter of credit (not clearly expressed in the Secretariat's Commentary, O. R. 45; accurate Huber, 511), unless this fails because the buyer, in spite of making all the required efforts, cannot create the prerequisites which concern relations to the authorities. Depending on the terms of payment, several other activities may have to be undertaken by the buyer (e.g. acceptance of a bill of exchange).

4. Mentioning the formalities that may be required by any laws and regulations, the CISG refers, and this is the only place where it is done so clearly, to foreign trade regulations, concretely to *foreign exchange regulations*. It is taken for granted in this context that keeping with those regulations is necessary for the payment to be made. Their observance becomes a contractual obligation of the parties. Those regulations are recognized as being a fact. This is also in line with the Uniform Rules for Collections according to which the sums collected have to be transferable at once under the foreign exchange control regulations (Articles 11, 12).

The formalities to be complied with can be extremely different and extensive so that the substance of the term, in quite a number of cases in the context of the regulations, goes far beyond the proper sense of the term. They cover the mere registration of payment claims, the depositing of the respective contracts (e.g. at the central bank) and even the obtainment of payment permits and furnishing of deposits in cash, to mention only a few examples. The buyer insofar has to undertake all the activities which are dependent on him; fulfilment of information obligations, making of applications, and probably invoking of remedies. And he also has to create all the conditions in his area of competence for the required decisions to be taken. But he cannot be made responsible, for the considerations made in note 6.1., for the success of his activities (likewise Tallon/Parker, 7-6; in less detail Plantard/Lausanne, 112). Granting the buyer the reasons for exemption under Article 79 would lead to the same result. There is an essential *difference in the substance of the obligations* of the buyer on a commercial basis and the relations with the authorities. This difference is not apparent when the seller relies on the failure caused by the other party under Article 80. He can do so when the buyer in the end is refused transfer of foreign currency.

5. It is not said *which country's currency regulations* are referred to. The statute of the contract is insofar not invoked in accordance with a widely held opinion which we share. The rule obviously proceeds on the assumption that all provisions of payment will have to be complied with by the buyer. These provisions will be those of his country and/or of the country from which the payment is to be made, because the payment of a sum generally requires greater formalities than the receipt of the sum. Where there are such formalities at the place of payment in another country (seller's country), they will have to be observed by the buyer (but see note 7).

6.1. For the payment to be made, the buyer has to undertake activities both on a *commercial basis* and *vis-a-vis the authorities*. Those obligations in our view vary as to their substance. The activities on a commercial basis are generally foreseeable in detail. The buyer has to be considered obligated to create the necessary conditions for their fulfilment, including recourse to third parties such as banks. In most of the cases, he will have alternatives at his disposal, e.g. engaging of another bank. In a vertical plane, the commercial partners cannot always foresee the prerequisites for the obtainment of the necessary decisions, for they depend on the judgement of the authorities concerned in accordance with the concrete political or economic situation. The commercial partners and, even more, the buyer alone can influence a positive decision, apart from keeping with procedural requirements, only if the prerequisites are defined, which is not always the case. Mostly there is no alternative when the authority concerned does not take a positive decision.

6.2. If the *place and date* of the steps and formalities are not determined, they can be inferred from the substance. The *place* of the steps to be taken depends on their nature and can be the same as the place of payment. It can also be the result of the kind of the agreed payment security. The place where formalities have to be fulfilled can be deduced from the relevant laws and regulations and the competence defined therein. The *date* of the steps and formalities has to be chosen in such a way as to effect payment in time. Legal processing or processing time required as from experience have to be taken into account.

7. Insofar as *formalities* for the payment to be made can be complied with *only by the seller*, e.g. applications with his authorities to open an account for the receipt of foreign currency; he will have to be considered as obligated to do so. This follows from Article 7 (good faith), and probably also from Article 9. If the seller failed to do so, the buyer could rely on Article 80.

Article 55[1]

(Calculation of the price)

Where a contract has been validly concluded2 but does not expressly or implicitly3 fix or make provision for determining the price[4], the parties are considered, in the absence of any indication to the contrary[5], to have impliedly made reference to the price[6] generally charged[8] at the time of the conclusion of the contract[7] for such goods sold under comparable circumstances[10] in the trade concerned[9].

1.1. Under the law of some countries, the agreement of a price is an essential part of the contract without which the contract is not made. According to the law of other countries, the conclusion of a contract is permitted without fixing a price and it is prescribed how that price is then calculated. (These differences are visible even within the western European industrialized countries, as shows the comparative analysis by Tallon.) The view held by the former countries is expressed in Article 14, paragraph 1, sentence 2, even though in a more feeble version. The fixing of a price is required as part of a contract offer, but it can be implied, and it is possible also that the offer only makes provision for it. The importance of fixing a price is also underlined in Article 19, paragraph 3. The opposite view finds its expression in Article 55. There is a *contradiction* between the two articles. It was covered in such a way that Article 55 would apply only when a State is bound by Parts I and III, but not Part II of the Convention and when the law applicable to the conclusion of the contract permits such conclusion without fixing a price (O. R., 45). This interpretation, however, is tantamount to evading the problem in the typical case, namely that the Convention is accepted as a whole. We believe that the total solution found at the diplomatic conference is also favourable to the *formation of a contract without fixing a price*. A point in favour of this view is, in particular, the fiction of a reference (note 6). Account of the opposite view is taken also by hinting to a valid conclusion of a contract (note 2). Therefore, the contradiction has to be overcome though delimiting the scopes of application of the rules where they do not harmonize.

1.2. In those cases where there is no agreement of a price, the *currency of the price* will not be agreed either. The CISG does not include a direct rule for such cases. Established practices may then serve to determine the relevant currency, e.g. it is customary to express and pay the price for a number of commodities in a specific currency, like $US. The same goes for usages in existence between the parties (Article 9, paragraph 1). Also international agreements to which the respective States are parties, e.g. bilateral payment agreements, may be consulted in this regard. If no solution can be found in this way, the currency is to be determined taking account of the foreign exchange rules of those States which have a close and relevant relationship with the contract in question (Article 4, subpara. (a)). In case of doubt, this can be the currency of the seller's country as Magnus (130) suggests, when that country allows international sales contracts to be performed in its own currency. The currency, should in the absence of a provision to the contrary, generally be considered as the *currency in which all payments under the contract are to be made*, including damages, liquidated damages, and refunding of expenditures. For foreign exchange reasons we have reservations of a general nature against the consideration of Magnus (135) to adopt the currency in which a damage is caused as the currency of the obligation to pay damages. Whereas, it seems indeed logical that claims for repayment are made in the currency in which the payment was made (ibid. 141).

2. Herewith reference can be made to the *prerequisites for validity* as contained in the CISG and to national validity conditions (Article 4, subpara. (a)). Some authors, therefore, proceed on the assumption that without having fixed a price there is no offer under Article 14, paragraph 1, sentence 2 and, therefore, no delivery can be taken. Hence, there will be no contract so that the rules governing the substance of the contract including Article 55 are irrelevant where there are no exceptions (Plantard/Lausanne, 112 fol). Others suppose, and the text speaks in favour of this assumption, that the validity of a contract in this case is to be judged only according to national law (Kahn, 980). Leaving the problems which this view also entails out of consideration (note 6), there are, as we believe, a host of *exceptions*. It may thus follow from established practices and usages that the contract can be formed even without an agreement of the price. Furthermore, Article 14 is not mandatory so that the parties may renounce it, e.g. in frame contracts, or may agree differently. Such modifications may be brought about when the contract provides for the parties to agree on a price later. This may even be considered as an agreement of the method of fixing the price. Sevon (Dubrovnik, 211) holds that an invoice sent in advance which is not protested by the buyer could mean his agreement with the price indicated therein. The *conclusion* of a contract by joint signature of

the relevant document at the end of negotiations *without a price agreement* could be considered as a modification of Article 14, paragraph 1 if the parties held the contract as valid (in this sense also Eörsi/BB, 497 and Lüderitz/Freiburg, 188).

Finally, mention should be made of the possibility of curing a possibly existing non-validity of the contract, which could be assumed when a delivery was made and taken already (ordering urgently needed spare parts). We believe that the possibility of a cure should be deduced from the CISG, namely from the analogous application of Article 29, paragraph 2, sentence 2 or directly from the prohibition of the *venire contra factum proprium* as a general principle of the Convention (note 10.1. of Article 7). In the case described above no party could rely on the non-validity of the contract, so that the price would have to be determined according to Article 55.

3. An *implicit fixing of the price* can be assumed, in particular, when the seller sells his goods according to price lists which the buyer knows or should know, or when constant prices were used in a continuing business relationship.

4. The methods of fixing the price can also be determined expressly or implicitly. Widely used methods of fixing a price are reference to a stock market or market price, to the valid price lists of the seller, to the price most favourable to the buyer which the seller asks third parties to pay, commercial most-favoured-party clause, etc. It is important in any of those cases to indicate the time relevant for the fixing of the price. We hold that it should be admissible that reference be made to a price which a party, in practice particularly the seller, has to fix individually, i.e. not on the base of generally applicable lists, (doubting even if it is the price generally calculated for this kind of goods at the time of the delivery, Sevon, 209). Even when no reservation is made in this context, e.g. that the price is reasonable, that it is the usual price on the market etc., and that there has to be a reasonable proportion between the price and the seller's prime costs, the fixing of an unjust price would nevertheless not be binding. This can be inferred from Articles 7, 8 or 9. The methods used to fix a price, which seemingly are gaining importance, include the calculation of the price on the basis of the procurement price plus fees, or of the prime cost plus reasonable profit. An agreement of price fixing methods eventually has also to include cases where a *third party* or an *arbitral tribunal* from the beginning, or only when the parties do not reach agreement, is instructed to fix the price.

5. *Clues to the contrary* may be an indication that the contract is to be formed only when there is agreement on the price. Those clues are in existence also when the price cannot be fixed pursuant to Article 55 because there is no generally calculable price for the goods concerned, e.g. collectors' prices as they are relevant in art trade.

6. The *legal assumption of a price agreement* which is substantiated herewith may be interpreted in such a way as to make ineffective the requirement to fix or make provision in the offer for determining the price insofar as such offer is accepted. This is what the arguments given by Bonell, DPCI (24 fol) and Honnold (164) aim at, the latter joining Tallon (Parker, 7-10 fol) in stressing the problem (compare also Lüderitz/Freiburg, 188 fol). Bonell, DPCI (25) basically believes that the determination of the price as a condition for a contract to be valid under national law applies only where a State has not ratified Part II of the Convention and where the law of the State which provides for such a condition is the decisive law.

There is thus an overwhelming trend in publications to *maintain the contract* by way of different juridical constructions (like, in the end, the comparative analysis of Tallon, too; note 1.1., particularly 107 fol). Article 55 is thus to be attached greater weight than Article 14, paragraph 1. However, account has to be taken of the fact that those domestic laws which, like the French law regard an agreement of the price as a condition for the contract to be valid, will rely on Article 4, subpara. (a) and circumvent application of Article 55 (Tallon/Parker, 7-11 fol). It is, therefore, a simplification when Bonell, DPCI (25) declares the Eastern European and developing countries as countries which require the price to be a condition for the validity of the contract, and the Western countries as not requiring it.

7. Since it is not the price which is decisive in the event of delivery, the seller will not enjoy later *increases* in, and the buyer will not enjoy later *reductions of, the price.*

8. By contrast to ULIS according to which that price is to be paid "which the seller at the time of the conclusion of the contract usually has requested" (Article 57), the CISG aims to achieve an *objectivization of the price determination.* Where there is a relatively uniform price level for the goods in question, from which only a few sellers deviate, this level has to be taken as a basis. Where the prices differ, however, an average price has to be calculated on the basis of the prices of representative sellers which hold the overwhelming share in the market concerned. Price modifications which are the result of economic considerations, e.g. technical parameters or other qualitative features, design and marketability of

the goods, for instance in connection with the trade-mark situation, have to taken into account.

According to Eörsi (BB, 408), in the case of doubt the prices on the world market take precedence over the regional or domestic prices of the goods sold. If a price can be calculated which is typically agreed between partners from the countries where the parties have their place of business, this should in our view be the decisive price even if it deviates from a price existing in the world market. If no price can be calculated for a *market covering both parties*, that price should be decisive which is generally calculated where parties of the kind of the buyer usually make their purchases. Under conditions of competition the buyer will naturally choose the most favourable offer. At any rate, it would serve economic effectiveness to make such conduct the norm.

Although the CISG does not define the party who is to take the *initiative in fixing the price*, it will in most cases be the seller for he makes out the bill. (This is absolutely necessary in very many cases if only for the customs clearance of the goods.) This being so, the seller is actually in a preferential position because the buyer has to prove that the price does not meet legal prerequisites. Honnold (339) goes even farther and concedes the price by the seller, unjustly in our view, *a priori* a certain dominance and thus interprets the CISG in the meaning of ULIS.

We hold that in the case of non-agreement of the parties a *decision regarding the price* can be taken by the competent deciding organ.

9. If the same *goods* are *traded in different trades*, e.g. sale of laboratory equipment to schools, hospitals, institutions of scientific research, or industrial enterprises, prices have to be based on comparable proportions.

10. Reference is made here to *circumstances that are relevant for the calculation of the price*, like the commercial terms, which takes into account territorial criteria which are not expressly provided for in the rule; ordered quantity, because of possible rebates; periods of order, in case special delivery charges are relevant; liability assumed by the seller, in particular guarantees such as price surcharges because of especially long guarantee periods; and terms of payment, discount in the case of payment in cash and others. All in all it matters which price the buyer would have had to pay had he bought a comparable good in comparable conditions from another seller.

Article 56[1]

(Price fixed by weight)

If the price is fixed according to the weight of the goods[2,] in case of doubt[3] it is to be determined by the net weight[4].

1. This article provides a *rule of interpretation* which complements an incomplete price agreement.

2. This is the case when the *price per weight unit* is named in the contract or can be deduced from the contract because the latter contains the total weight and the total price. In the latter case, however, it must be recognizable that the price is based on the weight. This is not so when the price was calculated for units, pieces etc. and the weight is given only as an information.

The price is determined according to the weight, for instance, when bulk goods are traded. And those goods are delivered in part unpacked. If there is a relevant legal (Article 35, subpara. (d)) or contractual obligation, the goods have to be packed, and the buyer does, as a matter of principle, not have to return the packaging, even if the seller is not allowed to calculate it either in the weight of the goods or separately. Practices or the contract may stipulate differently as in leased packaging.

Article 56 is to be applied, in our view, also to *weight clauses* which, even though it is contradictory to the trend toward reducing the weight, are still used sometimes in trading machinery and equipment. They allow a reduction of the price if a certain minimum weight is not reached. In the case of doubt the net weight would also be decisive to determine it.

3. *Doubt is excluded* to the extent to which there is an established practice according to which the weight of packaging is included in the weight of the goods because it is unimportant in proportion to the weight of the goods. There is no doubt either when the clause gross for net has been agreed, according to which the gross weight is decisive, and/or when there are other relevant agreements between the parties.

4. The *net weight* is the total weight minus the weight of the packaging. Should there be a change in that weight, for instance during transport a decrease in weight, the net weight at the place of delivery (Article 31) is decisive because the seller has to fulfil his obligations there.

Article 57[1]

(Place of payment)

(1) If the buyer is not bound to pay the price[2] at any other particular place[3], he must pay it to the seller[4]:

(a) at the seller's[6] place of business[5]; or

(b) if the payment is to be made[9] against the handing over of the goods[7] or of documents[8], at the place where the handing over takes place.

(2) The seller must bear any increase in the expenses incidental to payment[10] which is caused by a change in his place of business[11] subsequent to the conclusion of the contract.

1.1. There is a close *connection between* the rule governing the *place of payment and* that governing the *time of payment* (Article 58) because the place of payment under the Convention is dependent on the modalities of delivery to the same extent as is the time of payment, and because the time of payment can only be kept when the payment is made at the place of payment. Where the place of delivery and of payment are identical, the time of payment in several cases is dependent on when the required circumstances arose at that place. These *connections are blurred* by the different formulations and systematizations in Articles 57 and 58. Anyway, the comments on the provisions on the place of payment to a large part apply *mutatis mutandis* to the provision on the time of payment.

1.2. The determination of the place of payment, as it is made in this article, entails generally *four essential consequences for the buyer*. First, he must initiate the payment so early that it arrives on the settlement date (Article 58) at the place of payment. He thus bears the risk of a delay insofar as he is not exempted from liability under Articles 79 and 80. Second, he must take all measures and go through all the formalities at a commercial level and vis-a-vis the authorities so that the payment can be made at the place of payment, i.e. exceptionally also the fulfilment of formalities in the seller's country (Article 54). Third, he must bear the cost of the payment procedure up to this place. Fourth, he also bears the risks up to this place, i.e. when the initiated payment procedure is not successful because of the bankruptcy of a bank engaged it has to be repeated.

The institutions such as banks, which the buyer uses to fulfil his payment obligations, are *third parties in the meaning of Article 79, paragraph 2* (note 7 to that article). This means, and it can be inferred from this Article in its reverse conclusion, that the buyer is responsible for them, as far as he cannot be exempted. Such liability stops with the receipt of the payment by the seller and/or the first institution used by him, i.e. in particular the bank named by him for the transfer. Huber (512) expressed himself similarly on the draft but differs from the view explained here only in that he doubts whether the buyer is also liable for the engaged intermediaries. We do not share this doubt for when there is a party of the contract who can exert an influence, it is the buyer, e.g. in instructing his bank to avoid certain ways of transfer etc. The situation is different, however, when specific wishes of the seller have to be taken into consideration.

1.3. *Agreed payment guarantees* for lack of deviating agreements, as they occur regularly, in regard to the place of payment, and also the time of payment, have to be in line with the provisions of the Convention. When and where these guarantees have to be given is, however, not regulated by the Convention.

1.4. In some instances the problem was raised that the determination of the place of payment in Article 57, in the case of payment obligations, also affects the *jurisdiction* at the place of performance where it is provided by law. At the diplomatic conference, the FRG even submitted a proposal which aimed at preventing this, but was rejected (O. R., 122). Huber (513) and Honnold (343) rightly pointed out that this is no problem of the CISG. Unlike Huber we believe that clarification in this matter is incumbent on the respective procedural law and not on the CISG.

2. The rule only mentions the "price", but is to be applied, as we believe, also to *other payments under the contract*, like the payment of damages, liquidated damages, interests and reimbursement of expenses. Since there is not regularly a direct dependence between performance and counter-performance, and in particular no contemporaneous performance, this refers above all to subpara. (a) with the "seller" having to be read as the "obligee" and the "buyer" as "obligor".

3.1. The fact that this rule can be changed is stressed here once again irrespective of the general determination in Article 6, which can be regarded as an *orientation of the parties* towards an agreement of the place of payment. The parties, in general, attach great attention to the terms of payment which include the place of payment. Where an express agreement of the place of payment is lacking, an implicit agreement may be inferred from the way in which the payment is made. This may be done considering non-governmental codifications for specific categories of payment (Uniform Customs and Practices for Documentary Credits - Article 9 fol; Uniform Rules for Collections - Articles 11 and 12) which become binding through the agreements between the parties, business conditions of the banks engaged or directly as an established practice.

3.2. In view of the *bank transfer* widely used in international trade in which the payment does not go directly to the seller but to his bank, it can be assumed that relatively feeble indications in this direction are sufficient for the buyer to pay into the seller's bank account. The buyer, in our view, is entitled to pay to the bank named by the seller (also Sevon/Dubrovnik, 213). Where the seller has named several banks in connection with the contract in question, or with other transactions with the buyer, the buyer may choose between them, but will likely have to choose one from among the banks in the seller's country. A relevant decision could also be taken by the seller, which would be binding as payments must not be made to another bank.

4. The term payment generally includes *acceptance* of bills of exchange where such acceptance was agreed in the contract. It occurs, above all, in the cases covered by subpara. (b), but does not lead to the final fulfilment of the obligation to pay.

5.1. The principle on which the CISG is based, characterizes the obligation of payment as an *obligation to be performed at the creditor's place of business* in order to ensure that the seller can indeed dispose of the proceeds of the transaction without having to confront the foreign exchange rules of other countries (Secretariat's Commentary, O. R., 46; Honnold, 342).

5.2. Concerning the determination of the place of business compare Article 10. The place of business of the seller may change in the process of contract performance. As can be inferred from paragraph 2 it is decisive here what has been the *place of business at the time of payment*. However, payment at another place presupposes that the buyer is informed accordingly, namely before he has to initiate the acts and formalities of an orderly transaction in order to fulfil his payment obligation in time. We believe that the receipt of the information by the buyer is decisive because without it he would not be in a position to meet his obligation in the modified form, i.e. Article 27 cannot be applied. If the seller gives late notice, the buyer will is entitled to make the payment at the original place of business of the seller (Article 80). This may factually be impossible, but is of relevance insofar as the payment obligation will have to be regarded as fulfilled if the price was available at the original place of business. The buyer, of course, retains the obligation to take all measures he can to ensure that the price reaches the hands of the seller in the end. The buyer is also obliged to change his arrangements when he receives the information at a time that would allow him to do so. The seller, because of Article 80, does not have any right to claim delay in payment in such cases (Sevon/Dubrovnik, 213 fol, however relates to Article 79, paragraph 1, which in our view is less relevant here). As to the increase in the expenses, compare note 11.

6. Subpara. (a) applies where *no contemporaneous performance* as under subpara. (b) was agreed; but also in the latter case the place of payment can be the place of business of the seller. Subpara. (a), therefore, is of practical relevance in the event of advance payments and payments which are made after the goods are received, including the granting of unsecured credits (terms of payment as in "cash after receipt of the goods", "cash against open invoice" or "cash .... days (weeks etc.) after receipt of the goods").

Payment in these cases *is made* either in cash, which is very rare, or by handing over a cheque, respectively at the place of business of the seller. In the latter case it is assumed that the seller for lack of an agreement to the contrary, is entitled to reject a cheque if he does so immediately after having been offered one, unless the cheque is of such a quality that such conduct would constitute a violation of the principle of good faith such as a banker's cheque. Where the cheque is accepted it must be considered as a discharge by performance. The payment is regarded as made at the date of the handing over of the cheque, provided that it is honoured at its presentation. If this is not so, the payment is considered as not made (compare Caemmerer/Dölle, 363). Because of relevant agreements, a provisional payment can be made in a similar way by handing over a cheque, by way of handing out a promissory note, or of acceptance of a bill of exchange. When they are not sight bills, which can be used similarly to cheques, the bills contain generally a period for payment so that the payment in the context of the payment of interests cannot be referred to the date of the handing over or of the acceptance, and the interests have to be taken into consideration.

Payment at the *place of business* of the seller is required, but not necessarily inside that place itself. This obligation could be fulfilled also when the payment is made into the *bank account* of the seller at his place of business. From this situation follows the general question whether payment by way of bank transfer comes under the introductory part of paragraph 1 and whether such an obligation can be supposed as in existence under alleviated prerequisites (note 4), or whether it is a form of payment at the place of business of the seller. We are of the view that both variants are possible. Payment by bank transfer has to be considered as one of the legal options under the CISG, at least when it is customary and/or other options do not exist. The latter is the case, for instance, when international cash remittance is not one of the services offered by postal services, like in a number of countries, and the handing over of the money personally or by courier is excluded because of the modalities of the transaction, and when the sending of a cheque is not customary. In that event the seller must be regarded as having the obligation to maintain an account at his place of business and to inform the buyer of the number of that account. Otherwise, the buyer must have the right to pay into another account of the seller in the country of his place of business and/or he may invoke Article 80 if this not possible.

Hence, the *buyer can*, with some restrictions applying, choose between payment in cash and transfer and, where the seller agrees, the handing over of a cheque because he is the one to meet the obligation and thus able to fully exhaust the leeway granted by the legal provision.

7. If the *payment is bound only to the handing over of the goods*, the place of payment under the CISG is the place where the goods are handed over to the first carrier, the place where the goods are made available or the place of business of the seller (Article 31). As regards the first variant, we assume that the handing over referred to here also includes the handing over to the first carrier for transmission to the buyer. In that event it does not matter whether or not the goods are handed over directly to the buyer for in the case of a non-documented sale the seller in handing over the goods to the first carrier, who takes over the goods for the buyer, in general largely renounces his right to dispose of the goods. Where the contemporaneous principle is to be realized, which the CISG aims at, payment must be made at this place and at this time.

From the customarily agreed *trade terms* in the interpretation of the INCOTERMS the following could, for example, result: The term "Free Carrier" is used for the handing over to the first carrier, but very often the goods are handed over at a place which they pass through in transit, e.g. terms FOB, CIF etc. Payment at such places of handing over is very frequently impracticable so that these terms are linked with terms of payment which do not bind the place of payment to the place of the handing over of the goods, but rather to the handing over of the documents. And/or the possibility of Article 58, paragraph 2 is made use of. Insofar we can agree with Lüderitz (Freiburg, 189 fol) as regards the actual course. It is a condition, however, for the procedure discussed here that the payment is made against the handing over of the goods. This cannot simply be re-interpreted as a payment under subpara. (a) as Lüderitz does.

The term *"ex works"* is agreed for cases in which the goods are made available pursuant to Article 31, subparas. (b) and (c); the term *"named place of destination in the country of import (duty paid)"* is agreed for those in which the goods or documents are handed over at the place of destination which often is the place of business of the buyer. Both cases, as to their practical realization, cause less problems than the one discussed first, even though it is not a very widely followed practice that the collector pays for the goods. It happens frequently that the carrier of confidence is the one to collect or request, under an advice-note, the presentation of a proof of payment.

8.1. The documents mentioned here are obviously the same as under Article 58, i.e. the *documents which entitle to dispose of the goods*. Articles 30 and 34, however, refer to documents which relate to the goods. An extended version of the term "documents" is used there which may include certificates relating to quality and analysis, operating manuals, technical descriptions and drawings. Schlechtriem (74) wants to interpret the documents referred to in Article 58 in the meaning of Articles 30 and 34 because the right of the seller to refuse performance is at stake. We, too, are in favour of a functional interpretation and not of a limitation of the relevant documents to mere documents of title without wanting to consider the two groups of documents as identical. Reference is made here in the first place to shipping documents, like bills of lading, warehouse certificates, combined transport documents, international forwarding notes etc., i.e. the so-called *documents of title*. Depending on the basis for delivery agreed the *documents* can also be such *which* only *certify the taking over of the goods* (quay receipt, mate's receipt, forwarding agent's receipt) and/or such which *prove the conclusion of a freight or storage contract* which serve to substantiate an obligation to deliver (sender copies of the waybill in transportation by way of railroad, motor traffic, airship and inland navigation). The requirements for those documents are determined according to the rules applicable to the respective category of performance (regarding details see Richter, 12 fol). The category of transportation documents which will have to be presented can usually be inferred from the INCOTERMS referred to.

Where the buyer has to pay customs duties to obtain the goods the seller has to provide the necessary documents, such as invoices (if agreed having account of specific form requirements - consular invoices) and certificates of origin. Depending on what is agreed in the contract *other documents* are added, like insurance documents, certificates of quality etc. The Uniform Customs and Practices for Documentary Credits contain the requirements which most of these documents will have to meet.

8.2. Payment is to be made *only against the handing over of the documents* if the seller has determined it pursuant to Article 58 (subject to the right of the buyer to examine them, see Article 58, notes 8 and 9) or if the terms of payment "cash against documents" or "payment according to letter of credit" have been agreed.

8.3. *Where the documents are to be handed over* is made dependent in the Convention on the agreement between the parties (Article 34). But regularly established practices and/or rules referred to by the parties in one form or another intervene here. The places determined according to the handing over of the documents are different in the case of specific terms of payment. In the event of the term "cash against documents" the documents have to be submitted as a rule at the buyer's (Article 8, Uniform rules for collections). Payment is hence to be made there with the consequences described in note 1.2. However, the buyer has to be considered as obligated to satisfy all formalities which are necessary to allow transfer of the payment to the seller's country. But he is obliged only insofar as that one depends on him and, in particular, only to the extent to which he is legally entitled and actually in a position to do so (accordingly Article 54, note 4).

Where a *letter of credit* is agreed, all banks engaged act on behalf of the buyer, hence the issuing bank and also other banks engaged by it, including the bank in the seller's country which notifies the seller of the opening of the letter of credit. Its place of business is also the place of payment, which again entails the consequences described under note 1.2. This is also in line with the Uniform Customs and Practices for Documentary Credits according to which the bank sending the notification is under certain circumstances entitled to make the payment pursuant to the conditions prescribed (Article 2, (ii); Article 11, subpara. (d). Where a payment made under a reservation is reclaimed later, because the bank where the letter of credit is issued does not pay, the payment is considered as not having been made.

9. For lack of deviating agreements this is even the *rule* under the CISG (Article 58, paragraph 1, sentence 2 and paragraph 2), leaving out of consideration cases where credits are granted. The terms of payment agreed insofar are "cash against documents" (including forwarding agent's collection) and "payment according to letter of credit".

10.1. We believe that the buyer has the right to deduct the *increase in the expenses* from the amount to be paid if this is possible from a technical and financial point of view.

10.2. Of greater relevance should be the *other consequences which are unfavourable* to the buyer and which can be related to modifications of the place of business, such as earlier initiation of the payment procedure, increase in the risk, and more burdensome formalities. They can be financially compensated only partially without problems, e.g. loss of interests if the payment procedure has to be initiated earlier. The buyer, in our view, generally has the right here to rely on Article 80 (see also note 5).

11. This rule is invoked only when the *seller's place of business* is also the place of payment.

Article 58[1]

(Time of payment; payment as condition for handing over; examination before payment)

(1) If the buyer is not bound to pay the price at any other specific time[2], he must pay it when the seller places either the goods[3] or documents controlling their disposition[4] at the buyer's disposal in accordance with the contract and this Convention[5]. The seller may make such payment a condition for handing over the goods or documents[6].

(2) If the contract involves carriage of the goods, the seller may dispatch the goods on terms whereby the goods, or documents controlling their disposition[4], will not be handed over to the buyer except against payment of the price[7].

(3) The buyer is not bound to pay the price until he has had an opportunity[8] to examine the goods[9], unless the procedures for delivery[11] or payment[10] agreed upon by the parties are inconsistent with his having such an opportunity.

1.1. The main idea of Article 58 is the rule that the *delivery* and the *payment* have to be made *contemporaneously*. In the process, the buyer should, if possible, have the opportunity to examine the goods in order to guarantee the contemporaneous performance to the largest extent possible. Not only does the buyer have the rights provided for such cases, but time of delivery is also postponed where the seller falls behind with his delivery or where he in any other way does not deliver in conformity with the contract (note 3.3.). In the opposite case, the seller, depending on the commercial terms, either need not deliver the goods or at least need not hand them over as long as no payment is made. This article in a specific way also expresses the objection of the non-fulfilled contract (Art. 80) without, however, allowing a waiting game to be played in the performance of the contract (O. R., 369 fol, 377). The principle of contemporaneous performance is a more direct reflection of the immediate change in the possession of the goods than Article 80, and unlike the latter, does not require prior non-performance. But since we assume under Article 80 a non-performance caused by legal reasons (note 6 of that article), unlike Schlechtriem (75), we do not have to face the problems concerning a right of the seller to retain the goods when the buyer does not fulfil obligations other than payment contemporaneously. @P1 = We believe that this right can be easily deduced from Article 80 and thus arrive, on the basis of the CISG, at the same conclusion as he does using a complicated construction.

For the rule to be made operative, a *trigger* is needed. This is the obligation to deliver and, in the context of time, the setting of a date for it (note 4).

1.2. Also *advance payments* are generally not permitted. It does not seem to be excluded that the rule on delivery before the time for delivery is applied by analogy.

When the buyer wants to pay in advance to avoid losses which are looming because of an expected decline in currency, the *seller can reject* this. In accordance with the principle of good faith (Art. 7) he has to do so immediately. If not, the payment is considered as accepted, and the seller cannot later ascertain claims for damages. Even more so since he is basically in a position to use the received payment in such a way as to avoid losses. He can, however, ascertain claims when he accepts the payment making a relevant reservation (O. R., 370). The buyer, however, need not accept that reservation and can demand reimbursement when the reservation is made.

1.3. The payment of the price in regard to time (just as to place, Art. 57) includes that the full *price* is offered in the currency that was agreed. If this is not the case, the seller has the right to retain the goods to the extent that this would not violate the principle of good faith because of the smallness of the deviation to be calculated according to objective commercial criteria. After all, it is up to the seller to decide to what degree he would want to ascertain his right to retain the goods in the event of non-orderly payment. If he does not ascertain this right, this alone is not tantamount to a renunciation of possible claims because of a breach of contract on the part of the buyer.

2.1. Compare Article 57, note 3.1.

2.2. The *time of payment* can be determined in the contract by naming a calendar date for payment or its determination can be provided for in the contract, for instance, by tying the payment to the emergence of certain circumstances.

2.3. It must be derived from the functions of a *security for credit* the time such a security has to be procured. If nothing else can be derived, a letter of credit will have to be issued early enough as to allow its use from the beginning of the period for delivery at the place of payment. Where the procurement of a security is bound, however, to the delivery, it will have to be procured at the time of payment in accordance with this article (e.g. acceptance of bills of exchange, handing over of promissory notes).

3. Compare Article 57, note 7. The *time of payment* is the moment where the relevant steps mentioned there are being taken.

4. Compare Article 57, note 8.

5.1. Insofar as reference is made to the *rules under the Convention*, they relate, above all, to cases of Article 31, subparas. (b) and (c). But also the case of Article 31, subpara. (a) according to which the contract requires transport of the goods, can be made out in such a way that the goods are made available to the buyer at a certain point of the transport route or at the place of destination or at his place of business (Art. 57, note 7). Often it is commercially not practicable to pay the amount required at the time and the place where the goods or documents are made available. Therefore, terms of payment are agreed which do *not interlink the time and place of payment and the place of the making available of the goods or documents* (Article 57, paragraph 1, subpara. (b) calls it the handing over), but the documents controlling disposition of the goods reach the buyer differently from the goods. The handing over of the documents is made dependent on the payment, as paragraph 1, sentence 2, and paragraph 2 provide for. Payment is then made at the time when the documents have been handed over at the place of payment.

5.2. Where the buyer is not informed in advance and/or gets otherwise knowledge of the fact that the conditions for payments will soon be ripe (notification of readiness for dispatch, notice of dispatch etc.) he must, in accordance with the principle of good faith and/or established practices or usages (Articles 7, 9), be granted a reasonable, generally a *short, period for payment* (so already Huber, 515, on the draft). Payment cannot be demanded from him before he knew or had to be aware of the existence of the conditions causing payment, even when this leads to his missing the time for payment. The solution given by Lüderitz (Freiburg, 190) to assume that a breach of contract was committed in this case from whose consequences in terms of damages the buyer can be exempted under Article 79, paragraph 1 does not seem convincing to us. Normal commercial behaviour should not be incriminated in connection with belated justification. If one would wish to follow such way, it should rather be done pursuant to Article 80 (note 1.1.). But this, too, would mean making a detour.

5.3. *Payment* can be *refused* under the same conditions as acceptance (Art. 60, note 2).

6. When the handing over is done at the *place of business of the seller*, he can - for lack of other agreements - make it dependent on the payment, which could for instance be made by handing over a cheque. Payment in cash is not customary here. If proof of payment is submitted in this case, the buyer has already performed in advance.

Also in the context of paragraph 1, a handing over can be effected *on the way or at the place of destination* (place of business of the buyer), to which the explanations given in note 7 would apply.

7.1. The rule indicates that in the case of an existing obligation of dispatch the seller may *not* require payment *before dispatch* of the goods (Sevon/Dubrovnik, 216).

7.2. Like in the case described in note 6, in this event the seller must not, by way of unilaterally making the handing over of the goods or the documents dependent on the payment, restrict the right of the buyer to examine the goods under paragraph 3. For a contemporaneous performance, while the right to examination is retained and in a place other than that mentioned under Article 31, subparas. (b) and (c), there are, however, hardly any standardized *commercial techniques* because the various forms of collections preclude the examination right. After all, it is not customary, even where the legal stipulations for the relevant category of transportation allow it, to instruct the carrier to collect the price. Besides, this would hardly be compatible with the examination right, either. Insofar as the goods are not directly handed over between the parties to the sales contract, the engaged neutral intermediaries would have to be individually authorized to allow examination, where they are ready and willing to proceed accordingly.

8. The *possibility of examination* has to be included *in the orderly course of the transaction*, and the buyer cannot require that the seller takes special steps causing additional costs, e.g. giving a demonstration of machines in operation at the manufacturer's plant. The buyer has to do the examination at his own cost. The seller only has to provide the opportunity allowing him access to the goods. He may be obliged to do so before the dispatch (Honnold, 347 fol), which does not mean, however, that the seller would have to grant, by virtue of law, the buyer and/or impartial controlling organizations engaged by the latter access to his manufacturing facilities. The examination would thus possibly have to take place outside the latter. Such an interpretation of the right to examination speaks in favour of the version given in the Secretariat's Commentary. According to that version, the seller would have the obligation to make specific arrangements with the carrier in order to grant the buyer the possibility of examination when he, the seller, wants to ascertain his right under paragraph 2. If nothing is agreed to the contrary - which is what is assumed here - payment will have to be made generally at the place of business of the seller (Art. 57, paragraph 1, subpara. (a)). Where the seller deviates from this principle to his own disadvantage making use of the possibility given in Article 58, paragraph 2 (so that the contemporaneous principle of performance can be applied), he should not be burdened as a consequence with further risks.

9.1. The *right* of the buyer *to examination* is the general rule which is applied in particular when the seller, without a relevant agreement on his own, makes the handing over dependent on the payment under paragraph 1, sentence 2, or paragraph 2. In that event, he must not prescribe a term of payment which would exclude the examination right (note 8). The buyer is not obliged to pay as long as he is granted the right to examine the goods. Hence, he is not entitled to refuse acceptance if the latter is possible without payment.

9.2. This right to examine the goods in substance is not identical to the *obligation of examination under Article 38*. Even when the buyer pays the price after having examined the goods for the first time, he does not loose the possibility to examine the goods more carefully under Article 38 and to possibly claim a lack of conformity.

10. The terms of payment which are *incompatible with an examination* by the buyer include advance payment "cash against documents" (Uniform Rules for Collections, Art. 11 and 12), and "payment according to letter of credit" (Uniform Customs and Practices for Documentary Credits, Article 16, subpara. (a)). The procurement of securities for payment is done mostly also under conditions which preclude advance examination. And where they create an abstract payment obligation, later established lacks do not any more influence the payment procedure, so that the possibility for the buyer to examine the goods insofar, but not in regard to Article 38, is irrelevant (e.g. "documents against acceptance " - a differing view is seemingly held by Honnold, 349 - banker's indemnities). Terms of payment which offer the buyer an *opportunity to examine the goods* include, therefore, individually shaped collections instructions, "cash after receipt of the goods (and the invoice)" as well as the granting of open payment objectives.

It is *doubtful* in the case of some terms of payment whether they are compatible with the *possibility for the buyer to examine the goods*. Where the payment has been made dependent on the issuing or receipt of the invoice, it is generally assumed that the invoice is not dispatched before the goods. Otherwise it might arrive at the buyer's and the payment may become due even before the goods arrive and can be examined. The buyer, in our view, has in this case, and for lack of opposite clues, the right to stop payment until he has had an opportunity to examine the goods. He has that right at least when in the normal course of events the goods would have arrived before the expiry of the period for payment. Like Sevon (Dubrovnik, 217) we have doubts in regard to the view expressed in the Secretariat's Commentary (O. R., 47) that a term of payment according to which the price is to be paid against documents after arrival of the goods is not contrary to the examination right of the buyer. We rather believe that this term of payment should in general express that the documents need only be presented upon arrival of the goods, but have to be honoured then without inspection.

11. Where the terms of payment already preclude the possibility for examination, it is irrelevant to search the *terms of delivery* for such an opportunity. Hence, this is only of importance when the terms of payment offer such an opportunity. We hold that the possibility to examine the goods cannot be awaited, for instance, in the following case: The payment is to be made 30 days after the issuance of the invoice, but the goods are to be delivered directly to an inland construction site in a faraway third country where they will arrive only three months after dispatch.

Article 59[1]

(Payment due without request)

The buyer must pay the price on the date fixed by or determinable[2] from the contract and this Convention without the need for any request[3] or compliance with any formality[3] on the part of the seller[4].

1.1. The article makes it clear that *no* simple or even formal *reminder* is necessary as it is required, at least under certain circumstances, in some countries (examples given by Tallon/Parker, 7-14) to place the buyer in a situation of delay in payment.

1.2. Tallon (Parker, 7-14 fol) raised the question whether renunciation of requests etc. is an expression of a general principle of the Convention and answered it referring to Honnold (160) in that it should be considered as an exception, whereas in general, performance would have to be requested by a special act. We believe that these two should not be alternatives; what matters is whether the obligated party *has* all the required *information* regarding the period for delivery. If this is the case, he will have to act accordingly (in particular Art. 33). Only where he does not have it can information be requested as the condition for performance. Since payments under the contract other than that of the price, e.g. reimbursement of auxiliary costs which don't have to be paid together with the price, and payment of sums from claims for breaches of contract, are not fixed by law and often also not by contract with the exactness necessary for payment, a customary and *appropriate information* will be required as the condition for payment - if nothing different results from the circumstances.

2. The *determinability* under the Convention follows from Article 58 which generally in a more differentiating way again refers to the time of the actual delivery, which itself is characterized by the legal period for delivery (Art. 33) for lack of contractual determination.

3. The term *"formality"* apparently has a different content in this context than in Article 54 in that measures, which would have to be taken vis-a-vis the authorities, do not fall under it. The seller may be obliged to comply with such formalities in exceptional cases (Art. 54, note 4). Reference to the time for payment shows that formalities in the relationship between commercial partners are named here which had to be arranged for by the creditor.

4.1. It remains open whether the *issuing of an invoice* can be requested as a prerequisite for the payment. This is doubtlessly the case, in our view, when it is necessary for releasing the goods from customs and probably also when the exact price is to be determined on the basis of agreed conditions which are at first concretely known only to the seller. Therefore, the issuance of an invoice is very often agreed as a condition for payment. But irrespective of the existence of specific conditions, the invoice is in our view, generally a prerequisite for the payment (Honnold, 350; Sevon/Dubrovnik, 218), namely under the established practices of Article 9. Both parties need the invoice for their bookkeeping; often it is also a condition for complying with formalities in regard to the transfer of the money. But specific requirements for an invoice (consular invoices) will have to be agreed in any case.

4.2. The buyer is in our opinion entitled under established practices to request a *receipt* of payment where the latter, like in the case of a bank transfer, is not proven by document, especially in the event of payment in cash.

Section II

Taking delivery

Article 60[1]

(Obligation to take delivery)

The buyer's obligation to take delivery[2] consists[3]: (a) in doing all the acts which could reasonably[4] be expected of him[5] in order to enable the seller to make delivery[6]; and (b) in taking over the goods[7].

1.1. This article *fleshes out* with substance the *obligation to take delivery* as substantiated by Article 53.

1.2. *Recognition* of the goods *as conforming* to the contract is not required for taking delivery or also specifically for taking over the goods. If the goods are deficient in quality, the buyer will retain his relevant rights after having taken over the goods. Reception or taking possession of the goods does not necessarily constitute a taking over (Article 86).

1.3. There is no doubt, in our view, that taking delivery and payment are *independent obligations* so that payment in general cannot be refused because it is not possible to take delivery of the goods for reasons of exemptions (Hjerner/Lausanne, 143). This can be inferred, insofar as Article 79 is concerned, from the fact that article generally does not exempt from performance. But Article 80 will mostly lead to another result.

2.1. Although the *refusal to take delivery* is mentioned in the catalogue of the buyer's rights in Article 45, paragraph only indirectly or be reference to the special rule of Article 52, we believe that there is under the CISG a right to refuse taking delivery also in other cases which have to be defined more in detail. We do not refer here to avoidance of a contract because that would make the obligation to take delivery inapplicable. In favour of a refusal to take delivery speaks not only the express granting of that right under Article 52 for cases of early delivery and delivery of excess quantity (in regard to the quantity delivered in excess), but also the fact that Article 86 presupposes the existence of a right to refusal, and not in reference to Article 52 but generally. A point in favour also being that Article 86 uses a different terminology than Article 52. No difference in substance is, in our view, intended here insofar as the right to refuse taking delivery under Article 52 could at least be conceived as a special case of the right to rejection pursuant to Article 86. We will, however, use the term "right to refuse the taking of delivery". Its existence is substantiated also by the right of the buyer to examine the goods under Article 58, which is regulated in the context of payment, but which, as it seems, implies that not only the payment but also the taking delivery of the goods itself can be refused if certain kinds of non-conformity are noticed.

The exercise of the right to refuse the taking of delivery also corresponds with *commercial practice*. In the event of a tender of non-conform goods or documents, the buyer may very well want to retain the contract, even not be entitled to terminate the contract, but at the same time not be interested in taking delivery of the actually tendered goods or documents. When he exercises his right of refusal in this case, he may require the seller to deliver conform goods as follows from Article 46, paragraph 1 and Article 47, paragraph 1.

However, *the substance and the limits of the right to refuse the taking of delivery* have to be determined in detail according to the system of the buyer's rights under the CISG. We would, therefore, not go quite so far in regard to granting that right as Tercier (Lausanne, 132) has in mind affirming, following the Swiss law, that the goods will have to be offered conform to the contract in every aspect, otherwise there shall seemingly be a right to refusal. Where the buyer would not assert such a right, he would be considered as having renounced his rights. We believe that these interpretations are inappropriate in all their aspects.

In the event of a *late delivery* a refusal to take delivery would not make any sense without a termination of the contract because the time lost could not be made up. By contrast, there is a right to refuse the taking over of the goods where an *aliud* is delivered.

In the case of a *non-conform delivery*, a refusal to take delivery is practically possible only when the lack is discovered before the taking delivery, e.g. in the context of exercising the right to examination under Article 58, paragraph 3. A lack entitles, in our view, to refusal of the taking delivery if it constitutes a fundamental breach of contract which would also substantiate the right to delivery of substitute goods (Article 46, paragraph 2) because it would be absurd to assume an obligation for the taking delivery of goods which the buyer does not want or have to keep. If, on the contrary, the buyer is entitled to repair pursuant to Article 46, paragraph 3, and if he wants to claim, he has, as we believe, the obligation to take delivery. This is the case at least where the taking of delivery is possible without payment of the price. This interpretation, however, is not unequivocal for the buyer can also declare his willingness to accept after repair and take possession of the goods for some time only (Article 86 applies analogously). This cannot be considered as a breach of contract by the buyer. Where the buyer prefers the third solution he has in the event of a non-conform delivery, reduction of the price (Article 50), a refusal to take delivery is irrelevant (different a refusal to pay in the amount of the reduction entitlement).

It has to be proceeded similarly in the case of delivery of goods which are *not free from third party rights or claims* (Article 41 fol). Where the seller delivers only part of the goods, this is in general no reason for refusing to take delivery in regard to the goods delivered, unless the goods cannot be used for its purpose without the missing part. The same is true if only part of the goods is conform, in regard to the conform part of the goods. Summarizing the following *rule* could be deduced from the CISG in its entirety: The buyer is entitled to refuse the taking of delivery when the goods are tendered in such a way which substantiates a right that is incompatible with taking delivery and when he exercises that right at the latest by refusing to take delivery of the goods.

Under the same circumstances the buyer is entitled to *refuse the taking of delivery in regard to the documents* where the documents show the respective conditions in respect of the goods. A right to refuse the taking of delivery which would specifically relate to the documents, could only be inferred from the obligation of the seller under Article 43 to hand over the documents, namely in a similar way as this was explained as regards the goods. Banks have very strict requirements in regard to the adequacy of documents where letters of credit are issued (Uniform Customs and Practices for Documentary Credits, Article 16, subpara. (b), Article 25, subpara. (c), Article 26, subparas. (b) and (c)). Documents which are rejected as inadequate may, however, be submitted by the seller for collection. In so doing, he renounces the advantages of a letter of credit. The buyer, in general, could raise the same objections as the bank issuing the letter of credit, but only to the extent to which he does not violate the principle of good faith; hence, only within the scope of the restrictions mentioned above. Rejection of the documents includes a refusal to take delivery of the goods in cases where the goods cannot be accepted without documents.

2.2. Where the *taking delivery of the goods is refused without entitlement*, the seller can invoke the remedies under Article 61 fol. But he must take the measures required under Article 85.

3. The obligation to take delivery consists of *two essential elements*: the preparatory acts and the taking over itself. Under the CISG, no express distinction is made between obligations and participatory obligations. Anyway, the obligation to take delivery is a genuine obligation of the obligor.

4. *Unusual preparatory acts* are thus not considered as reasonable, e.g. procurement of confirmation of the future purpose of the goods which may be needed for obtaining approval, but which were never mentioned until the moment of the contract conclusion. The taking delivery insofar does not necessarily comprise all requisite preparatory acts (Schlechtriem, 75, Note 331).

5. These include not only *acts* which follow from the contract, the Convention, established practices and usages, but also such which, even though not mentioned, are to be taken by the buyer in accordance with normal commercial conduct and which are customary.

6.1. Depending on the contractual agreements, in particular in regard to the commercial terms, these acts comprise *in detail*, the giving of instructions for dispatch, calls for delivery (Huber, 515, generally classifies them as belonging to the obligation to take delivery), information on the means of transportation available, the procurement of import licences (Lüderitz/Freiburg, 192) etc. It follows from the essence of the preparatory acts that they have to be *performed before taking delivery*, namely so early that the seller, in the orderly course of the transaction, will be in a position to deliver within the period for delivery. Where a period for delivery has been set within which the seller can determine the concrete date of delivery (Article 33, subpara. (b)), the preparatory acts will have to be performed so early that he will be able, under normal circumstances, to deliver already at the beginning of that period. If it is required by the seller that the buyer performs preparatory acts unusually early before the time for delivery, the seller must bring about the relevant agreements.

6.2. Although the obligation to take delivery, specifically the obligation to perform preparatory acts, already comprises an important part of the buyer's participatory obligation. It does by far not include all, so that the participatory acts are to be distinguished from the *other obligations* of the buyer (Article 62). This is of relevance, for instance, because in the event of a breach of the obligation to take delivery, the seller, by setting a *Nachfrist* (Article 64, paragraph 1, subpara. (b)) which is not honoured, may create a condition for the avoidance of the contract which formally can be easily verified (Caemmerer/Dölle, 388). The obligation to take delivery in our view does not comprise, in particular, the obligation to participate in the manufacture of the goods, like supplying technical drawings, recipes, models (Sevon/Dubrovnik, 230, seems to have a different opinion), tools, auxiliary supplies etc.

7.1. The *taking over* may include the physically taking over of the goods, including rapid unloading of the means of transportation, hence the obligation to unload (Honnold, 353), provision of one's own or someone else's means of transportation, and acceptance of documents where they authorize controlling disposition of the goods. The forms of taking over in practice to an important degree depend on the agreed commercial terms (Maskow/BB, 440).

The *time* when the obligation to take over the goods emerges in the case where the sales contract includes carriage of the goods (Article 31, subpara. (a)) follows from the actual tender of the goods, provided that it is done in the customary way, hence at the times normally possible and at the respective places (railway station, quay). Where the goods have to be put at the disposal of the buyer (Article

31, subparas. (b) and (c)), the obligation to take over the goods emerges a reasonable time after the information on the putting at the buyer's disposal (compare note 3, art. 69; Huber, 516 fol, insofar mentions a time of receipt). Pursuant to Article 79, paragraph 2, the buyer is responsible for the carrier engaged by him.

7.2. *Further components* of the taking over of the goods could be the payment of customs and other duties as well as the procurement of import licences where the seller is not obligated to do so and/or where this is not already a condition for the fulfilment of his obligations by the seller. One and the same act can, therefore, fall either under subpara. (a) or subpara. (b) depending on the terms agreed for delivery.

7.3. Also the giving of a *receipt* when taking delivery must be considered as a part of the obligation to take over the goods. Receipt of the goods often is evidenced in the forms used for the several means of transportation. Where the goods are taken over against the handing out of documents of title, the latter are considered as a receipt.

Section III

Remedies for breach of contract by the buyer

Article 61[1]

(Seller's remedies in general; claim for damages; no period of grace)

(1) If the buyer fails to perform any of his obligations[3] under the contract[2] or this Convention[4], the seller may:

(a) exercise the rights provided in articles 62 to 65[5];

(b) claim damages as provided in articles 74 to 77[6].

(2) The seller is not deprived of any right he may have to claim damages by exercising his right to other remedies[7].

(3) No period of grace may be granted to the buyer by a court or arbitral tribunal when the seller resorts to a remedy for breach of contract[8].

1. This article gives an *overview of the rights of the buyer*, provides for a general right to claim damages and determines its relationship with other remedies. That overview, however, is not exhaustive insofar as Chapter V does not only describe in greater detail the legal consequences of claims for damages (Article 74 fol) and of avoidance of contract (Article 81 fol), but provides also other rights, in particular in the event of anticipatory breach of contract and of breach of instalment contracts (Article 77 fol). What is lacking also is the right to interest (Article 78) even though it is of special relevance to the seller. After all, the passing of the risk under Article 69, too, can be regarded as the legal consequence of certain breaches of the buyer's obligations. Here it shall only be indicated that in spite of the great progress made compared to ULIS, the aimed at consolidation of the rights of the seller (O. R., 48) has not fully been achieved; which was not possible anyway because of the complicated substance. Article 61 is insofar misleading to some extent.

2. The *obligations* can be agreed expressly or impliedly or they can be the result of an interpretation of the statements made by orother conduct of the parties (Article 8).

3. These are the obligations determined, in particular, in *Articles 53 to 60*. But they also follow from established practices or usages (Article 9), and include obligations that are provided for by the Convention or are determined by interpreting the Convention.

4. This covers, therefore, *all breaches of the obligations of the buyer*, irrespective of their nature, e.g. deviation in place, time, substance or also modalities of performance, and their importance, and places them under sanctions. It does, however, not include responsibilities like the obligation to examine the goods under Article 38 (differing view held by Knapp/BB, 445).

5. Reference is made here to the *right to performance and to avoidance* as well as to the specific legal consequence of Article 65 which finds no correspondence in the rights of the buyer. The system of the rights of the seller is easier than that of the buyer, for the obligations of the former are less complicated. The problems involved in the delivery of defective goods and in the existence of third party rights or claims are not existent at all. Regarding the supplementing of these provisions compare note 1.

6. The *right to claim damages* is determined here as being the most general sanction in the case of any breach of obligation by the buyer. Compare also note 5 of Article 45.

7. The right to claim damages is complemented in many cases by *more specific rights* which may supersede the former, but not replace it.

8. Compare note 7 of Article 45.

Article 62[1]

(Seller's right to require performance)

The seller may require the buyer to pay the price, take delivery or perform his other obligations[2], unless the seller has resorted to a remedy which is inconsistent with this requirement[3].

1. This article provides for the *right* of the seller *to obtain or require performance* which does not, however, constitute a sanction but a pursuance of initial rights under the contract (Knapp/BB, 453). Where they are disturbed, which makes up the substance of a breach of contract, they can no longer be fulfilled in the original manner whereby the right to obtain performance strictly speaking becomes a right to require approximate performance.

Concerning the right to obtain performance where impediments exist that are beyond the control of the debtor, compare note 13.6. of Article 79; where they are caused by the creditor under Article 80.

2. The *implementation* of the right to obtain performance *by way of the courts* is subject to the prerequisites of Article 28. The enforcement of the taking delivery of the goods and the performance of the other obligations is not only complicated under common law, but procedurally, tactically and above all in regard to enforceability also under continental European laws.

Under *common law*, the right to *payment of the price* can only be ascertained under restrictive conditions, and its recoverability often involves problems when the buyer has not yet taken delivery of the goods (Honnold, 355 fol). When the buyer neither pays nor takes delivery of the goods, the seller will, just to mention the most important options, do the following (Honnold, 358 fol; Sevon/Dubrovnik, 221 fol): Where he is still in possession of the goods he may, to the extent that the relevant conditions are given, resell them by way of self-help or emergency sale and require the buyer to pay the costs and damages (lower sales price) (Articles 85, 87 and above all Article 88; Article 74 fol). He can also, without setting a *Nachfrist* - however, a *Nachfrist* is more effective so as not to have to prove the fundamentality of the breach of contract - make the contract void (Article 63 fol) and claim damages, typically after a substitute sale.

Where a possible *suit* would have to be filed *not in a common law country*, the seller could concentrate from the beginning on the recovery of the sales price. Pursuant to Article 80, the non-taking delivery of the goods would not be an obstacle for it. But this is the way which the seller will generally choose when the buyer has already taken delivery. Avoidance of the contract with its further consequences may be chosen only when it might lead to the recovery of the goods and the goods are wanted.

3.1. In the event of an *avoidance of contract* the right to obtain performance becomes irrelevant (Article 64). The specification obligation is extinguished when the seller makes the specification himself (Article 65). This provision does apply, however, also when rights are given and exercised under the contract which are inconsistent with the right to obtain performance or right to termination.

3.2. On the other hand, the exercise of the right to obtain performance does not exclude *transition to other rights* which are also inconsistent with it (as explained also in note 3.1.) when the right to require performance does not lead to the intended result (Knapp/BB, 454 fol).

Article 63[1]

(Fixing of additional period for performance)

(1) The seller may fix an additional period of time[4] of reasonable[3] length for performance by the buyer of his obligations[2].

(2) Unless the seller has received notice from the buyer[6] that he will not perform within the period so fixed[7], the seller may not, during that period, resort to any remedy for breach of contract[5]. However, the seller is not deprived thereby of any right he may have to claim damages for delay in performance[8].

1. Article 63 grants the possibility to set a *Nachfrist* having the main consequence that the seller, during that period, in general has to stick to the contract while retaining his rights to claim damages. After that *Nachfrist* has elapsed fruitlessly he has the right to avoid the contract when the most important obligations are violated.

2.1. When the buyer does not fulfil according to his obligations under the contract, a *practical occasion arises for the seller* to relate to it. He can do so by abstractly, hence without setting a *Nachfrist*, insisting on performance. Also he can immediately upon the obligations becoming due resort to the deciding organs, which is done relatively seldom. The seller can, however, ascertain his right to obtain performance also in setting a *Nachfrist* of reasonable length. He can, at any time, give up in the event of the first-mentioned ways of ascertaining his right to obtain performance and can proceed to another right, which may even be inconsistent with it, insofar as the conditions for it are given, hence, in particular to avoidance of contract (c. Article 64, paragraph 1, subpara. (a)). But he is blocked in his movement in the latter case for the duration of the *Nachfrist* (paragraph 2, sentence 1). He has the advantage, however, that after the expiry of the *Nachfrist* without performance on the part of the buyer, the right to make the contract void becomes applicable anyway in regard to the right to payment of the price or also to taking delivery of the goods, i.e. even if the delay, which occurred first, in performance did not constitute a fundamental breach of contract (Article 64, paragraph 1, subpara. (b)). The setting of a *Nachfrist*, therefore, causes doubts as to the fundamentality of the breach of contract irrelevant. The effect is not the same in regard to other rights with respect to performance (note 5). Finally, the setting of a *Nachfrist* may result in that a right to avoidance of contract, which would have to be asserted within the period set under Article 64, paragraph 2, subpara. (b) (i), would then have to be ascertained only within the time limit under (b) (ii). In practice this will, however, only refer to exceptional cases (Article 64, note 13).

2.2. The setting of a *Nachfrist* is *governed by* the general rule of *Article 27*, i.e. the seller can rely on a *Nachfrist*, even if the relevant communication is received belatedly, contains errors or is not received at all. The opposite view held by Knapp (BB, 460) is understandable, however not tenable in our view. The rule under Article 27 is problematic. But since it has been adopted, certain cases, which clearly come under its scope of application, cannot be excluded for substantive considerations. Leser (Freiburg, 237 fol) tries to find an intermediary solution dissecting and analyzing the effects of dispatch. But this leads to further complicated distinctions for which reliable clues cannot be deduced from the text of the Convention.

2.3. By contrast to Knapp (BB, 459), we believe that a *Nachfrist* can be set *before there is a delay* (see also the comparable case of Article 88, paragraph 1 and note 3 thereto), e.g. when it can be anticipated and the buyer signals difficulties. This is not a one-sided modification of the contract, as Knapp believes. The buyer can still deliver at the time for delivery, and the reasonable time is to be counted starting at the end of the time for performance.

2.4. Like Knapp (BB, 461) and differing from Honnold (361 in connection with 306) and Sevon (Dubrovnik, 224), we hold that the *Nachfrist* must not be considered as final and/or the buyer must not be warned by the seller that he will declare the contract avoided. A formulation like "We set an additional period of time for payment on your part until May 31.." is in our view sufficient. Accordingly, we also are of the opinion that the *Nachfrist* can be extended, and upon its expiry a new one may be granted. The setting of a *Nachfrist* for performance of the most important obligations - in regard to the others the problem is uninteresting anyway - *gives the seller an option* to either stick to the contract, e.g. when non-payment is caused by foreseeable temporary difficulties of transfer, or make it void. The seller would be forced into too strict a scheme if in setting a *Nachfrist* he had to threaten the buyer with avoidance of the contract. The authors which spoke up in favour of this left open what would happen if the seller does not carry out his threat. One should not get too near again to the scheme of the *ipso facto* avoidance. However, the seller in setting the *Nachfrist* may declare the contract at the same time avoided in case it is not kept to by the buyer.

3. The vague term of *reasonableness* leaves some room to act at one's own discretion which can be used by the party who is entitled to set the *Nachfrist*, i.e. in this case the seller. If he fixes too short a period, the competent deciding body could determine the minimum *Nachfrist*.

In *calculating the additional period*, factors have to be taken into account which concern both parties. On the seller's part, these are: possibilities and costs for storage of the goods (compare also Article 88, paragraph 2) and price developments, e.g. the *Nachfrist* will be shortened in the event of a rapid decline in prices because the proceeds from a substitute transaction under Article 75, which presupposes an avoidance of the contract, would be reduced as a result. On the buyer's part it is the difficulties which he is confronted with during performance that are of relevance, e.g. when he needs more time than expected for complying with the so-called formalities in preparing the payment (Article 54) or also in importing the goods. The seller can take such factors into consideration only when the buyer informs him thereof.

In the setting of a *Nachfrist* the *postal handling time* needed for the information to reach the buyer has to be considered because the latter must have time to undertake the relevant activities during that *Nachfrist*. In the light of the fact that there is a breach of contract by the buyer here, we believe that the interests of the seller should be decisive. The reasonable period of time should in general be rather short in such cases. Sevon (Dubrovnik, 225) stresses this, in particular in regard to the obligation to pay the price.

In interpreting the term of a reasonable *Nachfrist, conformity* should be established with the interpretation of the formulation "unreasonable delay" in *Article 88, paragraph 1* (see also note 2 of that article), namely in such a way that an unreasonable delay is given when the reasonable *Nachfrist* has expired. Such conformity is required because the right to resell the goods under Article 88 will produce results that are similar to those of a substitute transaction under Article 75, so that the conditions in both cases will have to be aligned so as not to create unfounded alternatives. A substitute transaction presupposes avoidance of the contract and the latter again presupposes frequently the setting of an additional period of time for performance.

4. This time will have to be *fixed or be fixable according to the calendar* (O. R., 49). The mere invitation to deliver "as soon as possible", "promptly", "immediately" or within a similarly vaguely defined period of time is not sufficient because that would merely have to be considered as abstract reliance on the right to obtain performance under Article 62 (so believes also Honnold, 361 in connection with 306; Sevon/Dubrovnik, 224; Knapp/BB, 460 fol).

5. Among the rights granted by the CISG itself this refers to the right to avoid the contract under Article 64 and the right to resell the goods under Article 88, paragraph 1, from which another reason can be inferred to interpret the regulation concerning the periods of time in both articles in the same way. These are, therefore, *rights to early termination of the contract* and/or such which practically amount to it. But this does not refer to the emergency transaction under Article 88, paragraph 2, which has to be carried out as an obligation of the party obliged to preserve the goods. However, it is rarely of relevance in cases where an additional period of time was granted.

It is nevertheless indeed problematic when the seller must not exercise other rights ensuing from a breach of contract either, but rather has to wait and see whether the buyer performs within the *Nachfrist*. Hence, the seller can *within the additional period of time* not *require the buyer to perform* under Article 62 (so believes also

Plantard/Lausanne, 116). This is acceptable because the right to require performance and the right to set an additional period of time for performance are basically variants of the right to obtain performance between which the seller can choose from the outset. Also specification made by the seller himself as a specific legal consequence of the non-fulfilment of the obligation of the buyer for specification under Article 65 cannot be made during the additional period of time (more in detail Article 65, note 4).

It is thus the *rights to compensation* which constitute the real problem. Only the right to claim damages is expressly not blocked. The same should apply to the right to *reimbursement of expenses* under Article 85. Since the rights because of breach of contract are excluded in their entirety, but the right to compensation of expenses is granted specifically under Article 85, it has to be regarded as still existent when a *Nachfrist* is set. Apart from this formal deduction, there is also a functional interpretation which is orientated towards the objective of the rule. It would be absurd not to grant the seller the right to reimbursement of expenses in commercial practice - preservation of the goods may even be a condition for the setting of an additional period of time. This would also contradict the basic idea recognizable in the retention of the rights to claim damages that losses in the property of the seller should be compensated by the buyer also when a *Nachfrist* is set. Finally, with certain modifications, expenses can be considered as a specific form of damage in the meaning of Article 74.

For similar substantive and formal reasons we believe that the *entitlement to interests* under Article 78 is also not excluded when a *Nachfrist* is set. In this case it also has to be considered that otherwise reimbursement of the damage exceeding the interests could be required, but that there would be no entitlement to the interests themselves. And finally, we hold that a *right to penalty/liquidated damages*, e.g. because of late performance of participatory obligations in the manufacture of the goods, provided that there is no provision to the contrary in the contract, would not be excluded by setting an additional period of time. The considerations made so far also speak in favour of this, with one modification: depending on the agreement or the applicable law the penalty/liquidated damages constitute(s) either a standard damage or a standard minimum damage, less frequently a standard maximum damage. Hence, penalty/liquidated damages do(es) in any case constitute a form of damages for which the same exemptions apply. Therefore, there seems to be a clear possibility of subsumption under sentence 2.

Expenses, interests and penalties/liquidated damages can often be *claimed as damages*, but not in all cases and sometimes only under additional conditions. But why should the seller be penalized in such a way when he accommodates the buyer by setting a *Nachfrist*.

Specific discounts that would be granted for advance payment, immediate payment or similar reasons should certainly be lost in case of setting a *Nachfrist*.

It becomes evident as a *result of this discussion* that only comparable rights and comparable claims are excluded, not however claims for compensation. But the rule is not formulated very fortunately anyway.

When a *Nachfrist* is set for the fulfilment of a specific obligation under the contract, e.g. taking delivery of the goods, avoidance of the contract is not excluded during that *Nachfrist* because of *another fundamental breach of contract*, e.g. the cheque handed over for payment is not honoured (Sevon/Dubrovnik, 226).

The option to rely on a *failure caused by the other party* under Article 80 is not excluded by the setting of an additional period of time either. This may assume practical relevance among others when a *Nachfrist* is set for the fulfilment of obligations to participate in the manufacture of the goods or for the procurement of guarantees for payment.

6. No *form* is prescribed *for* the *notice*; it can be oral or in writing, but according to its character of a notice it cannot be given by other conduct, i.e. conduct implying an intent. As to its substance, the notice must be clear without having to include the formulations of the Convention (Knapp/BB, 463 fol). A so-called cancellation of the contract should be sufficient. Decisive is that the notice reaches the addressee so that the general rule of Article 27 is not applied.

7.1. Since the *notice* has to refer to that there will be no performance also during the *Nachfrist* it can *only be given after the Nachfrist has been set* and the buyer has received the respective information. When the buyer has named before a date of performance later than the expiry of the *Nachfrist*, the seller cannot rely on it because it is very well possible that the setting of an additional period of time inspires the buyer to make exceptional efforts to keep to the period granted. The situation is different when performance is rejected definitely and once and for all.

7.2. It is *not sufficient* in this case (by contrast to Article 71, paragraph 1, and/or Article 72, paragraph 1) that it becomes apparent or is clear that the buyer will not keep to the *Nachfrist*. If, however, the notice is given, the contract can be avoided at once, even when the delay does not yet constitute a fundamental breach of contract (Sevon/Dubrovnik, 226).

8. Compare note 5.

Article 64[1]

(Seller's right to avoid contract)

(1) The seller may declare the contract avoided[2]:

(a) if the failure by the buyer to perform any of his obligations under the contract or this Convention amounts to a fundamental breach of contract[3]; or

(b) if the buyer does not, within the additional period of time fixed by the seller in accordance with paragraph (1) of Article 63, perform his obligation to pay the price or take delivery of the goods[4], or if he declares that he will not do so within the period so fixed[5].

(2) However, in cases where the buyer has paid the price, the seller loses the right to declare the contract avoided[6] unless he does so:

(a) in respect of late performance[7] by the buyer, before the seller has become aware[9] the performance has been rendered[8]; or

(b) in respect of any breach other than late performance[10] by the buyer, within a reasonable time[11]:

(i) after the seller knew or ought to have known of the breach[12]; or

(ii) after the expiration of any additional period of time fixed by the seller in accordance with paragraph (1) of Article 63, or after the buyer has declared that he will not perform his obligations within such an additional period[13].

1.1. This article provides for the *conditions to govern the right to avoid the contract* and for the restrictions existing for its exercise. The effects of avoidance, however, are included in Article 81 fol.

1.2. Apart from the right provided for here, there is also the right to avoid the contract under Article 72, paragraph 1, and Article 73, paragraphs 1 and 2.

2.1. Avoidance is made by a written or oral *declaration* which has to be communicated to the other party (Article 26). Conduct implying an intent, e.g. sending back of the not accepted goods is, therefore, not sufficient. For the seller to rely on the notice it is not necessary that the latter reaches the other party (Article 27). But Knapp (BB, 468) seems to be right explaining that the avoidance becomes effective and irrevocable when the notice reaches the buyer (compare also note 3.1., Article 26). In view of the relevance of this decision it should be clear that its wording must be unequivocal. In the case of doubt it should, in our view, be interpreted as a mere threat of avoidance.

2.2.*An exclusion period* during which this right to avoidance must be exercised is not prescribed so that it comes under the general limitation period (e.g. Article 12, paragraph 1 of the Limitation Convention). There is nothing to complain about here because in the case of a delay in payment, the seller must be considered as entitled to decide how long he intends to wait. On the other hand, he shall not be allowed to speculate at the cost of the buyer, so that he will have to bring himself to take a decision within a reasonable time, at least at the inquiry of the buyer. Leser (Freiburg, 235 fol) wants to invoke Article 48, paragraph 2, and Article 77 in this context, which seems to us quite bold because there are only rather distant structural analogies. We prefer a deduction from the principle of good faith (Article 7 and note 10.1. thereto), even if it is very vague, insofar as one does not want to relate to the subsidiary statute, the relevant national law.

2.3. When the *buyer disputes* the justification of the avoidance of contract, the seller has to prove that the conditions required for it are given. This will in general be easier in regard to the conditions of paragraph 1, subpara. (b) because of their more formal and thus clearer character, than in regard to those of subpara. (a). It is recommendable for the seller, therefore, to fix an additional period of time. When it becomes evident that the contract was avoided without foundation, a non-performance by the seller that eventually follows from it is to be regarded as a breach of contract. Given the far-reaching consequences it entails, it is necessary to create clarity as speedily as possible on whether the buyer wants to dispute the avoidance. We, therefore, believe that he should be considered as being obliged to dispute the avoidance in one form or another, e.g. by reminding performance where the seller avoided the contract because of an overdue advance payment, within a reasonable time after he received the relevant declaration. Insofar only the receipt can be decisive. This follows from the principle of good faith (Article 7). If he does not do so, later contradiction in connection with other acts may be excluded also because of the prohibition of the *venire contra factum proprium* (Article 7, note 10.1.).

3. As regards the definition of a *fundamental breach of contract* compare Article 25 and comments thereon.

Since with respect to the obligations of the buyer deficiency in quality and the violation of third party rights or claims are hardly of any relevance, the typical breach by the buyer of an obligation under the contract is a delay, i.e. *non-keeping to the period for performance*. Since the time for performance of the buyer's obligations is in general not conceived in a way that time is of the essence, the mere non-performance at the time for performance will constitute a fundamental breach of contract only in rare instances. (The Secretariat's Commentary, too, O.R. 50, proceeds on the assumption that this will be the case only after the expiration of yet another period.) Such a situation is, however, imaginable. The time for performance can, for instance, in regard to fulfilment of the obligation to participate in the manufacture of goods, supply of drawings or sub-supply of material, be agreed as an essential date for the goods cannot be finished at another time because of different use of the facilities, planned changes in production, shutting-down of plant etc. Likewise, the late procurement of securities for payment can be a fundamental breach of contract because the seller needs those securities to secure the procurement on his part of the required materials and because at a later date he can procure the materials no longer and/or not anymore to the calculated conditions. Hellner (Dubrovnik, 353) even believes, somewhat exaggerated as we think, that the seller should always be allowed to declare the contract avoided if the buyer does not open a credit within a fixed time. Generally, late payment will constitute a fundamental breach of contract in the case of a rapid decline in currency. The late taking delivery will also be a fundamental breach of contract when the goods cannot be stored (similar view held by Schlechtriem/Freiburg, 76).

A longer delay in payment, or in taking delivery, should in general be reason for a fundamental breach of contract so that there will finally always be a right to avoid the contract in the event of non-payment, or also non-taking delivery.

4.1. By fixing a *Nachfrist* the seller will have the option to always avoid the contract when the buyer continues not to perform his obligation to pay the price or take delivery of the goods. This is interpreted partly in such a way that a non-performance of this most essential obligation by the buyer also within the *Nachfrist* and/or a respective declaration regularly constitute a fundamental breach of contract (Leser/Freiburg, 236). That this is indeed so does not only not have to be proved, but is irrelevant.

This does in no way preclude that a breach of other obligations, whose non-performance does not yet constitute a fundamental breach of contract at the time for performance, becomes such *as more time passes.* This may be emphasized by fixing a *Nachfrist.* In this event it will not suffice to prove that a *Nachfrist* of reasonable length was fixed and performance was not made nevertheless, but it must be proved that the conditions for the existence of a fundamental breach of contract are given. This is true, for instance, of the fixing of a *Nachfrist* for the performance of the obligation to participate in the manufacture of the goods, which we do not consider as being part of the obligation to take delivery of the goods (Article 60, note 6.2.).

4.2. The obligation to pay the price pursuant to Article 54 includes the *steps and formalities* required for it. Therefore, the rule applies also when agreed securities for payment are procured belatedly (e.g. a letter of credit, Honnold, 363); hence when preparatory measures which have a direct effect on the seller are not fulfilled in time. The Secretariat's Commentary (O. R., 50; similarly, even though hesitating, Knapp/BB, 469 fol) goes even farther including such preparatory steps which are not taken directly vis-a-vis the seller, such as procurement of foreign currency, registration of contracts. We have our reservations here because the buyer insofar is granted several options and he cannot be forced by the seller to choose one. Furthermore, not even a general date is fixed in regard to most of these steps vis-a-vis the seller so that there is neither a connecting point for the setting of a *Nachfrist.* To put it briefly, the relevant obligations of the buyer are not feasible enough so that such a far-reaching interpretation of the obligation to pay the price could lead to abuse by the seller.

5. Article 63, paragraph 2, is alluded to herewith where, however, a different wording is used and, in particular, the *receipt principle* is fixed. This one is decisive (notes 6 and 7 of Article 63).

6. Paragraph 2 presupposes that *there has been a right to avoid the contract*. This right lapses in certain cases when the price has been paid, and in full, if due ; partial payment is not sufficient (Secretariat's Commentary, O. R., 50; Knapp/BB, 470). The details, however, are not regulated convincingly, neither in language nor in substance.

From the reverse conclusion it follows that the *right to avoid the contract* (subject to limitation) *does not lapse* as long as the price is not paid (note 2.2.).

7. At the diplomatic conference several efforts were made to clarify what is meant in this case by "*performance*". The respective proposal submitted by a working group was to make clear above all that the seller could avoid the contract when the buyer did not take delivery of the goods, but had already paid (O. R., 412). This was rejected in the end by one voice more against (O. R., 125). The conclusion could be drawn now that performance is meant to be mainly the late payment which already the Secretariat's Commentary (O. R., 50) on the finally adopted version points to. Since the proposed amendment was to serve as clarification (O. R., 371), the rejection can also be interpreted as regarding the wording as clear enough. Its literal interpretation speaks in favour of the term "late performance" including both the late payment and the late performance by the buyer of his other obligations (Knapp/BB, 472).

8. In the event of *payment*, when such payment has already been made, e.g. at the place of business of the buyer being the place of payment, but the seller does not know of it yet, the latter may avoid the contract until he becomes aware of the payment. Even if the seller has got to know that the payment was made, he can avoid the contract so long as he has no knowledge of the taking delivery of the goods. In interpreting the wording in this way, it was assumed at the diplomatic conference that the seller could have an urgent interest in taking delivery because he might need his storage facilities for other purposes and that his interests would not be served either in having the option to resell the goods under Article 88 when there is an advantageous offer, i.e. when prices rise, because he would have to account to the other party (O. R., 371). It will, nevertheless, happen only in exceptional cases that the seller avoids the contract even though he has received the price.

The *right to avoid the contract lapses* thus when the obligation on whose breach it is based has been fulfilled and the seller has got to know it.

9. Unlike in many others, it is relevant in this case that there is *positive knowledge*. "Ought to have known" is not sufficient. Knapp (BB, 473 fol) believes differently; he wants to leave out of consideration that the wordings are different in paragraph 2, subparas. (a) and (b), (i). It is indeed hard to find reasons for it, but the text is clear and can, therefore, not be interpreted.

10. Since late performance constitutes the main case of a breach of obligation by the buyer, other breaches (all the more so since they have to be fundamental to substantiate a right to avoid the contract) will be of relatively little practical relevance. *Cases to which* that right could possibly be *applied* would be, for instance, sub-supply of defective materials, breaches of the prohibition to re-export goods, insofar as this can effectively be countered by avoiding the contract, and pledging of goods which were sold under the reservation of title (see also the examples given by Huber, 516). These will above all be non-conform activities by the buyer which are not specifically covered by the CISG.

11. To what the extent the *room left* by the Convention *at the parties' discretion* is used depends on the seller. In fixing the time it has to be taken into account what time would be needed to take a decision. This time commences upon the expiration of the periods mentioned under (i) and (ii) so that the overall period is fixed in two stages.

12.1. Unlike in the event of late performance (2.3.), there is a *time limit* for the exercise of the right to avoidance of the contract in the case of breaches of other obligations.

12.2. Since the right to avoid the contract emerges all the more when there is a fundamental breach of contract, the reasonable period can start to run only at the time when that degree of breach is reached. Where breaches become fundamental only by way of *quantitative accumulation* such as intensity or repetition, the degree of vagueness of the fixing of time is increased by the vagueness in determining its beginning. Activities which do not conform with the contract (note 10) may in several instances be considered, however, as fundamental breaches of contract already when they are committed.

13. The *expiration* of the Nachfrist under Article 63, paragraph 1, *without performance* being made and/or the refusal by the buyer to perform within that additional period of time is not a ground *per se* for granting the right to avoid the contract, but only when they come under the cases of Article 64, paragraph 1, subpara. (b). But these do not fall under the rule of paragraph 2, subpara. (b).

This rule addresses such cases where a *Nachfrist* was fixed for the *performance of another obligation*, whose breach is or becomes fundamental. As long as the *Nachfrist* continues to run and/or performance is not refused, an avoidance of the contract under Article 63, paragraph 2, sentence 1, is possible. To ensure that the buyer retains his right to avoid the contract, since he must not avoid the contract during the period under Article 64, paragraph 2, subpara. (b), (i), he is granted this additional period of time.

It shall be assumed that the price for the goods is paid and the seller becomes aware that the buyer resells the goods, technical consumer goods in large quantities, to a third country thus fundamentally breaching a contractually agreed export prohibition. He fixes a *Nachfrist* for the buyer to stop doing it. When that additional period expires without anything happening or when the buyer contradicts from the beginning, the possibility to avoid the contract is retained even though the seller has been aware of the breach of contract for some time already.

Article 65[1]

(Specification by seller)

(1) If under the contract the buyer is to specify[2] the form, measurement or other features of the goods and he fails to make such specification either on the date agreed upon[3] or within a reasonable time after receipt of a request from the seller[4], the seller may, without prejudice to any other rights[5] he may have, make the specification himself[6] in accordance with the requirements of the buyer that may be known to him[7].

(2) If the seller makes the specification himself[6], he must inform the buyer of the details thereof and must fix a reasonable time[8] within which the buyer may make a different specification[9]. If, after receipt of such a communication, the buyer fails to do so within the time so fixed[10], the specification made by the seller is binding[11].

1. This article provides for the seller's *right to specification* as a specific legal consequence of a case where the buyer does not perform his obligation to specify the goods. This is to avoid difficulties which might follow if damages would have to be calculated in a specification sale (v. Caemmerer/Dölle, 394; Honnold, 365). A more convincing argumentation is, however, that in this way problems are circumvented which would arise in the event of a right to performance of a specification obligation not only under common law (Article 28) (v. Caemmerer/Dölle, 393 fol). A procedure, which in spite of some inconsistencies, is effective if substantiated herewith which allows a regular continuation of the contractual relationship also in the event of non-specification by the buyer. It should be mentioned, finally, that the effectiveness of a specification sale is underlined in this rule.

2. It has to be assumed generally that the party who has to perform is entitled to specify that performance further in the framework of his contractual obligations (Tercier/Lausanne, 140). Where no specification of generally determined goods is made yet in the contract, it may have been agreed that the *buyer has to perform that specification*. Such agreements are made, for instance, in trading textiles and leather goods, but also bulk goods. It makes no sense, in our view, to differentiate in the typical cases whether there is a right or an obligation of the buyer as does the Secretariat's Commentary (O. R., 51). Where it is not clearly visible that something different is meant, e.g. a sales option, in the event of a contract without specification a right of the buyer to specification will at the same time have to be interpreted as his obligation for specification (obtaining the same result Knapp/BB, 482).

One could refer to a right to specification when the buyer can modify until a later date a specification already made in the contract. If he does not make use of this right, it will lapse and the agreed specification is retained. Then Article 65 does not come into play.

3. The right to specification of the seller emerges when the *date agreed is missed by the buyer* (but concerning the mandatory nature of the specification by the seller see note 11). When the seller does not receive the specification by the buyer in time, there will practically be no problems because a specification which arrives later can be considered as a reaction by the buyer under paragraph 2 and/or he can repeat the specification. It would, in our view, constitute a breach of the principle of good faith if the buyer relied on Article 27 even though it can be seen from the reaction of the seller that he did not receive the specification.

4. The seller can, on the other hand, *invite the buyer to make the specification*, which assumes practical relevance when no time was agreed. The latter then would have to specify the goods within a reasonable time after he received the invitation (Article 27 does not apply in this case). The room left for the parties' discretion in terms of reasonableness can be exhausted by the buyer for he is the one who has to act. In doing so he has to take account of the motives because of which the parties had planned specification without setting a date, and of the relationship between the dates on which specification is required; on the one hand, and on which the contract has been concluded and/or is to be performed, on the other. Where the seller invites the buyer only when the contract is nearing his performance, the period will be a short one for the buyer could adapt himself to the specification ever since the conclusion of the contract; and the mechanism regulated here cannot be abused so as to grant him additional options for observing the market situation to the detriment of the seller. As regards the reaction of the buyer, Article 27 is applied. As a result, the seller cannot exactly determine the date until which he would have had to receive the specification.

The interpretation given here is guided by the text and is comprehensible in substance in spite of the many uncertainties it involves for the seller. Another interpretation, which was given in the similar wording of ULIS (v. Caemmerer/Dölle, 395), assumes that the *seller* may fix the buyer a reasonable *Nachfrist*. In that case, he could reduce the buyer's time for reflexion and invite him to make a specification immediately upon the conclusion of the contract. This could be taken into account, however, in calculating the additional period. Generally speaking, this interpretation is preferable for reasons of substance. The wording and function of this rule could perhaps be brought into line as follows: When the seller fixes a *Nachfrist* at first, the buyer is considered obligated to contradict it if he regards it as unreasonable, and/or the additional period fixed by the seller is being taken into consideration when judging the reasonableness of the period's length.

Another corrective in the event of discrepancies in the case of both interpretations is offered by the *procedure of self-specification by the seller* (para. 2).

5. Those other rights refer above all to the *right to claim damages* (Article 61, paragraph 1, subpara. (b) and paragraph; compare also Article 63, paragraph , sentence 2). Furthermore, the seller can, under Article 80, rely on *failure caused by the creditor*, e.g. delay in delivery because of non-specification. A more differentiated approach should be followed in regard to the *right to avoid the contract*. The seller has such a right when the non-keeping to the specification

date either from the beginning or after a certain time turns out to be a fundamental breach of contract. The seller, however, cannot exercise this right when he fixes a *Nachfrist* for the buyer to specify the goods (Article 63, paragraph 1, sentence 1), and also when he invites him to make a specification without fixing a date. The two are incompatible (Article 63, paragraph 2, sentence 1 by analogy or violation of the prohibition of a *venire contra factum proprium* and/or Article 65, paragraph 1). When the decisive period has elapsed in each case, the seller can avoid the contract if the breach of the obligation for specification is fundamental at that moment. But there is no right to avoid the contract in our view when one *Nachfrist* fixed for specification did not bring about such specification (this view was expressed at the diplomatic conference, O. R., 373; a different view is expressed in the Secretariat's Commentary on the draft, O. R., 51) because unlike Huber (515, 518) and others we do not consider the obligation for specification as a part of the obligation to take delivery of the goods but rather as an obligation to participate in the manufacture of the goods. Hence, Article 64, paragraph 1, subpara. (b) does not apply here (Knapp/BB, 478, reaches the same result, which is a certain contradiction to what is said in another place, 482, namely that the obligation to specify is conceived as part of the obligation to take delivery; undecided v. Caemmerer/Dölle, 394).

6. The seller has no obligation to make the specification himself (likewise Loewe, 83). If he specifies, nevertheless, he insofar removes for himself the right to avoid the contract. He must then *accept a deviating specification* by the buyer under paragraph 2, sentence 1. An obligation for the seller to make the specification himself can exceptionally follow from the *obligation* of the seller *to mitigate losses* (Article 77). Of great relevance in this context is to what extent the seller can assess the needs of the buyer (note 7). Specification on the part of the seller presupposes a breach of contract by the buyer, for which there are possibly reasons for exemption, which is irrelevant, however, for the seller's specification, and is to remove or mitigate its consequences. This constellation of interests is to be considered when interpreting the details.

The seller should *specify early enough* to leave the buyer a reasonable time to react before manufacture must commence. Where this is no longer possible, the seller will reflect on whether he exercises this right at all.

7.1. The wording "may be known to him" does not require the seller, in our view, to make efforts to obtain such knowledge. But he *must not ignore clues*.

7.2. To the extent to which the seller is *not positively aware* of the buyer's needs he must not make any specification of which he knows that it will not meet the needs of the buyer. It is our belief that the requirement of taking into consideration probable or presumed needs of the buyer follows from the principle of good faith. The seller can, therefore, not take the chance to sell non-seller when he is aware of fashion trends in the buyer's country, even when he is not informed of the concrete needs of the buyer.

8.1. Compare explanations given regarding the *reasonableness* in Article 63, notes 3 and 4; compare also note 10. This will be a short time in general because the buyer is already in breach of contract and he is only required to take a decision.

8.2. When the seller does *not fix a reasonable time*, the consequence is, in our view, not necessarily that the specification is not binding on the buyer. The latter will rather have to specify within a time that would be considered reasonable. If this is too late for the seller, he will have to bear the consequences. When the buyer does not react, however, even though a specification within the reasonable time could have been taken into consideration by the seller, the latter's specification becomes binding.

9. We believe that *no express invitation is required* to make a deviating specification. It is sufficient that there is a time fixed for it, e.g. in a letter of August 15, it is said: "We will start preparations for manufacture on October 10, according to the following specification."

10. The seller thus has to take account of the *postal handling time* needed for the communication to reach the buyer. It is sufficient for the buyer to dispatch the communication within the time fixed (Article 27). Postal handling on the way back should not be considered in calculating the time. The risk of transmission is in both cases born by the seller being the party keeping to the contract.

11.1. According to Knapp (BB, 479), the specification made by the seller will not become binding on the buyer when the former *fails to take account of the requirements of the buyer*. We are not convinced by that interpretation as plausible as it may appear at first sight. It rather has to be expected from the buyer that he guard his interests, than from the seller that he take care of the buyer's interests. All the more so when the former is the party breaching the contract. When the buyer thus permits a possibility for contradiction to pass unused, it should not be to the detriment of the seller. The specification should, therefore, be generally binding in this case. Insofar as the seller, however, has breached his obligations in regard to specification, the buyer will have the right to claim damages (Article 45, paragraph 1, subpara. (b), which may be modified because of a prior breach of obligation of his own (Article 80)).

11.2. When the *specification* by the seller *does not reach the buyer* and therefore does not become binding, or when the seller does not receive a deviating specification by the buyer that was orderly dispatched and according to the rule obviously is to be binding, he will most likely manufacture the goods according to his own specification, which is not decisive. The buyer, as a consequence, can assert his rights under Article 45 fol because of lack of conformity. Such breach of contract in the end was caused, however, by a breach of contract of his own, so that it will have to be examined to what extent the seller may require the buyer to pay damages or, if this is excluded because of exemptions according to Article 79, can at least rely on failure caused by the other party under Article 80.

11.3. The exercise of the right to specification of the seller, generally speaking, harbours a number of *risks* for the seller which can be reduced by way of appropriate precise wording in the contract and effective commercial procedures.

Chapter IV

Passing of risk

Introductory remarks

1. The regulation of the risk bearing currently, at least for doctrinal considerations, constitutes a difficult problem. Like in several other areas, this is in our view to be seen in connection with the fact that theories, which in part have their origin in Roman Law or developed already in the Middle Ages (which at any rate are based on completely *different trade conditions* than those which exist today) have, so to speak, become independent from their social background and continue to have an influence without being able to fully meet today's realities.

In publications on the CISG (e.g. Hager/Freiburg, 388 fol) it has repeatedly been pointed out that the passing of the risk can be linked above all to *three fundamental aspects*: the conclusion of the contract, the passing of property in the goods, or the procurement of the goods which again can be defined differently. Those aspects overlap insofar as they relate to one another, e.g. in that the passing of property in the goods is made dependent on the conclusion of the contract or on the procurement of the goods.

The *conclusion of the contract* is not really suitable for determining the passing of risk especially in international sales contracts. Those are in general distance sales relating to non-specific goods to be delivered. At the time the contract is concluded they are thus not even specified, often not even manufactured, and are still in the hands of the seller or of the person acting on his behalf.

The *passing of property in the goods* is not suited to fit the purpose discussed here above all because in fixing the decisive criteria for it, security considerations quite often play a role, e.g. tying to the handing over of documents of title, reservation of title, and, therefore, other legal and political aspects come into play that have to be taken account of in determining the passing of the risk. The CISG has ruled out such procedure from the very beginning. Because of the differences in the domestic rules governing the passing of property, its deep integration into the national legal systems, the interests and ideologies it is burdened with, no unification could be achieved in this field (Article 4, subpara. (b)) a tying of the passing of risk to the passing of property in the goods would practically have meant to renounce a unification of this subject-matter which is, however, very important.

Only the third variant was left therefore: procurement of the goods. It is in line with contemporary trends and had been realized in ULIS in that the *passing of risk was tied to delivery*. This has been criticized for general and legal reasons (Neumayer, 958 fol), and rightly as far as the concrete implementation of that relationship is concerned (c. Introductory remarks 4.).

The CISG ties the passing of risk not that much to other legal terms for whose determination there are already actual or supposed solutions, but originally, so to speak, to the *stages of dispatch* (v. Hoffmann/Dubrovnik, 278, refers to a typological approach in this context). The trade requirements are the starting point (note 3) on whose basis the risk had to be distributed in a balanced way. What matters in this context is not justice but rather usefulness because the risk manifests itself in accidental happenings for which none of the parties can be blamed, but which have to be legally assigned.

It was exactly this autonomous or *genuine connection* of the passing of risk for which the general solution of this problem in the CISG was highly praised (e.g. Bucher/Lausanne, 216 fol; Hager/Freiburg, 411; in this spirit also Kahn/Lausanne, 975). But the cited authors also express themselves critically, in particular in regard to the concrete implementation of the applied principles (see also Sevon/Lausanne, 205 fol). Indeed, shortcomings cannot be overlooked as will be seen in the following detailed comments. In brief, we believe that there are problems which remain unsolved while others are regulated twice, which leads to misunderstandings, and that the trade requirements are not fully met in every instance. One gets the impression sometimes (e.g. Article 66, last part of sentence and also Article 70) that the passing, or better non-passing, of risk is used as an additional sanction and thus applied contrary to its real function. The interpretation given by us will therefore aim at restricting a respective use of this legal instrument.

2. The shortcomings indicated above can certainly not exclusively be put down to the general difficulties in the unification of law, but the latter are emphasized because this legal institute is undergoing a fundamental change. This is reflected differently in the individual laws. A clear signal that the national civil law regulations and their doctrinal legal interpretation have not fully met the requirements in many countries for quite some time now, was set by the fact that in practice a large part of those problems has been solved by relating to the *INCOTERMS* for more than 50 years. Without entering into detail as to their character, we wish to point out that in a case where the parties have agreed a customary delivery clause which is not further specified, it can be assumed that the interpretation given by the INCOTERMS is referred to (note 12 of Article 7). It

should be hard to disprove this, all the more so since proving that something deviating was agreed in regard to several points should not be sufficient for it. If there is no such connection, and the IN-COTERMS in their entirety are declared usages. This cannot replace the *choice* of the parties. Only in rare cases will there be proof that a certain clause of the INCOTERMS has become a usage in respect of a certain kind of trade. Hence, where the parties have agreed no trade term at all, the regulation under the CISG will apply. But those cases are rare.

Besides, the CISG would complement the INCOTERMS. Since they are generally more detailed, this will not occur very often. But as will have to be explained below, the rule governing the passing of risk under the CISG may well be considered as *supplementing the INCOTERMS*, in particular because of its broader angle of vision. Hellner (Dubrovnik, 346) even believes that the CISG is of greater relevance in regard to the passing of risk than to delivery. We, however, do not think that the CISG is an encouragement to *ignore* the traditional *interpretation of the INCOTERMS* and to destroy their fundamental interrelation, as H. de Vries affirms in his acerbic essay which is based, in our view, on many misunderstandings ("The passing of risk in international sales under the Vienna Sales convention 1980 as compared with traditional trade terms", European Transport Law, 1982/5, vol. XVII, p. 528).

3. We explained (Introductory remarks 1.) that the rule governing the passing of risk has to be orientated primarily towards *trade requirements*. In the following, we wish to summarize the relevant criteria, taking into account publications on the subject (in particular Secretariat's Commentary, O. R., 63; Roth, 291; Honnold, 367, 373 fol). In the relationship between the parties to the contract the rule governing the passing of risk should, if possible, be applied in such a way that the party who has the goods *in safekeeping* is also the one to bear the risk. He is best equipped to protect the goods and/or to save them from imminent danger, and is stimulated to do so if he bears the risk. Disputes that he will have to answer for loss or damage to the goods because of conduct contrary to his obligations even though he did no longer bear the risk, are avoided. A second criterion is that the *risk* is borne by the party who can *insure* the goods most easily and less expensively and/or has the most favourable prerequisites for submitting an insurance claim (aspect of simplicity). When one party has the goods in his safekeeping, all those criteria point to him. When a third party, in particular a store-keeper or a carrier, has the goods in safekeeping, it is important in the interest of an absolutely inexpensive insurance that one insurance covers the entire way of transportation or at least parts of it which are clearly delimitable, including the possibility of control on

the way. It is recommendable that the rule for the passing of risk follows that procedure. Less clear is the aspect of simplicity. It will point to the seller insofar as he is the one to organize transportation. But this does not include the bearing of the risk by the seller because he can also insure the goods on behalf of the buyer. Insurance for the latter is facilitated under Article 32, paragraph 3. The party who has the best opportunities to submit insurance claims is the one who receives the goods from the safekeeping by a third party, e.g. carrier, and who, accordingly, also has the required documents.

The third criterion refers to the best prerequisites for *asserting claims* vis-a-vis transport organizations. Again it points to the party who receives the goods from them. What becomes visible here is the usefulness of a congruence between the passing of risk in the relationship of the parties to the contract and points of intersection in regard to the liability of the carriers. Of no relevance in determining the passing of the risk should in our view be the aspect, as mentioned by Hager (Freiburg, 391) referring to Honnold, of who can best repair the goods. The measures which are of importance when the goods arrive relate first of all to securing claims.

These criteria do not always lead to the same results, but can to a certain extent serve as a guideline in interpreting difficult provisions of the CISG.

4. The *passing of risk and delivery* are not strictly bound to each other, but there is a close connection between them (Sevon/Lausanne, 193). When the CISG is applied for lack of deviating agreements, there are instances where the place of delivery and the place where the risk passes are the same, even when there is no formal relation between them. This follows in particular from the relationship between Article 31 and Articles 67 and 69 (Bonell, DPCI, 23; nuances are pointed to by Sevon/Lausanne, 193; Kahn establishes this relationship in a rather free and easy way - 976).

5. Regarding the relationship between the *risk* of having to pay the *price* and the risk of having to *perform*, compare Article 66, note 1.

6. Because of the close relations to the rights of the buyer and his obligation to pay the price the passing of the risk was, at a Norwegian proposal (O. R., 401 and 136), *placed* directly behind the Chapter which deals with the main obligations of the two parties. In ULIS the two relevant rules were found at the end.

7. While Article 66 defines the character of the risk passing, Articles 67 to 69 determine when the risk passes, and Article 70 implies that the passing of the risk has no influence on the rights of the buyer from a fundamental breach of contract by the seller.

Article 66

(Loss after risk has passed)

Loss of or damage to the goods after the risk has passed[2] to the buyer does not discharge him from his obligation to pay the price[1], unless the loss or damage is due to an act or omission of the seller[3].

1.1. From this formulation follows that the risk refers in the first place to the *risk of having to pay* (Huber, 453 fol; Schlechtriem, 78; Bucher/Lausanne, 207). Hager (Freiburg) has pointed out that the distinction between the risk to pay and the risk to perform is not made in many countries and that, where it is made, it is relevant only in the event where the buyer has to take the goods at the seller's place. In general, under the CISG the risk to pay and the risk to perform pass at the same time. This is also the attitude of the INCOTERMS in regard to this problem. The difference becomes obvious again when the fact that the risk has passed is later again put into doubt (note 3). We are referring here to different aspects which we want to examine separately.

1.2. The risk of having to pay informs of which conditions have to be fulfilled by the seller for the *obligation to pay the price* not to end and/or be reduced when the goods are destroyed or damaged. The totality of these conditions fulfilled characterizes the passing to the risk, of having to pay the price. From the view of the seller it can be deduced from the passing of the risk until the existence of which condition he will have to fear that his right to obtain the price might be lost, in other words, to what extent he is responsible for the intactness of the goods. This aspect of bearing the risk corresponds with the seller's liability under Article 36, paragraph 1 of the CISG, for a lack of conformity which exists at the time when the risk is passed. Apart from that, the bearing of the risk has no influence on the emergence or settlement date of the obligation to pay the price.

1.3. It follows from the rule on the *risk of having to perform* whether the seller is obligated to deliver again, to deliver missing parts, to repair etc. The seller might not only lose his right to obtain the price because the risk materializes, but he might also have to deliver once again, which of course would revive his right to obtain the price. As was said before, the risk of having to perform passes with the risk of having to pay the price; at least it passes with it at the latest and is not revived when the price risk comes back to the seller. Once the risk has passed, the seller does not have to deliver again. But what happens before? The seller has to tender the goods in a way prescribed in Articles 67 to 69. If he does not do that because the risk has materialized before it has passed and the orderly initiated process of tendering has failed because of this, the question whether the seller has to deliver once again or has to repair the goods etc. is answered according to the general rules. Since the cases which are of interest here are cases where the goods are destroyed or damaged (note 2) accidentally, the impediments under Article 79 will regularly be in existence. But this basically only frees the seller from damages because of non-observance of the time for delivery (Article 79, note 5). Only the buyer has the right to use the possibility of avoidance, which would free the seller from his obligation to perform. The seller, however, will be interested in obtaining a rapid decision in the matter, which he can bring about in the following way: He informs the buyer under Article 79, paragraph 4, of how long the impediment will exist in regard to the performance of his obligations or: when he will be able to deliver new goods. Provided that the information is formulated accordingly, this would amount to a notice of delivery after the date for delivery under Article 48, paragraph 3, which is assumed to contain an invitation to inform of performance under paragraph 2. This entails the consequences envisaged there, in particular exclusion of the right to avoid the contract before the indicated time for performance if there is no rejection within a reasonable time (in detail Article 48, notes 10 fol).

As regards *accidental damage to the goods before the risk has passed*, we assume that the goods were manufactured as planned and the problems emerged between the completion of manufacture and the passing of the risk. This case, too, is not specifically described in the Convention as being a reason for exemption, but can in its typical manifestations very well be subsumed under the impediments of Article 79, paragraph 1. Proceeding on this subsumption, the seller can repair the goods before the risk is passed, which leads us back to the procedure described in connection with the destruction of the goods.

A case which occurs rather often in practice is that the *risk is passed* without a repair having been made, e.g. because none of the parties knows that there is a damage. The same is true of theft of part of the goods. In that event the same rights of the buyer are to a large extent applied as in the case of delivery of non-conform goods. It is only the claims for damage which are excluded. There should be no great practical difference between whether the buyer refuses to pay part of the price because of an accidental damage or whether he relies on reduction of the price pursuant to Article 50. Where the destruction or damage of the goods before the passing of the risk is caused by an act or omission of the buyer, e.g. by sub-supplying unfit motor oil the motors to be delivered are destroyed during the test run, or the computers to be delivered are damaged because of the use of inappropriate packaging material, the buyer cannot rely on such non-conformity under Article 80.

1.4. It is understandable that the buyer cannot demand that goods are delivered or damaged goods are repaired twice, when the risk had already passed when the loss or damage occurred. However, where spare parts or parts of larger units are lost which can be delivered solely by the seller or which only he can repair, and where he can reasonably be expected to do so, grounds may be given for an obligation to accept a relevant contract against payment by following the principle of *good faith* (Article 7, paragraph 1).

2. Following the traditional understanding, reference is made here to *accidental destruction* and/or *accidental damage*. These include such effects which are not caused by either of the parties and/or by parties for which the former are responsible, but are the result of events that cannot be influenced by human beings and/or of the conduct of uninvolved third parties or possibly also of the carriers. There is no doubt that they cover the effects of impediments, accidents, loss including theft, the mixing up during transport, delivery etc. (c. Neumayer/Dölle, 605 fol). Where the buyer is responsible, he will bear the damage anyway (see also note 1.4.). As for the seller, see note 3. It is irrelevant after the risk has passed what has caused the loss or damage. We also believe that the buyer bears the risk of intervention by a State (obtaining a similar result, even though doubting, Neumayer, 957 fol). Hager (Freiburg, 409 fol) tries to substantiate his deviating view invoking the obligation to procure authorizations. This is, as we believe, a different problem which is frequently bound to the delivery and/or performance and thus the decisive place which often, as has already been mentioned above, is the same as the place where the risk is passed. When natural decrease or shrinkage (leakage, seeping away etc.) which is not caused by inappropriate packaging and similar things, is not taken into consideration during the making of the contract, it will in our view come also under the bearing of risk, i.e. the decisive weight is the weight at the time when the risk passes.

3. Obviously, the risk shall *not pass and/or fall back* to the seller when there is such an exception. This is an unfortunate rule. There were considerable difficulties of interpretation in the case of the similarly worded Article 96 ULIS (Neumayer/Dölle, 606 fol). Even the draft CISG was sometimes interpreted daringly (Huber, 565 fol). Neu-

mayer (966) had made the very good proposal to delete the reservation. But there was no substantial discussion at the diplomatic conference (O. R., 401 fol), and no proposals were submitted (O. R., 126).

The reservation, when interpreted narrowly, covers problems which are already solved in different places and, when interpreted broadly, leads to undesirable or even foolish results. The *commentators have to make a choice* between the two. There are those who want to have the reservation valid only when the conduct of the seller amounted to a breach of an obligation (Huber, 457; also Honnold, 370) and/or a breach of contract (in this direction Schlechtriem, 78 fol). The cases to be subsumed hereunder are already covered sufficiently by Article 36, paragraph 2. Others (like the Secretariat's Commentary, O. R., 63 fol) and Nicholas/BB, 485) rightly point out that such qualification is not contained in the text. Sevon (Lausanne, 196 fol) interprets that only possible regulations should be pointed to which give reason for the seller to be liable. Apart from that the text does not even provide for this. We are, generally speaking, back to the first solution.

Since the restriction cannot simply be ignored we are, in view of the existing dilemma, in favour of a *restrictive interpretation*. We assume here that the act or omission of the seller has to be in breach of contract or at least in breach of obligation. A difference which in our belief exists in comparison with Article 36, paragraph 2 (which could also justify a different wording) is that the seller cannot exempt himself pursuant to Article 79. The commented on half-sentence has thus the effect that the buyer in certain cases of performance in breach of contract, is granted further rights in regard to retaining the price apart from the rights provided for in such cases which actually are sufficient because of the not passing even the falling back of the risk. The conduct of the seller, which insofar is relevant, must have a close connection, in our view, with the motives because of which the regulation on the passing of the risk was established. Furthermore, there must be a direct relation to the contract and its performance in time and substance.

Instances which are possible in this context include, above all, a *lack of conformity* of the goods which starts to have an effect only after the risk has passed and possibly leads to the total destruction of the goods, damage to a part of the goods which is actually not affected by the lack of conformity, unfit packaging, e.g. omission of packaging for transport at sea. The acts of the seller must not necessarily be breaches of contract, although this will be the typical case. Anyway, the mentioned, but rather abstractly formulated rule should in general not be extended to *torts* because they require the examination of different conditions. It is, therefore, not advisable to grant the buyer for such reasons the option not to pay the price.

This refers, as we believe, also to the example mentioned and much cited(Sevon/Lausanne, 196 fol; Hager/Freiburg, 403 fol; Nicholas/BB, 485) in the Secretariat's Commentary (O. R., 163 fol). In a FOB contract the *seller damages* the *goods* when he removes his containers. Since this probably is no breach of contract but rather a tort and the buyer can, therefore, not invoke the rights he would have because of a breach of contract, the latter should at least be permitted to reduce the price to the extent to which this is allowed under the applicable law of tort. This example is proof that the rule does not meet its objective, for the fact alone that the seller damages the goods is no justification for presuming his responsibility for it, e.g. the buyer may have placed the goods in violation of regulations. Proceeding on the legal and political principle underlying the rule (Introductory remarks 4.) the buyer would have to bear the risk for he will be the one to have the goods normally insured. There was no reason for the seller to do so. When the insurance company indemnifies the buyer, the taking back the price wholly or in part would presuppose that he hands over the proceeds from it insofar to the seller. But this situation is not provided for in the Convention. Besides, we do not understand why the buyer should be in a particularly favourable position when the seller causes the damage, for the latter in this regard finds himself in a situation which is hardly different from that of any third party. Where the damaging of the goods by the seller was a tort and the buyer, therefore, has claims against the seller, the general possibilities of setting off against the price requirement are applicable under the decisive law, and the buyer is thus satisfied.

A very narrow interpretation could be used to counteract the fact that because of the lack of a time limit for the relevant conduct of the seller, such acts will be taken into account which happen a very long time after the risk has passed or whose effect is felt only that late, and that the *system of claims from breach of contract* is thereby fundamentally modified. This exceptional rule cannot, in general, be played off against the system of claims in the event of lack of conformity of the goods.

Furthermore, *lawful conduct* of the seller, which in interaction with accidents leads to loss or damage of the goods, should not be regarded as a reason for the falling back of the risk (rightly pointed out by Huber, 457; agreeing Schlechtriem, 79). This refers, for instance, to the case that the risk is passed in such a way that the buyer commits a breach of contract by not taking delivery of the goods under Article 69, paragraph 1, and the seller now takes appropriate measures under Article 85 to preserve the goods, which, however, accidentally lead to the destruction of the latter. The same applies where the seller exercises his lawful right to stop the goods in transit. Even more obvious is the non-applicability of this rule in its abstract form when the seller has chosen a carrier for that part of transportation for which the buyer bears the risk and when the goods perish in the keeping of the carrier. If this were not so, the scheme of risk bearing of the Convention would be completely distorted. The problems that may result between the seller and the buyer from the possible engagement of inappropriate carriers should also not be solved invoking the provisions on risk bearing.

Article 67

(Passing of risk when the sale involves carriage)

(1) If the contract of sale involves carriage of the goods[1] and the seller is not bound to hand them over at a particular place[2], the risk passes to the buyer when the goods are handed over[5] to the first carrier[3] for transmission to the buyer[4] in accordance with the contract of sale. If the seller is bound to hand the goods over[7] to a carrier at a particular place[6], the risk does not pass to the buyer until the goods are handed over to the carrier at that place[5]. The fact that the seller is authorized to retain documents controlling the disposition of the goods does not affect the passage of the risk[8].

(2) Nevertheless, the risk does not pass to the buyer until the goods are clearly identified to the contract[9], whether by markings on the goods[10], by shipping documents[11], by notice given to the buyer[12] or otherwise[13].

1. Compare note 4 of Article 31 concerning the same wording.

The contract requires *carriage* when the goods are at a place other than the place of destination as it follows from the contract, and when no such conditions for delivery apply which exclude carriage. The requirement of carriage thus is the rule and, for lack of rules to the contrary, comes into existence, in particular, when the mailing address of the buyer or ways of dispatch are mentioned. Being a bit more strict, Hellner (Dubrovnik, 344 fol) demands that the seller must have assumed the contractual obligation to transport the goods, without such clues there would only be an Ex Works contract. In agreeing customary trade terms, like in particular the IN-COTERMS, a carriage requirement is expressed in most cases. But this could also allude to other kinds of risk passing than the one envisaged here.

2. Compare sentence two and note 7 in regard to this case.

3.1. Reference is made here, and there is overwhelming agreement among the commentators (e.g. Honnold, 374 fol; Sevon/Lausanne, 199; Bucher/Lausanne, 214; Nicholas/BB, 490; Hager/Freiburg, 392, and already Neumayer/Dölle, 615 on ULIS; doubting Schlechtriem, 80 fol) which we share, to an *independent carrier* and not to the seller himself in his capacity as carrier. A point in favour of the interpretation that the seller acting as carrier has to bear the risk himself is that he regularly will be protected against all risks through his global insurances. Furthermore, this will help to increase his eagerness in meeting his obligation to keep the goods, and disputes on whether he breached it causing damage are restricted because he is always responsible. The counter arguments by von Hoffmann (Dubrovnik, 287) that this would serve to counteract a less expensive and more rapid transportation by the seller himself are in no way convincing for the above-mentioned reasons.

3.2. We are of the opinion that there is no reason to assume that the risk is not passed where goods are handed over to so-called *local carriers* as von Hoffmann (Dubrovnik, 286) offers as the uniform view (Neumayer/Dölle, 615 on ULIS, tends in the same direction; in spite of the same kind of rules in the Scandinavian sales law in regard to the CISG with the opposite trend Sevon/Lausanne, 200). This is justified neither by the wording nor the genesis of the Convention and also not desirable from the legal policy point of view. To provide the goods with uniform insurance it is not necessary to include the transport distance covered by the seller, but that of all other carriers. It would indeed be extremely complicated to make a distinction between local and international carriers. Is the train carrying the goods to the national port a local carrier or is it a motor traffic company carrying the goods from the factory to the train which also carries out international motor traffic transportation?

3.3. It is sometimes pointed out that *forwarding agents* are not carriers (Sevon/Lausanne, 199). This is true only insofar as they have not assumed such obligations by self-execution of the contract of carriage and/or act as forwarding agent working at fixed cost or on the basis of joint consignment (B. Wiesbauer, "Das Wiener Kaufrechtsübereinkommen aus der Sicht des Transportrechtes", Zeitschrift für den internationalen Eisenbahnverkehr, 1987/9/10, p. 97), which is what happens more frequently in connection with the development of modern container traffic.

4.1. Hence, the goods have to be *addressed* to the buyer or his firm in the form that is customary for the respective way of transportation, or to an intermediary, e.g. forwarding agent, to be forwarded to the buyer. Observance of this criterion is not impaired by the naming of additional conditions for the delivery/handing over of the goods to the buyer, like payment of the price or proof of it (in this meaning expressly sentence 3).

4.2. The wording is also not to express that the first carrier has to transport the goods to the buyer and does, therefore, not exclude transportation by *several carriers*.

5. Since losses occur or damages are caused often, especially during the process of unloading, it may be necessary, as Sevon (Lausanne, 200) rightly points to, to define the *handing over* more clearly. It should be useful in our view to proceed on the assumption that the risk bearing becomes effective at the end of the handing over because it is more exactly stipulated than the beginning of that process. We hold that one should insofar follow directly or analogously the quite clear and worldwide recognized INCOTERMS rules. According to those rules the handing over is generally ended when the goods are on the vehicle of the carrier taking them over and/or when the latter does the loading himself, the goods were provided ready for loading, or only handed over into the keeping of the carrier. Where the goods are composed of several units which are transported separately, nothing can be said against a risk passing per unit.

6. The obligation to hand over at a particular place can also be substantiated by a party during the process of contract performance making use of a *right to choice* granted to him, e.g. "depending on the choice of the buyer, the goods are to be tendered for shipping either in Rostock or Szczecin".

But we believe that less unequivocal *alternative clauses* are sufficient here. Von Hoffmann (Dubrovnik, 289) is of the opinion in this context that the identification of the "particular place" depends on an act of the carrier (which in our view is in general not true), and he wants the risk not to pass at a later specified place, which is not correct, as we think. Of course, decisive are the detailed arrangements made. Only two standard cases can be presented here. In the event of a F.O.B. contract the specification should generally be made by the buyer, and there is nothing which would speak against the risk passing at the port named by him. In a C.I.F. contract situation which is given as an example in the Secretariat's Commentary (O. R., 64, Article 79), the port of shipment is not even mentioned. Nevertheless, we see no problem in regard to the risk passing at a later, here by the seller, specified port, all the more so since the latter is the one having to insure the goods until the named port of destination. This, however, is not so in the case of a CFR transaction. But we do not consider an exception justified insofar as the buyer under Article 32, paragraph 3, is entitled to request the information needed for the conclusion of a transport insurance.

7.1. According to the view most expressed in publications (Secretariat's Commentary, O. R., 64; Roth, 308 fol; Sevon/Lausanne, 199; von Hoffmann/Dubrovnik, 287 and others) this is the case when the seller is to *tender* the goods *to* the agreed, or later to be specified, *carrier* at a port or airport. It can also be a carrier who sends containers in multimodal transport and who has, therefore, tendered several batches of goods from different sales contracts. In that case, INCOTERMS clauses like FAS, FOB, and FCA are used. As regards alternative clauses compare note 1.

When customary *trade terms* are agreed, the risk bearing rules contained in those terms become effective, too. And the Convention is pushed far into the background. But we could imagine that there are also cases for which a point of handing/taking over is agreed in situations which correspond to those aimed at in the trade terms without reference being made, so that the Convention comes into play again.

7.2. Honnold (376 fol) expresses an outsider opinion. According to him the risk shall pass at a particular place only when the goods are handed over by the *seller himself* and not by another carrier to a second carrier. This interpretation is based, *inter alia*, on the fact that in Article 67, sentence 2, (by contrast to sentence 1) a handing over by the seller is mentioned. But this is not convincing, if only because the Convention in other places implies that the respective party can also instruct a third party to act on his behalf. This leads to a sharing of the risk of transportation, which in itself is not desirable, but it presupposes the handing over of the goods from one person to another. In so doing, the goods can generally be examined for damages that might have been caused by transportation. Therefore, risk sharing is also usual in these cases. Should it not be possible, as in container transportation, the parties should be recommended not to agree the handing over of the goods at a particular place on their way.

7.3. Some authors become hesitant in regard to the application of Article 67, sentence 2, to a F.O.B. contract situation because Article 67, unlike Article 69, does not provide for the passing of the risk where the buyer does not make the means of transportation available in time, and want, therefore, to apply Article 69 (Nicholas

/BB, 506 fol - in our view there is a contradiction to his explanations on page 492). We too believe that the risk should pass, provided the other conditions apply, when the *means of transportation should have been made available*. The reason for this is in our view an analogous application of Article 69, but we also consider possible the solution given by Schlechtriem to deduce a respective principle under Article 7, paragraph 2, from Articles 67 and 69 which would amount to the same (the principle formulated by Hager/Freiburg on page 401 goes, however, too far - Article 69, note 5; of a different view Sevon/Lausanne, 201).

8. These documents are mainly the so-called *documents of title* (Article 57, note 8.1.). In accordance with their function, they do not accompany the goods, but reach the buyer via a bank or on a similar way because they are to ensure the payment or the use of payment guarantees. Their handing over is sometimes tied to the passing of property in the goods. It is expressly stated here that the passing of the risk is not affected by it whereby doubt is removed, for instance, where domestic stipulations to the contrary are concerned.

What is true of the *documents* of title is all the more true of such documents which contain less far-reaching legal positions (Article 57, note 8.1.).

9. This requirement is to prevent the seller from abusing the lacking *identification to the contract* in order to put the blame for losses or damages on a certain buyer. The requirements for an identification to the contract are determined by this function and hence must not be too strict in an abstract way.

10. They include, in particular, *markings* which are directly on the goods because of contractual agreements or because of regulations valid for the individual categories of transportation, like the number of the contract on whose basis the delivery is made or also of the addressee. Packing lists which are added to the goods may also contain identifying information. Also copies, which usually exist, can prove the identification of the goods to the contract even if they are totally lost. It is clear that markings made by the seller, which point to the buyer, like his name, his trademarks or other means of advertising, also have an identifying effect.

11. One of the clearest forms of identification is certainly the *addressing* of the goods to the buyer, which is reflected above all in the carriage documents.

12. Compare Article 32, notes 3 and 4.

In sending *bulk goods* which are not marked as such, it is recommended to indicate not only the ship by which the goods are sent, but, as far as possible, that part of the ship where the batch of goods for the buyer is stored (c. note 13.2.).

13.1. The above enumeration (notes 10 to 12) is to serve as an example and concentrates on particularly evidential means of identification. The wording *"otherwise" may*, for example, *indicate* that the goods have been manufactured according to specific requirements requested by a certain buyer; that its quantity is exactly the one agreed with a certain buyer and/or also the time for delivery, other equally due orders lacking; that they are adapted to the technical standard of a country or a region when the seller has no other clients there; and, that a characteristic category of carriage was used etc.

Where one or the other criterion in itself is not sufficient, several *features taken together* may permit an unequivocal identification. If such an identification cannot be made, the existing features might suffice to give rise to such a strong supposition that the burden of proof is reversed. (But then the buyer proves that the textiles marked with his trademark can nonetheless not been have handed over to the carrier for transmission to him because they were supposed to go to a place of destination and at a time other than those agreed.)

13.2. Identification becomes extremely difficult where the buyer is to be supplied goods from a *totality of goods* which is not separated during carriage, like for instance in the case of liquids which are supplied to the customer in tankers of a special transportation company. Under the INCOTERMS this can be done using the trade terms "carriage paid to" and "carriage and insurance paid to - named place of destination" which include the same rule for the bearing of the risk. But they do not expressly solve the problem mentioned here so that the CISG has to be invoked. The latter, however, does not offer a solution, but because of its complexity and its principles, opens up greater possibilities of interpretation. We believe that in this case the risk should pass with the taking over of the liquid which is destined for several named addressees because it is clear that the goods intended for every one of these buyers is contained in it. Thus, when because of an accident the liquid is spilled before even one of the buyers is supplied, there is no doubt that any one of the buyers is affected (in this sense even though in another context-Neumayer/Dölle, 640; Neumayer, 984). In the event that only part of the liquid is spilled, it has to be assumed, so we believe, that the buyers not supplied yet (insofar as one has already been supplied, there has been a clear identification for him, and the matter is closed for him) bear the risk *pro rata* of their part in the delivery. The remaining goods would have to be delivered accordingly (similarly as here Neumayer/Dölle, 640; holding a different view Sevon/Lausanne, 202).

Article 68

(Passage of risk when goods sold in transit)

The risk in respect of goods sold in transit passes to the buyer[1] from the time of the conclusion of the contract[2]. However, if the circumstances so indicate[3], the risk is assumed by the buyer from the time the goods were handed over to the carrier who issued the documents[4] embodying the contract of carriage. Nevertheless, if at the time of the conclusion of the contract of sale the seller knew or ought to have known[6] that the goods had been lost or damaged and did not disclose this to the buyer, the loss or damage is at the risk of the seller[5].

1.1. This solution was not part of the draft CISG and was adopted at the diplomatic conference only after extensive discussion in the First Committee (O. R., 403 fol) and in the Plenary (O. R., 213 fol), in particular at the insistence of Pakistan which was supported by other developing countries. It does prevent a retroactive passing of the risk, but has to be considered as *inappropriate* from the point of view of trade requirements because it is in general difficult to establish, when a loss occurred or damage was caused to goods in transit. This difficulty becomes irrelevant when the passing of the risk takes place with the handing over to the carrier. Furthermore, in that event it is the buyer, hence the party who receives the goods and can initiate the necessary measures against the carrier or insurer, who bears the risk. Goods in transit are often such goods as raw materials and other bulk goods which indeed count among export commodities of the developing countries. It is, however, often the basic rule adopted in this article which causes difficulties, in particular, to the exporter of such goods. It is not quite understandable why this should clearly be in the interest of the developing countries as it appeared to be the case at the diplomatic conference. In publications it was Neumayer (Dölle, 646 fol) who advocated a solution as it has now been adopted, and Bucher (Lausanne, 216) obviously agrees. Hager (Freiburg, 411) has expressed some reservations, and Sevon (Lausanne, 202) seems to have doubts, too.

5.4. The rule also covers those cases where the goods at the time of the conclusion of the contract have already completely been destroyed so that the contract was aimed at an *impossible performance*. Such a contract is void under the law of many countries. Hence, a question of validity is touched here which the Convention under Article 4, subpara. (a) has expressly excluded from its scope of validity. The question has now to be asked of whether one should consider the rule as irrelevant to the extent to which the contract in question is void under the applicable national law, or whether, conversely, it should be used to deduce from it an exception to the self-limitation of the CISG. We believe that the latter is accurate (Article 4, sentence 2, first half-sentence; of a different view regarding ULIS Neumayer/Dölle, 652 fol).

From the legal policy point of view, a satisfying solution can be obtained when one stays *within the framework of the Convention*. The seller is bound to the contract. He will not be able to rely on the grounds which led to the loss or damage of the goods as impediments, since he could have taken account of them at the time when the contract was concluded (Article 79, paragraph 1). He will thus have to face all the consequences of a breach of contract insofar as he cannot ensure performance otherwise.

6. In our view the "*ought to have known*" should *not* be *overly stretched* as does Neumayer (Dölle, 652 fol) in commenting on the very similar formulations of ULIS when he wants the seller to retain the risk when the worsening or the total destruction of the goods are only the consequence of a dangerous situation which was emerging even before the contract was concluded and of which the seller knew. The wording, at least of the CISG, requires in our view that the seller ought to have known of the effect on the goods that has taken place and that it is not sufficient that he can assume it at best because of any dangerous situations in which the goods find themselves, e.g. the ship passes through a region where there are acts of war. At the most, a damage is included which is connected with the original damage of which the seller knew or ought to have been aware, as Nicholas (BB, 499) sees it.

Article 69

(Passage of risk in other cases)

(1) In cases not within articles 67 and 68[1], the risk passes to the buyer when he takes over the goods[2] or, if he does not do so in due time[3], from the time when the goods are placed at his disposal[4] and he commits a breach of contract by failing to take delivery[5].

(2) However, if the buyer is bound to take over the goods at a place other than the place of business of the seller[6], the risk passes when delivery is due[7] and the buyer is aware of the fact[8] that the goods are placed at his disposal at that place[9].

(3) If the contract relates to goods not then identified[10], the goods are considered not to be placed at the disposal of the buyer until they are clearly identified to the contract[11].

1. The cases referred to here cover instances in which carriage of the goods is not planned (Article 67) and in which no transiting goods are to be sold (68). Therefore, those cases are covered in which the *buyer fetches the goods* (corresponds approx. to the INCOTERMS clause "Ex works"). A distinction is made insofar whether:

- the buyer fetches the goods at the place of business of the seller (Article 69, paragraph 1, which corresponds to the place of delivery under Article 31, subpara. (c),

- or fetches them at another place (Article 69, paragraph 2, which corresponds to the place of delivery under Article 31, subpara. (b).

Those cases are also taken into consideration where the *seller hands the goods over to the buyer* (there is no respective INCOTERMS clause because a different rule governs the risk bearing for "carriage paid to" and "carriage and insurance paid to").

2.1. Unlike in paragraph 2, the *actual taking over of the goods* by the buyer is requested and not only the creation of the relevant conditions by the seller.

2.2. Here, where the buyer is required to act, the *"taking over"* is mentioned. Whereas Articles 67 and 68, which want to stress the seller's activities, refer to the "handing over" (Article 67, note 5). The processes in both cases are very similar.

3. The taking over is done *in due time* when, in the case where no information is necessary (note 4.3.), it is done within the planned time for fetching the goods and, in the opposite case, within a reasonable time after the information on the intended, provided it was indeed made available, or real placing of the goods at the buyer's disposal. This applies under the condition that the goods are not made available before the admissible time. When the buyer does not comply with this time and/or the contractually agreed time, he will not take over the goods in due time. The risk, nonetheless,

passes to him. The passing of the risk occurs also when in the event of the late placing of the goods at the buyer's disposal, the goods cannot be taken over in due time, unless the seller exercises his right to avoidance.

4.1. The *placing at the disposal* presupposes that the goods can be identified to the contract (notes 10 and 11). The goods have to be ready to be fetched.

4.2. Although it is not prescribed that the goods have to conform with the contract, the seller cannot, in our view, by tendering an *aliud*, cause the risk to pass. He must place the goods at the disposal of the buyer at the envisaged place.

4.3. According to the formulation in paragraph 1, the placing of the goods at the disposal of the buyer does *not necessarily include information* on it. Cases are indeed thinkable where the information can be left out, for instance when in the contract the following is agreed: "Pick up of the goods at the seller's from May 15 to May 31, 1990." Where there is no concrete date agreed for picking up the goods and/or having them ready for pick up, a relevant information must be regarded as part of the placing at the disposal of the buyer for the latter cannot reasonably be expected to have a means of transportation ready over a longer period of time or to come more than once.

Whether or not a required *information needs to reach the addressee* is not said here, unlike in paragraph 2, so that there is a choice between the general rule of Article 27, according to which dispatch is sufficient, or the analogy to paragraph 2. Because of the similarity of the problems and because in the event the goods are with the seller himself even greater demands can be made on the latter as when they were in a different place, we are in favour of an analogy. However, it has to be taken into account that this only refers to the effect of the information in regard to the passing of the risk. Where there are other consequences tied to it, e.g. the information in due time is a condition for complying with the time for delivery, the general rule of Article 27 applies.

5.1. The term of *taking delivery* is taken up here which pursuant to Article 60 is broader than the term of taking over. But the former, too, does in no way cover all obligations of the buyer and, in particular, a breach of the obligation to pay the price, which *de facto* leads to the non-taking delivery of the goods, cannot be subsumed under not taking delivery. The problems involved here have been expounded above all in German publications (Schlechtriem, 83; von Hoffmann/Dubrovnik, 295; Hager /Freiburg, 401).

We believe that the requirement of taking over and/or taking delivery embraces that the *buyer creates all the conditions that are necessary for it*. This, of course, includes that he provides the means of transportation, and, if so agreed, that the one picking up the goods brings along cash or a cheque or a guarantee (Nicholas/BB, 507, holds a different view). In our opinion it is decisive, therefore, that the act itself of handing over the goods is thwarted by the buyer displaying a non-conforming conduct, even if this does not constitute a breach of the obligation to take delivery in the strict sense. The buyer has no possibility for exemption because of impediments (Article 79). Having the consequence of deferring the passage of the risk because those impediments would only exempt from the payment of damages (Article 79, paragraph 5 - Schlechtriem, 83). But the buyer could well rely on failure of the other party under Article 80, e.g. wrong information on the placing at the disposal of the buyer.

However, it goes too far in our view when Hager (Freiburg, 401) wants to infer from Article 69, paragraph 1 in connection with Article 7, paragraph 2, the *general principle* that the risk passes on to the buyer always when the seller, because of non-conforming conduct of the buyer, cannot cause the passing of the risk under the general rules. The requirement of identification under paragraph 3 would in any case have to be complied with, which in many cases would lead to the thwarting of reliance on the passage of risk in the event of many breaches of contract by the buyer. But what is to become of the placing of the goods at the disposal of the buyer? Must the seller place the goods at the disposal of the buyer declaring at the same time that the buyer must not get them before he has, for instance, opened up an agreed letter of credit? When is the risk to pass, always provided that the goods are identified to the contract? When should the letter of credit be opened up, at the beginning of the time for delivery? at its end? There is no well-founded answer to all of these questions, and this is not coincidence. The passing of the risk is no sanction which can be used to react to all breaches of contract by the buyer. This would greatly overstretch the functions of this legal institute. Besides, the seller would not be helped. Because of the passing of the risk the goods might not be protected by his insurance. To stick to the example, the buyer who has not opened up a letter of credit, has not yet entered into an insurance for the goods. When they are destroyed, the seller has claims under the law of contract, but their assertion will often be very uncertain when there are problems already in regard to the opening up of the letter of credit. The CISG does contain a sufficient number of appropriate sanctions for breaches of the obligations of the buyer.

5.2. The risk passes, in our view, at the latest when a *surrogate*, like in particular storage or deposit, replaces the taking over by the buyer. In the event of a re-sale by the seller the new owner takes the risk.

6. This case differs from that of Article 67, paragraph 1, sentence 2, in that the seller does not have to hand over the goods at a particular place, but that he only needs to *place them at the disposal of the buyer*. This applies to Ex works deliveries when the plant is not located at the place of business of the seller, hence when the goods manufactured in several factories are sold by specialized sales companies. Other examples include Ex ship and Ex quay deliveries like those starting at the storage facility. We are of the opinion that the buyer can have himself represented by a carrier when taking over the goods. For Bucher (Lausanne, 215) it is exactly the fact that the buyer himself acts which is the decisive criterion for the application of this provision; otherwise he would want to rely on Article 67. We fail to see any reason why personal acting should be required here because the CISG generally allows the inclusion of third parties.

There is a problem in deciding whether *FOB deliveries* should be covered by this rule. Hager (Freiburg, 401) seems to proceed on this assumption, and Nicholas (BB, 506 fol) has, in our view contrary to earlier explanations (491), provided extensive grounds for it. They take into consideration, above all, that the risk would not pass in applying Article 67 when the buyer fails to provide the hold needed. This is indeed a hardly desirable result; and in regard to such questions it would be useful if the INCOTERMS were supplemented by the Convention. Therefore, we are in favour of the solution offered in note 7.3. of Article 67.

7. The *becoming due* follows from Article 33 which, on its part, refers to the contract in the first place. Nicholas (BB, 506) following Roth (306) rightly points out that where the goods are placed at the buyer's disposal before delivery is due, the risk is passed when the buyer takes over the goods, hence not, as we would wish to add, where he has received the goods only in order to meet his obligation to preserve them (Article 86 fol).

8. *Positive knowledge* is therefore required. This means, on the one hand, that in deviation from the general rule of Article 27, dispatch of the notice is not sufficient to cause the passing of the risk. On the other hand, it has to be proceeded on the assumption that a notice which was received in the meaning of Article 24 suffices, even when exceptionally it has not informed the buyer. Article 24, which expressly relates to the conclusion of the contract, thus has to be ap-

plied by analogy to other cases where the receipt or similar conditions are required.

The information can in our view also refer to a *future placing at the disposal*, but would then naturally cause the passing of the risk only when the goods are indeed placed at the disposal of the buyer. Pursuant to the general provisions of the CISG, the seller is responsible for the correctness of the information.

Notice does, of course, not necessarily have to be given by the seller, but can also originate from the *carrier or* the *warehouse keeper* etc. (Sevon/Lausanne, 205).

9. Apart from the factory where they are manufactured, the *goods will be placed at the disposal* of the buyer very often *in a warehouse*. Notice of it can be given by handing out a relevant document relating to the goods (warehouse certificate) or also other documents, probably a delivery note which only instructs the warehouse keeper to deliver. The view has been expressed in publications that in the former case the risk passes when the documents are handed over, in the latter, however, only when the warehouse keeper declares that he wants to follow the instruction (Hager/Freiburg, 400). This differentiation is not supported by the CISG, as we believe. It would amount to adding, in certain cases, a fourth to the three conditions under the Convention for the passing of the risk; (becoming due, placing at the disposal, including identification, and notice). When the manufacturer or the warehouse keeper refuse to hand the goods over to the buyer, they will not have been placed at the latter's disposal. The risk has, therefore, not passed even when a document relating to the goods has been handed over.

10. *Identification* is basically a form of attribution of the goods to the contract. It is done by separating the goods in question from the rest of the goods. The separated goods are clearly identifiable, in particular, because their quantity corresponds to the quantity that was agreed in the contract and because they may be marked with the name of the buyer. Frequently, there are also other identification features.

11. Compare Article 67, notes 9 to 13.

There was a specific article contained in ULIS (98, paragraph 3) which referred to *non-selectable unascertained goods* (in particular Neumayer/Dölle, 640 fol). We hold that under these circumstances the rules developed in note 13.2. of Article 67 should be applied to the passage of the risk where the goods are not taken over and/or placed at the disposal of the buyer. This means, in particular, that in the event of the destruction of part of the goods, the defaulting buyers, have to bear, possibly *pro rata*, the risk in regard to the price and performance.

Article 70

(Effect of fundamental breach on passage of risk)

If the seller has committed a fundamental[2] breach of contract, articles 67, 68 and 69 do not impair the remedies available to the buyer on account of the breach[1].

1. This article essentially states that the buyer is not deprived of rights because of a fundamental breach of contract where the risk has passed. This relates basically to the *avoidance of the contract and the delivery of substitute goods* because it is a general prerequisite for the exercise of these rights under Article 82, paragraph 1 that the buyer can restitute the goods in essence in the same condition in which he had received them. Paragraph 2, however, provides for considerable restrictions of this principle of which the one under subpara. (a) is of particular interest here. According to it, the restitution of the goods cannot be made a condition when it is impossible for reasons which are not related to the activities of the buyer. But these are exactly the coincidences as they are covered by the bearing of the risk, so that actually the objective of Article 70 is attained to a large extent already in Article 82, paragraph 2, subpara. (a) (see also Sevon/Lausanne, 198 and 220; Neumayer/Lausanne, 219). Anyway, it does not appear very useful to search for a meaning in Article 70 which would go beyond the eventually required closing of gaps which are left by Article 80, paragraph 2, subpara. (a).

Hence, where non-conforming goods are delivered and the non-conformity constitutes a fundamental deficiency, the buyer can require the avoidance of the contract or delivery of substitute goods. This is true even where the goods *accidentally perish or are damaged* after the risk has passed, and also where those events have nothing to do with the deficiency. A batch of 200 electric motors are delivered for instance. During a test it is discovered that 100 of them are defective. Before a complaint can be lodged, all motors are destroyed in a fire. When it is assumed that the individual deficiency of each motor was fundamental and that the batch as a whole had a fundamental deficiency because of the high degree of faultive motors, the buyer will have two options (c. also Nicholas/BB, 510): He can either require a delivery of substitute goods in regard to the defective motors (Article 46, paragraph 1) and has to keep the rest, i.e. the destruction is at his risk, or he can avoid the entire contract (Article 49, paragraph 1, subpara. (a)) and will be freed from the obligation to pay the price and/or can demand restitution of it (Article 81).

We do not believe that Article 70 should be interpreted in such a way as though it would defer the passing of the risk, like in the case of a hidden defect, as long as the rights in regard to avoidance of contract or delivery of substitute goods are excluded or fall under the statute of limitations because the time limits have expired (Hager/Freiburg, 406 - such an interpretation seems to go better with Article 97, paragraph 2 ULIS). Even the view held by Nicholas (BB, 510) according to which the risk is retrospectively passed back by the remedy of avoidance does, in our opinion, not fully meet the wording of the provision. Rather, the *risk bearing* is *not influenced* at all by the rule (so believes also Honnold, 388). But the buyer is freed from his obligation to restitution where the contract is avoided or substitute goods are delivered insofar as such restitution is made impossible because of an event for which he already bears the risk. This may amount to the same in some cases and, in particular, to the rare instance where the goods are not insured. In the typical cases where the goods are insured there will, in our view, be a great difference when the insurance covers only such assets for which the insurant bears the risk. It will not happen regularly that the seller insures the goods already delivered, considering that in connection with a fundamental breach of contract the risk might be on him. On the other hand, it is normal that a factory insures its assets. When goods counting among those assets are lost or damaged, there will be an insurance claim which replaces the goods. The buyer is not obligated to insure the goods. But if he is insured, the insurance company shall not be in a position to rid itself of its obligations pretending that the insurant did not bear the risk.

When the buyer, in the event of a non-conformity, has *decided* in favour of *a claim*, he cannot pass on to another if the seller does not offer an additional reason for it. Hence, when he has demanded repair, he cannot change his mind during the time for repair and require the avoidance of the contract because the goods have perished in the meantime (Hager/Freiburg, 406).

Even if the *delay* constitutes a fundamental breach of contract, the contract can still be avoided pursuant to Article 49, paragraph 1, subpara. (a) after the goods have been delivered. (Should it be avoided before the delivery takes place, the risk will because of the regular connection between delivery and the passage of the risk in most cases not have passed yet so that the problem discussed here will not exist.) The destruction or damage of the goods after the risk passing do not deprive the buyer of the right to avoid the contract. When the seller delivers only after the expiration of a *Nachfrist* set by the buyer, the buyer will also have the right to avoid the contract (Article 49, paragraph 1, subpara. (b)) without a fundamental breach of contract having to have been committed. It is, at least, a question of interpretation whether one wants to consider such breach as being existent in this case. But this does, in our view, not cause such problems as Nicholas (BB, 511) supposes. For Article 82, paragraph 1, subpara. (a), which does not make such a distinction, provides for the same rule as Article 70.

The option given by Article 70 and Article 82, paragraph 1, subpara. (a) to avoid the contract or to require delivery of substitute goods, even where the goods after the passing of the risk perish or are damaged by accident, will considerably increase the buyer's temptation to make use of a factual or supposed right to avoidance. This can be counteracted in setting reasonable *periods for the assertion of* these *rights* under Article 49, paragraph 2 (Honnold, 388 fol; Nicholas/BB, 511). To put it in other words, when the buyer after the occurrence of an accidental event, suddenly gets the idea that a fundamental breach of contract had been in existence even before that event, it will have to be very carefully examined whether he would have had to assert his relevant claims already before the occurrence of that event.

2. If *another breach of contract* is committed, the rights of the buyer are generally not affected because of the passing of the risk. Claims for damages (Article 45, paragraph 1, subpara. (b) are retained and can at best be modified by this other breach of contract. In the event of a non-conformity the right to repair (Article 46, paragraph 3) lapses with the perishing of the goods, whereas it remains in existence in the case of their damaging insofar as it is not changed in its substance by the damage. This solution also has to be applied, as we believe, where the buyer has chosen repair in the event of a fundamental breach of contract. But one could probably assume in the latter case that the damage which occurred because of the risk, has to be removed at least to the extent to which this is necessary in order to remove also the original non-conformity. In this surely rare constellation Article 70 would indeed take on a meaning of its own. Claims for reduction of the price (Article 50) will also continue to exist because they are aimed at re-establishing the disturbed equivalence.

Chapter V

Provisions common to the obligations of the seller and of the buyer

Section I

Anticipatory breach and instalment contracts

Article 71

(Suspension of performance)

(1) A party may suspend[1] the performance of his obligations if, after the conclusion of the contract, it becomes apparent[2] that the other party will not perform a substantial part of his obligations[3] as a result of:

(a) a serious deficiency in his ability to perform or in his creditworthiness[4]; or

(b) his conduct[5] in preparing to perform or in performing the contract.

(2) If the seller[6] has already dispatched the goods before the grounds described in the preceding paragraph become evident, he may prevent the handing over of the goods to the buyer even though the buyer holds a document which entitles him to obtain[7] them. The present paragraph relates only to the rights in the goods as between the buyer and the seller[8].

(3) A party suspending performance, whether before or after dispatch of the goods, must immediately give notice[9] of the suspension to the other party and must continue with performance if the other party provides adequate assurance[10] of his performance.

1. There was an unusually lengthy and controversial discussion of Article 71 at the diplomatic conference because representatives of some developing, but also other, countries were apprehensive that this rule could be abused to the detriment of less strong countries (O. R., 218 fol, 374, 377, 419 fol, 431 fol; see also G. Strub, "The Convention on the International Sale of Goods: Anticipatory Repudiation Provisions and Developing Countries", ICLQ, 1989, p. 475 fol). A party may *suspend performance of his obligations* under certain circumstances. This relates to *any party* and to *any obligation*. What we are referring to here is chiefly the obligation of the seller to deliver the goods and the obligation of the buyer to pay the price. According to Honnold (393) Article 71 also refers to the obligation of the seller to deliver substitute goods under Article 46, i.e. an obligation which presupposes an earlier breach of contract. It is quite logical to include the obligation to deliver substitute goods if it has become doubtful as a consequence that the price will be paid.

It is a logical condition for the suspension of performance of an obligation that the *obligation to perform is already due*. Hence it was concluded that the party who had to perform first was empowered to suspend performance (see the 1985 CISG Commentary, 140; likewise Welser/Doralt, 123; critically Reinhart/Freiburg, 379). What are required are not only acts in performance of the contract, but also those in *preparation of performance* which, therefore, can *also* be *suspended*. Thus production of goods may be stopped and procurement of materials put off (O. R., 52; Honnold, 393; Schlechtriem/Lausanne, 154, has certain doubts).

As a practical consequence of the inclusion of preparatory work the question arises as to how long a party may suspend performance of his obligations (see here note 10).

If a party is granted the right to suspend performance of his obligations, *non-performance* by that party is *not a breach of contract*.

While a party under Article 71 can suspend the performance of his obligations, he may pursuant to Article 72 avoid the contract under similar conditions. Proposals made at the diplomatic conference in order to combine both rules were not adopted (O. R., loc. cit.; as to the differences in the conditions required compare note 2).

Also national laws contain the right, however often more restricted, of the first party to perform under certain circumstances to retain the goods or stop them in transit, e.g. 312 German BGB; Article 83 OR; sec. 41 (1) SGA; sec. 22-609 (1) UCC.

2. If the reasons which allow a party to suspend performance of his obligations were known to him at the time the contract was concluded, that party could not refer to them to suspend performance. It is, however, not a condition that those reasons emerge only after the conclusion of the contract. It will suffice that they become *apparent* only *after the conclusion of the contract*. This rule is the result of the discussions at the diplomatic conference. Preparatory work by UNCITRAL and the draft submitted to the conference only consider those circumstances which emerge after the conclusion of the contract. (For greater details see Reinhart/Freiburg, 371 fol). One of the arguments brought forward by the International Chamber of Commerce against the inclusion of circumstances existing at the conclusion of the contract was that a party, who could not insist on assurances at the time the contract was concluded, could obtain such assurances later by invoking the right to suspend performance of his obligations (UNCITRAL Yearbook, VIII (1977), p. 47 fol; also Bennett/BB, 514).

The right to suspend performance must not lead to a situation where contracts are thoughtlessly concluded. In spite of the inclusion of the circumstances existing at the conclusion of the contract, the first party still has the *obligation to examine the creditworthiness* of the other party (Schlechtriem/Lausanne, 152).

Therefore, the right to suspend performance cannot be invoked if the bad economic situation of the other party is generally apparent but not in fact known to the party wishing to suspend performance (Bennett/BB, 524).

A party would have the right to suspend performance only if he was aware of the bad economic situation of the other party at the conclusion of the contract and can prove that the other party's economic situation considerably worsened (Reinhart/Freiburg, 380). An *objective measure* should be used to judge the reasons which would give rise to a suspension of performance; subjective fear by one party will not be sufficient. There must be a high degree of probability of non-performance (Honnold, 395). The reasons must become apparent to a reasonable person in the same circumstances (Welser/Doralt, 124; Schlechtriem, 87; Schlechtriem/Lausanne, 151; Reinhart/Freiburg, 381).

Decisive is not just the relevant information, but whether the party wishing to suspend performance could hold it to be true. It is disputed, however, who shall be the one to bear the *risk of a wrong assessment*; the party wishing to suspend or the other party (c. Reinhart/Freiburg, 370, listing further sources). If the party suspending performance could hold the information available to him to be true, the risk falls to the other party. If the first party, however, refuses to perform his obligations unfoundedly, he commits a fundamental breach of contract (Reinhart/Freiburg, 381). Risks of this kind cannot be fully avoided in international trade (Vilus/Dubrovnik, 242).

The right to suspend performance supersedes all domestic rules in regard to changes of the *Geschäftsgrundlage*, error etc. *Avoidance of a contract based on a mistake* about the other party's ability to perform *is excluded* (Schlechtriem, 86; Reinhart/Freiburg, 378). An exception here is the contesting of a mistake on grounds of fraud (Schlechtriem/Lausanne, 153).

While Article 71 says "*it becomes apparent*" that the other party will not perform a substantial part of his obligations, Article 72 mentions that "*it is clear*" that the other parties will commit a fundamental breach of contract. Thus the standards of Article 71 are less strict than those of Article 72 (Honnold, 393). Schlechtriem (Lausanne/151) refers to a linguistically somewhat lower ceiling but not to a fundamental difference. A *worsening of the economic situation* of the other party has *to be feared* by a reasonable obligee, but *no absolute certainty* is required. A situation where a totally insolvent obligor suddenly obtains credit does not have to be taken into consideration (Schlechtriem, 87).

3. Non-performance of a substantial part of obligations will, however, not always amount to a fundamental breach (Bennett/BB, 521; Huber believes differently, Article 73 ULIS; critical remarks by Schlechtriem/Lausanne, 152). If the expected *non-performance* were *at the same time a fundamental breach of contract*, the obligor would have a choice between a suspension of performance under Article 71, or avoidance of the contract under Article 72.

An anticipated minor breach of contract by the other party is insufficient.

4. Here *deficiency in the ability to perform and deficiency in the creditworthiness* are placed next to each other. A deficiency in the seller's ability to perform may arise for the seller, e.g. in the event of a forthcoming strike (Bennett/BB, 519), an official order, a prohibition of export, embargo measures et. A deficiency in the buyer's creditworthiness can be the result of a FOB business where there is insufficient storage room on board a ship. There may be a deficiency in the ability of a party to perform a contract even if that party's financial situation is excellent. The reasons for insufficient ability are irrelevant, they don't have to be anybody's fault nor

does anybody have to be responsible for them (Schlechtriem/Lausanne, 150; Reinhart/Freiburg, 377).

Creditworthiness, too, *can relate to both parties;* not only to the buyer who is obligated to pay the price of the goods, but also to the seller who may find himself incapable of financing manufacture of the sold goods. Another serious deficiency could also be that the other party did not perform his obligations under earlier contracts (Bennett/BB, 520) or attempts at obtaining pledges were unsuccessful (see Article 83, OR).

The *creditworthiness of the buyer* may even play a role *when he is the one to perform first,* e.g. in the case of advance payment or the opening of a letter of credit. Should it become apparent that the buyer will at the time of delivery not be in a position to open a letter of credit, the seller may cease or postpone manufacture of the goods (see note 2).

A deficiency in the creditworthiness of the buyer is no reason for suspending performance when the financial situation of the buyer has not changed since the conclusion of the contract and when there are growing doubts on the part of the seller in regard to setting the buyer a time limit for payment.

Deficiency in creditworthiness should, in our view, be interpreted broadly and cover the event where the economic situation of a guarantor or provider of a guarantee deteriorates.

5. Such conduct may also refer to the fulfilment of other contracts (O. R., 52) and is *independent of the financial situation* (Reinhart/Freiburg, 377), e.g. frequent complaints. It may also cover the use of certain unfitting raw materials in performing obligations under similar contracts (Bennett/BB, 520).

6. In contrast to paragraph 1 we are dealing here only with the *right of the seller to stop the goods in transit.* One could have imagined that the buyer, too, should have been granted such a right, i.e. that he should have had the opportunity to revoke a money transfer order. A relevant proposal was rejected, however, during the drafting of the CISG because there was fear of a serious impairment of the international payment transactions and because in many countries the non-payment of a cheque constitutes a criminal act (c. UNCITRAL Yearbook, VIII (1977), p. 54). No such protection is needed in the case of the opening of a letter of credit because the seller usually cannot have access to the letter of credit before having delivered.

If the seller has already dispatched the goods he can only prevent the handing over of the goods to the buyer by giving relevant *orders to the carrier or forwarding agent in question*. To what extent the latter follows those orders in the first place depends on the contract concluded for carriage. (As to the possibilities of the sender to change plans, compare Handbuch 3, 246, 267 fol, 287, 300.) If the buyer's country has acceded to the CISG or if the domestic rules of that country also provide for a right to stop the goods in transit, the seller may try to enforce this right through the courts, e.g. by way of *distress or temporary injunction*.

7. Hence even when the *buyer has obtained title in the goods* through the handing over of the documents.

8. The right to stop the goods in transit, therefore, does not relate to the relationship between the buyer and his other partners if he has already resold the goods and a third party has obtained title in the goods (Schlechtriem/Lausanne, 155). Also *the relations between the buyer and his obligees remain untouched*. If an obligee of the buyer has the goods or if he has pledged title in the goods from a document, the rights of the seller are not governed by the CISG but by the otherwise applicable domestic law (c. also Article 4 according to which property issues are not covered by the CISG; Bennett/BB, 521).

Finally, the right to stop the goods in transit does not touch upon the relationship between carrier and buyer. There are *no obligations for the carrier under the CISG* to respect the seller's request for stoppage. If he voluntarily stops the goods in transit he exposes himself to a claim for damages on the part of the buyer. The seller, on his part, could, because of the right to stop performance, request the buyer not to take measures against the carrier.

Because of the contractual relationship with the carrier the seller could perhaps give orders to the former thus exercising his right to stoppage. Otherwise, he would have to call in a court.

9. It is sufficient to give *notice after the performance of obligations has been suspended*; the entitled party does not have to indicate his intention earlier because frequently there will be no time to do so (Bennett/BB, 519). *Notice* here is subject to Article 27 and *need not*, therefore, *to be received*. The risk of transmission is borne by the addressee (Reinhart/Freiburg, 381). It should, however, be in the interest of the suspending party to see to it that the notice reaches the other party.

It is not required in the rule to indicate grounds in the notice. But it may be inferred from the principle of good faith that grounds should be stated so as to enable the other party to decide what action is to be taken (Bennett/BB, 521).

If the entitled party fails to give notice of suspension he will not lose the right to suspend performance, but he may have to satisfy the claims for damages by the other party (Schlechtriem/Lausanne, 156).

10. Three questions are involved here: first, what is adequate assurance; second, when does a party have to continue with performance; and third, what happens when the other party does not provide adequate assurance.

Adequate assurance depends on the circumstances which have led to the suspension of performance. If export of the goods sold was prohibited, but the seller later obtained an export license, the requirement of adequate assurance would be fulfilled. The same is true for cases where a strike in the sellers factory was thwarted or settled, or where the seller obtained new sources of materials for the manufacture of the goods. According to Honnold (398) this includes the event in which the buyer, who had suspended payment of this obligations, has reestablished them. If performance was suspended on the basis of the mere statement by the other party that he did not intend to perform his obligations, a later statement that he would now be performing as required by the contract may be adequate (Bennett/BB, 523). Such assurance could also be given by way of offering immediate performance of his obligations or performing them without delay (Bennett/BB, 522).

In the event of a deficiency in creditworthiness, a banker's guarantee would for instance offer adequate assurance.

Adequate assurance need not include full performance; a slight delay should be accepted. In this context, however, reference should be made to assurance in the sense of security for damage claims in case of non-performance (O. R., 53; Honnold, 399; agreeing also Schlechtriem, 87).

When the other party provides adequate assurance, such assurance may cover two events: (a) the grounds which led to the suspension of performance have been overcome, and (b) the grounds were not existent at all. In the latter case the suspending party may already have committed a breach of contract including all the consequences ensuing from it. *Suspension of performance* may, however, also *entail a certain risk* (c. note 2). The other party might, in certain circumstances, not only claim damages because of the delay but also because of the costs incurred in providing additional assurances.

Even though there is no express requirement under the CISG, the suspending party should inform the other party that he considers the offered assurance as adequate and will continue with performance (Bennett/BB, 523).

It is generally assumed that the suspending party, who has to *continue with the performance of* his *obligations,* can extend the period for performance by the time that has passed since he has stopped his preparatory work (Schlechtriem/Lausanne, 157; Reinhart/Freiburg, 379). That time may also be shorter (Honnold, 399). In any case the party who is entitled to suspend performance can reasonably adjust the time for performance in accordance with the circumstances (Bennett/BB, 523 fol). If the other party provides no assurance, this can be seen as an indication of an anticipatory, fundamental breach of contract, and the party empowered to suspend performance of his obligations can avoid the contract under Article 72 (Honnold, 400; Schlechtriem/Lausanne, 156, Reinhart/Freiburg, 382; Bennett/BB, 524). He may, however, also wait until the time for performance has passed and, in the case of non-performance, avoid the contract under Articles 49 or 64 (Honnold, 400; Bennett/BB, 524).

Article 72

(Avoidance prior to the date for performance)

(1) If prior to the date for performance of the contract it is clear[1] that one of the parties will commit a fundamental breach of contract[2], the other party may declare[4] the contract avoided[3].

(2) If time allows[5], the party intending to declare the contract avoided must give reasonable[6] notice[7] to the other party in order to permit him to provide adequate assurance[8] of his performance.

(3) The requirements of the preceding paragraph do not apply if the other party has declared that he will not perform his obligations[9].

1. As already explained in note 2 of Article 71, a *greater certainty than* in Article 71 *regarding the right to suspend performance of obligations* is required here. It is clear that a fundamental breach of contract will be committed when the other party declares that he will not perform his obligations (c. paragraph 3). There is the same clarity when the other party denies the very existence of a sales contract (c. the ruling of the Corte d'Apello di Milano concerning ULIS of March 1, 1976, Schlechtriem/Magnus, 399). It is also clear that a fundamental breach of contract will be committed when the seller resells to a third party the goods that he had contracted to deliver to the buyer, or when he sells the machines with which he had agreed to produce the goods for the buyer (Honnold, 402).

A breach of contract is also clear in the case of insolvency and the initiation of bankruptcy proceedings (Schlechtriem/Magnus, 399). The circumstances mentioned in notes 4 and 5 of Article 71 can be so serious that it is clear that a fundamental breach of contract will be committed. There need *not*, however, be *absolute certainty*. Since paragraph 2 envisages the possibility that adequate assurance be provided and the contract be performed in the end, there need not be a fundamental breach of contract.

If a party declares the contract avoided without a fundamental breach of contract by the other party being anticipated, the former commits a fundamental breach of contract (Bennett/BB, 528).

2. As to the fundamental breach of contract, compare Article 25. An example that is given quite often is bankruptcy (see also Vilus/Dubrovnik, 244). We believe, however, that a distinction has to be made of whether it is the seller or the buyer who goes bankrupt since, depending on the circumstances, his receiver may still perform the contract. An *anticipatory, fundamental breach of contract is*, except when there is an express statement by the obligor, *a presumption* which is based on objective factors. Article 72 thus *combines in one rule the refusal to perform and an anticipated objective impossibility to perform.* Stoll criticizes such combination because, in his view, different conclusions have to be drawn when it comes to the right of the entitled party to claim damages. Hence there would be an immediate right to claim damages in the case of a refusal to perform, whereas in other cases there would not be such a claim before the performance is due and/or there would be no such claim at all if the obligor is not liable under Articles 79 or 80 (H. Stoll, "Zur Haftung bei Erfüllungsverweigerung im Einheitlichen Kaufrecht", RabelsZ, 1988/3-4, p. 618 fol). This consequence is in our view not covered by the wording of the CISG (note 3).

3. Whereas a contract can usually be avoided only *after* a fundamental breach of contract under Article 49 and 64, a party may, under the prerequisites of Article 72, already declare the contract avoided before. He may, however, under Article 71 also suspend performance of his obligations and wait until the time for performance has expired. But in this context Article 77 should be taken into consideration. A contract should definitely be avoided where an immediate avoidance would mitigate the losses (Bennett/BB, 528 fol). But even if there is no *obligation to mitigate losses*, clarity can be obtained by avoiding contract and the way could be opened up for new contracts (Bennett/BB, 527). When a contract has been declared avoided, the entitled party can immediately claim damages, the amount of which is fixed by resale or repurchase (Honnold, 403; Bennett/BB, 528).

4. There is no time limit for such a declaration. If the entitled party first decided to wait, he may avoid the contract at any time before the period for performance expires. This is advisable also when there are still doubts as to the seriousness of the conditions impeding performance. The declaration is subject to Article 27. In general, a declaration will be preceded by a notice under paragraph 2 (note 7).

The declaration leads to prompt avoidance of the contract; no further steps are required, neither agreement by the other party nor assistance by the courts (c. also Article 49). Therefore, a declaration cannot be withdrawn once it has become effective.

5. Paragraphs 2 and 3 were added to the draft convention at the diplomatic conference because the developing countries were concerned that the *right to suspend performance could be abused* (Honnold, 403; Vilus/Dubrovnik, 245).

Given the sophisticated means of communication it is hardly imaginable that time would not allow to give notice to the other party of the intended avoidance of the contract. (Compare also the obligation to give notice under Article 88.) This is also in the interests of the party who considers himself entitled in order to preclude unjustified avoidance of contract (Honnold, 403; Bennett/BB, 529).

Time also relates to the *time-span between the giving of notice and the expiration of the time for performance*. The other party must have sufficient time to provide assurance.

6. In the very interest of the obligee it should be *reasonable* in most cases *to give notice of an avoidance of contract*. This is contradicted by circumstances only where there is absolute certainty of future fundamental breaches of contract (c. also paragraph 3). Even in the event of the other party's bankruptcy could his receiver prefer fulfilment to avoidance of a contract (Bennett/BB, 527). A notice is reasonable whenever there is a chance that the other party will provide assurance of performance.

7. This *notice, too, is subject to Article 27*. If it is lost, the party entitled to avoid the contract does not lose that right. But he should in his own interest make sure that the notice reaches the other party.

In practice, the notice of an intended avoidance of contract is frequently linked with the notice of the suspension of performance (Article 71, note 9)(Bennett/BB, 529).

8. As to what adequate assurance is, compare Article 71, note 10. *The way in which such adequate assurance is to be provided depends on the expected fundamental breach of contract.* The simplest means is to provide assurance by way of paying a sum, e.g. banker's guarantee. If there is serious doubt as to the seller's performing of his obligations, he could also provide a guarantee of performance. He could also explain in which way he can and will deliver the goods in time, in the agreed quality and free from third party rights or claims (e.g. use of sub-contractors, increase in the production capacity, cancellation of other obligations to deliver, acquisition of licenses etc.).

9. Thus there is no need to give notice in advance of the intention to avoid the contract. But also in this case the other party has a right and *no obligation* (except in regard to mitigation of losses, note 3) *to declare the contract avoided*. If the entitled party does not avoid the contract, and if the obligor changes his mind, the latter may still fulfil the contract. On the other hand, the obligee does not have to wait and see whether the obligor changes his mind; he can avoid the contract immediately. In such a case the declaration of an intended non-performance of the contract is irrevocable (Honnold, 402).

Article 73

(Avoidance of instalment contracts)

(1) In the case of a contract for delivery of goods by instalments[1], if the failure of one party[2] to perform any of his obligations in respect of any instalment constitutes a fundamental breach of contract[3] with respect to that instalment, the other party may declare[6] the contract avoided[4] with respect to that instalment[5].

(2) If one party's failure to perform any of his obligations in respect of any instalment gives the other party good grounds to conclude[7] that a fundamental breach of contract will occur with respect to future instalments[8], he may declare[6] the contract avoided for the future[10], provided that he does so within a reasonable time[9].

(3) A buyer who declares the contract avoided in respect of any delivery may, at the same time[11], declare[6] it avoided in respect of deliveries already made or of future deliveries[12] if, by reason of their interdependence[13], those deliveries could not be used for the purpose contemplated by the parties[14] at the time of the conclusion of the contract[15].

1. It is a *condition* for the avoidance of a contract under Article 73 that the *contract provides for the delivery of goods by instalments*. If a party commits a breach of contract, and the obligee wishes to draw conclusions for *other* contracts, he may probably do so on the basis of Article 72.

A contract on the delivery of goods by instalments does not require delivery of similar goods at all times, or agreement of fixed dates. Deliveries may include different goods or   partial deliveries, e.g. for production facilities, (Bennett/BB, 534). Instead of setting dates for delivery, there might be agreement in that deliveries can be asked for when needed.

The basic problem here, on the one hand, is to make the *rules governing avoidance of contract* (Articles 49 and 64) *applicable to each and every partial delivery* and, on the other, to punish the violation of obligations in regard to a partial delivery only in regard to that partial delivery. Under certain circumstances, however, there will be consequences for the contract as a whole. In this regard the provisions of Article 73 are similar to those of Article 51. Vilus (Dubrovnik, 245) believes that Article 73 represents application of the rule of Article 72. This is true, however, only in respect of paragraphs 2 and 3. For Article 73, paragraph 1, to be applied, a fundamental breach of contract *has* to have *occurred*, whereas under Article 72 a breach of contract is *to be anticipated*.

2. Article 73 is *not limited to the obligations of the seller*. The buyer, too, can breach a contract in regard to some of the partial deliveries, either by not taking delivery of the goods or not paying for them (e.g. advance payment may have been agreed in respect to each instalment, Bennett/BB, 534). The rule is applied here directly and not merely by analogy (as says the 1985 CISG Commentary; c. also Honnold, 404; Bennett/BB, 533). Article 73 is not applied to cases where the buyer of a delivery, as a whole, has the right to pay in instalments (Knapp/BB, 447, wants to have Article 73 applied here analogously.) In this context, non-fulfilment of the obligation to pay in instalments may lead to avoidance of contract under Articles 64 or 72.

3. As to the characteristics of a fundamental breach of contract compare Article 25. Whether or not non-performance of an obligation relating to an instalment constitutes a fundamental breach of contract, will in the first place have to be clarified in regard to that instalment itself. Only from the *context of the contract as a whole* can it be judged whether conclusions will have to be drawn for future (paragraph 2) and earlier (paragraph 3) instalments (O. R., 54).

If the buyer is not sure whether a fundamental breach of contract occurred he can proceed following Article 51 and set the seller a *Nachfrist* to perform his obligations. If the latter does not do so within the additional period so set, the former will have the right to avoid the contract (Bennett/BB, 536).

4. Regarding the consequences of an avoided contract compare Articles 49 and 64.

5. The obligee can, as a rule, suspend performance of the contract only in respect to the instalment in question, which would amount to a *modification of contract* (a reduction of the quantity and the price of the goods) (Bennett/BB, 534).

6. The declaration to avoid a contract is subject to Article 27. *No prior notice* is required (as in Article 72). *Neither* is there under paragraphs 1 and 3 *a time limit for making the declaration*, whereas a reasonable time is required under paragraph 2 (note 9).

7. Unlike in paragraph 1, the failure by one party to perform any of his obligations in respect of any instalment need not be a fundamental breach of contract. *Also a simple breach of contract* may lead to the conclusion that a fundamental breach might be committed in the future (Bennett/BB, 535).

The grounds for this assumption are similar to the circumstances explained in the context of Articles 71 and 72. However, neither a deterioration of the creditworthiness nor a declaration of an intention not to perform are sufficient; there must be an actual breach of contract (Bennett/BB, 536 fol).

8. Since the breach of contract in regard to former installments does not necessarily have had to be fundamental in character, the *contract cannot be avoided in respect of instalments already delivered.*

9. What *time is reasonable* depends, among other things, on the length of the interval between the latest and the next instalment and/or its reception and payment.

10. Reference is made here, like in Article 72, to a fundamental breach of contract to occur in the future. While under the preceding article the entire contract may be avoided, it can here *only* be an *avoidance for the future* (Bennett/BB, 536).

11. Unlike paragraphs 1 and 2 which grant both parties the right to avoid the contract, paragraph 3 refers exclusively to the rights of the buyer.

If the buyer wants to avoid the contract not only in regard to the latest, but also to earlier and future instalments, he has to declare so at the same time.

12. Earlier deliveries may well have been faultless, and a fundamental breach of contract does not necessarily have to be expected in regard to future deliveries (Bennett/BB, 535).

13. Honnold (406 fol) mentions as an example the delivery of several machines which were designed to perform a series of interrelated production operations, the second of which was so defective that the defect could neither be cured nor repaired, not even by a machine of another manufacturer.

The Secretariat's commentary (O. R., 54) notes that the purpose for which the goods are to be used may require that all instalments of raw materials, colouring, semi-finished products etc. come from the same source.

14. It is not sufficient that the buyer alone knew of the interdependence; the *seller, too, has to be aware of that interdependence.* If the interdependence of the instalments is not clear from itself, the buyer has to inform the seller accordingly.

15. It does not suffice that the buyer informs the seller of the interdependence of the instalments during performance; he should rather *reveal the purpose* of the goods to the seller already *at the conclusion of the contract* (c. here Article 35, paragraph 2, subpara. (b)).

Section II
Damages

Article 74

(General rule for calculation of damages)

Damages for breach of contract[1] by one party consist[6] of a sum equal to the loss[4], including loss of profit[5], suffered by the other party[2] as a consequence[3] of the breach. Such damages may not exceed the loss which the party in breach foresaw or ought to have foreseen[8] at the time of the conclusion of the contract[7], in the light[9] of the facts and matters of which he then knew or ought to have known[10], as a possible consequence of the breach of contract.

1. Irrespective of which obligation was not performed, *any breach of contract* by one party who causes damage to the other party, under Articles 45 and/or 61 (c. note 6), *entails the right* for the latter *to claim damages.* Damages mostly are caused by delay in delivery, non-delivery, or delivery of non-conforming goods. They are not so often caused by the buyer's refusal to take delivery. Damages caused by delayed payment of non-payment of the price are in general cured by the entitlement to interest under Article 78 (Honnold, 409). *As an exception, compensation for damages is granted in the case of breaches of contract which have not been committed* but are expected to occur in the future, and which, for the purposes of Article 74, have to be interpreted as committed (Article 72; Stoll/Freiburg, 258). *Damages may also be claimed in the case of violations of auxiliary obligations,* i.e. non-provision of information under Article 32, paragraph 3, or failure to give notice under Article 32, paragraph 1 (differently Stoll/Freiburg, 260). Some of the acts described to be obligations under the CISG are, however, nothing but mere incumbencies whose non-performance does not entail the right to claim damages but results in a loss of rights (like the obligation to examine the

goods and the buyer's obligation to give notice under Articles 38 and 39, Stoll/Freiburg, 260).

Unlike in ULIS in regard to the claiming of damages, it does not matter under the CISG whether or not the contract has been declared avoided. The CISG, nonetheless, in Articles 75 and 76 contains *specific rules to be applied to the measurement of damages after the contract has been avoided.* In contrast, Article 74 provides the more general rule which is applied whenever Articles 75 and 76 cannot be invoked, irrespective of whether or not the contract has been avoided (Knapp/BB, 539).

Damages can be claimed no matter whether the breach of contract has been *culpably* committed intentionally or negligently or in any other way. The mere fact of a breach of contract is sufficient. Compensation for damages is, however, limited by the foreseeability of the loss (note 8), on the one hand, and by the exemptions provided for in Articles 79 and 80, on the other (Knapp/BB, 540).

2. Third parties cannot deduce claims from the CISG. *Claims outside the contract* that are asserted against the parties of the international sales contract have to be invoked pursuant to the applicable *domestic law.* If a third party has suffered a loss which the other party would have to compensate, such loss could be cured by recourse when it was the result of a breach of contract.

3. Apart from the breach of contract and the damages suffered is the relationship between them, the *causality of the damage,* which is the third condition for damages to be claimed. The CISG does not give a direct answer to the question of whether compensation is to be made only in regard to the losses suffered directly as a result of the breach of contract or whether it extends to losses that are the result of that causality. It can be deduced from the context that also indirect losses are to be compensated, provided that they were foreseeable by the party in breach (Knapp/BB, 540).

4. It is the *entire loss* suffered as a result of the breach of contract (excluding the non-foreseeable, c. note 8) which has to be compensated, *including possible losses that are the result of defects.* Article 74 is, however, not applied to claims for damages in the case of the death or the bodily injury of a person caused by the goods, irrespective of whether or not the buyer himself or a third person is involved (c. Article 5). Injuries to persons cannot be claimed, not even by recourse (Stoll/Freiburg, 291 in response to Basedow/Freiburg, 289).

The CISG only knows of compensation in money; *restitution in kind* as foreseen in some legal systems (e.g. 249 German BGB) is *excluded*. (See, however, the possibilities for the cure of defects prior to (Article 37) and after the period for delivery (Article 48). Possible losses are not compensated in this way, the right to claim damages persists.)

The principle of full compensation includes both the effective loss, i.e. a *reduction in the fortune* of the party in loss (*damnum emergens*), *and the loss in profit* (*lucrum cessans*).

Article 74 does not provide for multiple claims for damages as it is given, e.g. as punitive damage, in American law. The CISG does, however, not exclude relevant contractual agreements.

The *calculation of the damage* in detail may cause *manifold problems*, not only when the buyer suffers a loss because the delivered machines do not function properly; the delivered materials cannot be used as planned; there is a delay in repairs or in the delivery of spare parts and repairs have to be effected by the buyer himself; but also when the seller having been notified by the buyer that he would not take delivery of the goods purchased, discontinues production of the same goods (for examples see the Secretariat's Commentary, O. R., 59; and Knapp/BB, 545 fol).

It is *disputed* to what extent damage can be claimed for losses suffered in connection with the *decline of exchange rates* (J. Hellner, "The Limits of Contractual Damages in the Scandinavian Law of Sales", 10 Scandinavian Studies, p. 60). While Basedow (Freiburg, 288) is against it, Stoll (Freiburg, 266) believes that an abstract calculation should not be permitted, but that concrete proof of damages should be possible where there was a decline in the exchange rate or the purchasing power of the buyer's money during the delay in payment.

5. As to the loss of profit, there are several possibilities. It may be questioned whether the injured party is entitled to recover the loss of profit he actually suffered, the exact profit he could have expected, or an average profit to be expected at a certain time in a certain place. It is unclear also for which period of time the loss of profit can be measured. In this context, however, the obligation to mitigate losses under Article 77 is to be taken into account.

Honnold (416) holds that what matters is the *loss which the injured party in fact suffered*. The seller would suffer no loss if he could sell the goods not taken by the buyer elsewhere in times of great demand. The buyer would suffer no loss if he could continue production by purchasing substitute goods meeting his needs. According to Knapp (BB, 544), one should proceed from the loss which the injured party suffered in fact or from the profit that could have been expected, setting no time limit but only the condition that the loss was foreseeable. He rejects a calculation of future profit by a lumpsum. He does not exclude, however, that the injured party may repeatedly be adjudicated the loss of profit by the courts if the conditions of Article 74 apply.

A loss of profit is, therefore, not a category which can be calculated only for the sale or resale of goods; it also includes the loss incurred because of interruptions of production as a consequence of the delivery of defective machinery (von Hoffmann/Freiburg, 302).

6. Article 74 itself does not stipulate a claim for damages, but is applied when a party under Articles 45 or 61 is entitled to claim damages. In compensating the loss suffered, the injured party shall be placed in the same economic position he would have been had there been no breach of contract by the other party (Honnold, 408; Knapp/BB, 543). Insofar as the contract is avoided the specific provisions of Articles 75 and 76 are to bring about the same result (losses which cannot be compensated invoking the two Articles, can be so compensated under the broader rule of Article 74).

The party who claims damages has to provide evidence of the damage and must, at the same time, prove the causality between the breach of contract and the loss suffered.

7. It is not sufficient that the party in breach could at the time of the delivery of the defective goods or at the time of performance of the non-delivered goods foresee the damage to be caused by the breach of contract. The party in breach rather should have been able to *foresee* the damage *at the time of the conclusion of the contract*. He should at the time of the conclusion of the contract be in a position to calculate his risk (c. also Article 35, paragraph 2, subpara. (b); and Article 42, paragraph 1, subpara. (a)).

8. What is meant here is to *foresee subjectively* (Vilus/Dubrovnik, 247), but the Convention does not stop at that. Insofar as damage is a completely normal consequence of a breach of contract, it should have been foreseen (note 10). However, it is not quite exact to state that the subjective foreseeability does not matter (so Stoll/Freiburg, 260). Subjective foreseeability plays a role when the resulting loss is

above what would have been regarded as the normal measure by any reasonable person, but actually was foreseen by the party in breach.

The *foreseeability does* not *refer* to a certain sum of money equal to the loss, even though the wording of this rule may suggest it, but *to the possibility of a loss* as a consequence of the breach of contract as such and the extent of the possible loss (Knapp/BB, 541).

It is above all the Anglo-American (e.g. 2-715, paragraph 2 UCC) and the French legal families (Article 1150 Code civil) which provide for a limitation of damages by way of foreseeability. Other legal systems come to similar conclusions using the so-called theory of adequacy.

In some legal systems the *limitation of damages* by foreseeability as such is *restricted when the breach of contract was committed intentionally*. No such rule exists in the CISG (O. R., 60). Such a rule could at best be deduced from the underlying general principles of the Convention (Article 7, paragraph 2; Article 40 and Article 43, paragraph 2).

9. The *facts and matters must* have existed at the time of the conclusion of the contract and/or must *be foreseeable at the conclusion of the contract*, like seasonal market fluctuations, difficulties in transport caused by bad weather etc. They may, however, also result from the specific purpose of the goods which the buyer has made known to the seller. In the leading English decision, Hadley v. Baxendale (1854, 9 Exch. 341; explained in detail in Cheshire/Fifoot, The Law of Contract, 1969, p. 546 fol), the defendant did not know the purpose and the facts and matters, the essential condition for the use of the goods. (A carter was supposed to carry a broken crankshaft for a miller from Gloucester to Greenwich where it was to serve as a model for a new one. Since the carter was late in transport, the mill was inoperative longer than it would have been without the committed breach of contract.) To what extent the party in breach is capable of taking the circumstances into consideration also depends on his position (e.g. manufacturer or trader, c. Article 35, note 8).

10. This wording serves to *objectify the foreseeability*. What matters is not anymore the actual foreseeability, rather, it is the foreseeability which can be expected from a reasonable party in the same situation.

A party in breach can thus not be freed from his obligation to pay damages by proving that he did not foresee the damage. Knapp (BB, 541) mentions that the party claiming damages need not prove that the party in breach really foresaw the loss; rather it will be enough if he proves that the party in breach was objectively in a position to foresee it. We believe that the party who claims damages need not prove one nor the other. It will be sufficient for him to prove the breach of contract, the damage and the causality between them (note 6).

It is up to the party in breach to object that the damage could not be foreseen. He would have to prove that the loss could not be foreseen by him.

It is obvious that a party who fears suffering an extraordinary loss as a consequence of the breach of contract by the other party, should make this known to the latter at the conclusion of the contract so as to enable him to calculate the risk. *What should have been foreseen* in each case will often have *to be judged* retroactively *by a court or an arbitral tribunal.* Already in the jurisdiction in regard to ULIS, which in Article 82 contained the same rule of foreseeability, the following cases became apparent:

(a) the cost of a substitute transaction and the loss of resale profit are foreseeable;

(b) missed uses of the goods to be delivered are also part of the generally foreseeable damage;

(c) additional costs for transportation, storage and insurance are also foreseeable; and

(d) even the loss of clients of the buyer because of the defect in the goods was characterized as foreseeable.

Only the loss suffered from a decline in the currency which occurred as a consequence of the delay in payment was predominantly rejected as not foreseeable.

(In this context see Schlechtriem, Kaufrecht, p. 51 fol; and Schlechtriem/Magnus, 410 fol.)

Article 75

(Damages in case of avoidance and substitute transactions)

If the contract is avoided[1] and if, in a reasonable manner[2] and within a reasonable time[3] after avoidance, the buyer has bought[4] goods in replacement or the seller has resold[4] the goods, the party claiming damages may recover the difference[5] between the contract price and the price in the substitute transaction as well as any further[6] damages recoverable[7] under article 74.

1. It is a *condition for the calculation of damages* under Article 75 *that the contract has been avoided* (before) (c. Articles 49; 61 and 72; 73; and 81). Otherwise, if the seller has declared the contract avoided, he can sell the goods and if the buyer has declared the contract avoided, he can procure the goods.

2. It is to be interpreted in such a way that the party who is true to the contract must try to effect the substitute transaction either as the buyer at the lowest possible price or as the seller at the highest possible price (Vilus/Dubrovnik, 248). Other contractual stipulations may have to be taken into account, e.g. the duration of the period of guarantee. *An unreasonable substitute transaction cannot be considered to measure the damages.* This follows, *inter alia*, from the obligation under Article 77 to mitigate losses. Jurisdiction in regard to Article 85 ULIS, which contains a relevant rule, in respect of the reasonable manner, called for a cautious and circumspect businessman (Schlechtriem/Magnus, 454 fol).

3. The *substitute transaction* has to be effected *within a reasonable time*. This is to prevent the loss from further increasing under worsening market conditions. ULIS made no mention of a reasonable time. It was probably assumed that the reasonable time followed from the condition of a reasonable manner (Knapp/BB, 549).

4. It is not at issue here which substitute transaction could be carried out. This is provided for in Article 76. The claim for damages on the basis of *Article 75 presupposes a substitute transaction or a substitute sale to have taken place.* Mere offers are not considered (also in regard to the reasonableness of the substitute transaction; c. Schlechtriem/Magnus, 455).

The party who is true to the contract does not always have an obligation to effect a substitute transaction, unless the loss can be mitigated in comparison to the calculation under Article 76.

5. The *difference between the price of the substitute transaction and the price of the avoided original contract is the loss to be recovered*. Here we are dealing with a concrete calculation of damages (in contrast to the abstract way of Article 76) as is preferred in many legal systems, including the UCC (2-706 and 2-712) (Honnold, 413).

If the party who is true to the contract can carry out the substitute transaction according to the original terms, he does not suffer losses (but compare Article 74, note 5). If the terms he can agree are even better, he may keep the difference and need not hand it over, for instance to the party in breach.

The difference in price between the avoided contract and the contract which was newly concluded can, however, be the result of different terms, e.g. guarantee, or of different auxiliary costs, e.g. packaging, transportation). Due account has to be taken of this situation, i.e. the price difference has to be adjusted accordingly (Knapp/BB, 550).

6. To carry out a substitute transaction requires *additional costs* which are *not covered and compensated for by the difference in price*. If the substitute transaction had been possible without avoidance of the original contract, the seller would suffer further losses in regard to the profit he missed.

7. *Further damages* are recoverable under the general rule of Article 74. This means, however, that any further damage is limited as to its foreseeability. In this case, too, it is a prerequisite that the injured party claims damages and proves the loss.

Article 76

(Damages in case of avoidance and no substitute transactions)

(1) If the contact is avoided[1] and there is a current price[2] for the goods, the party claiming damages may, if he has not made a purchase or resale under article 75[3], recover[7] the difference[4] between the price fixed by the contract and the current price at the time of avoidance[5] as well as any further[6] damages recoverable under article 74. If, however, the party claiming damages has avoided the contract after taking over the goods[8], the current price at the time of such taking over[9] shall be applied instead of the current price at the time of avoidance.

(2) For the purposes of the preceding paragraph, the current price is the price prevailing at the place[10] where delivery of the goods should have been made or, if there is no current price at that place, the price at such other place as serves as a reasonable substitute[11], making due allowance for differences in the price of transporting the goods.

1. Just like Article 75 this rule presupposes that the original contract has actually been avoided (c. Article 75, note 1). To avoid speculation the *time limit for avoidance has to be taken into consideration*. Insofar as there are no time limits for avoidance of a contract, Article 77 is to be consulted in regard to the obligation to mitigate losses.

2. The concept of a *current price does not presuppose official or unofficial market quotations* as is required in the case of stock exchange goods. Any goods that are available on the market or elsewhere do have a market price. An exception could be goods which are made under special order by the buyer and for which damages would have to be calculated under Article 74 and not Article 76 (Knapp/BB, 557).

3. The *abstract calculation of the damages* provided for in Article 76 is *possible only when the obligee has not effected a substitute transaction* (Schlechtriem, 91). The reasons for his inaction are irrelevant here (Knapp/BB, 553).

If the obligee effects a cover transaction and then measures his damages according to the abstract method because this is more favourable to him, he acts dishonestly and violates the principle of good faith. In such a case, the obligor can remind him of his duty to mitigate losses under Article 77.

The abstract method of calculating damages does not require the obligee to have tried concluding a substitute transaction (Stoll/Freiburg, 266).

It cannot be excluded that the obligee *first measures the loss abstractly and then proceeds to a cover transaction*. There can be no objection against it if this is more favourable to him and if, in so doing, he uses the market developments in his favour. Should it become clear, however, that a cover transaction is possible only under more unfavourable terms and this is transaction carried out within a reasonable time, additional differences in price can be claimed as further damages (note 6).

When the obligee purchases and sells continuously and, therefore, no contract can be qualified as a substitute purchase or sale, losses can also be calculated abstractly under Article 76 (O. R., 60 fol). Some authors assume that it is always at the buyer's discretion to decide whether he measures his losses according to the abstract or the concrete method, hence an abstract calculation would be admissible in the case of a substitute transaction (so Herber, 45 fol).

But an abstract calculation that is preceded by a cover transaction is admissible and advisable only when the cover transaction was not effected in a reasonable manner (Article 75, note 2).

4. Compare Article 75, note 4. No foreseeability is required in regard to this price difference (Knapp/BB, 558).

5. This time of avoidance was the result of a lengthy discussion at the diplomatic conference (O. R., 222 fol, 394 fol, 415). The draft CISG stated as the *decisive time* such time at which the injured party first had the right to declare the contract avoided. This was supposed to prevent speculation on the part of the obligee. There was also fear of too much discretion on the part of the courts, and a decision was taken in favour of the *actual time of avoidance*. However, to largely exclude speculations, at least on the part of the buyer, another time was fixed for the taking over of the goods (note 9).

Hence the time of avoidance is relevant for cases of non-delivery (Article 49) or not taking delivery and/or non-payment (Article 64) as well as early avoidance of the contract (Article 72).

6. Such further damages may occur when the loss is calculated abstractly at first, but it becomes clear later that a cover transaction is possible only under more unfavourable terms.

Additional cost in doing business or lost profit (Article 74, note 5) can also constitute further damages, even if there is no difference between the contract price and the price in the substitute transaction, e.g. if prices have fallen in the case of an intended resale of the goods. In such a case further damages are the only losses suffered (Knapp/BB, 554).

7. In the case of such further damages the foreseeability rule again applies. Compare also Article 75, note 7.

8. Thus this can only be the buyer. To ensure the *symmetry of the rights and obligations of both the seller and the buyer* the Convention generally uses an abstract language. This is criticized by Hellner (85) who considers it a serious mistake to believe that impartiality could be achieved in establishing identical rules to govern the obligations of both parties and breaches of contract by both sides.

9. At that time the buyer may not have been aware of the reason for avoiding the contract. This is hardly understandable according to Schlechtriem (Lausanne, 92).

The intention of fixing such an early time is *to prevent the buyer from speculating* on the movement of market prices and delaying avoidance of the contract (Knapp/BB, 556). On the other hand, an economic disadvantage may result for the buyer because of price movements from the time of the taking over of the goods to the time of avoidance. He may prevent this, however, in carrying out a cover transaction and claiming damages under Article 75.

10. The *decisive place is the place where the delivery was supposed to take place or* the place, if the goods were taken over, *where the delivery actually took place*. According to Article 31 this is the place of delivery. While this place may indeed be reasonable to the seller, it may well entail difficulties for the buyer. Since the place of delivery in many cases, e.g. handing over to the first carrier, is located in the seller's country, it can be difficult for the buyer to prove damages based on market prices in the seller's country (Honnold, 415).

11. It cannot be generally defined which other place might be considered as reasonable. One may find it difficult to imagine why there should be no current price at the contractual place of delivery. Rather it suggests that there is no current price at all (note 2).

When another place is found, the differing cost of transportation is to be included in calculating the price difference.

Article 77

(Mitigation of damages)

A party who relies on a breach of contract[1] must take such measures as are reasonable[2] in the circumstances to mitigate the loss, including loss of profit[3], resulting from the breach. If he fails to take such measures, the party in breach may claim a reduction in the damages[4] in the amount by which the loss should have been mitigated[5].

1. A party who relies on a breach of contract can chose among several remedies (compare in particular Articles 45 and 61). Reference is made here only to a party claiming damages. The rule of Article 77 does not apply to other remedies (c. also note 4).

2. The *party who is true to the contract* cannot sit and wait for the other party to breach the contract, but *must become active in order to minimize the loss* or to prevent it at all (Knapp/BB, 560).

No exceptional efforts are required from that party; he only has to take such measures as are reasonable under the circumstances. Such measures may frequently include a cover purchase or sale. It can also include the possibility that the buyer himself remedies defective goods delivered to the buyer (Knapp/BB, 560).

Costs which the party threatened by loss incurs for the measures he takes to mitigate his losses can also be *claimed compensation for* even when the, otherwise reasonable, measures were taken in vain (Knapp(BB, 561).

Although there is *no obligation to avoid the contract* even if the other party has committed or is expected to commit a fundamental breach of contract (Articles 49 and 64), avoidance of the contract may be one of the reasonable measures which help to mitigate the losses of the injured party.

If reasonable measures can be taken before an impending breach of contract, they have to be taken by the party threatened by loss (Knapp/BB, 566 fol). Such measures could include for instance suspension of performance under Article 71. We are faced here with an *obligation to mitigate losses.* But non-fulfilment of this obligation by one party does not entail a claim for damages but rather leads to a situation where the party who is true to the contract cannot claim full compensation for damages. The rules governing the mitigation of damages are consistent with normal commercial practices (Honnold, 420) and can be found in many legal systems.

3. Compare Article 74, note 5.

4. Of particular importance at the diplomatic conference was the question of whether the obligation to mitigate losses indeed referred only to the reduction of damages. An American proposal to *extend that principle to other remedies* was rejected. The example given related to a seller who continues manufacture of a machine even though the buyer has informed him that he has no more use for the machine ordered and would refuse to take delivery of it. If the seller nonetheless continues manufacture of the machine and sues

for performance, i.e. taking delivery and payment, he will have no obligation to mitigate losses because he claims the price and no damages (O. R., 396).

Regarding this problem it was suggested to treat the obligation to mitigate losses under Article 77, paragraph 1, as a genuine obligation whose breach will entail the obligation to compensate for damage. In the case of the example given, the buyer would have to pay the full price, but he would also have the right to claim damages (Hellner, 99; agreeing Schlechtriem/Lausanne, 170; like before Schlechtriem, 93).

Other authors obviously do not see any solution to this problem but rather believe that the obligation to mitigate damages does not have priority over the right to performance (Knapp/BB, 564; like the 1985 CISG Commentary 1985, 150).

One could also imagine invoking Article 77 analogously on the basis of the principle of good faith. As can be seen from the genesis of the diplomatic conference, it was a lack of time at the end of the conference which prevented a proper solution (Honnold, 421). There was agreement in that Article 77 should be broadly interpreted (Knapp/BB, 566).

Stoll, too, (Freiburg, 269) holds that the basic idea of Article 77, i.e. that the obligee should have taken measures to mitigate losses, must not be lost because of the obligee's choosing of other remedies, i.e. that he claims payment of the price instead of damages.

5. If the loss could have been prevented, there would have been the chance of *reducing the damages down to zero*. Here the CISG follows the rule of avoidable loss as applied by the Anglo-American legal family. In contrast to 254 BGB, the CISG does not know of any participatory fault, and thus offers no room for the judge's discretion (Stoll/Freiburg, 268; critical Schlechtriem, 92, who compares Article 77 to 254 BGB). Several examples of how to reduce the damages are given in the Secretariat's commentary (O. R., 61; also Knapp/BB, 562 fol).

Section III

Interest

Article 78[1]

(Interest)

If a party fails to pay[3] the price or any other sum that is in arrears[4], the other party is entitled to interest[2] on it, without prejudice to any claim for damages recoverable under article 74[5].

1. The regulation of interest has caused considerable *difficulties*, both in preparing and holding the diplomatic conference. Those difficulties are reflected in the modesty of the results. In ULIS there was a rule for interest in arrears in the event of payment in arrears of the price which provided for one per cent above the official discount rate in the creditor's country (Article 83). No agreement could be achieved in preparing the draft CISG, however, so that the interest is mentioned only in what is now Article 84, paragraph 1, hence interest on the price to be paid back (Nicholas/BB, 568).

The subject was taken up repeatedly at the diplomatic conference. Religiously motivated prohibition or restriction of interest in Islamic countries played a role in the debates, but by no means a decisive one (O. R., 416 fol). The main contentious issue was rather how the *interest rate* should be calculated. Given the considerable movement in the money market, there were only few delegations which, like that of the FRG, were in favour of a fixed interest rate, as a minimum (O.R., 416).But flexible interest rates were only possible through reference to an existing interest level. Insofar the discussion revolved around the question of whether the interest level in the *creditor's country* or the one in the *debtor's country* should be decisive. At the time of the diplomatic conference there were serious differences between the Western industrialized countries, where the amount of interest is formed in the market (naturally influenced by political measures) and had at that time reached considerable amounts, and most of the at that time called socialist countries where the interest was fixed by law and relatively low. It was against this background that the Western industrialized countries aimed towards interest to be set according to the level of the creditor's country. This would have meant that debtors from those countries would have had to pay low interest to creditors from Eastern countries, but by contrast, debtors from the latter countries high interest. It was pointed out in favour of this variant that the creditor would have to procure financing in replacement in his country. The Eastern countries, and also many developing countries, opted for the reverse solution pointing to the fact that they would have to procure the means needed in their commercial relations with Western partners in high-interest countries (c. in regard to the overall subject O. R., 223 fol; 388 fol, 415 fol, 429 fol). These differences of opinion caused by the differing interests could not be overcome even by compromise proposals (O. R., 138). Furthermore, in light of the divergent methods used in forming interest in the countries involved, difficulties of a substantive and legal, technical kind become apparent in *concretely determining* the level of interest by reference. It was impossible, in the end, to come to a basic rule.

2.1. One of the main ideas of this article is the *general entitlement* to interest which is rather far-reaching (note 3) in substance. The entitlement to interest under the CISG is, in our view, characterized above all by two features: its normativity and its absoluteness.

Its *normativity* consists in that the amount of interest (however not by the Convention itself - note 2.2.) is fixed *a priori* and irrespective of the damage which is caused by the arrears in payment. Insofar the interest is comparable to a penalty. There seems to be far-reaching agreement on this principle.

Absoluteness means that the existence of grounds for release cannot remove the entitlement to interest. But, a reservation has to be made here, namely that this is not true of a failure caused by the other party's act or omission (Article 80). The impediments under Article 79, however, do not free from the obligation to pay interest (see also Schlechtriem, 94, and following him somewhat restrainedly, Nicholas/BB, 571, and Stoll/Freiburg, 279). A point in favour of this is that the entitlement to interest is not mentioned in Article 79, paragraph 5, but could be explained with the genesis of the Convention. We believe, however, that the economic background is also justification for such a solution. The party who does not pay a debt that is due, disposes of the sum of money required for it and/or does not have to procure it. He thus has an advantage vis-a-vis the other party which is compensated by the entitlement to interest of that party. This applies, in particular, to restrictions in the transfer of currency, often cited as an example, which shall not have the effect of a reason for exemption here.

But there are also voices who, assuming that interest is a part of the damages, want to permit an *exemption* on the ground of impediments (van der Velden, 405). But for the reasons given above we cannot join them.

2.2. Since the amount of interest is not determined, this shortcoming is to be compensated above all by *agreement between the parties*. These cannot, because of the CISG, be countered anymore by national prohibitive rules for interest, which in many Islamic countries have been considerably relaxed in regard to the economic sector (e.g. Article 455 fol, Algerian Civil Code). Insofar a specific rule of the Convention supersedes the general rule of Article 4, sub-para. (a) according to which the Convention does not cover questions of validity (c. also Honnold, 424; for a similar consideration see Article 68, note 5.4.).

The entitlement to interest in abstract terms is not limited by a ceiling so that in our view also, *national restrictions in regard to* the amount of *interest* do not prevail over farther-reaching party agreements. But these could be measured against relevant general provisions of national law which are aimed against unfair (immoral) behaviour (Article 4, notes 5 and 6).

When the parties have agreed the amount of interest, only in regard to *specific claims for payment*, e.g. delay in paying the price, it is in our view recommendable, because of the difficulties in determining the amount of interest (which we will discuss in the following) to apply this solution analogously to other financial claims. Hence, the agreements between the parties should, so to speak, serve as the general basis for taking a decision (Article 7, paragraph 2) by analogy, insofar as there are no other clues.

Where the parties have agreed nothing, the amount of interest will have to be calculated on the basis of the *applicable domestic law* (Schlechtriem, 94; Nicholas/BB, 570; Magnus, 140 fol). This is, in general, the subsidiary law applicable to the sales contract. No special connecting points seem to have developed for the entitlement to interest. When the applicable law does not provide for the calculation of the amount of interest, as can be the case in countries which do not generally forbid an entitlement to interest, e.g. Algeria, the claim does not in our view become unenforceable as Schlechtriem thinks (94, Note 414). Rather, recourse should be had to the level of interest applied in the respective country to similar transactions. This may seem formal, in particular when the parties have agreed to invoke a neutral law as the subsidiary law applicable. Such approach corresponds, as we believe, best to the structures founded in the CISG. Besides, the way pointed to by Nicholas (BB, 570) to take into consideration the cost of credit at the creditor's place of business, without examination of the concrete costs incurred, does not seem practicable because the solution aspired to by the Western industrialized countries, which was not adopted at the diplomatic conference, would in part be introduced by way of interpretation. Other countries could then be inclined to interpret into the Convention their own rejected proposals. This would give rise to disharmony in the taking of decisions. The suggestion by Stoll (Freiburg, 279 fol), who seeks to provide grounds for special connecting factors leading to the law of the seller's country, is aiming towards a similar solution. The seller is the typical but not exclusive creditor. Therefore, the reasoning of Stoll is not conclusive, in particular not in the case where the buyer demands refunding of the price (Article 84, paragraph 1). Where a way is really to be sought via special connecting factors, and when account is taken of the arguments expounded in Vienna, more speaks in favour of following the proposal by Basedow (Freiburg, 288 fol) and relying on the statute of currency.

Toward a similar direction tends the proposal by Honnold (424), with which van der Velden (406 fol) obviously sympathizes, namely to take into account the *cost of credit* at the place where the creditor has indeed gotten his supplies. Better account could so be taken of the interests of those countries which do not have their own domestic currency markets. But, as the author notices himself, the fact that the interest claim would thereby move very near a claim for damages speaks against it. This could be further objectivized insofar as the interest that is customary at the international level in relation to currency could serve as a basis where such is in existence. The proposal in this regard includes ideas worth reflecting on where the filling of the gaps of domestic law is concerned. But it is conceived still further and makes reliance on national law superfluous.

3. Of greatest practical relevance is interest on price claims. It was, however, useful to go beyond ULIS and mention *other claims*, if only to avoid reverse conclusions. In this context, however, the question arose among authors from the Anglo-American legal family whether other sums were only meant to be such which are already liquidated, for which interest could be claimed under that legal system, or sums that have not yet been specified (in particular Honnold, 424 fol - see note 4).

4.1. From the formulation that interest is to be paid on sums in arrears we draw the conclusion that interest is to be paid *from the time when the respective sum is due.* For lack of deviating agreements the becoming due is, in the event of price claims, determined by Article 58 .

4.2. It is less clear when most of the other claims become due. It could be reflected on whether this can be determined by analogy to Article 10 of the Limitation Convention. Such a complex interpretation of Conventions which relate to one another is desirable even when it comes across difficulties where the States Parties are not identical. In the present case, however, it does not seem to be of great help because, in the context of limitation, the becoming due has to be determined in such a way that it becomes effective when the parties do not call in their claims, whereas the assertion of claims is to be demanded under the aspect of interest.

Without being able to enter into detail in respect of each concrete claim, we believe that in regard to claims for damages, reimbursement of expenses and reduction of the price, hence secondary claims which emerge only when primary obligations under the contract are breached, from the aspect of interest, one should proceed on the assumption that they become due when they have been *liquidated* vis-a-vis the other party and in the amount in which later they turn out to be justified. Another aspect is that they should have accrued at the time when they were charged and were not just expected in the future.

It should be admitted, however, that a *general principle* of this substance, in the meaning of Article 7, cannot simply be deduced from the Convention. Indicators for it are offered in general by the reverse conclusion from Article 59 as well as, more specifically, in Articles 39, 43 and 46, which are limited, however, to non-conformity or lack of freedom from third party rights or claims.

We wish to bring the developed principle up for discussion. It places the decisive time between others that are possible or practiced, like the time of the breach of contract and of the assertion of a claim, and does in a way also consider the liquidation requirement of the Anglo-American law.

The principle developed here for secondary claims is, in our view, also applicable to *primary claims* whose becoming due is not determined otherwise, like claims for reimbursement of auxiliary/additional expenses which are not included in the price, hence expenses for packaging, transport and insurance, as well as customs duties and taxes. They would become due with the issuance of the invoice.

4.3. Article 84, paragraph 1 expressly stipulates that on a *price to be refunded*, interest must be paid from the date on which the price was originally paid. The same should apply to the refunding of the reduced price under Article 50.

4.4. The *obligation to pay interest ends* with the time of payment which is relatively uncomplicated. The same rules apply for the payment of interest as for the payment of the principal claim. To the latter in turn Articles 56, 57 and 58 should apply directly or by analogy. Since the payment in many cases is considered as effected only at a later date than that on which the debtor has caused it, a guess will have to be made as to the actual time of payment in calculating interest if the transfer of the principal claim and the interest is made simultaneously.

4.5. *Interest* is usually calculated *on an annual basis.* Hence the question arises whether it should be capitalized respectively after one year, or whether the annual interest rate should be used as the multiplying factor and be multiplied by the entire delay period. In other words: whether compound interest can be claimed. In our view, this is not the case because, among other things, it is not customary in international sales law. There would have to be specific clues for it.

5.1. Another important aspect under the provision on interest in the Convention (Vilus/Dubrovnik, 252) is to clarify that the entitlement to interest does not preclude *claims for damages.* This clarification indicates that damage which exceeds interest can be claimed (Rudolph/Moscow, 92), hence interest can be counted towards the damages even when the two claims have different features.

A claim for damages presupposes a breach of contract, as is the case in regard to the entitlement to interest when one assumes, as we do, that an excusable breach of contract is nonetheless a breach. The main difference, however, is that *exemption* under Article 79 is possible in respect of the obligation to pay damages. Hence, it may happen that there is an entitlement to interest and a damage exceeding interest can be proved, but there will be no right to claim damages because there is an impediment, such as restriction of the transfer of currency. However, as the entitlement to interest and the claim for damages both exist, the claim for damages can compensate for the lack of an interest rate in the CISG, as proves the ruling in a case before the Landgericht Aachen (Judgment of April 3, 1990 - 41 0 189/89, in: RIW, 1990/6, p. 491 fol).

5.2. The *reference to Article 74* here is unfortunate as it suggests the reverse conclusion. Article 77 is not be applied in cases where the calculation of the amount of damages is concerned. This would be completely unjustified and can, therefore, not be meant in our view. A party who had to provide himself with a bridging loan has of course done so at low cost. We hold that the right to claim damages generally follows from Article 45, paragraph 1, subpara. (b) and Article 61, paragraph 1, subpara. (b), and not from Article 74.

Section IV
Exemptions

Introductory remarks

1. The regulation under the law of contracts has two main functions: to optimize cooperation between the parties and to guarantee reliability on the reciprocal promises. In the latter respect it is the provision on responsibility which plays a decisive role insofar as it determines the *consequences of unreliability*. This presupposes a rather clear determination of when there is indeed unreliability. And this is the concern of this Section.

Great demands have to be made on observance by the parties of their contractual promises in international trade. A party who participates in it has to create the necessary prerequisites. This means that *obligations* assumed generally *have to be fulfilled* and that subjective reasons for exemptions, which could amount to the party personally doing his best, cannot be taken into account. Best is not sufficient if it is below standard. Normally, international economic relations do not involve individuals but companies whose efficiency is determined by the totality of its employees and their appropriate management. Also, inability in regard to management or fulfilment of tasks cannot be tolerated. On the other hand, the fact that a party has concluded a contract cannot allow him under any circumstances to rely on the rights attested therein, irrespective of which impediments relate to the other party. Conversely, he cannot absolutely guarantee the fulfilment of his obligations. In concluding a contract, each and every party commits himself to fulfilling his obligations and overcoming normal or contractually assumed difficulties, however not accepting completely unusual difficulties which are the consequence of extraordinary risks. What we are dealing here with is the splitting of risk.

2. There can be no doubt that there is a close kinship with the rule on *risk bearing*. That rule supplements the one on exemptions insofar as it determines the point, in regard to location and time, up to which the seller bears responsibility for the delivery of the goods, hence for the fulfilment of his main obligation. Influences on the goods beyond that point are generally to the detriment of the buyer. When they occur before that point, they cause the seller to lose the right to payment of the price. In regard to further consequences in respect of the obligation to deliver, the rule on responsi-

bility remains decisive in which reasons for exemption play an important role.

3. Exemption is possible for two reasons: because of *impediments* (Article 79) and because of *the act or omission of the other party* (Article 80). The effects of the former are less far-reaching than those of the latter (Article 79, note 13 and Article 80, note 3). As to terminology, we use the term "exemptions" as the generic term for both cases. The notion "impediments" is used in the Convention to describe the disturbance causing the breach of contract (Article 79, paragraph 1) and the disturbance characterized by certain further features which constitutes the ground for an exemption (Article 79, paragraphs. 3 and 4). It is in this latter meaning that we will speak of "grounds for exemption".

A third ground which produces a similar effect as an exemption, *changed circumstances*, including hardship or imprevision, whose typical consequence would be an adjustment of the contract, was not included. This is a relatively new phenomenon in legal relations, and it corresponds to the conservative trend of the CISG in that it does not provide for it. The question arises, therefore, whether recourse is to be had under domestic law as assumes Vischer (Lausanne, 176 fol). At any rate in respect of the work contract covered by the CISG, or whether the Convention in not taking up this problem, has turned against the taking account of changed circumstances. In that case, there would be no gap to be filled by national law, like Honnold (443) and Tallon (BB, 591 fol) suppose.

We also believe that in this matter, recourse should not be had under domestic law because of the great differences which exist and because otherwise damage would be caused to the unification of law. The problem should, however, not be dramatized. Taking a not doctrinal but rather operative approach to its solution, it becomes obvious that the Convention offers *sufficient prerequisites* for it.

To start with, the majority of authors, while making a differentiation in each particular case, recognize that changed circumstances can be impediments in certain cases (note 6.3.). We believe that they constitute a permanent objection not only to claims for damages because of non-performance but, as will still have to be shown (note 13.6.), to the realization of the right to performance. The aggrieved party, hence the partner of the party who is affected by the changed circumstances, thus has only two options left: either to avoid the contract or to accept in this way or another the wishes of the other party to adjust the contract - or wait for better times. This solution resembles the typical legal consequences from changed circumstances. The party who is affected by the changes does not have the right to avoid the contract. This is a general insufficiency of the Convention, which is also true of the impediments (note 13.2.). The partner of that party cannot be forced to accept the adjustment under the CISG. This is not possible under quite a number of other laws. Under common law, courts do not shape contracts. After all, the mentioned objection in fact exercises a pressure to adjust which the courts and above all the arbitral tribunals could use to achieve such adjustment.

4. The grounds for exemption to a certain extent excuse from the *non-compliance with specific obligations,* as it corresponds to continental European legal tradition, and do not refer to the fate of the contract as a whole as is the case under common law (Nicholas, 234 fol). However, the breach of contract caused by the grounds for exemption can constitute a reason for exemption to the other party. Only in this way, as we believe, can the problem of a counter-performance already made be solved. The other party is refunded that payment and also the advantages drawn by the first party from it when he avoids the contract (Article 81 fol - c. also Honnold, 427 fol). Where the grounds for exemption are only temporarily in effect and the contract is to be retained, e.g. when the goods have already been delivered, but the payment is delayed because of restrictions in transfer, we do not see under the Convention any possibility for the restitution of the performance made. Insofar as it has not been made yet, the party who should actually perform, has manifold options to substantiate a suspension of his performance where grounds for exemption as to the payment exist. The provisions on which he would rely include those which require a concrete synallagmatic connection of specific obligations, like those of Articles 57 and 58, and/or those which generally require such a connection, like those of Article 80 and also Article 71 fol.

5. There is, in our view, no doubt in regard to the Convention that a *breach of contract* is always given when the objective facts of a breach have occurred, hence irrespective of whether there are grounds for exemption or not. Exemptions, as can be seen particularly well from the context of impediments, only lead to the removal of certain legal consequences of the breach of contract while others continue to exist. The reason for it is a breach of contract which cannot be eliminated as such by way of exemptions. From this it follows that the term "breach of contract" does not necessarily include an accusation.

Article 79

(Impediments beyond debtor's control)

(1) A party is not liable[1] for a failure to perform any of his obligations if he proves that the failure[2] was due to an impediment[3] beyond his control[4] and that he could not reasonably be expected to have taken the impediment into account[5] at the time of the conclusion of the contract or to have avoided or overcome it or its consequences[6].

(2) If the party's failure is due to the failure by a third person whom he has engaged[7] to perform the whole or a part of the contract, that party is exempt from liability only if:

(a) he is exempt under the preceding paragraph[8]; and

(b) the person whom he has so engaged would be so exempt if the provisions of that paragraph were applied to him[9].

(3) The exemption provided for in this article has effect for the period during which the impediment exists[10].

(4) The party who fails to perform must give notice to the other party of the impediment and its effect on his ability to perform. If the notice is not received by the other party[11] within a reasonable time after the party who fails to perform knew or ought to have known of the impediment, he is liable for damages resulting from such non-receipt[12].

(5) Nothing in this article prevents either party from exercising any right other than to claim damages under this Convention[13].

1.1. It can be seen from paragraph 5 (note 13) that *not being liable* does not go so far as it might seem at first sight.

1.2. It is in our view important to stress that the Convention has developed a *concept of its own in regard to impediments*, which cannot be directly traced back to any national law. This saves from borrowing from a domestic law in interpretation, which could be very misleading, especially when it comes to one's own domestic law. We, therefore, believe that it is not very helpful when Nicholas (Freiburg, 286 fol) tries to prove that the Convention is based on a concept of fault. Possible clues for it from its history can be interpreted differently (Schlechtriem, 95), and representatives of the legal systems which provide for liability in the case of fault do not see that concept implemented in the Convention (Stoll/Freiburg, 270). Vischer (Lausanne, 174) who wants to recognize in the rule of liability under the CISG what he considers as the Anglo-Saxon model, is the - though considerably more restrained - counterpart of Nicholas.

For this reason we are, like Tallon (BB, 595), also *skeptical* in regard to the recommendation by Honnold (434) to adopt the *comparative law approach* when it comes to the interpretation of the grounds for exemption. There are no generally recognized methods which could be used to comprehensively identify the prevailing patterns and trends of modern domestic law which he recommends.

There is, however, another proposal by Honnold (434 fol) which we consider as acceptable, namely to obtain ideas for the interpretation of the grounds for exemption from *contractual practice*. Clauses, model contracts etc. which have prevailed in a certain context, can play a role in this regard. However, the General Conditions of the ECE Nos. 188 and 574 mentioned by Honnold, *inter alia*, do not seem to be the best examples to give because they are quite favourable to the seller and are criticized by the developing countries.

2 . The term *"failure to perform"* is to be conceived here in the broadest sense of the word. Apart from late performance and non-performance it includes, in particular, non-conform performance and relates to the obligations of both the seller and the buyer.

The *possibilities of exemption in the case of non-conformity* are unusual for the common law, so that differences of opinion become visible where interpretation is concerned. The CISG uses the notion "impediments" (in this case in the meaning of disturbances, compare Introductory remarks 3) and no longer mentions "circumstances" as in Article 74 ULIS, the discussion of which had been controversial already at that time. Honnold (430 fol) has tried to assess this fact in such a way as to explain that this modification was to exclude exemption in the event of non-conformity. This is doubted even by other common law representatives (Nicholas, 240), and this has been rightly contradicted by others (Tallon/BB, 579). The clear wording of the introductory part of the article cannot be changed by pretending that an impediment could not cause non-conformity (in this sense also Vischer/Lausanne, 177 fol). But we, too, are of the opinion that these differences of opinion are of little practical weight, because impediments as defined in Article 79, paragraph 1 will seldom be the cause of non-conformity (c. also Stoll/Freiburg, 275).

3.1. The exemption becomes effective when the non-performance, breach of contract, is based on an impediment which cumulatively fulfils *three conditions* (notes 4 - 6). The decisive prerequisite for an impediment to be taken into consideration is its *causality* in regard to the breach of contract. It is also possible that the impediment excuses only part of the breach, like for instance one part of the period of delay where the delivery is not made within the period for delivery.

3.2. When the impediment occurs *during the delay*, its causality for the breach of contract is given only if it had an effect in the case of delivery within the period prescribed (Rudolph/Moscow, 82).

3.3. The causality of the impediment for the breach of contract, in this case by the seller, depends on how much the goods have been *individualized*. The two extremes in this regard are specific and generic obligations. With respect to specific obligations, it should be sufficient for an exemption that the impediment has an effect on the goods themselves. Where limited generic obligations are concerned, which have to be fulfilled by delivering goods from a certain manufacturing plant or by delivering goods from a certain region, from an agreed stock etc., exemption will be granted when the limited generic goods are affected. When it is affected only partly, the buyers to be delivered would have to be supplied in part, where this is possible. Otherwise, the seller should have a choice to decide in good faith who he supplies. In the event of obligations in regard to unlimited generic goods, it will generally be difficult to grant an exemption. The seller may, however, prove that because of impediments he was not in a position to obtain supplies of the generic goods in question. Similarly to Vischer (Lausanne, 178) and unlike Tallon (BB, 582) we are of the opinion that the principle "*genera non pereunt*" cannot be used within the scope of the CISG to prove that exemption is excluded where generic obligations are concerned. Like in the case of obligations in regard to specific goods it will be granted when the goods are clearly identified to the contract with a view to fulfilling generic obligations.

3.4. Unlike Tallon (BB, 583) we believe that it cannot be required that the impediment is the exclusive cause of a breach of contract. This is true not only of cases in which it covers the breach of contract only partially, but the impediment should in our view also be accepted *when a cause overtakes another cause*. In an example given by Tallon improperly packed goods later perish because of an accident which constitutes an impediment. Tallon does not want to allow an exemption. We believe that it must be possible. It is only the damages which are affected by the exemption, and the damage to the buyer has not become worse because of the fact that the perished goods were packed improperly. (We neglect here that Tallon distorts the problem by demanding accident-proof packing.) It is decisive, as we hold, whether the impediment lastly has caused the breach of contract. If this is so, it consumes other breaches of contract for which there are no grounds for exemption insofar as those no longer appear independently.

3.5. The *burden of proof* for the existence of impediments lies with the aggrieved party.

3.6. A *list of impediments* which takes into account such typical categories as natural phenomena; decisions by the State; other extraordinary events (war, blockade, accidents); acts by third parties (sabotage, robbery); and forms of industrial action was not included. Many of the above-mentioned phenomena will generally become impediments. But they are not such per se and without any examination; further criteria must serve as the measure for them. From this it may result, for instance, that a fire, which in most cases will constitute an impediment, will not be such in a specific case because the person concerned has violated the most elementary requirements of protection against fire so that the result was within his control.

3.7. The *parties* often agree concrete impediments which can be examined in regard to their causality for the breach of contract, but not to their character as impediments (note 4 - 6).

4.1. In requiring that the impediment must be *beyond the control* of the party concerned, the scope of risk of the latter is determined, though only roughly.

Within the control of the seller are all those factors which are connected with an orderly organization of his manufacturing and/or procurement process. To explain this in giving an example, he must have the necessary capacities in terms of personnel and technical equipment, use them appropriately and maintain his equipment according to his expert judgement so as to prevent any breakdown.

His control also includes that he disposes of the required financial means to ensure manufacture and procurement, timely takes care of needed sub-supplies, and does all that is in his power to obtain authorizations by the State.

4.2. Opinions may differ as to whether *strikes* are beyond the control of the party concerned, for their causes are often found in the enterprise. We believe that one should follow those authors who like Vischer (Lausanne, 179) take a careful stand in the matter and do not exclude strikes as impediments, except when they are internal confrontations at a factory and provided that the other conditions of impediments are fulfilled, too (c. also Tallon/BB, 584). Rudolph (Moscow, 84) even believes that strikes could generally be considered as possible in the context of negotiations on pay and therefore would not constitute an impediment (note 5) because they happen at specific intervals. This is true of strikes which can be foreseen at the time of the conclusion of the contract. Lockouts are, at least to a certain extent, not exterior to the activities of the debtor and can, therefore, not be considered as impediments (Rudolph, ibid).

5.1. This second condition, which an impediment to cause an exemption will have to fulfil, describes in a very flexible manner the criterion of *foreseeability*, which is known from the *force majeure* clauses.

Insofar the impediment was in existence even *before the contract was concluded*, it has to be required that the party concerned neither knew nor, as we believe, ought to have been aware of it because otherwise he would have had to take it into consideration.

5.2. Where the impediments occur before the contract is concluded, they will in part be such as to *render performance impossible*, e.g. a specific good is lost before the time of the conclusion of the contract, and in part such as to hinder it only temporarily. In respect of the former case, national laws often stipulate that declarations and/or contracts regarding impossible performances are void. For this reason, some authors (Tallon/BB, 578) believe that because of Article 4, subpara. (a) domestic law will have to be applied so that the Convention becomes irrelevant in this context. We can, however, not join such a view because of the considerations expounded already in another context (Article 68, note 5.4.).

5.3. The rule does *not require foreseeability per se*. Here we see a difference compared to the usual rules and clauses governing cases of *force majeure*. In the end, most of the phenomena that might become impediments are foreseeable. It is, however, not expected that such events are taken into account which, given general foreseeability, are not expected to materialize before the contract is performed and/or if they do nevertheless, they are at least not expected to have an effect on it.

These expectations are further qualified in stipulating that they will have to be *reasonable*, i.e. that it is proceeded in the customary way, like comparable parties would do. Thereby, an objectivization is effected.

6.1. It is in line with the general liability of the parties in regard to the obligations they have assumed that they have to *counteract impediments*. The two main forms of doing so are mentioned here.

First, *disturbances* will have to be *avoided*. In order to achieve this, measures will have to be taken against such impediments which are generally looming ahead but cannot, *a priori*, be put in relation to the fulfilment of concrete obligations. These include measures of protection against accidents and specifically fire; a factory management which guarantees peaceful labour relations; etc. Above all, measures have to be taken against disturbances which are clearly approaching.

Second, where a *disturbance has already revealed itself* it has to be overcome as speedily as possible invoking, for instance, remedies against hindering decisions by the State insofar as they have a chance of succeeding. It is the requirement of overcoming which is aimed at removing the consequences of disturbances. Hence, the effects of accidents have to be removed fast. No clear distinction can be made between avoidance and overcoming when it comes to looking for a replacement for a supplier lost.

6.2. The yardstick used to measure the efforts of the party concerned is again what can reasonably be expected from him. And that is what is customary, or what similar individuals would do in a similar situation. The exemption is thus granted when efforts would have been necessary that go beyond the former.

6.3. The Convention provides no specific rule as to whether a disturbance which does not fully exclude performance, but *makes it considerably more difficult*, such as change of circumstances, hardship, can be considered as an impediment. The facts of that case would have to be considered in the context of Article 79. The majority of commentators, therefore, want to allow changes in the circumstances in serious cases to be impediments (Schlechtriem, 96; Honnold, 443; Vischer/Lausanne, 178 fol). Herein we also see the best way for finding a solution. There is nonetheless a conspicuous reticence on the part of the authors in regard to their general commitment to it and also in regard to its importance. But if one takes the wording of the CISG literally (and what is at issue here is the obligation to avoid and/or overcome) and applies it to the main case of changed circumstances, to the changes in the ratio between performance and counter-performance, one has to note that the subsumption actually is not that extraordinary. It is in our view not the essential criteria whether the party concerned would be put on the way to ruin in the event of non-recognition of the exemption (Vischer/Lausanne, 179) because then the subjective financial liquidity would be decisive. Neither can one, like Schlechtriem (96) does, infer the non-recognition of the impediment from the liability for financial liquidity. The criterion for it is the limit of what can reasonable be expected. It may be different in the different sectors, and speculative transactions hardly permit reliance on such impediments. It seems to us that in shifting the equivalence by 100 per cent, the extent of efforts which can reasonably be expected is surpassed; and this is frequently the case when the discrepancy is much smaller. This is true, however, of both directions, wherefrom follows a pressure to adjust in most cases (Introductory remarks 2). Stoll (Freiburg, 274) who represents the outsider opinion that economic impossibility and *Wegfall der Geschäftsgrundlage* (which is the terminology used in the FRG), do not constitute impediments in the meaning of Article 79, concedes, however, that insistence on unchanged performance could contradict the *requirement of good faith* under Article 7, paragraph 1. This view is more flexible than the one held by a majority because it does not tie to the inflexible scheme of legal effects under Article 79, in particular paragraph 5. Without wanting to speak in favour of rejecting changed circumstances as impediments, we do not want to exclude reliance on good faith in these cases. This follows from the fact that one form of changed circumstances, frustration of purpose (the plant for whose reconstruction a machine is to be delivered is destroyed by an earthquake), cannot be solved by invoking Article 79. What good is a possible exemption from payment of damages because of not taking delivery, when the obligation to pay the price is retained and is probably secured irrevocably, and when the obligation to take delivery of the goods continues to exist (note 13). Tallon (BB, 593 fol) has good reasons to attack recourse to good faith, but the same reasons, vagueness, in the end, unfortunately also apply to the other solution.

Anyway, the discussion shows that at present it cannot be determined with sufficient security how the issue of changed circumstances can be decided on the basis of the CISG. The parties are, therefore, urgently recommended to make *arrangements* in the matter and/or to exclude adjustment (Maskow, Bewältigung, 16, as well as other solutions in PICC, Article 5.2.1. to 5.2.3.).

7.1. It is to be welcomed that the CISG, by contrast to Article 74 ULIS, directly bears on the problem of exemption where a breach of contract is caused *by a third party*, even if an interpretation of the relevant rule in detail proves to be difficult.

7.2. A third party whose non-performance can also lead to exemption of the debtor is *defined in the Convention itself* so that supplementary recourse to national law, e.g. in regard to a sub-contractor, is not necessary. From the possibility of exemption granted as an exception follows basic liability of a third party.

In respect of the categories of persons involved in the performance of the contract, apart from the actual parties to it, most commentators distinguish *three groups*: (a) the employees of the parties; (b) those, who on the basis of relevant contracts with one of the contracting parties, create the general prerequisites for the party in question to conduct his business (in the following referred to as suppliers); and, (c) those who are described in paragraph 2 (in the following referred to as sub-contractors). Every party basically has the right to engage such third parties. Insofar nothing to the contrary follows from the circumstances or the contract for a Pakistani proposal, which aimed at making that right dependent on agreement, was rejected (O. R., 134 fol).

Apart from a few exceptions, the first category includes mostly natural persons, whereas the other two are composed of mostly legal persons. Every party is responsible for the conduct of his *employees*, at least where the latter are used in the organization of contract performance and where their behaviour is concerned. We would, however, not go so far as Stoll (Freiburg, 276) who presumes that the party should always vouch for them. If a party had employed, in excusable ignorance, a saboteur or an arsonist, he should not be liable when that person becomes active. The exemption would, however, have to be granted on the basis of paragraph 1 in this case.

There are problems when it comes to delimiting categories two and three. We have already given a definition of the *supplier*. These include suppliers of raw materials and parts, electric companies, providers of communal services, etc. In the context of omission on their part, the party can, according to an apparently unanimously held view, be exempted only under paragraph 1, but not paragraph 2.

A *sub-contractor*, finally, can be defined as taking charge of part of the contract performance. His performance is, therefore, regularly aimed at fulfilling a certain contract. This notion includes companies which manufacture or produce the goods to be delivered on instruction by the seller and deliver them to the buyer. It also includes carriers who work for the one or the other party. The fact that a third party carries out a performance directly vis-a-vis another party may indicate that he is a third party in the meaning of the CISG. As to its definition, the *third party* has to be *legally independent* of the party for whom he works. But it is, in our opinion, not required and not necessary that he be economically independent. The rule requires the existence of grounds for exemption on the part of both the contracting party and the third party and hinders, therefore, a conspiracy between them (seemingly of a different view Tallon/BB, 585).

7.3. There was no agreement at the diplomatic conference as to *how far the exemption under paragraph 1* would reach and whether or not the one under paragraph 2 would entail stricter liability (O. R., 378 fol). A more detailed analysis, in our view, produces the result that the differences between the two paragraphs are not that great and that, above all, it cannot be said whether the one or the other of the two paragraphs offers a basis for stricter liability. We wish to demonstrate this in comparing a classic supplier and a classic sub-contractor. When a supplier fails to deliver, the seller (the same applies to the buyer who, for instance, is to supply sub-deliveries) does not have to prove that there were grounds for the exemption of the former, but only that this was the case in regard to himself. In this context he can even rely on failure by the supplier, and it will then be examined whether this constitutes a reason for exemption. In general this will not be the case because recourse can be demanded to other sources. Where there are, in exceptional instances, no such sources, e.g. because only one electric power company can be engaged or the only possible supplier of certain microelectronic chips has sold elsewhere, exemption can be granted even though especially in the latter case the supplier has obviously not breached his obligation because of grounds for exemption (c. also Honnold, 439 fol).

Let us consider now the case of the *sub-contractor*. The impediment is, similar to the case of the supplier, a breach of contract by the third party. But by contrast to the former example, the breach of contract is not a ground for exemption of the third party when the reason for exemption is given for the seller. It must have been given also for the sub-contractor. Because of this cumulation, greater requirements are made for an exemption to be granted. Conversely, the requirements that are made for the seller's own conduct to be a ground for exemption are less far-reaching (note 8).

It can thus be summarized that the exemption under paragraph 2 is granted for such impediments which are based on non-perform-ance by a certain category of partners of the seller. It is judged according to criteria which, because of the different actual circumstances, diverge from those of paragraph 1. Constellations that are comparable in structure can, therefore, lead to an exemption under paragraph 1, but not under paragraph 2 or vice-versa. The attempt to compare the strictness of the two norms is therefore misleading.

A differentiation of the rule aims toward finding proper solutions for different circumstances. It has to be admitted, however, that the distinction between supplier and sub-contractor is not always easy (so already the Danish delegate at the diplomatic conference - O. R., 379). Often this question can only be answered considering the function of the rule. Insofar we can agree with Honnold (441) who does not want to apply paragraph 2 in the event of a pure re-sale, assuming that the goods resold are goods which have already been manufactured and are the subject of an obligation to deliver unascertained goods. In that case there would be an obligation to procure the goods (so also Oberlandesgericht Hamm in a decision of December 19, 1983 in the case 24310/82 on the similar Article 74 ULIS - printed in Schlechtriem/Magnus, 294 fol). Where, by contrast, equipment that is tied to a project is ordered for re-sale and is destroyed when almost finished, paragraph 2 will apply.

7.4. In the discussions at the diplomatic conference and in publications the question of an *imposed sub-contractor* was also dealt with. According to our experience, it plays a role in regard to all categories of persons engaged in the performance of the sales contract, even though there are differences as to the degree. We believe that the imposed engagement of third parties in the fulfilment of the contract does not *per se* lead to a change in liability for him (in this sense also Tallon/BB, 585; of a different view apparently Loewe, 97). However, if the buyer requests the seller to employ workers from the buyer's country to assemble the machines delivered and/or to engage specific suppliers, hence in the event that liability in the meaning of paragraph 1 is invoked, the feature "beyond his control" would be affected because the scope of influence of the buyer would be diminished to this extent. We can subsume (note 8) also a reduction in the liability for the sub-contractor under this rule. This is relevant for an exemption only insofar as it caused an impediment. Exemption can, for instance, not be granted when the forcedly employed workers have been insufficiently organized and instructed, but it can very well be granted when the personnel made available has not been sufficiently qualified.

If one assumes under paragraph 2 the existence of liability for the *orderly choice* of the sub-contractor, as it is done in some publications (note 8), exemption should be granted from it, fully or partially, depending on the situation in the event that the sub-contractor was imposed. But the buyer is not helped when the third party does not supply without grounds for exemption being given. Therefore, the solution offered by Vischer (Lausanne, 180) is understandable and should not be neglected insofar to reject liability relying on Article 80. It has to be taken into consideration, however, that the engagement of a third party regularly will have been fixed up to the conclusion of the contract, so that the seller acts in performing an obligation under the contract. There is an indirect causality of the buyer's acts in regard to the breach of obligation by the seller in these and similar circumstances. Therefore, additional contractual agreements are recommendable.

7.5. The rule will be of practical relevance mainly for the obligations of the seller. But it refers, as already repeatedly indicated, to both parties. It may gain relevance for the *buyer*, for instance, when he engages a carrier in the event of Ex works deliveries or when the delivery in a distance sale is to be made to a third final purchaser who is to fulfil the obligation of the buyer to take delivery of the goods. Here, too, the question may arise whether the party is to be considered the counterpart of a supplier or a sub-contractor, which is to be answered in accordance with the criteria indicated. We cannot follow Stoll (Freiburg, 278) who for such cases seemingly assumes a general parallel to the case of the supplier.

7.6. The fact of *full performance by a third party* is given above all, when he, in a distance sale, delivers directly to the buyer. A *splitting* of performance can be done in regard to the goods (the third party delivers only part of the goods) or also in regard to the completion of a successful delivery (the third party carries out only one of the necessary partial operations, e.g. transport).

8. It is spelled out in publications that the exemption under paragraph 1 in this context refers above all to the *choice of a third party* (Tallon/BB, 585). We doubt that this is what is meant. To start with, this argument strongly resembles the civil law principle of liability for fault in choosing a third party and may insofar cause suspicion among common law jurists. But also, apart from this fact, it is not convincing. When grounds for exemption have arisen on the part of a third party, it is not understandable why the correct choice of the third party should matter. It is irrelevant because unsuitability is no

reason for exemption. Conversely, a correct choice does not help the party concerned when there are, at the same time, no grounds for exemption on the part of the third party. An interpretation of subpara. (a) which aims at integrating into the acts of the third party the engaging party by way of the obligation to a correct choice of the former leads, therefore, to absurd results.

By contrast, the principle of *correct choice*, taken by itself, is of relevance in the context of paragraph 1, namely both in connection with the scope of influence of the party concerned and its obligation to avoidance. The engaging party has a responsibility for choosing a suitable third party of which he can discharge himself when he could not fulfil it because of impediments. But this does not concern the issue discussed here.

The discussion at the diplomatic conference could not convince us that there is consensus on the substance of subpara. (a). It has, therefore, to try to give an interpretation following objective criteria. In our view the rule should be conceived to apply only when an engaging party and a third party *jointly undertake an act* which proves to be a breach of contract. Hereby they can act successively (grounds for exemption because of belated delivery and delay in transportation) and jointly. The exemption always reaches as far as it applies to one or both of the parties. Where the breach of contract is committed only by the third party, subpara. (a) becomes irrelevant. Hence, when the goods identified to a contract, because of a seaquake, perish during transportation before the risk has passed, exemption will be granted even when the seller has not orderly chosen the carrier. This interpretation is not customary, but it seems to us that it meets the idea of the rule best.

9. Irrespective of whether the CISG applies to the relations between the engaging party and a third party, the grounds for exemption provided by it are used as the measure for judging whether or not exemption will be granted. This fiction has the effect that there will not necessarily be *congruence in assessing* the claims which are asserted vis-a-vis the engaging party, on the one hand, and his claims for recourse vis-a-vis the third party, on the other. This is the case, in particular, where the non-performance is caused by a carrier who can obtain exemption for other reasons. Therefrom results the requirement to diminish discrepancies in the process of shaping the contract. It has to be taken account that it will not be easy for the engaging party to prove impediments when the third party can obtain exemption on completely different grounds.

10.1. While at the end of paragraph 1 a distinction is made between the *impediment and its consequences* because under that paragraph, they are addressed separately in relation to the obligation of avoidance or overcoming. Such a differentiation is not made here. But the "period during which the impediment exists" has to be conceived in those cases in which there is a difference between it and his consequences, e.g. earthquake and its consequences in contrast to temporary ban on transportation, as including the period during which its consequences have an effect. However, not every period actually used to overcome the consequences is to be taken into account, but only that which is necessary provided that the party concerned makes appropriate efforts. A proposal by the former GDR, which provided for expressly mentioning the consequences, was referred to the Drafting Committee and taken into consideration and, in accordance with the Norwegian proposal, the word "only" before "period" was deleted (O. R., 135 fol).

10.2. In particular, where the overcoming of impediments is concerned, this *temporary exemption* can be of great relevance. When, for instance, a supplier (note 7) fails to deliver, there is no permanent ground for exemption because of the general obligation to supply. But the delay, which, depending on how long before the period for performance the failure occurred, arises because another supplier will have to be found, may be excused.

In our interpretation (note 13.6.) this rule, even though not with the desirable clarity as to the substance and the legal techniques, has the effect of *suspending the obligation to perform* as it is often prescribed in international economic contracts and in some instances also in laws as the primary consequence of *force majeure*.

11. Account is insofar taken of the *receipt of a notice*. This is done in deviation from the rule of dispatch as spelled out in Article 27, but corresponds with Article 48, paragraph 4. This is important insofar as that notice can be conceived as a notice under Article 48, paragraph 2 or 3. The term "received" should be interpreted by analogy in the same way as the term "reaches" in Article 24.

12. This is the damage which is caused and/or could not have been avoided because the creditor of the performance concerned was *not given proper notice* of the impediment.

13. This laconic formulation offers many tough nuts to crack in regard to interpretation.

13.1. First of all, it will have to be clarified how far the notion of damages reaches. A proposal by the former GDR to expressly include *penalties* under the contract in their different manifestations (penalties and liquidated damages) was rejected without being put to a vote (O. R., 135), but above all because penalties under the contract are not a claim following from the Convention and the shaping of contracts in that respect should not be influenced (O. R., 385 fol). This objection is not realistic insofar as penalties are agreed frequently without the question of possible exemptions being touched upon. If the latter happens, the contractual agreement will in any way supersede the Convention. The reasons given for the rejection do not exclude that, other contractual clues lacking, the grounds for exemption will also be extended to penalty claims (so also Loewe, 96. The Secretariat's Commentary (O. R., 55), however, is in favour of applying domestic law). This does not apply to interest claims (Article 78, note 2.1.).

13.2. The existence of grounds for exemption without any doubts (but see Tallon/BB, 589 fol) does not preclude the right to *avoid the contract*. That right is given above all when there is a fundamental breach of contract. The character of a conduct being a breach of contract is not affected by the existence of impediments (Introductory remarks 5.). It is, in our view not excluded that the existence of impediments is taken into consideration where a breach of contract is classified as fundamental. From a doctrinal point of view, this may be substantiated by the principle of good faith. But this indicates that the risk for the emergence of such grounds should not be located adopting a one-sided approach. A point in favour of this opinion is furthermore that the definition of a fundamental breach of contract in Article 25 in a certain way refers to the conduct of the party in breach, even though it relates mainly to the effects the breach of contract has on the other party. The expectations of the latter may, however, be influenced by the possibility of impediments.

It is problematic though that even where grounds for exemption exist the right to avoid the contract *remains limited to the party* against which the breach is committed. Considerations by the former GDR following a less far-reaching Norwegian proposal to introduce such a right also for the other party (O. R., 134 fol, 381 fol) did not meet with a response so that the problem is now to be solved in the context of the right to performance (note 13.6.).

13.3. The rights to *delivery of substitute goods* (Article 46, paragraph 2) or repair (Article 46, paragraph 3), persist where there are grounds for exemption. When the latter, however, hinders the satisfaction of exactly those rights, and is taken into account in the conditions for repair claims, the general problem of the right to performance will arise (note 13.6.).

13.4. The *right to reduction of the price* (Article 50) is not affected because it is aimed at maintaining the originally agreed equivalence and does not constitute a claim for damages.

13.5. The fact that claims under notes 13.3. and 13.4. which emerge in the event of delivery of non-conforming, hence defective goods, are retained by all means shows that there is no reason to exclude liability for non-conformity from the grounds for exemption. The claims of the greatest practical relevance continue to exist. Many laws are still cautious when it comes to approving damage claims because of non-conformity.

13.6. There will still be the *right to performance* when there are impediments. This seems to amount to an obvious contradiction because it is supposed that performance is not possible. Requests by Norway and the FRG, which had intended to avoid this, could not be carried through (O. R., 134 fol). Given today's far-spread practice of credit sales in international trade, the following situation is characteristic: The seller has delivered the goods, but because of currency transfer regulations introduced later, payment is prevented. The seller could withdraw from the contract in this case, but may not be interested in doing so because for commercial (the goods have effectively been sold to a third party) or foreign trade reasons (re-exportation is prohibited) he cannot again obtain possession of the goods or because he cannot use them for another purpose. Should he therefore be hindered to require payment? Such concerns as they have been articulated, in particular by Soviet delegates (O. R., 384), have prevented many delegations from supporting the FRG proposal. At the diplomatic conference it was not possible to find a flexible answer to the question of what is to become of the right to performance. The rigid solution that has been adopted led to the most diverse interpretations which were guided by the idea of making it manageable in practice.

It has become clear at least that the right to performance continues to exist in the event of *temporary grounds for exemption* and that auxiliary claims that are related to it, like interest, continue to accumulate thus stimulating, as in particular the Swedish delegate stressed at the diplomatic conference (O. R., 384), the parties concerned to make greater efforts to overcome the impediments. Furthermore, the synallagmatic connection to the corresponding right of the other party is underlined.

On the other hand, the prevailing opinion at the conference (O. R., 383 fol) was that a non-fulfillable claim must *not be granted*. This is reflected in publications. But there are differences in details. Tallon (BB, 589 fol) is in favour of dissolving the contract by virtue of law in the event of a total and definitive failure to perform, but it is not clear whether it should be based on national law or the Convention. The view expressed by Rudolph (Moscow, 86 fol) in 1983 amounts to something similar. We do not consider that interpretation as correct. It contradicts the wording of the Convention and also the renunciation of the *ipso facto* avoidance as it was completed with the transition from ULIS to the CISG. The argument that a party could be forced to perform although the other party is hindered by impediments, is not conclusive because the functional synallagma is secured by the Convention in many ways (e.g. Article 71 fol; 80). Others would have wanted to invoke domestic law by way of Article 28 in order to avoid a sentencing by a court in respect of performance (Schlechtriem, 51 and 97; Vischer/Lausanne, 175 fol). We do not think that this is the optimum way but believe that, in general, it is well-founded and acceptable. Even though national laws diverge in the matter, it is not to be reckoned with that this would lead to serious differences in the practical application of the CISG. The rights to performance should, at any rate, be seldom asserted where there are impediments, whether disputable or not. Claims for damages will generally dominate because the creditor of the characteristic performance cannot wait until a decision is taken on a right to performance whose possibility of realization may be doubted after all. Claims for payment which are granted cannot be realized easily either when there are impediments in their way, but the interest continues to accumulate until performance. And, furthermore, there might be opportunities for execution which are not touched upon by grounds for exemption, e.g. assets of the debtor in countries where there are no currency transfer regulations which may constitute grounds for exemption.

If one wanted to avoid the *unequal treatment of obligations in money and goods* which is entailed, one would have to try to develop an interpretation that conforms to the Convention and would apply to both obligations as the optimum solution. It could amount to that a right to performance must not be awarded insofar as the grounds of exemption are in effect. A relevant sentence could thus only require performance after they have ceased to be effective. Interest would continue to accumulate until that time. It is difficult, however, to discover a respective principle (Article 7, paragraph 2) in the CISG which avowedly does not provide for issues of validity (Article 4, subpara. (a)).

In some cases the problem can be solved in that it is assumed that the right to performance is aimed to deliver a commercially reasonable *substitute* (Nicholas, 241; Secretariat's Commentary, O. R., 55). We believe that the party affected by impediments can only be obligated to deliver such substitute in exceptional cases because this otherwise could lead to a far-reaching and, above all, undefined modification of his obligation to perform. When, for instance, payment in the agreed freely convertible currency is prohibited, but can be made in other such currencies, it will have to be assumed that the buyer has the obligation to switch to those currencies. By contrast, it may be too far-reaching when the seller in the event of a prohibition of fluorocarbons as propellant is obligated to use other propellants because he might lack the technological prerequisites for it. When the party concerned, because of the performance requirement offers substitutes, the other party would contradict his own behaviour and thus violate the principle of good faith in international trade (Article 7) were he to reject them, even though they are commercially equivalent. This offers in our view a basis for permanent objection to the claim for performance. The same applies when the seller offers the substitute on his own and its rejection would be considered as an harassment (Article 7).

13.7. This may have served to show that the rule governing grounds for exemption, as rigid as it may seem at first sight, in practice might well help to initiate a *process of negotiation* among the parties to solve the problems that have arisen. It is exactly in this direction that often aim the contractual clauses on *force majeure*.

Article 80[1]

A party[2] may not rely[3] on a failure of the other party to perform[2], to the extent[6] that such failure was caused[5] by the first party's act or omission[4].

1.1. At the *proposal of the former GDR* this article was unanimously adopted and included in the Convention (O. R., 386 fol, 135 fol). Its content is obviously an expression of general principles, in particular that of good faith, respectively a concrete manifestation of it, the prohibition to contradict one's own behaviour (*venire contra factum proprium*). When one, however, wants to deduce too many concrete solutions from general principles, the latter are overextended and become void of substance, which in practical terms means that the decisions are shifted to judges. It was useful, therefore, to include such a rule (Tallon/BB, 596).

1.2. Article 42, paragraph 2, subpara. (b) provides for a concrete manifestation of the principle of Article 80. This *special norm* existed before Article 80 was drafted and continues in existence, although it is consumed by the latter.

2. Failure to perform refers to *any breach of contract* just like Article 79 (note 2 of Article 79).

3.1. The party in breach can, therefore, *not assert any claims* because of a breach of contract. It not only has no right to claim damages, as in the event of grounds for exemption in the meaning of Article 79, it has no right to performance nor to avoidance. When the debtor is hindered in performing in time by the party in breach, e.g. because of belated communication of instructions for dispatch the seller cannot dispatch the goods, the party in breach will have to accept the late delivery without having the right to require any sanction. When the party in breach has caused the non-conform or defective delivery, e.g. sub-supply of material having non-apparent defects; he cannot require delivery of substitute goods or repair or reduction of the price etc.

3.2. The acts by the creditor which cause the breach of contract will generally represent themselves as *breach of contract* committed by the former (note 4) so that the debtor being the creditor of those acts can assert the respective claims. He will have the right to claim damages only to the extent to which the party in breach cannot rely on impediments. Among the rest of the claims, which are retained in any case, the right to avoid the contract is of special relevance. In asserting that right, the fate of the blocked contract can be decided once and for all.

3.3. There is no general *obligation* (Stoll/Freiburg, 280) for the debtor *to overcome or avoid the failure* with respect to his own performance, as under Article 79, paragraph 1 in regard to the disturbances emanating from the party in breach.

The debtor will in many cases be interested, however, to overcome a disturbance in order to be able to perform himself. Article 65 of the CISG provides for such a possibility. Furthermore, the debtor can, under the CISG, be considered as being entitled and in part also obligated to avoid or to overcome disturbances which emanate from the other party in the customary way. This follows, above all, from the principle of good faith (Article 7, paragraph 1), e.g. when the failure because of the creditor's act or omission is minor compared to the breach of contract (note 5). It could play a role whether the creditor's act or omission was caused by impediments. The principle of cooperation between the parties, which can be regarded as implemented in the Convention (Article 7, paragraph 2), has a similar effect.The debtor could also be obliged to take such measures in the frame of his obligation to mitigate losses (Article 77). Hence, the seller himself instead of the buyer could provide the means of transportation, procure himself material or parts to be supplied by the buyer after he had granted the party in breach an additional possibility to do so. The additional expenses incurred by the seller from those acts could, under the CISG, be claimed by him as damages where the disturbance caused by the party in breach was a breach of contract and where there are not grounds for exemption. Since this is not always the case, the debtor insofar runs a risk. He might, however, claim the additional expenses as an increase in the price without impediments becoming effective. The seller might have other rights under national law which allowed him to compensate for additional expenses, e.g. from unjust enrichment when material was procured in replacement. It should be mentioned in this context that there are also such rules under domestic law relating to *surrogates for performance* or services without mandate or, less frequent, fictitious declarations or vicarious performance.

The acts carried out by the debtor in replacement are covered by the CISG only insofar as they do not change the *character of the contract*. Hence a contract on the delivery of a medal stand cannot be turned into one on the delivery of a machine because the buyer has not delivered his sub-supplies.

4. These will mostly be *breaches of contract on the part of the creditor*. Whether or not there are impediments is irrelevant to the extent to which the exemption of the debtor is at issue. To speak in this context of fault as does Schlechtriem (100), is contrary to the system of the Convention in our view because this would unjustly presuppose that the CISG is based on the principle of fault, which is exactly what should be counteracted.

The act or omission can also be a conduct which is not directly related to the contract, thus in particular an, *infliction of damage* (tort). The workers employed by the buyer, for instance, because of negligence destroy the goods at a production facility of the seller.

5.1. The *causality* required here of the conduct of the party in breach in regard to the breach of contract has been defined by Tallon (BB, 599) as a high degree of probability. To put it in our own words, the breach of contract must be a characteristic consequence of the act of the creditor which can be expected in international trade. Where the former carries out legal acts which, because of a completely unusual chain of cause and effect, lead to the breach of contract, there will be no reason for exemption in our view. This will be the case, for instance, when the goods perish while the risk is still with the seller because the buyer has asserted his right to give instructions for dispatch in a specific way, i.e. accident on the road. This, however, does not exclude exemption under Article 79.

5.2. The conduct of the creditor can *actually* cause the breach of contract, e.g. when technical drawings according to which the goods would have to be manufactured are not delivered, or can break the envisaged functional synallagma so that the debtor would worsen his *legal position* were he to continue his performance, e.g. when the seller does not deliver because the letter of credit has not been opened yet, and the buyer does not pay because he has not received the goods. Article 80 insofar constitutes a nominative expression of the objection of the non-performed contract.

6. Problems will arise when the breach of contract has *not* been caused *exclusively by the creditor*, but in part by the conduct of the debtor. With respect to the debtor it would again have to be differentiated whether or not he can rely on impediments. There are many constellations possible. We limit ourselves to presenting principles which could, in our view, be inferred from the regulation governing the most important case groups.

(a) When the consequences of the different *causes* can be *delimited from one another*, every cause has to be attributed its legal remedy. A distinction will, however, have to be made of what caused the breach of contract.

(aa) When the *breach of contract*, a delay offers insofar the best example, was caused by an act or omission of the creditor, but *later continued* because the debtor did not display an orderly conduct, the remedies under failure caused by an act or omission of the creditor apply to the first period, but for the second those applicable under breaches of obligation by the debtor. The latter may then be assessed less strictly, e.g. considering their fundamentality being the prerequisite for an avoidance, when they are preceded by an act or omission of the creditor.

(ab) In the event that the breach of contract becomes fundamental only as a consequence of the cumulation of failures of the two parties, that change in the character of the breach which is caused by an act or omission of the creditor is irrelevant in our view. To put it in other words, the creditor may have a right to claim damages but not the right to avoid the contract. Insofar we come to a similar conclusion as Tallon (BB, 598), even if under more precise conditions and with a different doctrinal deduction (compare also (c)).

(b) When a breach of contract by the debtor and an act or omission by the creditor *act in combination* having the same effect, i.e. the seller is not ready to deliver and the buyer does not give the agreed instructions for dispatch or does not open up an agreed letter of credit, the act or omission of the creditor dominates. But exemption will become effective only in regard to the conduct concerned. The party in breach can, therefore, not claim a breach of contract because of the consequences of the act or omission of the creditor. The result can be a stalemate in which the contract is neither performed nor can it be avoided by any of the parties.

(c) The last case to be considered here is the one where the failures of the two parties are so closely interwoven that their *effects cannot be delimited and attributed to the breach of contract* which is the result of that situation, such as when the buyer provides drawings which cannot, in part, be realized, and the seller, without referring back to the buyer, proceeds with modifications in the realization which do not meet the intentions of the buyer. In our view, it is appropriate in these cases to reduce, in a similar way as Tallon (BB, 598) suggests, the legal consequences which would be the result of a breach of contract where the causes of the breach are not taken into consideration. The reduction can be merely quantitative as in the case of damages, insofar also grounds for exemption on the part of the debtor would have to be taken into account. But it may also take on a qualitative character when the right to avoidance of the contract is turned into a claim for damages, which might then be thwarted because of grounds for exemption, for it is assessed that the breach of contract because of the act or omission of the creditor has passed the threshold toward a fundamental breach. Or, the right to performance may be judged to have elapsed and the part of the debtor in the breach of the contract is paid off because of a claim for damages by the creditor.

Section V
Effects of avoidance

Introductory remarks

1. Avoidance under the CISG appears as a possible reaction to *breaches of contract*, including anticipated breaches (Articles 49, 51, 64, 72 and 73). Since an avoidance of a contract constitutes a very far-reaching sanction which signals the breakdown of the contract and excludes its belated approximate performance, it is tied to further conditions such as the fundamentality of the breach of contract or the expiry of certain periods of time. In the articles under which avoidance is one of the legal consequences, no further explanation is given. Rather, it is summarized in this section.

2. The *term "avoidance"* denotes an *early end* in a neutral form. Terms like "termination" or" withdrawal", which have a defined meaning in the national legal language, are deliberately omitted. It is stressed in this way that the Convention has developed an original concept of putting an early end to the contract.

3. We proceed on the assumption that the right to avoid the contract applies *irrespective of the cause* of the respective breach of contract, hence also in the event of impossibility. But also those who through the national law (Article 4, subpara. (a)) want to include an automatic early termination of the contract by virtue of law (notes 13.2 and 13.6. of Article 79), believe that an analogous application of "certain provisions" of this section is possible in the matter (Tallon/BB, 602).

4. This section is applied both to *total avoidance and* to *partial avoidance* as provided for in Articles 51 and 73. Criteria are indicated there for when in the event of a breach of contract in regard to part of the performance part of the contract going beyond the former (Article 73, paragraph 3) and/or the entire contract (Article 51, paragraph 2 and Article 73, paragraph 3) can be avoided.

Furthermore, important problems of the delivery of substitute goods (Article 46, paragraph 2) are dealt with (Article 82 and 84, paragraph 2) which are not covered by the heading of the section.

5. We believe that Section V does not only apply to legal but also *contractual rights* of avoidance (Weitnauer/Dölle, 503 on ULIS). This goes also for functional equivalents like the right to withdraw from a contract. However, where terms other than those of the CISG are used, it is to be examined with particular care whether because of the ideas which the parties usually have in regard to the former certain rules of the CISG have to be regarded as having been abrogated or modified.

6. Even though the regulation is meant as avoidance because of a breach of contract, its decisive operative Articles (81 and 84) are balanced and do not place a greater burden on the *party who has committed the breach.* A possibly required redistribution of costs will be achieved only through damages insofar as there are no grounds for exemption. This section also becomes applicable to an agreed avoidance of the contract insofar as the parties have not determined its effects. Articles 82 and 83 would be irrelevant anyway in this context.

Article 81[1]

(Release from obligations; contract provisions for settlement of disputes; restitution)

(1) Avoidance of the contract releases both parties from their obligations[2] under it, subject to any damages[3] which may be due. Avoidance does not affect any provision of the contract for the settlement of disputes[4] or any other provision of the contract governing the rights and obligations of the parties consequent upon the avoidance of the contract[5].

(2) A party who has performed the contract either wholly or in part may claim[6] restitution from the other party of whatever the first party has supplied or paid under the contract. If both parties are bound[7] to make restitution, they must do so concurrently[8].

1. This article clearly shows that the avoidance of the contract *does not nullify* the latter and clarifies which are the obligations that are terminated or returned, respectively, and which remain in existence. It does not meet the character of the provision that there is a dispute on whether the avoidance has the effect of *ex nunc* or *ex tunc*. While Kahn (978) stresses that the parties are, to the extent possible, in the same situation as they were at the conclusion of the contract, insofar alludes more to an *ex tunc* effect; Schlechtriem (102) attaches importance on that the contract schedule is only reprogrammed but the contract is not destroyed *ex nunc* (similarly already Weitnauer/Dölle, 504; in favour of an *ex nunc* effect also Vischer/Lausanne, 181). But the contract is not terminated, neither *ex nunc* nor *ex tunc*; it remains in existence as long as there are still claims of the parties under it, including claims for returning the goods or the price (in this spirit also Leser/Freiburg, 238 fol). The latter under the Convention are thus contractual claims and not claims for unjust enrichment under national law. The obligations which characterize the contract as a sales contract and which are stipulated in Articles 30 and 53 end or have to be returned in goods or in price so that a situation is achieved which is similar to the original one. This is at the centre of efforts when there is talk of the *ex tunc* effect of an early termination of the contract. The right to avoid the contract is insofar *nearer a right to withdraw* from the contract than a right to terminate the contract. On the other hand, a partial avoidance under Article 51, paragraph 1 in regard to non-

delivery of goods, or under Article 71 in regard to partial deliveries due, can entail the effects of a termination.

In detail, the rule is casuistic, on the one hand, but not very precise in their general formulations, on the other, and leaves important problems unsolved.

2. What matters in particular are the obligations of the seller to deliver the goods and to transfer property in them as well as to hand over the documents (Article 30), and those of the buyer to pay the price and to take delivery of the goods (Article 53). Insofar as they are not fulfilled at the time of the avoidance of the contract (notice to the other party - Article 26), they will not have to be fulfilled later, i.e. the other party could *refuse to accept performance.*

3. This refers in particular to claims for damages which have arisen in connection with the obligations from which he is now released. Damages, for instance, have to be paid because of delay, even if the contract is later avoided because of that delay and even if damages arise because of avoidance, which in our view come under sentence 2 (note 5). Articles 45 and 61 have already made it clear that claims for damages can be asserted apart from other legal consequences of breaches of contract, thus also apart from avoidance. The term "damages which may be due" is in this context conceived as a *bit tight,* for the same should apply to obligations to pay penalties under the contract in their different manifestations.

4. Hereby a widely recognized rule is repeated (Convention on the law applicable to contracts for the international sale of goods, note 6 of Article 5).

The rule *does not remedy deficiencies* which lead to non-validity of an arbitral clause under national law, including that based on other conventions (Article 4, subpara. (a) - O. R., 57). This is true by analogy of the rights and obligations discussed in note 5.

5. This formulation is not very fortunate, for what is referred to here is not only those rights and obligations which are ancillary to an avoidance of the contract, like a respective penalty, but such which are to *help solve a conflict* between the parties (Tallon/BB, 603 fol) and which, of course, are of special importance when that conflict aggravates so that the contract is terminated early. The Secretariat's Commentary (O. R., 57) makes an attempt to reach this result in that it declares non-exhaustive the two named conditions which continue in existence. This is not convincing because the second condition actually is a description of general features.

The surviving conditions can *be multifaceted* (Leser/Freiburg, 239). They relate to general questions of cooperation between the parties, like agreement of general business terms whose individual elements again have to be examined according to that criterion, agreements on the form of declarations, a general obligation to cooperate, obligations to maintain secrecy, a reservation of title up to restitution, limitation of claims, and the applicable law (on the latter c. Vilus/Dubrovnik, 256). Another group of conditions refers to the modalities of performance, i.e. commercial terms, risk bearing, packaging, procurement of licenses, which can play a role where the return of the goods or of the price is concerned. Of particular practical relevance are those agreements which deal with liability, such as penalties, liquidated damages and damage clauses, including possibilities of exemption and restrictions, the amount of interest etc.

Concurring with the majority of authors who have expressed themselves on the subject (Honnold, 447; Vilus/Dubrovnik, 256; van der Velden, Koopvertrag, 331) we believe that the provisions regarding the *obligation to preserve the goods* have to be enumerated here. In part, they even proceed from an avoidance (this refers to certain cases of Article 86, paragraph 2) so that Tallon's doubts (BB, 604) in regard to applicability are not convincing. The remark that it is useless because all legal systems provide for this problem questions the sense of the unification of law all the more so when one takes into consideration the detailed manner in which some of the provisions of Section V are drafted.

6.1. In the case of a *partial avoidance* this, naturally, applies only insofar as the performance already made is concerned.

6.2. It is, therefore, a condition for the claim to return what has been supplied or paid that the *right* to such return *is asserted*. This is justified because the parties may wish to leave what has been supplied or paid, respectively, with the other party.

When the contract has been legally avoided, the goods delivered or the price paid have to be returned, subject to sentence 2, within a reasonable period after the receipt of a respective claim, (for goods Article 33, subpara. (c) by analogy). Since the subject of the performance is generally available, such period will usually be a *short one*. Normally, the party who declares the contract avoided will at the same time claim the return of what has been supplied or paid. Where the other party agrees with the avoidance, he will on his part demand the return of what has been supplied or paid when he is interested in it. This might not be the case when the contract is avoided because of non-conformity and the seller himself does not know what to do with the goods delivered either.

6.3. As regards the *modalities* of the above-mentioned return, the provisions governing the respective performance can be applied analogously (Schlechtriem, 103; Leser/Freiburg, 342). Where a party is responsible for the breach of contract which gave rise to the avoidance, in our view, the other party may require as damages that he pay the costs he incurs returning what has been supplied or paid.

6.4. The right to demand return of the goods delivered or the price paid is *irrelevant* insofar as the conditions of Article 82, paragraph 2 apply.

7.1. This is *not the case* where the other party has not asserted the right to such return (note 6.2.) or where it is irrelevant (note 6.4.).

7.2. It is concluded from this rule that the seller cannot make a *delivery of substitute goods* dependent on whether the buyer returns the delivered goods. A Norwegian proposal, which aimed towards this goal, was rejected by a large majority (O. R., 136). It has to be admitted that the restitution of the replaced goods is insufficiently provided for in the CISG, but it does not necessarily belong in this context. It is problematic that in Article 82 (note 3 of that Article) an aspect of the delivery of substitute goods is taken up in isolation. As to the substance, a concurrent performance is insofar unusual, and from a technical point of view it would be much more difficult to effect it than the usual transaction goods in exchange for money.

8. As convincing as this rule may sound, it will be *difficult to implement* it. Since in international trade concurrence does not mean a direct change from one hand into the other, there can be several forms in which this requirement is to be fulfilled. Article 58 can provide an orientation for it. We believe, however, that in choosing the forms of concurrence, it has to play a role whether a party is liable for a breach of contract. The concrete form to be applied would then have to be chosen to the disadvantage of that party. When the contract is avoided because the seller has delivered grossly non-conforming goods, the buyer may demand that a letter of credit be opened up as a condition for the restitution. Where the avoidance, however, is caused by the buyer who stops paying instalments, the seller will at best be willing to repay the refundable part of the price on the condition of cash against documents, and require the granting of an opportunity to examine the goods to be restituted. This means that arrangements will in any event have to be made between the parties. When they do not succeed, the competent decid-

ing organ should proceed according to the principles mentioned above.

The situation, however, is further complicated because it will in most cases not be clear in which amount the performance in money will have to be restituted. In this regard, the CISG offers little help to clarify the situation. Every party will, of course, be interested in having the sum of money to which he will be entitled or which he will have to pay under Article 84 and refundable expenses related to the restitution included in the concurrent restitution as either surcharges or reductions. In general, this has to be considered as justified since restitution relates to the claims as they actually stand. The parties, therefore, have to agree the sums and/or obtain a decision on them before the concurrent restitution takes place.

Article 82

(Buyer's loss of right to avoid or to require delivery of substitute goods)

(1) The buyer loses the right to declare the contract avoided[1] or to require the seller to deliver substitute goods[3] if it is impossible for him to make restitution of the goods substantially in the condition in which he received them[2].

(2) The preceding paragraph does not apply:

(a) if the impossibility of making restitution of the goods or of making restitution of the goods substantially in the condition in which the buyer received them is not due to his act or omission[4];

(b) if the goods or part of the goods have perished or deteriorated as a result of the examination provided for in article 38[5]; or

(c) if the goods or part of the goods have been sold in the normal course of business or have been consumed or transformed[6] by the buyer in the course of normal use before he discovered or ought to have discovered the lack of conformity[7].

1.1. The norm relates merely to the *right of the buyer* to avoid the contract.

1.2. The right to avoid the contract *lapses* when the goods can no longer be restituted. But there are so many important exceptions to this principle that the principle itself should constitute an exception.

1.3. In FRG publications (Huber, 494 fol; Schlechtriem, 503) the question was raised what happens when restitution becomes *impossible after the buyer has declared the contract avoided*. We believe that basically it should be proceeded analogously to how one would have proceeded before the declaration of avoidance. Where the impossibility is caused because of circumstances under paragraph 2 (of which only subpara. (a) is of relevance here), the right to avoid the contract remains in effect on the general conditions. This is justified because it presupposes a fundamental breach of contract by the seller. Where the impossibility is caused by grounds which would have led to the lapsing of the right to avoidance, the implementation of the avoidance of the contract would also be thwarted by it (see also Huber, 495). This also follows from the synallagmatic connection of the obligations involved in restitution. There may be modifications to the disadvantage of the seller when he delays a justified avoidance or does not demand restitution of the goods within a reasonable period. Even more radical solutions, even though not applicable in our view, are offered by those authors who infer from Article 70 a deferral of the passing of risk or a falling back of the risk on the first party (Article 70, note 1).

2.1. *Normal wear and tear* of the goods would not be in the way of their restitution. It would be different, however, in the case of greater damage which has its cause in the improper use or maintenance of the goods by the buyer. The latter can insofar not rely on grounds for exemption. They would only refer to claims for damages.

2.2. We hold that what is at issue in regard to the obligation to restitute the goods is exact restitution of the delivered goods. Obligations *cannot be fulfilled by delivering substitute goods* as Tallon (BB, 608) believes. Typically, the buyer will withdraw from a contract on goods which have already been delivered and taken by him on grounds of non-conformity of the goods, and then, only those goods will have to be restituted.

3. Here the *conditions* for the right to delivery of substitute goods are rendered *more precise*, but in a not very fortunate way from a legislative point of view (reference to Article 46, paragraph 2, would have been better).

4.1. The right to avoid a contract *must have existed*. Hence, in general, it will have nothing to do with the event which causes the impossibility of restitution.

In note 2 we have given examples for when the buyer has caused the impossibility of restitution. This is not the case where the perishing or deterioration was accidental (Article 70, note 1), unless they occurred because the buyer did not protect the goods in the customary manner. He will also be responsible for an impossibility of restitution because of omission on his part. This, however, does not apply when the goods could not be restituted even earlier for grounds which were not caused by the buyer.

4.2. It happens sometimes that the buyer himself is in a position to restitute the goods in the manner required, but that he is *prevented* from doing so *because of foreign trade rules*. The right to avoid the contract remains in our view untouched, but its realization may be thwarted insofar as concurrent restitution (Article 81, paragraph 2) cannot be made. This may also happen when the price cannot be refunded. Applying the underlying legal idea of Article 71 fol we are of the opinion that an avoidance is blocked when it is clear that there can be no concurrent restitution.

5. The goods should, in general, withstand examination so that cases are referred to here where the goods do not survive it because of *non-conformity*, e.g. a motor gets stuck during an orderly test run. In most cases the goods would later be damaged during normal use, but it is specifically registered when higher demands are made on the customary goods during the examination. Where the buyer has overstrained the goods, however, or has not examined them in the prescribed way, he may have caused the impossibility of restitution.

6. Reference is made here to goods with *hidden defects* (note 7). Material, for instance, is used to manufacture goods, and later when the goods are finished it becomes apparent the goods delivered do not conform to the contract. It is obvious that the right to avoid the contract shall not be influenced by the manufacturing process. Less convincing is that a normal re-sale relieves from the obligation to restitution (c. also Vischer/Lausanne, 183 fol.; Tallon/BB, 609). Either the final purchaser avoids the contract and has to restitute the goods or he retains them and asserts other claims because of

breach of contract. Where he declares the contract avoided, he can restitute the goods to the buyer; where he retains them, it is not understandable why he should be allowed to avoid the contract. This undesirable consequence under a legal policy point of view, which has been interpreted very differently in publications (Honnold, 452), can best be circumvented when it is assumed that a breach of contract cannot be fundamental in that event. It does, therefore, not entitle to avoidance or delivery of substitute goods when the goods are resold and the final purchaser does not avoid the contract. In that case the buyer will not lose what he could have been entitled to expect under the contract (Article 25). This aspect of the rule would thus apply only when the final purchaser declares the contract avoided without having the obligation to restitute the goods, e.g. for the reasons given under subparas. (a) and (b) if the CISG applies also to that contract.

This applies similarly to the right to delivery of *substitute goods* when the final purchaser cannot restitute the goods.

7. The buyer must have *examined the goods* under Article 38, and there must have been a non-conformity which could not be established during the examination.

Article 83

(Buyer's retention of other remedies)

A buyer who has lost the right to declare the contract avoided or to require the seller to deliver substitute goods in accordance with article 82 retains all other remedies[1] under the contract and this Convention.

1. It follows from this article, for instance, that the right to reduction of the price is retained even if the goods have been destroyed later by the buyer.

Article 84[1]

(Accounting for benefits in case of restitution)

(1) If the seller is bound to refund the price, he must also pay[2] interest[3] on it, from the date on which the price was paid.

(2) The buyer must account to the seller for all benefits which he has derived from the goods or part of them[4]:

(a) if he must make restitution of the goods or part of them[5]; or

(b) if it is impossible for him to make restitution of all or part of the goods or to make restitution of all or part of the goods substantially in the condition in which he received them, but he has nevertheless declared the contract avoided[6] or required the seller to deliver substitute goods[7].

1. Going beyond the obligation to restitute the goods under Article 81, paragraph 2, this article stipulates that the *benefits* have to be accounted for which the party having to restitute the goods obtained from the performances in goods or in price, have to be returned. This obligation arises irrespective of the grounds which have led to the avoidance of the contract. But its results can in the end be considerably modified. The party who has declared the contract avoided because of a breach of contract by the other party will, as a rule, have the right to claim damages which he can set off against payment obligations under this article. Furthermore, the parties may set off against each other the claims they might have under this article (note 8 of Article 81).

2. This rule proceeds on the assumption that the seller, within the period in which he has disposal over the price, *has a benefit* from it, at least in the form of interest, and, therefore, sets the date of the payment as the date from which on interest begins to run. This is the day when the payment is actually made according to the contractually or legally (Article 57 and 58) provided procedure; in our view also in cases where the seller in individual cases had disposal of the means only later. Interest runs until the demand for the restitution of the price lapses, in particular by performance or effective setting off.

3. In regard to the *amount of interest* there is the almost uniform view that the calculation of interest should be based on the interest rate used in the seller's country because it is the return of benefits drawn from use that are at issue and not claims for damages (so already O. R., 58). Tallon (BB, 612), however, expresses doubt. Actually, we do not see why we should, in this context, depart from our general opinion, that the amount of interest to be claimed is to be calculated according to the general subsidiary statute (note 2.2. of Article 78). However, the view held in publications by a majority of colleagues is also acceptable. This does, in our view, not exclude the buyer from claiming further damages when the avoidance of the contract is based on a breach of contract by the seller and/or the latter commits another breach of contract which leads to buyer be-

ing withdrawn means. Late repayment would also constitute such a breach, and our view corresponds with the one held by Schlechtriem (102, note 449).

4.1. Basically, the buyer does not have to return the equivalent of the benefits which he omitted to draw. This again does not exclude that the seller may assert *claims for damages* because of loss in value of the goods delivered where the avoidance is based on a breach of contract by the buyer and/or the latter restitutes belatedly. These claims for damages may indeed come close to benefits not drawn.

4.2. The benefits do not have to be returned in kind, but according to the requirements of international trade, in *money*.

5.1. In this case, possible benefits may exist in the *use of the goods*. In calculating them one should, in our view, proceed as a rule from how a temporary placing at the disposal of the relevant goods would have been compensated for, e.g. in the framework of a leasing contract, provided that the goods were actually used. This also meets the legal ideas as contained in Article 76. The opposite to this rule consists in that the seller has to accept normal wear and tear of the goods to be restituted. A payment of the equivalent of fruits as it is seemingly envisaged by Leser (Freiburg, 250) cannot be excluded. All the more so since it brings close to the actually drawn benefits, but will often be impractical because the expenses for the fruit bearing will have to be deducted again. In many cases the drawing of benefits will not be possible anyway because of the reasons for the avoidance, non-conformity of the goods, or because of the category of goods, (consumer goods.

5.2. In the event of a delivery of *substitute goods* this rule will hardly be of practical relevance. The buyer generally has the right to the benefits of use which he draws from the goods because they are satisfied by the payment of the price in the context of the agreed terms of payment. It is not customary to require an additional payment in the event that the buyer twice receives new goods. As required, these did not conform to the contract in the first instance so that it would be more likely for the buyer to claim damages.

6. It follows from Article 82, paragraph 2 when a contract can be avoided without restitution being made. In these events, benefits from use are to be compensated to the extent to which the goods could be used until the possibility of restitution was lost. The advantages nonetheless include *claims for damages vis-a-vis third parties*, the party in breach or the insurance company, in connection with a damage or a destruction of the goods as well as price demands vis-a-vis third parties. It cannot be left to the discretion of the buyer, in

our view, to decide whether or not he draws the benefits, hence no-tifies and pursues in time a claim vis-a-vis an insurance company. He is obligated to do so, both according to the principle of good faith (Article 7, paragraph 1) and the general principles of the CISG (Article 7, paragraph 2); in the latter case particularly because of the obligation to cooperate (note 10.1. of Article 7). But the buyer must be considered as having the right to fulfil this obligation by ceding claims against third parties to the seller. This is the obvious choice when the claims are uncertain because of those grounds which also led to the avoidance of the contract, i.e. price claims vis-a-vis third parties to which defective goods were delivered).

7. The inclusion of the delivery of substitute goods in this context should be of *minor practical relevance* and was obviously supposed to establish a correspondence with Article 82. A case to which this rule could possibly be applied is the one where non-conforming goods, for which substitute goods are delivered, are in addition af-fected by an insured accident so that the buyer obtains a refund which he has to return to the seller.

Section VI
Preservation of the goods

Introductory remarks

1. The reciprocal obligation of the parties to preserve the goods is an expression of the *general obligation to cooperate*, as it can be de-duced from this or that provision of the CISG as one of the Conven-tion's underlying general principles (Article 7, paragraph 2 and note 10.1. on it). The rule amounts to that in the case of hindrances in the process of delivery, which may occur at one of the parties', the other party is obligated to take care of the goods, provided that he disposes of the better opportunities to do so and is not overly burdened thereby. The facts try to cover the typical situation as concretely as possible, but cannot enter into all of the details and are insofar to be interpreted in the meaning of the above-mentioned basic concern. The obligation to preserve the goods and the further consequences it entails, arise irrespective of whether or not the party under whose risk the hindrance occurred is responsible for it.

2. The section is *structured* in such a way that Article 85 formulates the conditions for the obligation of the seller to preserve the goods. Article 86 does the same in regard of the buyer. Both articles also determine the basic content of these obligations. Finally, the re-quirements for both parties concerning the substance of the preser-vation obligation is specified, namely storage with third parties (Article 87) and sale of the goods in the form of resale (Article 88,

paragraph 1) and/or of emergency sale (Article 88, paragraph 2). The general structure of the Convention (Introductory remarks 2.4.) is repeated here in a tighter context.

3. The CISG makes the obligation to preserve the goods a contractual obligation of the parties. Since the CISG does not make any legal difference between main and auxiliary obligations, it is irrelevant whether the obligations to preserve are considered as auxiliary obligations as is done by some authors (Eberstein/Dölle, 575 on ULIS). A breach of these obligations entails *claims for damages* when there are no grounds for exemption (note 1 of Article 74).

Article 85

(Seller's obligation to preserve)

If the buyer is in delay in taking delivery[1] of the goods or, where payment of the price and delivery of the goods are to be made concurrently, if he fails to pay the price[2], and the seller is either in possession of the goods[3] or otherwise able to control their disposition[4], the seller must take such steps as are reasonable in the circumstances to preserve them[5]. He is entitled[6] to retain them until he has been reimbursed his reasonable expenses by the buyer[7].

1. It is decisive here that the seller *cannot deliver*, and it is, therefore, sufficient that the buyer does not fulfil one of the two elements of his obligation to take delivery under Article 60. The non-taking of delivery may also hide a rejection of the goods by the buyer (notes 2, 8 and 10 of Article 86) which the seller does not accept so that he continues to proceed according to the contract.

2. This amendment was added at the diplomatic conference at the proposal of the FRG (O. R., 398, 139). It *presupposes the right of the buyer to retain* the goods (Article 58). Non-payment becomes manifest when the goods are tendered. Then the risk has in general already passed to the buyer (Article 67) so that there will be every reason to substantiate an obligation of the seller to preserve the goods. Where the delivery is hindered by non-payment of a sum that was due and/or there is no payment security, it may be supposed that the seller, because of his right to retain the goods, does not even initiate delivery. The risk will not pass in this event so that it will be on the seller to take care of the goods already since he still bears the risk.

3. This is the case, in particular, when he has *not handed them over* to a carrier for delivery to the buyer. Preservation in this context generally requires the least additional expenses.

4. This happens mainly when the seller has *already handed over* the goods to the carrier, but is still in possession of the documents on whose basis he can instruct the carrier on how to proceed with the goods and/or when he can induce the holder of the documents, like in a particular bank, a trusty forwarding agent or others, to give such instructions and/or take steps.

5.1. This half-sentence characterizes the *substance* of the preservation obligation. It is of relevance when the risk (like under Article 68; c. also note 2) has already passed to the buyer (Schlechtriem, 104; also Honnold, 457).

5.2. What is to be considered as "steps as are reasonable in the circumstances" will have to be determined using the measure which the CISG applies (e.g. Article 8, paragraph 2) to flesh out such vague descriptions. It amounts to taking such steps as they would be taken by a *reasonable person* in the same circumstances.

Steps to be taken with *priority* are described in Articles 87 and 88. They can be applied in such a way that they constitute performance surrogates in the meaning of the subsidiary applicable law, not only steps to preserve the goods. The call for instructions of the buyer and their implementation, where they are appropriate, may be such a step. But this will be more seldom the case than in regard to the steps to be taken by the buyer to preserve the goods, because the seller can preserve the goods which are still in his possession and his further stocks.

5.3. The *duration* of the period for preservation can be deduced by reverse conclusion from Article 88, paragraph 1 (note 2.2. on it). It will continue to exist, however, as long as there is no resale.

6. Where steps to preserve the goods have been taken, not only does the buyer have to create the original conditions in regard to taking delivery and payment, but he must also, where there is doubt, refund the *reasonable expenses* concurrently when the seller requires so. But the latter can also pursue a refunding separately if he wants to avoid another delay after the buyer has removed the decisive obstacles. The seller must, in accordance with the principle of good faith, be considered as having the obligation not to make the delivery dependent on the reimbursement of expenses for the steps he has taken to preserve the goods; where the buyer procures

an appropriate security (in this sense Barrera Graf/BB, 618 fol) when they are completely irrelevant.

7. The reimbursement of expenses is *no payment of damages* even though the two may overlap. This is of importance where the buyer can exempt himself from damages he caused in breaching the contract. But he must always pay the expenses for measures taken to preserve the goods.

Article 86[1]

(Buyer's obligation to preserve)

(1) If the buyer has received the goods[2] and intends to exercise any right under the contract or this Convention to reject them[3], he must take such steps to preserve them as are reasonable in the circumstances[4]. He is entitled to retain them until he has been reimbursed his reasonable expenses by the seller[5].

(2) If goods dispatched to the buyer[6] have been placed at his disposal at their destination[7] and he exercises the right to reject them[8], he must take possession of them on behalf of the seller[9], provided that this can be done without payment of the price and without unreasonable inconvenience or unreasonable expense[10]. This provision does not apply if the seller or a person authorized to take charge of the goods on his behalf is present at the destination[11]. If the buyer takes possession of the goods under this paragraph, his rights and obligations are governed by the preceding paragraph[12].

1. The article deals with two *different situations*: first, the buyer has already received the goods (note 2) and second, the goods have only been tendered to him (notes 6 and 7). The latter is provided for in greater detail, i.e. the obligation to preserve the goods is tied to additional conditions because the buyer is required additional activities in this case.

2. We believe that the *term "received"* has the same meaning as the terms "take over" in Article 60, subpara. (b) (notes 7.1. and 7.2. of that article) for what matters is that the buyer has indeed taken possession of the goods. It is regrettable that different terms are used. The receipt or taking over of the goods on the face hardly differs from the taking possession of the goods under paragraph 2. But the

latter is done only after the right to rejection has been exercised (note 8).

3.1. The view was expressed at the diplomatic conference that the right to reject the goods is given only when there are the prerequisites for an avoidance of the contract or for the right to delivery of substitute goods (O. R., 399; so also believes Schlechtriem, 104). These are in particular the cases of Articles 49 and 46, paragraph 2, but probably also of Articles 72 and 73, hence without any doubt the most important and typical applications. From an overall point of view, however, this approach is too narrow for Article 52. It grants a *right to refuse to take delivery* of the goods, which is not linked with an avoidance of the contract, but which also leads to a right to rejection in the event of early and excess delivery. The right to suspension of obligations under Article 71 could lead to a right to rejection, e.g. when the buyer refuses to take over, as agreed, parts for a machine form a company that has declared bankruptcy as partial deliveries before he has a security for that the rest will also be delivered. Therefore, we have in another context (note 2 of Article 60) interpreted the right to reject the goods in broader terms, so to speak as an expression of general principles that underlie the Convention and are reflected in the cited articles. Article 86, however, does not offer an independent basis for the ascertainment of a general right to rejection because of a breach of contract. Barrera Graf (BB, 621) nonetheless seems to hold such a view. Such a right has to be provided for in the Convention or in a contract.

3.2. The *period* within which the right to reject will have to be exercised depends on the norms which provide for it, hence in particular, the periods fixed for the avoidance of a contract or the claim for delivery of substitute goods. The facts given under this article are based on the assumption that rejection is made after the receipt of the goods so that the affirmation by Barrera Graf (BB, 622) that the buyer will have to manifest his intention at the moment of receipt, is not convincing.

The intention to exercise the right to reject the goods has to be *manifested* vis-a-vis the seller. Where this is not done, the buyer has to take charge of the goods as being his own. Only after such manifestation this provision will become applicable, all the more so since under Article 70 and 82, paragraph 2, subpara. (a) the effects of the risk will, at least in that case, fundamental breach of contract, be on the seller.

4. Reference is made here to the *same steps* as described in note 5 of Article 85. In most cases the buyer will in his own interest preserve the goods in order not to lose his right to avoid the contract (Article 82, paragraph 1; Schlechtriem, 104).

5. Compare notes 6 and 7 of Article 85.

6. It is obviously assumed that a contract is referred to here which provides for *carriage of the goods* (Article 67). It is of no relevance in this case what should be considered as place of delivery or place of risk passing. According to Eberstein (Dölle, 587) it is not necessary (under the identical wording of ULIS) that transmission of the goods has been agreed, e.g. the seller finally dispatches the goods because the buyer does not fetch it as agreed. While agreeing to his idea because in that event measures might have to be taken to preserve the goods, we see problems involved in this interpretation for there is actually no place of destination in the meaning of the following text (note 7). One might agree with the author, however, in those cases where there is no doubt about the destination.

7. Reference is made hereby to the *contractual place of destination*. If the goods are delivered at a completely different place, there will, in our view, be no obligation of the buyer to preserve them for it will have to be assumed that he has no representation there. Where the buyer has delivered the goods to a third party in a distance sale, it will be problematic to determine whether or not that third party has to assume the obligation of the preservation of the goods. In the case of deliveries at construction sites or similar places the buyer will have to have an appropriate representative ready.

It is spelled out in the Secretariat's Commentary (O. R., 62) that the buyer need not take possession of the goods when he has already rejected the documents. We believe that there is no reason for doing that. On the contrary, when the rest of the conditions are fulfilled, he may be obligated to *take possession of the documents* in order to be able to take charge of the goods.

8. Regarding the right to rejection, compare note 3.1. It will have to be *exercised at the latest* at the time when the goods are tendered to him because the obligation to preserve the goods will commence at the same time, at least, however, before the buyer has taken possession of the goods. Otherwise the conditions of the case under paragraph 1 are fulfilled. It will, in particular, be the so-called rights to refuse receipt of the goods as mentioned in note 3.1. which will be of relevance here.

9. The buyer *physically takes possession* of the goods after having made it clear that he does not intend to take them over. The passing of the risk is tied to the taking over of the goods only in the cases referred to in Article 69 which are not relevant here. But a justified rejection of the goods should have such effects on the seller which are similar to those involved in the risk bearing (Article 70 and note 1 of it).

10.1. The *obligation* to preserve the goods *does not apply* in particular when the payment term "cash against documents" is used. The case in which the goods can be obtained only against payment is in our view identical to the one in which security will have to be procured as a condition for the taking possession of the goods, e.g. "documents against acceptance". When the payment was made earlier, e.g. from a letter of credit, or when it is not tied to the taking possession of the goods, an obligation to preserve the goods will arise.

10.2. *Unreasonable inconvenience* may, for instance, be caused when the buyer in a distance sale has the goods sent to a third party who cannot be expected to receive them or when he himself has no facilities for preserving the goods at the place of destination (but compare notes 7 and 12).

10.3. *Unreasonable expense* is incurred in the cases described in Article 88, paragraph 2 so that a concurrence is caused between the two provisions. We believe that the concern of the overall rule is best met when the approach of Article 88, paragraph 2, is given priority and this part of Article 86, paragraph 2 is not interpreted in such a way as to pretend that in this case there will be no obligation of preservation and thus no obligation of an emergency sale.

11. These are the seller's own duly authorized *employees* or his trade *representatives*. Unlike Honnold (460) we believe that a bank, which is only to present the documents on behalf of the seller, does in general not meet these requirements.

12. This amendment was included at the suggestion of Australia (O. R., 139). It relates to the steps to be taken to preserve the goods and the right to retain them, hence "...take such steps as are reasonable in the circumstances..." It is in the same sense that the relevant Article 92 ULIS, in which the amendment is missing, was interpreted (Eberstein/Dölle, 586).

Article 87

(Deposit with third person)

A party who is bound to take steps to preserve the goods may deposit[1] them in a warehouse of a third person at the expense of the other party provided that the expense incurred is not unreasonable[2].

1.1. There was no discussion of this article, which was already contained in ULIS as Article 93, at the diplomatic conference. It makes clear that the goods can be deposited with *third parties* from which follows that the party having the obligation can keep them at his own place. This can be deduced from the wording of Articles 85 and 86 but is not directly said there.

No requirements have to be met by the storerooms of the third party, like that it would have to be a warehouse (Barrera Graf/BB, 626) or that specific documents would have to be issued or similar conditions, which is understandable since the party having the obligation to preserve the goods can even store them at his place. It is also understandable, and follows from the obligation to take "such steps as are reasonable..", that the storerooms have to fit the respective storage purpose (O. R., 62).

1.2. Where the primary or subsidiary applicable law connects further consequences with the deposit of the goods, the conditions set forth therein must also be fulfilled, e.g. issuance of a warehouse certificate by an authorized organization.

2. What is at issue is the *ratio between cost and value* of the goods. In particular, in the case of goods which are to be returned because of non-conformity, an expensive deposit will usually be out of the question.

Where a deposit at reasonable cost with a third party is not possible and where the obligated party cannot store the goods himself, the latter would have to proceed to an *emergency sale* under Article 88, paragraph 2.

Article 88

(Sale of the preserved goods)

(1) A party who is bound to preserve the goods in accordance with article 85 or 86 may sell them by any appropriate means[1] if there has been an unreasonable delay[2] by the other party in taking possession of the goods or in taking them back or in paying the price or the cost of preservation, provided that reasonable notice of the intention to sell has been given to the other party[3].

(2) If the goods are subject to rapid deterioration[4] or their preservation would involve unreasonable expense[5], a party who is bound to preserve the goods in accordance with article 85 or 86 must take reasonable measures to sell them[6]. To the extent possible he must give notice to the other party of his intention to sell[7].

(3) A party selling the goods has the right to retain out of the proceeds of sale an amount equal to the reasonable expenses of preserving the goods and of selling them[8]. He must account to the other party for the balance[9].

1.1. The resale to which paragraph 1 refers is to prevent the disturbed contractual relationship from being blocked permanently. The resale is *not bound to particular requirements*, it only has to be done by any appropriate means. It is in our view inappropriate to measure the appropriateness against the yardstick of national laws, as does the Secretariat's Commentary (O. R., 63) and also a number of subsequent authors (Schlechtriem, 105; Barrera Graf/BB, 628). We believe that the wording of the provision clearly indicates that there shall be exemption from particular requirements which the national laws indeed provide for in the event of resale, e.g. resale by certain persons, by specific procedure, Eberstein/Dölle, 595 fol. As appropriate will have to be regarded here as what a reasonable person of the same kind as the party obligated to preserve the goods would consider as appropriate in the same circumstances. It will thus have to be a method which promises appropriate proceeds. Appropriateness follows more from commercial than legal criteria. The resale can be made by the obligated party and not only by a neutral third party (of a similar view Eberstein/Dölle, 594; Vischer/Lausanne, 184).

1.2. Whether or not the resale is *justified* can be inferred from the CISG. The consequences which follow where the party was not entitled to resell the goods, in particular to what extent an acquisition in good faith was possible, will be guided by the national law as determined by the conflict-of-law rules (O. R., 63) (even where the CISG, which does not cover such cases, applies to the resale, too).

2.1. The *right to resell* the goods *will arise* for the seller when the buyer has unduly delayed the taking possession of the goods, the payment of the price, or the cost of preservation.

Where the right to reject the goods is based on that the buyer has avoided the contract and the price has already been paid in full or in part, the buyer may make the restitution of the goods dependent on the repayment of the price. This applies also, in our view, when he has taken possession of the goods on behalf of the seller (Article 86, paragraph 2). When the right to reject the goods has emerged because the buyer has required delivery of substitute goods, he may make the restitution dependent on the delivery of such substitute goods. One can assume that the seller being the party in breach has the obligation to perform first (note 7.2. of Article 81). The buyer will have the right to resell the goods when the seller causes an undue delay in the repayment of the price, its tendering, and/or the substitute performance, by way of analogy as the equivalent of the price.

The mentioned conditions may be fulfilled partly or completely.

2.2. Where the right is clear and undisputed the required measures have to be performed in the orderly course of transaction. And a delay is undue when it exceeds this time frame plus a *Nachfrist*. In the *event of disputes* between the parties it will have to be delayed, however, until the most essential arguments have been exchanged and the confrontation has come to a deadlock, but not until it is decided.

2.3. Whether or not *resale leads to performance,* according to the situation this is only possible when the seller is the one to resell the goods, would have to be deduced from the applicable subsidiary law whose possible, additional requirements will then have to taken into account.

3.1. This additional condition in regard to the resale is to point out to the other party the *consequences of its conduct*, and give him a chance to remedy the delay. Less important seems to us, the aspect of giving him an opportunity to send a representative to attend the sale (but see O. R., 400) because this would presuppose a public sale, which under the CISG seldom takes place.

Given this situation it will now have to be determined what is to be understood by "reasonable notice". We believe that from this wording, requirements can be deduced in regard to the *time and content* of the notice. It has to be given so early that the other party, in reacting speedily, still can remedy his fault. As the discussion at the diplomatic conference (O. R., 400 fol) has proved, it is possible for the notice to be given before the conditions for the resale are fulfilled (also Schlechtriem, 105), in that event it is to be conceived as a warning for possible conduct. The party entitled to resell the goods should not have to wait twice. In regard of the content it is relevant, above all, to indicate how long the entitled party wants to wait. The notice is not bound to any form requirement and need not be received (Article 27).

3.2. Where the *obligation to give notice is not fulfilled*, the resale is not justified. The consequences of that transaction will follow from the applicable law for which the CISG can only create the facts (of a different opinion Eberstein/Dölle, 594). There might by claims for damages in the relationship between the parties when the resale is considered as valid even though it was not justified.

3.3. An *objection* by the other party does not hinder the resale when the conditions are fulfilled (Eberstein/Dölle, 594), but the arguments voiced can make it clear whether this was indeed the case.

4. This condition is fulfilled in the case of *easily perishable goods*. But the view is held that a rapid loss of the *economic value* of the goods can also be subsumed hereunder (Schlechtriem, 105, who unjustly relies on the Secretariat's Commentary, O. R., 63, because the latter is based on another text). We are of the opinion that from the debates in the plenary of the diplomatic conference (O. R., 227 fol) which led to the deletion of the word "loss", the conclusion can rightly be drawn that there is no obligation to sell in that event (Vischer/Lausanne, 184). It may often be difficult for the obligated party to foresee a price decline, certainly less in the case of highly fashionable bathing clothes at the end of the season than in the case of raw materials, so that he cannot be burdened by this additional risk. All the more so since the remaining conditions which have led to the situation of resale will frequently be disputable. It would be appropriate, however, to substantiate a right of the owner to sell

the goods. This can to a certain extent be done within the framework of paragraph 1 interpreting correspondingly the undue delay and the obligation to give notice. The seller who actually should have the greatest interest in it, could then rapidly resell the goods. He could also authorize the buyer to do so or the latter could act accordingly in the presumed interest of the seller. But this would be legal constructions that lie outside the CISG.

5. This can be the case where the feeding and care of living animals, cooling, air-conditioning etc. are required. This rule should, in our view, apply in the cases of Article 86, paragraph 2, not only when it becomes apparent that the preservation of the goods would involve excessive costs after possession of the goods has been acquired, as believes Barrera Graf (BB, 631), but when the *relevant goods are tendered* and the remaining conditions are fulfilled (see also note 10.3. of Article 86). This, however, presupposes chances to sell the goods.

6. The conditions commented on in paragraphs 4 and 5 characterize the urgent necessity to sell, which makes it an emergency sale. The party who has the responsibility to preserve the goods is obligated not necessarily to carry out such a sale, but to *make the relevant efforts* for it. His obligation is not geared toward being successful but toward engaging in the respective measures.

The seller will have to be required to include the goods in his customary sales transactions attributing them their due rank; the buyer also when he is a trader in the branch. Where the buyer acts as the final purchaser and lacks sales opportunities of his own, he must probably be regarded as having the obligation to engage a third party. If he is to act himself, he cannot be measured by the yardstick used for a professional businessman when the relevant branch is not his usual branch.

When the *owner* of the goods *breaches this obligation* and when, for this reason, there is no sale or only one on very unfavourable terms, i.e. dumping, he has the obligation to pay damages to the other party.

As to the consequences of an emergency sale for which the conditions have not been fulfilled, compare note 1.2.

7. The possibility of giving notice has arisen when its *function* (note 3) *can be fulfilled* before the sale has been performed.

8. If the party has stored the goods himself or sold them, he can demand *reasonable payment for them* (Huber, 517, therefore rightly considers the accounting for a resale more favourable than for a substitute transaction; Schlechtriem, 105) just as he can charge services provided to him by third parties.

9. This does in no way exclude that the *balance is set off* against other claims as Barrera Graf (BB, 631) apparently believes, even when or because the setting off is regulated neither in this place nor elsewhere in the CISG and therefore has to be taken from national law. Since the obligation to preserve the goods presupposes that the other party has committed a breach of contract, there will regularly be such claims. Payment of at least part of the balance will, however, be made for instance when the buyer, who himself has not paid the price yet, has sold the goods.

Part IV

Final Provisions

Introductory remarks

The debate on part IV at the Diplomatic Conference in Vienna was held in the Second Committee (O. R., 141 fol, 434 fol). These final provisions *largely follow from the Vienna Convention on the Law of Treaties* (Vienna Treaty Convention). This was, however, forgotten in respect of the term used for the States Parties. Hence the entire CISG mentions the *"Contracting State"* when referring to the *"State Party"*, e.g. Article 1 or Article 101. A State is a State Party when the Convention has become effective for him; it is a Contracting Party when the Convention has not yet become effective for him, but when he has already deposited his instrument of ratification, acceptance, confirmation or accession (Article 2, paragraph 1, Vienna Treaty Convention). In regard to specific issues the CISG was also aligned with the Limitation Convention and the United Nations Convention on the Carriage of Goods by Sea (Hamburg rules), i.e. earlier Conventions drafted by UNCITRAL, which do not take the terminology of the Vienna Treaty Convention into account. Insofar as those provisions were further developed at the Diplomatic Conference, the former were laid down in the Protocol to the Limitation Convention.

The provisions of Part IV can be divided into three categories: provisions which serve to administer the Convention (e.g. Articles 89, 99 and 100); others which govern the Convention's relation to other international conventions (Article 90; 99), and finally those in which possible reservations and declarations are stipulated (Articles 92 to 96) (Winship/Parker, 1-39).

Article 89

(Depositary)

The Secretary-General of the United Nations[2] is hereby designated as the depositary[1] for this Convention.

1. The tasks of the depositary of an international treaty have been explained in detail in Articles 76 fol of the Vienna Treaty Convention. The *functions of a depositary* comprise in particular:

(a) *keeping custody of the original text* of the treaty and of any full powers delivered to the depositary;

(b) *preparing certified copies* of the original text and preparing any further text of the treaty in such additional languages as may be required by the treaty and transmitting them to the parties and to the States entitled to become parties to the treaty;

(c) *receiving* any *signatures* to the treaty and receiving and keeping custody of any instruments, notifications and communications relating to it;

(d) *examining* whether the signature or any instrument, notification or communication relating to the treaty is in due and proper form and, if need be, bringing the matter to the attention of the State in question;

(e) *informing* the parties and the States entitled to become parties to the treaty of acts, notifications and communications relating to the treaty;

(f) informing the States entitled to become parties to the treaty when the number of signatures or of instruments of ratification, acceptance, approval or accession required for the *entry into force* of the treaty has been received or deposited;

(g) *registering* the treaty with the Secretariat of the United Nations; and

(h) performing the functions specified in other provisions of the present Convention (Article 77, paragraph 1, Vienna Treaty Convention).

In the CISG, *additional functions* of a depositary are stipulated, e.g. *in Article 99, paragraph 6*. References can be found also in Article 91, paragraph 4; Article 93, paragraph 2; Article 97, paragraphs 2, 3 and 4; and Article 101, paragraphs 1 and 2.

2. For international conventions which are concluded within the framework of the United Nations, it is *usually the Secretary-General of the United Nations* who is designated as depositary, irrespective of the country in which the relevant diplomatic conference was held. For conventions which are concluded outside of the United Nations framework, it is usually the government of the country where the diplomatic conference was held which is designated as depositary.

The Secretary-General *annually* publishes *a register* of signatures, ratifications, accessions etc. in respect of multilateral conventions for which he acts as depositary. (This register is published under ST/LEG/SER.D/...)

The Secretariat of UNCITRAL also publishes a report on the status of ratifications and accessions every year (see e.g. *A/CN.9/337* Status of Conventions of *1 July 1990*).

Article 90

(Relationship with Conventions containing provisions dealing with matters governed by this Convention)

This Convention does not prevail[1] over any international agreement[5] which has already been[2] or may be entered into[3] and which contains provisions concerning the matters[4] governed by this Convention, provided that the parties have their places of business in States Parties to such agreement[6].

1. This article regulates the relationship between the CISG and earlier or later international agreements on the same subject. This is a complicated problem because the simple principle that agreements which are concluded later prevail over those which were concluded earlier cannot be applied here, among others because of the fact that the *Contracting States to the different conventions are seldom identical.* Article 90 stipulates that other international agreements are not affected by the CISG. This corresponds to Article 30, paragraph 2, of the Vienna Treaty Convention. Because of the rule laid down in Articles 30 and 59 of the Vienna Treaty Convention there was doubt that Article 90 was needed at all.

When it is stated that earlier or later conventions on the same subject are not affected, this means that those prevail over the CISG, but they do not fully exclude the CISG. The provisions of the CISG fill the gaps to the extent to which those are contained in the other agreements (Winship/Parker, 1-42).

2. The agreements on the same subject which are already concluded include, *inter alia*, the Hague Conventions and the General Conditions of Delivery of Goods of the Council for Mutual Economic Assistance (GCD/CMEA). While the Hague Conventions are to be replaced by the CISG (c. Article 99, paragraphs 3-6), the Member States of the CMEA have not declared such intention in regard to the GCD/CMEA. Besides, the *matters which the GCD/CMEA provides for* are *not* fully *congruous with those of the CISG.* The GCD/CMEA rules a number of matters which are not contained in the CISG and, vice-versa, certain matters are only regulated by the CISG so that in regard to those the CISG is to be applied as a subsidiary.

3. The *Contracting States can conclude deviating agreements* in the future, both bilateral and multilateral. Agreements to be concluded in the future are not meant to be a revision of the CISG. The Hague Conventions (Articles XIV and/or Article XII), in contrast, contained specific provisions on the possibilities of revision which were not included in the CISG (Evans/BB, 638). Should there be in the future a modification of the CISG, it would not be regulated by Article 90, but rather would provisions be agreed that are similar to those found in Article 99.

4. There need *not be congruence*. The Contracting States can regulate specific questions in deviation of or amending the provisions of the Convention.

There is differing interpretation of what is meant by "the matters governed by this Convention". It is clear that the subject of the Convention are international sales of goods, but is reference made only to the substantive rules of the international sale of goods or also to the conflict-of-law rules? Vékas (342 fol) and Winship (Parker, 1-41) include the conflict-of-law rules in their considerations, which is of significance above all for the Hague Convention on the Law Applicable to Contracts for the International Sale of Goods, while Kindler (780) obviously understands matters to be governed by the convention as not only covering the social situation to be taken into account but also the character of the regulation itself, and therefore excludes the latter Convention from the matters referred to under Article 90.

According to Kindler (780), referring to Evans (BB, 637), Article 90 was meant to relate in particular to the two Hague Conventions.

The latter, however, expressly points to the fact that reference is not made to the Hague Conventions because the CISG in regard to those Conventions contains the special rule of Article 99.

5. The notion "international agreement" is used here as the generic term for international conventions. Besides, there is no difference between *treaty, convention, charter, covenant, pact, concordat or certified recommendation*. Article 90, however, is to cover only multilateral agreements. When Contracting States conclude bilateral or multilateral contracts, they have the possibility to make a reservation invoking Article 94.

6. The application of this provision presupposes that the parties to the sales contract have their *place of business in States that are parties to the other conventions*; it is, however, no condition that they have their places of business also in the States that are parties to the CISG (namely when the CISG is applied on the basis of Article 1, paragraph 1, subparagraph (b)).

Article 91
(Signature, ratification, acceptance, approval, accession)

(1) This Convention is open for signature[2] at the concluding meeting[3] of the United Nations Conference on Contracts for the International Sale of Goods and will remain open for signature by all States[1] at the Headquarters of the United Nations, New York until 30 September 1981[4].

(2) This Convention is subject to ratification[6], acceptance or approval[7] by the signatory States[5].

(3) This Convention is open for accession[8] by all States[1] which are not signatory States as from the date[9] it is open for signature.

(4) Instruments of ratification[10], acceptance, approval and accession are to be deposited[11] with the Secretary-General of the United Nations.

1. As already in the case of the Limitation Convention, the *clause "all States"* was included in the CISG, which corresponds to the principles of general and democratic international law. Article 6 of the Vienna Treaty Convention stipulates that any State is capable of concluding treaties. By contrast, it was general custom for a long time to accept only those States which are a member of the United Nations or of one of their specialized agencies.

2. The Convention is *not approved of through the mere act of signing* it (note 5). But in any case, signature is one step by which States affirm their serious intention to become a party to the Convention.

It would, of course, be possible to accept the signature as sufficient (c. Article 12, Vienna Treaty Convention).

3. The CISG was adopted at the concluding meeting of the Sales Conference by 42 States *without a vote against* and nine abstentions. At the final meeting of 11 April 1980 it was signed by Chile, Ghana, Yugoslavia, Austria, Singapore and Hungary.

4. The *period of time* during which a convention remains open for signature is *determined individually* and mostly is between 12 and 18 months to allow the States domestic consultations, if need be, e.g. with the economic circles concerned.

By September 30, 1981 the Convention had been signed by the following further States: China, CSFR, Denmark, Finland, France, FRG, former GDR, Italy, Lesotho, the Netherlands, Norway, Poland, Sweden, USA and Venezuela.

5. An international convention can be *approved in several ways*:

(a) by signature alone (but c. note 2);

(b) by signature followed by ratification, acceptance or approval; and

(c) by accession without prior signature.

In regard to the CISG only (b) and (c) are admissible. As to the effect, there is no difference. But there are agreements according to which the signatory States have farther-reaching rights than the member States which acceded later.

6. *Ratification, acceptance and approval* are terms which *define the same situation*, they reaffirm a signature. These differing terms have been developed more recently to satisfy the various procedures which have developed in the different countries (c. Article 11 Vienna Treaty Convention). Article 42 of the Limitation Convention only speaks of ratification.

Whether a signature is reaffirmed by ratification, acceptance or approval, and which government authority is to do it follows from domestic law.

From among the 21 signatory States of the CISG only Ghana, the Netherlands, Poland, Singapore and Venezuela did not ratify the Convention (as of 1 June 1990). Some of them have already announced their intention to do so.

7. According to Article 14 of the Vienna Treaty Convention agreement by a State to be bound by a treaty is expressed through ratification, acceptance or approval, when the treaty itself provides for it, or when it is otherwise established that the *Contracting States have agreed on the need for ratification*, or when the representative of a State has signed the treaty subject to ratification, or when the intention of a State to sign the treaty subject to ratification appears from the full powers of its representative or was expressed during the negotiation.

8. *Approval of a State* to be bound to a contract is according to Article 15 of the Vienna Treaty Convention expressed *through accession* when the contract itself provides for it, or when it is clear otherwise that the Contracting States have agreed on the possibility for a State to express approval by acceding to the Convention, or when all Contracting Parties have agreed later that such approval by a State can be expressed by way of his accession.

As of 1 June 1990, Egypt, Argentina, Australia, Byelorussia, Iraq, Mexico, Zambia, Switzerland, Syria and the Ukraine had acceded to the Convention.

9. Accession is usually possible only after the period envisaged for signature has expired. Since, however, *no difference* is made *in assessing the importance of signatory States and States which had acceded later* (note 5), States should have the opportunity to accede to the Convention from the beginning without having to sign first.

10. The documents expressing the agreement of States, no matter in which way it is given, are usually made out by the Ministries of Foreign Affairs.

11. Compare Article 89. As to the effects of deposition compare Article 99.

Introduction to Articles 92 - 101

Articles 92 - 96 contain the reservations permitted under this Convention (but c. note 2, Article 98). Concerning the possibility of reservations in general, compare note 1 to Article 98. The possibilities for reservations that are reflected and commented on in the following have been included in the Convention at the request of groups of States. They refer to questions relating to the *content of the Convention*, like Articles 92, 95 and 96, or to such which relate to the *territorial structure of a Contracting State*, e.g. Article 93 (compare Article 98, note 2) *or* to its *legal system*, e.g. Article 94.

While some declarations have to be made at the time of the approval of the Convention (like in the case of Article 92 or 93), others can be made at any time (like under Articles 93, 94 and 96).

Article 92

(Partial ratification, acceptance, approval or accession)

(1) A Contracting State[1] may declare[3] at the time of signature, ratification, acceptance, approval or accession[2] that it will not be bound by Part II of this Convention or that it will not be bound[4] by Part III of this Convention.

(2) A Contracting State which makes a declaration[5] in accordance with the preceding paragraph in respect of Part II or Part III of this Convention is not to be considered a Contracting State within paragraph (1) of article 1[6] of this Convention in respect of matters governed by the Part to which the declaration applies.

1. In the 1964 *Hague Conventions* the *conclusion of an international sales contract and* its *content* were provided for *in separate uniform laws* offering to the States the possibility to accede to either one or the other or to both conventions. As a matter of fact, all Contracting States of the Hague Conventions acceded to both conventions; Belgium and Israel, however, acceded first to the one and later to the other. This possibility was to be retained, in particular, at the request of the Scandinavian States. However, since during preparatory work by UNCITRAL a majority of States had spoken out in favour of combining the rules for conclusion and content, *the possibility of a reservation* had to be created *for interested States*.

It is possible now to exclude parts II or III of the Convention. Denmark, Finland, Norway and Sweden made use of the possibility to exclude part II. It is not expected that other States will perhaps exclude part III.

2. Compare here Article 91, note 8. The *declaration* can be made already *at the time of signature*; it will not be late, however, if made when that signature is confirmed through ratification, acceptance or approval; and it must be repeated in any case when the signature is confirmed (c. Article 97).

3. *Once* a State has *acceded* to the Convention, it may *no longer* make a *reservation* under Article 92; there is, however, a possibility of a partial denunciation (c. Article 101, paragraph 1).

4. A *reservation can be withdrawn at any time* (c. Article 97). If the reservation was made at the time of signature, it will suffice not to confirm and/or repeat it at the time of ratification, acceptance or approval. Ratification of the non-signed part of the Convention, and/or of the part of the Convention that is excluded from signature, is then considered as accession.

5. Insofar as the declaration was made in accordance with paragraph 1, it was not made by a State Party but rather by a signatory State, in the case of signature, or a Contracting State. Only when the Convention comes into effect in regard to the Contracting State the latter becomes a State Party (c. preface of part IV).

6. Hence the reservation is *relevant also in respect of the scope of application of the Convention* (Article 1, paragraph 1). This becomes relevant, for instance, in the relations of Germany with Sweden, and/or other Scandinavian States. When companies of the two above-mentioned States conclude sales contracts, the Convention is not applied to the conclusion of the contract according to Article 1, paragraph 1, subparagraph (a) because only one of the parties has his place of business in a Contracting State. The provisions to be applied to the formation of the contract follow from the rules of the international private law. If they refer to Swedish law, then this is to be invoked. If, however, they refer to German law, then the CISG is applied irrespective of the Swedish reservation because the Convention is part of German law, and is to be applied under Article 1, paragraph 1, subparagraph (b) even when the rules of international private law refer to the law of one Contracting State, even if only one, or none, of the parties has his place of business in a Contracting State (c. Article 1, note 6).

Article 93

(Federal State clause)

(1) If a Contracting State[1] has two or more territorial units[2] in which, according to its constitution, different systems of law are applicable in relation to the matters dealt with in this Convention, it may, at the time of signature, ratification, acceptance, approval or accession[3], declare that this Convention is to extend to all[4] its territorial units[2] or only to one or more of them, and may amend[6] its declaration by submitting another declaration at any time.

(2) The declarations are to be notified to the depositary[7] and are to state expressly the territorial units[2] to which the Convention extends.

(3) If, by virtue of a declaration under this article, this Convention extends to one or more but not all of the territorial units[2] of a Contracting State, and if the place of business[8] of a party is located in that State, this place of business, for the purposes of this Convention,[9] is considered not to be in a Contracting State, unless it is in a territorial unit to which the Convention extends.

(4) If a Contracting State makes no declaration under paragraph (1) of this article, the Convention is to extend to all territorial units of that State[5].

1. The reservation of Article 93 (but compare Article 98, note 2) was included, in particular, at the request of Canada and Australia. It relates to *federal States which* for matters governed by the Convention *have no central or no exclusive legislative competence.* Federal States like Germany or Austria do not need such a reservation. But the federation clause was vividly discussed at the diplomatic conference also by other States for it is in the interest of legal security to know exactly which is the effect of the accession by a federated State.

2. The term *"territorial unit"* was regarded as sufficiently *neutral* to cover federal States, federal countries, provinces, republics of a union or cantons. Regarding the difference between this term and a colonial clause, compare Article 31, note 3, of the Limitation Convention.

3. Compare Article 91, notes 5, 7 and 8. A declaration under Article 93 can only be made at the time of, non-technical, accession to the Convention, but not later. Although Australia made great efforts at the diplomatic conference to having the possibility of such reservation, it nonetheless did not make a relevant declaration at the time it acceded.

4. Also *without* making a relevant *declaration*, the Convention applies *to all territorial units*, compare paragraph 4. A positive declaration is sometimes necessary for the internal purposes of a Contracting State (O. R., 446).

5. This provision does not correspond to Article 29 of the Vienna Treaty Convention and *customary international law* and was, therefore, considered superfluous by some delegations.

6. If possible, such amendment should increase the number of territorial units, up to extending to all of them, to be included into the scope of application of the Convention rather than reduce it. If the Convention is to *apply to all territorial units* under paragraph 4, a reduction of that number will no longer be possible. Evans (BB, 649), however, considers a reduction as feasible; it would, as he believes, presuppose a relevant declaration. But this would amount to a partial denunciation.

As to the taking effect of the declaration compare Article 93.

7. Compare Article 89, note 1.

8. Compare Articles 1 and 10.

9. Compare Article 1, paragraph 1, subparagraph (a). In the light of Article 10 it was regarded as superfluous to go back here once again to the case where a party has several places of business (c. O. R., 445).

Article 94

(Declaration of non-application of Convention)

(1) Two or more Contracting States[1] which have the same or closely related legal rules on matters governed by this Convention may at any time declare that the Convention is not to apply to contracts of sale or to their formation[5] where the parties have their places of business in those States[2]. Such declarations may be made jointly[3] or by reciprocal unilateral[4] declarations.

(2) A Contracting State which has the same or closely related legal rules on matters governed by this Convention as one or more non-Contracting States[6] may at any time declare that the Convention is not to apply to contracts of sale or to their formation[5] where the parties have their places of business in those States.

(3) If a State which is the object of a declaration under the preceding paragraph subsequently becomes a Contracting State[7], the declaration made will, as from the date on which the Convention enters into force in respect of the new Contracting State, have the effect of a declaration made under paragraph (1), provided that the new Contracting State joins in such declaration or makes a reciprocal unilateral declaration[8].

1. This reservation is suited for *States which have the same or closely related legal rules*, irrespective of whether the same legal rules came into existence by way of international agreements (but c. Article 90), unilateral reception or in another way. At the diplomatic conference there was indication of a possible application of such reservation by the Scandinavian States as well as to the relations between the Netherlands and Belgium/Luxembourg, or between Australia and New Zealand (O. R., 436). Eörsi (Convention,...) suggested that the CMEA States make a joint declaration under Article 94. Honnold (466) in regard to Article 94, referred to the member States of the CMEA. A very similar provision can be found in the Hague Conventions (Article II) at the time of whose adoption the interests of the CMEA States did yet not play a role (c. also Evans/BB, 651). It is up to the States involved to decide for themselves what is to be considered as "closely related". So far, only the Scandinavian States made statements under Article 94, namely Denmark, Finland, Norway and Sweden pursuant to paragraph 1 in their relations with one another and the same States pursuant to paragraph 2 in their relations with Iceland.

2. When one of those States is a federal State, Article 93 is applied. The CISG excluded, domestic law is invoked. To the extent to which the States involved have the same legal rules, there will be no difference in whether the law of State A or State B is applied. When, however, the legal rules are only closely related, the *international private law of the forum will* in the first place *decide which law is to be applied*. Evans (BB, 653) mentions the hypothetical case that the parties have chosen as the applicable law that of a third State, which is a Contracting State of the CISG, the law of that State not being the same but being very closely related. Which is then the law to be applied by the courts? Evans does not answer this question. We believe that in such a case the courts of the States making the declaration should invoke the CISG as the right of that third State since the Convention was to be excluded under Article 94 only in favour of the application of the domestic law of the States of the declaration. There is no reason why the CISG should also be excluded in favour of the law of a non-involved third State.

Since a declaration under Article 94 only refers to the parties in the Contracting States themselves, parties in third States are not affected.

3. Joint declarations have the advantage of being unequivocal also in regard to time. As to the taking effect compare Article 97, paragraph 3.

4. Declarations which relate to one another *require prior arrangement* by the States concerned. A unilateral declaration may, of course, *also refer to* a *future declaration* by another State. Regarding the taking effect, compare Article 97, paragraph 3. If there is no second declaration, the first one is up in the air and does not take effect.

5. The declaration can also refer to *sales contracts and their formation.* The word "or" relates to the case where States might not be parties in regard to parts II and III; thus also to the case where the States concerned have the same or very closely related legal rules only in respect to one or the other part of the Convention.

6. Since pursuant to Article 1, paragraph 1, subparagraph (b) the CISG under certain conditions also applies to contracts between parties which have their place of business in non-Contracting States, paragraph 2 of Article 94 provides for the possibility of excluding application of the Convention where the legal rules of one Contracting State are the same or are closely related to those of non-Contracting States. Such reservation is not required where a reservation under Article 25 is made.

7. When a non-Contracting State, to which a declaration under paragraph 2 relates, becomes a Contracting State of the Convention, it has *two options*: It may join the view of the State which has made a declaration under paragraph 2 and declare a reservation on its part as a result of which paragraph 1 takes effect; or, if it believes otherwise, renounce making a declaration of its own. (It is thus not obligated to reject the declaration of the other State. An obligation of rejection was considered as politically undesirable; O. R., 448.) The result is a situation under paragraph 1 in which the first declaration is not followed by a second one.

8. When the non-Contracting State at the time of accession does not make a declaration, the Contracting State, which has made a declaration under paragraph 2, now has to apply the Convention also vis-a-vis the new Contracting State. Hence, there is the same effect as when the new Contracting State has withdrawn its declaration (Article 97, note 10).

Article 95

(Declaration concerning the exclusion of reference to conflict-of-law rules)

Any State[1] may declare at the time of the deposit of its instrument of ratification, acceptance, approval or accession that it will not be bound[2] by subparagraph (1) (b) of article 1 of this Convention.

1. Without this reservation, which was integrated in the Convention at the request of Czechoslovakia, an accession to the Convention would have the effect of putting the *CISG in the place of what has been the domestic rule for international sales contracts*, irrespective of whether or not the parties to the sales contract have their places of business in the Contracting States.

This would create a *uniform rule* for all international sales contracts to which the law of one Contracting Party is applicable. On the other hand, a specific rule for international economic contracts, e.g. the Czechoslovak law on international trade, would be excluded in regard to international sales contracts to the extent of which the CISG contains relevant rules.

There was a rather controversial discussion of Article 95 at the Vienna Diplomatic Conference. The Czechoslovak proposal was rejected in the Second Committee (O. R., 439), but adopted in the plenary (O. R., 230). Also as to publications, Article 95 has been the one most commented on among the final provisions (see, for instance, Vékas, 342 fol; Kindler, 776 fol; B. Piltz, "Internationales Kaufrecht", NJW, 1989/10, p. 615; Lando, The 1985 Hague Convention, 60 fol; Siehr, 587 fol). Winship (Parker) has explained in greatest detail the various possibilities for the application and/or non-application of Article 1, paragraph 1, subparagraph (b) (see the scheme on p. 1-53). The extensive *discussion* is *out of proportion to* the provision's *practical significance*. The reservation under Article 95 loses importance the more States accede to the CISG (c. preface 1.2.).

The Federal Republic of Germany has not made use of the reservation provided for in Article 95. The introductory law, however, stipulates that Article 1, paragraph 1, subparagraph (b), in the case of reference to the law of a Contracting State applies only when that Contracting State has itself not invoked the reservation under Article 95 (see Schlechtriem, Kaufrecht, 43). This can happen only when the partner of a German company has his place of business in a non-Contracting State (because otherwise Article 1, paragraph 1, subparagraph (a), would apply) and when it was agreed that the law of a third State will be the applicable law, e.g. a sales contract between the FRG and Canada for which application of US law was agreed. In such a case, German courts would have to invoke the UCC instead of the CISG.

In contrast, we believe it correct in such event to apply the CISG, providing the more adequate rules in respect of international sales contracts, i.e. to ignore the US reservation. We also hold that only the courts of the State making the reservation are bound by the reservation of Article 95. (Lando is of the same opinion, The 1985 Hague Convention, 82; Siehr, 621).

Only China, Czechoslovakia and the USA have declared a reservation under Article 95 so far.

2. The States having made the reservation, hence only apply the CISG when the two parties to the sales contract have their place of business in Contracting States. Publications (c. note 1) consider as a problem, on the one hand, the case where the court of a Contracting State, which has not declared a reservation, through a reference to international private law has to apply the law of another Contracting State, which has declared a reservation, in regard to a sales contract of whose parties only one or none has his place of business in a Contracting State (e.g. the examples mentioned in note 1); and, on the other, the opposite case where the Forum of the State has declared a reservation but, through a reference to international private law , has to apply the law of a Contracting State which has not declared such a reservation (this would be the case where a US court would have to apply German law to a sales contract between Germany and Canada). It remains a *question* though *whether a Forum must take account of the reservation of his own or of the one made by another State.* The answers published in this regard differ from one another. Evans (BB, 656), for instance, suggests that a Forum of the State, which has declared a reservation, when applying the law of another Contracting State, which has not taken a reservation, invoke the domestic law of that other State instead of the provisions of the CISG. We fail to see the sense of such solution because the State when making a reservation does so only in favour of his own domestic law.

The Hague Sales Convention provided for the same reservation of which, by the way, the majority of the Contracting States, e.g. Germany, Gambia, Britain, the Netherlands and San Marino, made use. Only Belgium, Israel and Italy renounced to do so.

Article 96

(Declarations relating to contracts in writing)

A Contracting State[1] whose legislation[2] requires contracts of sale to be concluded in or evidenced by writing may at any time[3] make a declaration in accordance with article 12 that any provision of article 11, article 29, or Part II of this Convention, that allows a contract of sale[4] or its modification or termination by agreement[5] or any offer[6], acceptance[7], or other indication of intention[8] to be made in any form other than in writing, does not apply[10] where any party has his place of business in that State[9].

1. This reservation goes back to a proposal by the USSR. Argentina, Byelorussia, Chile, China, the Ukraine and Hungary have so far made a relevant reservation.

Concerning the importance of the written form in international trade compare notes to Articles 11 and 12.

2. It is a condition for the reservation to be taken that the State in question has a legislation which either requires that international sales contracts be concluded in writing or does not permit evidence for the conclusion and the content of a sales contract other than in writing. It is left *open, whether* that legislation *only* includes *civil law and the law of civil procedure or also administrative law.* This should be left to any State which wants to declare the reservation.

3. This is to allow such States to make the reservation which only *at a later date* include the *requirement of the written form* in their legislation (O. R., 444). As to the effectiveness of a declaration compare Article 97.

4. Compare Article 18, paragraph 1.

5. Compare Article 29.

6. Compare Article 14.

7. Compare Article 18.

8. Compare Article 26.

9. Thus the *reservation* is at all times *effective only for one's own companies.*

10. The effect of the reservation is disputed. Mostly the view is held that, when excluding the relevant provisions of the Convention pursuant to the PIL rules, the *law which would otherwise apply* is to be identified which *will then determine the form of the contract*. (So e.g. H. Stoll, "International-privatrechtliche Fragen bei der landes-rechtlichen Ergänzung des Einheitlichen Kaufrechts", in Festschrift fur Murad Ferid, Frankfurt on Main, 1988, p. 506; also Czer-wenka/Freiburg, 170 fol). According to these views the reservation has no other effect than to have the provisions of the Convention replaced by the respective domestic law. A court in a non-reserva-tion State would, therefore, not automatically apply rules of the res-ervation State which concern the written form. On the other hand, a reservation State would probably, for reasons of public policy ,ap-ply its own rules of form, even when otherwise the law of the other State would have to be invoked. An option providing for a relevant reservation was also integrated in the Hague Convention on the Law Applicable to Contracts for the International Sale of Goods (see also Winship/Parker, 1-47).

On the other hand, the view is held that the declaration of a *reserva-tion automatically entails an obligation in regard to the form* of sales con-tracts (so L. Vékas, "Das UNO-Abkommen über den internationalen Warenkauf vor seinem Inkrafttreten I.", Magyar Jog, 1987/5, p. 385 fol). Rehbinder (Freiburg, 154 fol) holds that the reservation of a State where the written form is required must be respected in the other Contracting States. This could be done in such a way that Article 12 is interpreted extensively in that the form rules of States making reservations are considered as being valid everywhere, or that foreign form rules, which have their roots in economy, be applied in the frame of international private law (*Son-deranknüpfung*).

Article 97

(Declarations)

(1) Declarations made under this Convention at the time of signature[1] are subject to confirmation[2] upon ratification, acceptance or approval[3].

(2) Declarations and confirmations of declarations are to be in writing[4] and be formally notified to the depositary[5].

(3) A declaration takes effect simultaneously with the entry[6] into force of this Convention in respect of the State concerned. However, a declaration of which the depositary receives formal notification after such entry into force takes effect on the first day of the month following the expiration of six months[7] after the date of its receipt by the depositary. Reciprocal unilateral declarations under article 94 take effect on the first day of the months following the expiration of six months after the receipt of the latest declaration by the depositary.

(4) Any State which makes a declaration under this Convention may withdraw[8] it at any time by a formal notification in writing addressed to the depositary. Such withdrawal is to take effect on the first day of the month following the expiration of six months[9] after the date of the receipt of the notification by the depositary.

(5) A withdrawal of a declaration made under article 94 renders inoperative, as from the date on which the withdrawal takes effect, any reciprocal declaration[10] made by another State under that article.

1. This refers to declarations made under Articles 92, 93, 94 and 96.

2. This corresponds with Article 23 of the Vienna Treaty Convention.

3. Compare Article 91, note 5 fol.

4. The considerations regarding Article 11 do not relate to the written form in diplomatic relations. Reference is made here always to *notes*.

5. As to the functions of a depositary compare Article 89.

6. Concerning the taking effect compare Article 99.

This, of course, presupposes that the *declaration and* the *instrument of confirmation* are notified to the depositary *simultaneously*.

7. This *period of time* is *necessary* in order to communicate the declaration to the other Contracting States so that they are able to bring the declaration to the notice of interested economic circles.

8. A withdrawal of reservations is *in the interest of the uniform application* of the Convention and can, therefore, be made at any time. See also Article 22 of the Vienna Treaty Convention.

9. Compare note 7. A *withdrawal cannot become immediately effective* because, in the interest of legal security, information to the circles involved has to be ensured.

10. Such other declaration becomes ineffective without being withdrawn because there is no longer reciprocity.

Article 98

(Reservations)

No reservations are permitted[1] except those expressly authorized[2] in this Convention.

1. In general, reservations to international agreements are permitted in order to allow as many States as possible to join in spite of diverging views on individual issues. On the other hand, the reservations *impair the unification of law as envisaged* with the Convention. Therefore, Article 19, subparagraph (b) of the Vienna Treaty Convention provides for the possibility to restrict the reservations. Article 98 creates clarity as to the admissibility of reservations.

The depositary will inform the other Contracting States of the reservations declared by Contracting States, which in the case of the CISG, however, do not need confirmation (but c. Article 20, paragraph 1 Vienna Treaty Convention). In regard to its subject-matter the reservation has the effect of preventing the Convention from becoming effective between the State which declares the reservation and the other Contracting Parties. The relationship between the other Contracting States, however, is not affected (c. Article 21, paragraph 1, Vienna Treaty Convention).

2. These are *declarations under Articles 92 to 96*. It can be doubted, however, whether Article 93 provides for a reservation in the strict sense. The Limitation Convention does not deal with the federal State clause under Article 31 in the part entitled "reservations". There is often a *fluid boundary between reservations and other declarations*.

Article 99

(Entry into force)

(1) This Convention enters into force[1], subject to the provisions of paragraph (6)[4] of this article, on the first day of the month following the expiration of twelve months[3] after the date of deposit of the tenth[2] instrument of ratification, acceptance, approval or accession, including[5] an instrument which contains a declaration made under article 92.

(2) When a State ratifies, accepts, approves or accedes to this Convention after the deposit of the tenth instrument of ratification, acceptance, approval or accession[6], this Convention, with the exception of the Part excluded, enters into force in respect of that State, subject to the provisions of paragraph (6) of this article, on the first day of the month following the expiration of twelve months after the date of the deposit of its instrument of ratification, acceptance, approval or accession.

(3) A State[7] which ratifies, accepts, approves or accedes to this Convention and is a party to either or both the Convention relating to a Uniform Law on the Formation of Contracts for the International Sale of Goods done at The Hague on 1 July 1964 (1964 Hague Formation Convention) and the Convention relating to a Uniform Law on the International Sale of Goods done at The Hague on 1 July 1964 (1964 Hague Sales Convention) shall at the same time denounce, as the case may be, either or both the 1964 Hague Sales Convention and the 1964 Hague Formation Convention by notifying the Government of the Netherlands[8] to that effect.

(4) A State party to the 1964 Hague Sales Convention which ratifies, accepts, approves or accedes to the present Convention and declares or has declared under article 92 that it will not be bound by Part II of this Convention shall at the time of ratification, acceptance, approval or accession denounce the 1964 Hague Sales Convention by notifying the Government of the Netherlands to that effect.

(5) A State party to the 1964 Hague Formation Convention which ratifies, accepts, approves or accedes to the present Convention and declares or has declared under article 92 that it will not be bound by Part III of this Convention shall at the time of ratification, acceptance, approval or accession denounce the 1964 Hague Formation Convention by notifying the Government of the Netherlands to that effect.

(6) For the purpose of this article, ratifications, acceptances, approvals and accessions in respect of this Convention by States parties to the 1964 Hague Formation Convention or to the 1964 Hague Sales Convention shall not be effective until such denunciations as may be required on the part of those States in respect of the latter two Conventions have themselves become effective[9]. The depositary of this Convention shall consult with the Government of the Netherlands, as the depositary of the 1964 Conventions, so as to ensure necessary co-ordination in this respect.

1. This article regulates the entry into force of the Convention in two ways: it *determines the required number of Member States and* the *period of time* to expire *after the required number of Member States has been attained.*

2. There is no general rule as to the number of approvals required for a Convention to enter into force. For this Convention to take effect ten Member States were needed, i.e. the same number as in the case of the Limitation Convention. A suggestion made at the diplomatic conference, according to which the number of six Member States would be sufficient, was not adopted (O. R., 456). The Hague Sales and Formation Conventions entered into force after five accessions. *At times* a *tendency* could be noted *to agree on a greater number of Member States*. The Hamburg Rules require, for instance, 20 Member States, and the United Nations Convention on the International Multimodal Transportation of Goods even 30. Since the entry into effect can be greatly delayed in this way, because many States consider accession only after a Convention has taken effect, the required number of approvals was reduced again in the case of later conventions. The Convention on Bills of Exchange, therefore, requires ten States, the draft Convention on the Operator of Transport Terminal five, and the Leasing Convention and the Factoring Convention enter into force after the third approval. This procedure greatly *facilitates the entry into force* for those States which are interested in a unification of law.

3. This period of time has to be seen in connection with the period of denunciation of the Hague Sales and Formation Conventions which is also 12 months. The Limitation Convention, in contrast, takes effect already six months after the tenth instrument has been deposited. As for the transportation of goods at sea and the multimodal transportation of goods,too, a period of 12 months is required. This time is usually needed domestically to take all measures needed to broadly inform of the changes in the legal situation in due form.

4. Paragraph 3 to 6 exclusively refer to the States Parties to the Hague Conventions, i.e. Belgium, Britain, Gambia, Germany, Israel, Italy, Luxembourg, the Netherlands and San Marino. The first to denounce the Hague Conventions was Italy which did so on 11 December 1986.

5. For the purposes of the entry into force *States* are *counted which have acceded only to parts of the Convention.* The first ten States to accede, however, did not make relevant declarations.

6. For States, which later, prior to or after the entry into force, accede to the Convention the period of twelve months applies too.

7. Paragraphs 3 to 5 are dealt with in such great detail in order to cover all variants of membership to only one of the Hague Conventions and/or of accession of only part of the CISG. These paragraphs contain the *obligation to denounce the Hague Conventions.* If this were not so, the CISG and the Hague Conventions would exist in parallel (c. Article 90). However, the Hague Conventions would cease to be in force without denunciation as soon as all its Member States have acceded to the CISG (c. Article 59 Vienna Treaty Convention). The requirement of denunciation of the old conventions might have delayed accession to the CISG because no State would want to give up the old convention without being sure of the new one taking effect. A joint action of the European Member States of the Hague Convention envisaged originally did not come about.

8. The Government of the Netherlands is the depositary of the Hague Conventions.

9. According to the Hague Conventions, the denunciations will become effective twelve months after notification. In order to avoid a time gap between the expiration of the denounced Hague Convention and the entry into force of the CISG, Italy has declared that the Hague Conventions will continue to be effective for Italy until 31 December 1987 (the period of twelve months for denunciation expired on 11 December 1987). As to the effect of this declaration

there are differing views (see E. Jayme, "Das Wiener Kaufrechtsübereinkommen und der deutsch-italienische
Rechtsverkehr", Tagung in Ferrara, IPRax, 1989/2, p. 128 fol). In the
view of the FRG the *legal situation* has become *confusing for a transition period* because the German judge is not bound by the unilateral
Italian declaration (see G. Reinhart, "Vom Haager zum Wiener Einheitlichen Kaufrecht", in: Jahrbuch fur Italienisches Recht, Band 2,
Eherecht - Schadensregulierung - Wiener Kaufrecht - Sprachrisiko,
p. 65 fol).

Article 100

(Date of application)

**(1) This Convention applies to the formation[1] of a contract
only when the proposal for concluding the contract is
made on or after the date when the Convention enters into
force in respect of the Contracting States referred to in
subparagraph (1) (a) or the Contracting State referred to in
subparagraph (1) (b) of article 1.**

**(2) This Convention applies only to contracts[2] concluded
on or after the date when the Convention enters into force[3]
in respect of the Contracting States referred to in
subparagraph (1) (a) or the Contracting State referred to in
subparagraph (1) (b) of article 1.**

1. In order to be applied to the formation of contracts *it is not sufficient that a sales contract was concluded after the Convention enters into
force* for the Contracting States concerned (for both when the parties
to the sales contract have their place of business in Contracting
States, and/or for one Contracting State whose law is applicable on
the basis of reference to the conflict-of-law rules), rather the offer
must have been made already after the entry into force of the Convention.

2. For the contracts to be applied it will suffice that the *statement of
acceptance has reached the offeror after the entry into force of the Convention.*

3. Article 100 is in accord with Article 28 of the Vienna Treaty Convention which stipulates that international treaties are non-retroac-
tive.

Article 101

(Denunciation)

(1) A Contracting State may denounce[1] this Convention, or Part II or Part III[2] of the Convention, by a formal notification in writing addressed to the depositary.

(2) The denunciation takes effect on the first day of the month following the expiration of twelve months[3] after the notification is received by the depositary. Where a longer period for the denunciation to take effect is specified in the notification, the denunciation takes effect upon the expiration of such longer period after the notification is received by the depositary.

1. The Convention as a whole or Part II or Part III can be denounced at any time; this is, however, unlikely in view of the growing importance of the international uniform law. Should, because of such denunciation, the *number of Contracting States fall below ten*, i.e. the number needed for the entry into force of the Convention, this *would have no effect* (Article 55, Vienna Treaty Convention).

2. Compare Article 92.

3. The time for the denunciation to take effect is *twelve months at least*; this *time may be extended but not shortened*.

DONE at Vienna, this day of eleventh day of April, one thousand nine hundred and eighty, in a single original, of which the Arabic, Chinese, English, French, Russian and Spanish texts[1] are equally authentic[2].

IN WITNESS WHEREOF the undersigned plenipotentiaries, being duly authorized by their respective Governments, have signed this Convention.

1. The CISG is made in the *six official languages of the United Nations* with each text being equally authentic. It is presumed that the terms of the Convention have the same meaning in each authentic text (Article 33, paragraph 3, Vienna Treaty Convention).

2. As to the interpretation of the CISG compare Article 7, paragraph 1. The Vienna Treaty Convention establishes, *inter alia*, the following general rules to govern the *interpretation of international treaties*:

(a) A treaty shall be interpreted in good faith in accordance with the ordinary meaning to be given to the terms of the treaty in their context and in the light of its object and purpose (c. Article 31, paragraph 1).

(b) Recourse may be had to supplementary means of interpretation, including the preparatory work of the treaty and the circumstances of its conclusion (c. Article 32).

B.
COMMENTARY ON THE CONVENTION ON THE LIMITATION PERIOD IN THE INTERNATIONAL SALE OF GOODS OF 14 JUNE 1974[1] IN THE VERSION OF THE PROTOCOL OF 11 APRIL 1980[2]

Introduction

The Convention on the Limitation Period in the International Sale of Goods (Limitation Convention) was the first result of the work of the *United Nations Commission on International Trade Law (UNCITRAL)*. At its second session in 1969 UNCITRAL in accordance with its programme of work, which included as one of the main issues the consideration of the legal questions involved in the international sale of goods, set up a working group to prepare a draft convention on the limitation period in the international sale of goods.

The Working Group was composed of the representatives of Egypt, Argentina, Belgium, the UK, Japan, Norway and Czechoslovakia (and after the latter retired from UNCITRAL - Poland). The selection of those States was based on the idea to have the main legal systems represented in the drafting of uniform rules to govern limitation.

As early as in 1972 the Working Group at its fifth session submitted a *draft convention* to UNCITRAL which was adopted unanimously. At the same time, it was decided to invite the Secretary-General of the United Nations to convene a diplomatic conference to consider the draft convention.

[1] United Nations Conference on Prescription (Limitation) in the International Sale of Goods, New York, 20 May - 14 June 1974, Official Records, Documents of the Conference and Summary Records of the Plenary Meetings and of the Meetings of the Main Committees, United Nations, New York 1975, p. 101.

[2] United Nations Conference on Contracts for the International Sale of Goods, Vienna, 10 March - 11 April 1980, Official Records, Documents of the Conference and Summary Records of the Plenary Meetings and of the Meetings of the Main Committees, United Nations, New York 1981, p. 191.

On 28 November 1972, the General Assembly of the United Nations in resolution 2929 (XXVII) decided to hold such a conference in 1974.

The conference then was held at United Nations Headquarters in New York from 20 May to 14 June 1974. 66 States participated in the conference and another three attended as observers.

The Limitation Convention was adopted without a vote against (with five abstentions) on 14 June 1974, but not all attending States participated in the vote. *The UNCITRAL draft was in part considerably amended* with initially included provisions not meeting with the required support (see in this context F. Enderlein/Ch. Paul, "Bericht über die Konferenz der Vereinten Nationen über die Verjährung beim internationalen Warenkauf", RiA, 3. Beilage zu DDR-AW, 1975/18, p. 1 fol).

The relatively speedy drafting and adoption of the Limitation Convention testified to the efforts of UNCITRAL to obtain visible results as early as possible. On the other hand, the States were not ready to join the Limitation Convention as long as UNCITRAL could not present results in regard to the unified sales law itself. Therefore, there were also critical voices who expressed that they would have considered it more favourable to include the provisions on limitation in the CISG or at least to adopt the Limitation Convention *after* the CISG had been adopted (c. Th. Krapp, "The Limitation Convention for International Sale of Goods", Journal of World Trade Law, 1985/4, p. 343).

Those provisions of the Limitation Convention which are particularly related to the CISG have been formulated so as to correspond to the state of work on the CISG draft at the respective time. The final version of the CISG did not always take account of the initial formulations so that later the Limitation Convention had to be adapted to the CISG.

Paragraph 3 of resolution 33/93 of the General Assembly of the United Nations authorized the diplomatic conference, convened at Vienna with a view to adopting the CISG, to make the needed adjustments, even though the States which attended the 1980 Vienna Conference were not identical with the States participating in the 1974 New York Conference.

While in general there was no doubt of the need to adapt the Limitation Convention to the CISG, this is expressed also in the preamble to the Protocol amending the Limitation Convention, opinions differed rather often on the scope of the required amendments.

Comparing the Limitation Convention and the CISG one can note a differing approach to the rule governing the scope of application:

Some provisions, which in the Limitation Convention appear under the heading "sphere of application", have actually nothing to do with it and are, therefore, regulated in the CISG in Chapter II "General Provisions", like some definitions (c. Articles 10 and 13 CISG).

Having a look at the *substance* of the introductory provisions one notices that they are *mostly identical*. But there are also specific rules in the Limitation Convention (Articles 1 and 5) or the CISG (Article 4) for which there is no counterpart in the other Convention.

It was, therefore, not possible, to simply replace the section on the sphere of application of the Limitation Convention by the respective section of the CISG. Rather, the provisions had to be adjusted individually. This adaptation referred, on the one hand, to provisions on the sphere of application (Articles 3 and 4 Limitation Convention) and, on the other, to some of the final provisions (Articles 31, 34, 37 and 40 Limitation Convention). But not all provisions whose wording differed were taken into consideration, in particular not when there are no different decisions to be expected (e.g. Article 2, subpara. (c) Limitation Convention in relation to Article 10, subpara. (a) CISG or Article 7 Limitation Convention in relation to Article 7 CISG).

As a *consequence* it can be noted that the *adaptation* was *successful* in a number of cases, but a *complete harmonization* could *not* be *achieved* because of the hesitation on the part of many delegations (c. note 4 of Article 30 Limitation Convention).

The new version of the Limitation Convention was pursuant to Article XIV, paragraph 2 of the Protocol Amending the Convention on the Limitation Period in the International Sale of Goods transmitted by the Secretary-General of the United Nations as a draft to the States on 17 April 1989 and finally made known on 1 August 1989.

Insofar as the original and the new version differ from each other, the text of the Convention is printed below in two columns with the original version appearing on the left and the amended version appearing on the right.

The former GDR ratified the Convention on 23 February 1989 and acceded to the Protocol amending it. It had, therefore, been a Member of both the original and amended version of the Limitation Convention. The relevant instruments were deposited with the Secretary-General of the United Nations on 31 August 1989.

As of 28 April 1992 the following States have acceded to the Limitation Convention in its original and/or amended version:

1. Convention on the Limitation Period in the International Sale of Goods

State	Signature	Ratification Accession Approval	Entry into force
Argentina		9 Oct. 1981	19 July 1983
Belarus	14 June 1974		
Brazil	14 June 1974		
Bulgaria	24 Febr.1975		
Costarica	30 Aug. 1974		
Czechoslovakia	29 Aug. 1975	26 May 1977	1 Aug. 1988
Dominican Rep.		23 Dec. 1977	1 Aug. 1988
Egypt		6 Dec. 1982	1 Aug. 1988
Germany */			
Ghana	5 Dec. 1974	7 Oct. 1975	1 Aug. 1988
Guinea		23 Jan. 1991	1 Aug. 1991
Hungary	14 June 1974	16 June 1983	1 Aug. 1988
Mexico		21 Jan. 1988	1 Aug. 1988
Mongolia	14 June 1974		
Nicaragua	13 May 1975		
Norway	11 Dec. 1975	20 March 1980	1 Aug. 1988
Poland	14 June 1974		
Romania		23 April 1992	1 Nov. 1992
Uganda		12 Febr. 1992	1 Sept. 1992
Ukraine	14 June 1974		
Russian Federation **/	14 June 1974		

Yugoslavia   27 Nov. 1978   1 Aug. 1988

Zambia   6 June 1986   1 Aug. 1988

*/ The Convention was signed by the former German Democratic Republic on 14 June 1974, ratified by it on 31 August 1989 and entered into force on 1 March 1990.

**/The Russian Federation continues, as from 24 December 1991, the membership of the former Union of Soviet Socialist Republics (USSR) in the United Nations and maintains, as from that date, full responsibility for all the rights and obligations of the USSR under the Charter of the United Nations and multilateral treaties deposited with the Secretary-General.

2. Protocol amending the Convention on the Limitation Period in the International Sale of Goods

State	Accession	Entry into Force
Argentina	19 July 1983	1 August 1988
Czechoslovakia	5 March 1990	1 October 1990
Egypt	6 December 1982	1 August 1988
Germany */		
Guinea	23 January 1991	1 August 1991
Hungary	16 June 1983	1 August 1988
Mexico	21 January 1988	1 August 1988
Romania	23 April 1992	1 November 1992
Uganda	12 February 1992	1 September 1992
Zambia	6 June 1986	1 August 1988

*/ The Protocol was acceded to by the former German Democratic Republic on 31 August 1989 and entered into force on 1 March 1990.

By contrast to the CISG, on which there are already numerous commentaries, little has been published concerning the Limitation Convention. Apart from articles, there has to this day been only the known commentary by Kazuaki Sono which he wrote on behalf of the Office of Legal Affairs of the United Nations at the request of the diplomatic conference convened to adopt the Limitation Convention (quoted as Sono, UNCITRAL).

Preamble

The States Parties to the present Convention,

Considering that international trade is an important factor in the promotion of friendly relations amongst States,

Believing that the adoption of uniform rules governing the limitation period[1] in the international sale of goods would facilitate[2] the development of world trade,

Have agreed as follows:

1. The legal institute of limitation is known in most legal systems (except of some African countries, but also of Iran, see IECL, Vol. II, Chapter 1, p. 147). It is in the interest of legal certainty to allow the enforcement by legal proceedings of claims to come under the statute of limitations because there are increasing difficulties to present a case as time lapses (c. in particular Article 25, paragraph 1).

2. There are, however, considerable differences between the various national laws in regard to the juridical construction and classification of limitation, the commencement and duration of the limitation periods as well as to the effects of limitation. A first essential difference is that the limitation of actions is conceived as either a limitation of claims or a limitation of law suits. As regards the limitation of claims, the claim itself comes under the statute of limitations (so for instance Article 1234 C.c.), i.e. the claim lapses with the commencement of the limitation. In that case, the satisfaction of a lapsed claim constitutes a performance without a legal basis and can be demanded back under the rules governing unjust enrichment. In the event of a limitation of law suits, however, the claim remains in existence but can no longer be enforced through a court. This is the model on which the Limitation Convention is founded, but also FRG law (222 German BGB), English law (Limitation Act 1939 and 1963) and Italian law (Article 2940 CC).

A second essential difference lies in whether the expiration of the limitation period *ex officio* has to be taken into consideration (so in a number of developing countries, c. note 2 of Article 24) or whether the limitation period is taken account of in court proceedings only when they are brought forward as a plea by the debtor (so under the laws of the FRG, Britain and France). According to Italian law the plea is not considered by the court when the debtor has admitted that the obligation has not been paid off (Article 2959 CC). Also under numerous other laws the plea in bar is not recognized when it violates the principle of good faith.

A distinction is made between the limitation periods and the exclusion periods which will always have to be taken account of *ex officio* and prevent, for instance, the emergence of a claim (like in particular where no notice of non-conformity is given - c. Article 39 CISG, 377 HGB).

A third difference relates to whether the limitation is considered as procedural law, like in most common-law countries, or substantive law, like in most other laws. This difference has an effect on the determination of the law applicable to limitation.

From these and other differences follow uncertainties in the enforcement of laws, which can be reduced through the adoption of uniform rules.

PART 1

SUBSTANTIVE PROVISIONS

Sphere of application

Article 1

(Introductory provisions; subject-matter and definitions)[1]

(1) This Convention shall determine when claims of a buyer and a seller against each other[3] arising from a contract of international sale of goods[2] or relating to[5] its breach, termination or invalidity[4] can[7] no longer be exercised[6] by reason of expiration of a period of time. Such period of time is hereinafter referred to as "the limitation period".

(2) This Convention shall not affect a particular time-limit[8] within which one party is required, as a condition for the acquisition or exercise of his claim, to give notice to the other party or perform any act other than the institution of legal proceedings.

(3) In this Convention[9]:

(a) "Buyer", "seller" and "party" mean persons who buy or sell, or agree[10] to buy or sell, goods, and the successors[11] to and assigns of their rights or obligations under the contract of sale;

(b) "Creditor" means a party who asserts a claim, whether or not such a claim is for a sum of money;

(c) "Debtor" means a party against whom a creditor asserts a claim;

(d) "Breach of contract" means the failure of a party to perform the contract or any performance not in conformity with the contract[12];

(e) "Legal proceedings" includes judicial, arbitral and administrative proceedings[13];

(f) "Persons" includes corporation, company, partnership, association, or entity, whether private or public[15], which can sue or be sued[14];

(g) "Writing" includes telegram and telex[16;]

(h) "Year" means a year according to the Gregorian calendar[17].

1. The headings used here were put in brackets because they do not belong to the official text of the Convention. They are taken from the commentary by Sono (Sono, UNCITRAL), except Article 41 fol.

2. In the meantime the term "contract on the international sale of goods" has largely prevailed, which appears also in the heading of the Convention.

3. Reference is made here to claims between buyer and seller and not to claims by third parties which, however, could become relevant in connection with Article 18. Excluded are also claims against third parties, e.g. of the seller against the bank that issued a letter of credit.

4. The Limitation Convention covers claims under the contract (but pay attention to Article 5), including claims from the withdrawal from the contract or from unjust enrichment where the contract is void. Not covered are, however, claims outside of the contract (from tort).

5. Included are claims which arise from an international sales contract, and those which refer to such a contract. This can, in particular, be of relevance for claims which follow from the invalidity of a contract or also where such invalidity of the contract has to be established by the courts (Sono, UNCITRAL, 73). By contrast, questions relating to the validity of a sales contract are excluded from the scope of application of the CISG (see Article 4).

6. The Limitation Convention, apart from its heading and preamble, does not use the terms "limitation" and "prescribed". Rather, limitation is paraphrased by mentioning that claims can *no longer be exercised*, i.e. implemented, because of the expiration of a period of time. (Insofar this is rather an "implementation convention".) This "neutral" term had to be chosen to cover the different conceptions existing in national laws. Under Anglo-American law the limitation is mostly regulated by procedural law, whereas it belongs to substantive law in other legal systems. But practical consequences follow from this situation only in regard to connecting factors under the conflict-of-law rules.

7. When a claim comes under the statute of limitations it does not lapse as claim. Therefore, it *cannot be demanded that a performance made in spite of limitation be returned* (Article 26) and a set-off can be made also with claims that are prescribed (Article 25, paragraph 2).

8. Exclusion periods, in particular periods for giving notice of non-conformity (Articles 39 and 43 CISG), are not covered by the Limitation Convention. It has to be taken into consideration, however, that there is no uniform delimitation between exclusion and limitation periods in all countries and that the differences become blurred when both periods have to be taken into account *ex officio* (Article 24). From a legal point of view certain functions can be fulfilled invoking either one of the two periods.

9. The *catalogue of definitions* which is described hereunder *follows the Anglo-American legislative practice*. This is to ensure that the defined terms are used and interpreted in a uniform meaning.

10. According to the CSIG (c. Article 3) any sales contract is an agreement on the purchase and/or sale of goods, irrespective of whether the goods already exist or not. The English law, however, makes a distinction between contracts on existing and contracts on future goods. For this reason the duplication had to be included here. (Compare also Article 6, paragraph 2).

11. Among the successors of a party count parties who have taken over the debt or who have been assigned a claim. They include, for instance, and to a growing extent factoring companies (Handbuch 2, 471 fol). Even an insurance company may be assigned rights from a sales contract. Generally, a distinction is made between individual and total legal succession. Manifestations of the latter are bankruptcy, fusion or other forms of reorganization of a company. But one can safely assume that questions of inheritance play a role in international contracts only in very rare instances.

12. Compare in this context Articles 10 and 12.

13. Compare in this context Article 15.

14. Hence, not only legal persons are included because associations not possessing legal personality have the ability to take legal action, e.g. the BGB society (705 BGB) or the Partnership (124 HGB).

15. Therefore, this applies irrespective of the legal basis of such a person, like trade law, administrative law etc. The property situation is not directly reflected in the distinction made in some countries, usually between persons of private law and persons of public law; also State enterprises could be organized in the form of private corporations. The subjects of public law include the States themselves which may act as parties in international sales contracts. The Limitation Convention does in no way influence the extent to which they can request immunity before their own or foreign courts.

16. Compare Article 13 CISG.

17. This provision was necessary because other calendars are used in many countries, especially in Arabic countries.

Article 2

(Definition of a contract of international sale)

For the purposes of this Convention[1]:

(a) A contract of sale of goods shall be considered international if, at the time of the conclusion of the contract[3], the buyer and the seller have their places of business in different States[2];

(b) The fact that the parties have their places of business in different States shall be disregarded whenever this fact does not appear either from the contract[4] or from any dealings between, or from information disclosed by, the parties at any time before or at the conclusion of the contract[5];

(c) Where a party to a contract of sale of goods has places of business in more than one State, the place of business shall be that which has the closest relationship to the contract and its performance[6], having regard to the circumstances known to or contemplated by the parties at the time of the conclusion of the contract;

(d) Where a party does not have a place of business, reference shall be made to his habitual residence[7];

(e) Neither the nationality of the parties nor the civil or commercial character of the parties or of the contract shall be taken into consideration[8].

1. These provisions follow the former draft CISG and in their substance correspond to its Articles 1 and 10.

2. Compare Article 1, paragraph 1, first half-sentence CISG. Compare also the possibility of a reservation under Article 38.

3. The requirement "at the time of the conclusion of the contract" is not contained in Article 1 of the CISG. It was considered necessary here to exclude the application of the Convention in those cases where one of the parties of what was first a national contract after the conclusion of the contract transfers his place of business to a foreign country. It is quite another story whether the application of the Convention in such cases would be in the interest of the two parties.

4. Sono (UNCITRAL, 75) giving an example of that a party is not aware of the fact that he has concluded an international sales contract mentions that a party might act as an agent for a foreign "undisclosed principal". The question whether an agent or his principal has become a party to a sales contract was of relevance in the arbitration proceedings SG 373/84 (see RiA, 111th supplement to AW documents, 1989/22, p. XIV fol). During those proceedings the plea by the defendant that he had concluded the contract with an agent was dismissed as unfounded.

5. Compare Article 1, paragraph 2 CISG.

6. Compare Article 10, subpara. (a) CISG.

7. Compare Article 10, subpara. (b) CISG.

8. Compare Article 1, paragraph 3 CISG.

Article 3[1]

(Application of the Convention; exclusion of the rules of private international law)

(1) This Convention shall apply only if, at the time of the conclusion of the contract[2], the places of business of the parties to a contract of international sale of goods are in Contracting States[3].	**(1) This Convention shall apply only (a) if, at the time of the conclusion of the contract[2] the places of business of the parties to a contract of international sale of goods are in Contracting States[3]; or (b) if the rules of private international law make the law of a Contracting State applicable to the contract.[4]**

(2) Unless this Convention provides otherwise, it shall apply irrespective of the law which would otherwise be applicable to the contract of sale[5].

(3) This Convention shall not apply when the parties have expressly excluded its application[6].

(2) This Convention shall not apply when the parties have expressly excluded its application[6].

1. Article 3 was redrafted in the Protocol amending the Convention. The modification of the sphere of application of the Limitation Convention was fiercely debated at the Vienna Conference (O. R., 464 fol). Many delegations pointed out that the New York Conference had purposefully excluded the application of the Limitation Convention on the basis of private international law and spoke up, therefore, against the inclusion of the formulation of Article 1, paragraph 1, subpara. (b) CISG in the Limitation Convention. Other delegations, however, pointed to the fact that a State which accedes to both Conventions would have to have a uniform sphere of application for both in order to avoid contradictions. The latter opinion prevailed, but one did not succeed in realizing the consequence that followed from it, namely to amend also Article 30 of the Limitation Convention (c. note 4 of Article 30). As a result of the discussion, paragraph 1 was adapted to Article 1, paragraph 1 CISG, and paragraph 2 was deleted. Article XII of the Protocol amending the Convention, however, provides an opportunity for States to make a reservation in order to exclude the new version of Article 3 (c. Article 36 (a)).

2. According to Article 23 CISG the *receipt of the acceptance* by the offeror is conceived to be the time of the conclusion of the contract. The fact that the parties during the time of legal proceedings have their places of business in the same State does not prevent the application of the Convention.

3. Since the Limitation Convention finds its way into the respective national law, this provision as well as other provisions concerning the sphere of application constitutes only the internationally required minimum. A Contracting State can also apply the Limitation Convention to international sales contracts when the *parties to the contract do not have their places of business in Contracting States*. This is expressly clarified in paragraph 1, subpara. (b) of the new version of Article 3.

4. When the remaining conditions are fulfilled, the Convention shall be applied without reference to private international law. In particular, its application shall not be excluded on the ground that the conflict-of-law rules of one Contracting State refers to the law of a non-Contracting State. Paragraph 2 in its old version was deleted by the Protocol amending the Convention without the intention of the former being lost, namely to prevent the exclusion of the Convention whenever it should be applied because of the fact that the parties have their places of business in different Contracting States.

5. This rule serves to achieve an adaptation to Article 1, paragraph 1, subpara. (b) CISG (compare also the respective comment of the CISG and of Article 96 CISG).

6. Just as under Article 6 CISG the parties can exclude the international uniform law; in that event the national law chosen by them or determined by private international law is applied. The *exclusion has to be expressly declared*. Where a Contracting State has integrated the Limitation Convention in his national law in such a way that the former replaces the existing national law in regard to every international sales contract, its rules can be globally excluded only when the law of another non-Contracting State is chosen. The parties can, however, deviate also from individual provisions (but compare Article 22).

Article 4[1]

(Exclusion of certain sales and types of goods)

This Convention shall not apply to sales:
(a) of goods[2] bought for personal, family or household use;

(b) by auction;
(c) on execution or otherwise by authority of law;

This Convention shall not apply to sales:
(a) of goods[2] bought for personal, family or household use, unless the seller, at any time before or at the conclusion of the contract, neither knew nor ought to have known that the goods were bought for any such use;

(b) by auction;
(c) on execution or otherwise by authority of law;

(d) of stocks, shares, investment securities, negotiable instruments or money;	(d) of stocks, shares, investment securities, negotiable instruments or money;
(e) of ships, vessels or aircraft;	(e) of ships, vessels, hovercraft and aircraft;
(f) of electricity.	(f) of electricity.

1. Compare note 1 on Article 2.

This provision corresponds with Article 2 CISG. Compared to its earlier draft the modification of the CISG only consisted in adding to subpara. (a) the seller's ignorance and in subpara. (e) hovercraft.

2. Non-commercial sales are to be excluded, which had to be made clear, in particular, because of the rule in Article 2, subpara. (e). The Limitation Convention is, therefore, only applied to international sales contracts.

Article 5

(Exclusion of certain claims)

This Convention shall not apply to claims[1] based upon:

(a) Death of, or personal injury to, any person[2];

(b) Nuclear damage caused by the goods sold[3];

(c) A lien, mortgage or other security interest in property[4];

(d) A judgement or award made in legal proceedings[5];

(e) A document on which direct enforcement or execution can be obtained in accordance with the law of the place where such enforcement or execution is sought[5];

(f) A bill of exchange, cheque or promissory note[6].

1. While Article 4 excludes certain sales and Article 6 certain combined contracts or certain contracts for the supply of goods, Article 5 deals with the *exclusion of specific claims* which may arise from or in the context of sales contracts.

2. This serves to largely exclude claims from product liability. Insofar as personal injury is claimed outside of the contract or by third parties, they do not come anyway under the scope of application of the Limitation Convention (c. notes 3 and 4 of Article 1). Not excluded are claims that are based on such damages which the goods sold cause to other goods because of their non-conformity (c. also Article 5 CISG).

3. Nuclear damage is excluded because radiation damage might be noticed only after a long time. Periods of ten and 20 years are agreed on in the Vienna Convention on Civil Liability for Nuclear Damage of 21 May 1963.

4. *Claims in rem are excluded* because in some legal systems they are governed not by the *lex causae* but by the *lex rei sitae*. This refers also to the claim of a seller for the restitution of unpaid goods when a reservation of title has been agreed. (Compare also the exclusion of effects which the sales contract has on the title of the goods - Article 4 CISG.)

5. *In many laws* there are *specific limitation periods* for claims of this kind, which are often regulated under procedural law. Their unification was regarded as being to complicated.

6. Claims that are based on bills of exchange, cheques or promissory notes are excluded because they are not always asserted between the parties of the sales contract itself (but compare note 11 of Article 1). Furthermore, international conventions contain specific periods of time for the limitation of such claims. (According to Convention Providing a Uniform Law for Bills of Exchange and Promissory Notes of 7 June 1930, limitation periods of between three years and six months are in effect.)

Article 6

(Mixed contracts)

1. This Convention shall not apply to contracts in which the preponderant part of the obligations of the seller consists in the supply of labour or other services[1].

(2) Contracts for the supply of goods to be manufactured or produced shall be considered to be sales, unless the party who orders the goods undertakes to supply a substantial part of the materials necessary for such manufacture or production[2].

1. This provision corresponds with Article 3, paragraph 2 CISG.

2. This provision corresponds with Article 3, paragraph 1 CISG. (C. also note 10 of Article 1.)

Article 7

(Interpretation to promote uniformity)

In the interpretation and application of the provisions of this Convention, regard shall be had to its international character and to the need to promote uniformity[1].

1. This provision is similar to Article 7 CISG. The latter, however, includes also the observance of good faith. (See in this context also Enderlein, Interpretation.)

The duration and commencement of the limitation period

Article 8

(Length of the period)

The limitation period shall be four[1] years[2].

1. In regard to the length of the limitation period the Limitation Convention does not differentiate between claims for the payment of the price and other claims from an international sales contract. Neither does it make a distinction in this context between apparent and latent defects. This *uniform length of the limitation period* is the *most important result of the unification of law* since it is, in particular, periods of different length (and with a different commencement, c. Article 9) which lead to legal uncertainty. The period of four years constitutes a justifiable compromise. At the conference periods of between two and six years had been called for with, in particular, the developing countries opting for longer periods and establishing a connection between the duration of use of the goods, above all of plants and machines, and the limitation period.

In fixing the length of the period other articles of the Convention, which have an influence on the course of the limitation period, were taken into account. Those include Articles 9 - 12 on the commencement of the limitation period, Articles 19 and 20 on the commencement of a new limitation period, Articles 17, 18 and 21 on the extension of the limitation period and Article 22 on modification of the limitation period.

2. Under the Limitation Convention there is only one uniform period. The initial draft provided for a shorter limitation period (two years) for claims from non-conforming performance.

The view prevailed, however, that although shorter periods of notice would have been needed in the interest of legal certainty and in order to prevent difficulties in furnishing proof, no short limitation periods would be required at the same time and in addition.

Article 9

(Basic rule on commencement of the period)

(1) Subject to the provisions of articles 10, 11 and 12[2] the limitation period shall commence on the date on which the claim accrues[1].

(2) The commencement of the limitation period shall not be postponed by:

(a) A requirement that the party be given a notice[3] as described in paragraph 2 of article 1, or

(b) A provision in an arbitration agreement that no right shall arise until an arbitration award has been made[4].

1. The *time when a claim accrues* (c. note 2.2. of Article 58 CISG) generally serves as the *point of commencement of limitation periods. Claims from breaches of contract* accrue on the day of the breach (Article 10, paragraph 1), *claims from non-conforming performance* accrue on the day the goods are handed over to the buyer (Article 10, paragraph 2). 201 German BGB even fixes the first day of the next calendar year as the date of commencement.

2. The general rule does not apply to the extent to which the Convention for certain facts, in particular claims from breaches of contract, specifically provides for the commencement of the limitation period.

3. This provision was necessary because in some legal systems claims do arise only when such a notice is given (Sono, UNCITRAL, 84). The general limitation period and its uniform commencement also apply to claims whose implementation presupposes the observance of a period of notice (Articles 39 and 43 CISG).

4. This provision was included because in some common-law countries it is customary to integrate the Scott-Avery clause into sales contracts. This clause implies that a claim arises only, and that court proceedings can be instituted only, after an arbitration award had been rendered (O. R., 198). A Soviet motion to delete this passage was rejected with a majority of two (O. R., 64).

Article 10

(Special rules: breach; defect or non-conformity of the goods; fraud)

(1) A claim arising from a breach of contract[1] shall accrue on the date on which such breach occurs[2].

(2) A claim arising from a defect or other lack of conformity[3] shall accrue on the date on which the goods are actually handed over[4] to, or their tender is refused by, the buyer.

(3) A claim based on fraud committed before or at the time of the conclusion of the contract[5] or during its performance[6] shall accrue on the date on which the fraud was or reasonably could have been discovered.

1. As to the definition of a breach of contract compare Article 1, paragraph 3, subpara. (d). The term *"breach of contract"* is used there *as* the *generic term* which also includes lack of conformity. The present article, however, covers lack of conformity separately in paragraph 2. The Limitation Convention furthermore deviates from the basic rule of paragraph 1 in regard to fraud (c. paragraph 3) and to claims under a guarantee (c. Article 11). No distinction is made between the claims of the buyer and those of the seller. Concerning claims from breach of contract compare also Article 45 fol and Article 61 fol CISG.

2. The commencement of the limitation period sometimes plays a role in arbitration, like in SG 242/82, SG 48/85 and SG 255/86. The latter, for instance, referred to Article 10, paragraph 1 of the Limitation Convention, namely to the principle according to which a claim from breach of contract accrues on the day when the breach is committed (c. RiA, 103th supplement to AW documents, 1988/28, p. XIV). The arbitration committee granted that this rule could lead to unjust results when the entitled person does not know of the breach of contract and/or of the damage.

3. Such defect or lack of conformity includes both defects in title and third party claims (c. Articles 35, 41 and 42 CISG). The Convention, by contrast to the draft, does *not differentiate between apparent and latent defects*.

4. This is *not always the date when the delivery is made*. It is of no relevance here whether the goods are handed over to the buyer at the time of delivery, early or belatedly. The passing of risk and title in the goods do not have influence either. A refusal by the buyer to take delivery of the goods will have the same effect. The commencement of the limitation period presupposes that the buyer can really examine the goods. Otherwise the Convention orientates toward an immediate examination of the goods by the buyer (c. Article 38 CISG).

5. This claim is not provided for in the CISG (c. there also the exclusion of the validity of the contract, Article 4, subpara. (a)). Hence, *claims* are referred to *which one of the parties may assert because of the national law to be applied* to the contract. The Limitation Convention in this regard goes beyond the substance of the CISG. It also covers claims from contracts that are void, e.g. repayment of a deposit. But compare note 4 of Article 1.

6. What is referred to here is *fraud* vis-a-vis the buyer *in regard to the quality of the goods*. (But compare Article 35 CISG and the exclusion of claims because of mistake in respect of the quality of the goods.)

Article 11

(Express undertaking)

If the seller has given an express undertaking relating to the goods which is stated to have effect for a certain period of time, whether expressed in terms of a specific period of time or otherwise[3], the limitation period in respect of any claim arising from the undertaking shall commence on the date[1] on which the buyer notifies[2] the seller of the fact on which the claim is based, but not later than on the date of the expiration of the period of the undertaking[4].

1. This rule is an *exception to Article 10, paragraph 2*. Frequently, it is of practical relevance in foreign trade because the seller in exporting mechanical engineering products, usually gives an express guarantee.

2. Compare Article 39 CISG. The limitation periods starts to run on the day of *dispatch* of the notice of lack of conformity. This is inferred from the fact that the above notice need not reach the addressee (c. note 9 of Article 39 CISG).

3. The guarantee given may also refer to the operating hours or the running time in kilometres or to a combination of both.

4. The period of limitation begins to run on the day the guarantee expires even when the buyer is entitled to give notice later.

Article 12

(Termination before performance is due; instalment contracts)

(1) If, in circumstances provided for by the law applicable to the contract[1], one party is entitled to declare the contract terminated[2] before the time for performance is due, and exercises this right, the limitation period in respect of a claim based on any such circumstances shall commence on the date on which the declaration is made to the other party[3]. If the contract is not declared to be terminated before performance becomes due[4], the limitation period shall commence on the date on which performance is due.

(2) The limitation period in respect of a claim arising out of a breach by one party of a contract[5] for the delivery of or payment for goods by instalments[6] shall, in relation to each separate instalment, commence on the date on which the particular breach occurs. If, under the law applicable to the contract, one party is entitled to declare the contract terminated by reason of such breach[7], and exercises this right, the limitation period in respect of all relevant instalments[8] shall commence on the date on which the declaration is made to the other party[3].

1. Article 72, paragraph 1 CISG, for instance, allows the creditor to assert *claims from breach of contract before* the contractual obligations of the debtor become *due*.

2. The notion "termination" is used here which by contrast to the term "avoidance" (c. Articles 49 and 64 CISG) usually designates an *ex nunc* termination of the contract.

3. *Decisive* is here the *day of dispatch* of the declaration. The limitation period commences on this day. Under Article 27 CISG, too, declarations become effective on the day they are made.

4. This is the day when performance is due and/or on this day the breach of contract is committed so that the limitation period commences both under Article 9, paragraph 1 and under Article 10, paragraph 1. The creditor, in certain circumstances, has the right to terminate the contract early, but he is not obligated to do so, except where he has an obligation to mitigate losses (Article 77 CISG). The

application of Article 12 always presupposes a *declaration*. Automatic termination, like in ULIS, does not come under Article 12.

5. The basic rule for the commencement of the limitation period is contained in Article 10, paragraph 1.

6. This specific rule for delivery and payment by instalments has been included to avoid doubt. It is completely clear in itself that each delivery becomes due on a different date where delivery by instalments has been agreed. The contract can insofar not be breached only once but in the case of each and every delivery. The same is true of an agreed payment by instalments.

7. Whether or not the creditor will have the right to terminate the contract in regard to a delivery by instalments or to a breach of the obligation to pay by instalments is regulated differently. Under Article 73, paras. 2 and 3 CISG the buyer has under certain circumstances the right to terminate the entire contract.

8. In terminating the contract the possibility of a uniform commencement of the limitation period is created; not only for future but also for earlier delivery or payment by instalments. The limitation period for breaches of contract in regard to earlier delivery or payment by instalments, which has already elapsed, is disregarded when the contract is terminated. In the case of long-term agreements, which exists over several years, the claims from breach of contract in regard to earlier deliveries may have already lapsed. It remains to be seen whether or not a court in applying Article 12 would assume the claim to be revived and the limitation period to start again.

Cessation and extension of the limitation period

Introductory remarks

The following articles regulate the cessation and extension of the limitation period through acts by the parties or other events. The Limitation Convention refers to that "the limitation period ceases to run". This term has been created to prevent the concept of the Convention from being equated with the concepts underlying national laws.

According to the Limitation Convention, full new limitation periods do not always commence after a limitation period ceases to run, so that there is a similarity between the former and the notion of suspensions which exists in many legal systems. Given this structure, the Limitation Convention accommodates the development of international trade and its legal basis for it undoubtedly stimulates a rapid liquidation of disputes under international sales contracts. Acts by the parties which affect the course of the limitation are, in the first place, the institution by the creditor of court or arbitral proceedings against the debtor, but also counterclaims by the debtor against the creditor as well as acknowledgement of an obligation.

Article 13

(Judicial proceedings)

The limitation period shall cease to run[3] when the creditor performs any act which, under the law of the court where the proceedings are instituted, is recognized as commencing judicial proceedings[1] against the debtor or as asserting his claim in such proceedings[2] already instituted against the debtor, for the purpose of obtaining satisfaction or recognition of his claim.

1. Judicial proceedings are instituted, first of all, by *bringing a charge*, but also by *requesting the issuance of a payment order* or a temporary injunction etc. In some countries the service of a claim by a lawyer without recourse to a court is considered as the institution of court proceedings. Which steps are required at which time is determined by the *lex fori*.

2. Whether or not in proceedings that are under way *further claims* may be asserted and in which way this is to be done is also determined by the procedural law applied by the court. Claims which were not asserted when the claim was instituted first and which are barred cannot be "revived" invoking Article 13.

3. The cessation here does not refer to an interruption followed by the commencement of a full new limitation period; but in connection with the rule under Article 17 of the Limitation Convention this is practically a *suspension*.

Article 14

(Arbitration)

(1) Where the parties have agreed[3] to submit to arbitration, the limitation period shall cease to run when either party commences arbitral proceedings[1] in the manner provided for[2] in the arbitration agreement or by the law applicable to such proceedings.

(2) In the absence of any such provision, arbitral proceedings shall be deemed to commence on the date on which a request[4] that the claim in dispute be referred to arbitration is delivered[5] at the habitual residence or place of business of the other party or, if he has no such residence or place of business, then at his last known residence or place of business.

1. In regard to the cessation of the limitation period in the meaning of the Limitation Convention the institution of arbitral proceedings can be equated with the institution of court proceedings. This is not true of the institution of other proceedings with a view to settling disputes alternatively, e.g. conciliation proceedings.

2. The manner in which arbitral proceedings are to be instituted follows from the arbitration agreement or from the law applicable to the arbitration. There will be differences, above all, between proceedings before institutional and ad hoc arbitral tribunals. Since the General Assembly of the United Nations in resolution 31/98 of 15 December 1976 recommended the use of the *UNCITRAL arbitration rules*, the parties will frequently refer to those rules in their agreements. The way of instituting arbitral proceedings can also be deduced from the rules of a permanent arbitral tribunal. Under some laws, a suspension or the interruption of the limitation period is caused only when the arbitral tribunal has constituted itself and the

charge has been serviced to the opposing party via the arbitral tribunal. Only when a relevant provision cannot be inferred from the arbitration agreement or from the law applicable, is the uniform rule of paragraph 2 to be applied.

3. The institution of arbitral proceedings only affects the limitation period when the parties have agreed to submit their dispute to an arbitral tribunal. When the creditor addresses an arbitral tribunal without the parties having agreed to do so, and when the debtor accepts such proceedings, this is considered in many legal systems as a belated implicit agreement which also fulfils the condition of Article 14. An agreement of the parties is requested here to delimit arbitral proceedings from such which are obligatory without any party agreements (e.g. pursuant to the *General Conditions of Delivery of the CMEA*). According to the structure of the Limitation Convention these fall under Article 13 (O. R., 22).

4. Compared to many known procedural provisions, this rule constitutes a *considerable advantage for the creditor*. According to it, it is sufficient, for instance, in ad hoc arbitral proceedings that the plaintiff informs the defendant of his will to institute proceedings, and usually at the same time the arbitrator named by him.

5. Likewise in Article 3, paragraph 2 of the UNCITRAL arbitration rules. Such an effect is achieved by way of delivery even without the addressee actually knowing of it. On the other hand, dispatch of the request is not sufficient. It is thus the plaintiff who bears the risk of transmitting his request.

Article 15

(Legal proceedings arising from death, bankruptcy or a similar occurrence)

In any legal proceedings[1] other than those mentioned in articles 13 and 14, including legal proceedings commenced[2] upon in the occurrence of[3]:

(a) The death or incapacity of the debtor,

(b) The bankruptcy or any state of insolvency affecting the whole of the property of the debtor, or

(c) The dissolution or liquidation of a corporation, company, partnership, association or entity when it is the debtor.

The limitation period shall cease to run[4] when the creditor asserts his claim in such proceedings for the purpose of obtaining satisfaction or recognition of the claim, subject to the law governing the proceedings[5].

1. Articles 13 and 14 cover the *principal cases* of legal proceedings which exist in foreign trade relations. Occasionally, there are further possibilities for asserting claims which pursuant to Article 15 interrupt the course of the limitation period. This is the case when the creditor asserts his claim in proceedings other than those already regulated under Articles 13 and 14 in order to obtain satisfaction or recognition of his claim.

2. Reference is made here to *proceedings* which are not instituted by the creditor, but mostly *ex officio*.

3. The enumeration provides examples only.

4. Compare note 3 on Article 13.

5. The law applicable to the proceedings determines also whether or not the creditor of an international sales contract can assert his claim in any such proceedings at all and, possibly, within which period of time and with which further consequences he can do so.

Article 16

(Counterclaims)

For the purposes of articles 13, 14 and 15, any act performed by way of counterclaim[1] shall be deemed to have been performed on the same date[2] as the act performed in relation to the claim against which the counterclaim is raised, provided that both the claim and the counterclaim relate to the same contract or to several contracts concluded in the course of the same transaction[3].

1. Countercharges will in the cases of Articles 13 and 14 mostly be asserted in raising *counteractions*. (Regarding set-off compare Article 25, paragraph 2.)

2. In the case of counterclaims this means *retrospective cessation of the limitation period*. Given this rule, a counterclaim can be raised even when the claim has already come under the statute of limitations, but had not lapsed when the action was brought forward. This provision has the advantage that the debtor and first defendant may wait to see the course of the proceedings and the outcome of possible settlement negotiations without being forced, because of the expiry of the limitation period for his counterclaims, to raise immediately a counterclaim.

3. An example of such transaction could be an agency contract with a dealer in the frame of which several sales contracts are concluded.

Article 17

(Proceedings not resulting in a decision on the merits of the claim)

(1) Where a claim has been asserted in legal proceedings within the limitation period in accordance with articles 13, 14, 15 or 16, but such legal proceedings have ended without a decision binding on the merits of the claim[1], the limitation period shall be deemed to have continued to run[2].

(2) If, at the time such legal proceedings ended, the limitation period has expired or has less than one year to run, the creditor shall be entitled to a period of one year[3] from the date on which the legal proceedings ended.

1. There may be different reasons for the ending of legal proceedings without a decision binding on the merits of the claim. For instance, the claim may have been rejected because of incompetence of the court. This includes the case where the decision by an arbitral tribunal is rescinded and set aside by a court of law. It is of no relevance in regard to Article 17 whether the creditor has withdrawn the claim or not continued to pursue it, whether the arbitral tribunal has abandoned the proceedings by a relevant decision or whether the court, also by a relevant decision, has referred the claim to another court.

2. The cessation of the limitation period pursuant to Articles 13 - 16 is deemed not to have occurred; the limitation period is deemed to have continued to run.

3. This provision is to *prevent undue hardship* for creditors. When the larger part of the limitation period has not yet expired, then there will be no need for a special *Nachfrist*.

Article 18

(Joint debtors; recourse actions)

(1) Where legal proceedings have been commenced against one debtor, the limitation period prescribed in this Convention shall cease to run[2] against any other party jointly and severally liable with the debtor, provided that the creditor informs such party[1] in writing[3] within that period that the proceedings have been commenced.

(2) Where legal proceedings have been commenced by a subpurchaser[4] against the buyer, the limitation period prescribed in this Convention shall cease to run in relation to the buyer's claim over against the seller[5], if the buyer informs the seller in writing[3] within that period that the proceedings have been commenced.

(3) Where the legal proceedings referred to in paragraphs 1 and 2 of this article have ended[6], the limitation period in respect of the claims of the creditor or the buyer against the party jointly and severally liable or against the seller shall be deemed not to have ceased running by virtue of paragraphs 1 and 2 of this article, but the creditor or the buyer shall be entitled to an additional year[7] from the date on which the legal proceedings ended, if at that time the limitation period had expired or had less than one year to run.

1. In the case where another *party is jointly and severally liable with the debtor* it is up to the creditor to decide which debtor to address his claim to and/or against which debtor he institutes legal proceedings. In taking this decision he is guided by which debtor is the wealthiest or against which debtor, probably also for other reasons, an enforcement may have the greatest chance to succeed.

According to Article 18 the creditor has the opportunity to cause the limitation period also against one or more other debtors to cease to run by way of giving notice of the institution of proceedings.

2. Regarding cessation compare note 3 on Article 13.

3. The written form later facilitates the presentation of the case. For the information to be effective it has to be received.

4. Paragraph 2 was very much disputed at the diplomatic conference because it starts out from a case which regularly will *not* be *an international sale*, namely of the relations between the buyer of an international sales contract and his, mostly domestic, subpurchaser.

The inclusion of paragraph 2 in the Limitation Convention was nonetheless considered as justified in order to allow the buyer to have recourse against the seller of an international sales contract.

5. The claim referred to here must be a *claim resulting from the same facts*, e.g. because of lack of conformity.

6. When the proceedings that have been instituted by the creditor against a party jointly and severally liable with the debtor or by the subpurchaser against the buyer have ended, the *limitation period* continues to run. It *had ceased to run only for the duration of the proceedings*.

7. Irrespective of the actual course of the limitation period vis-a-vis the other debtors and/or the seller, the *creditor or* the *buyer* is always *granted one additional year* within which he can assert his claims. This rule may indeed be considered as successful. On the one hand, it does not force the creditor to proceed immediately against all debtors and the buyer to institute proceedings against the seller as long as the outcome of the first proceedings is still uncertain. On the other, the period of one year after the end of the first proceedings allows a direct clarification of the relationship between the creditor and the other parties jointly and severally liable with the debtor and/or between the buyer and the seller.

Article 19

(Recommencement of the period by service of notice)

Where the creditor performs, in the State in which the debtor[2] has his place of business and before the expiration of the limitation period, any act[1], other than the acts described in articles 13, 14, 15 and 16, which under the law of that State has the effect of recommencing a limitation period[3], a new limitation period of four years shall commence on the date prescribed by that law[4].

1. In some countries the *limitation period can cease to run without legal proceedings* having been instituted, e.g. by personal request for payment (like in Belgium and France). Such and similar acts are referred to here.

2. In deviation from the remaining provisions of the Limitation Convention, which aim at creating an independent international uniform law, Article 19 expressly refers to the national law of the debtor's country. This is, firstly, to offer the creditor a chance to have the limitation period cease to run without the institution of legal proceedings where the relevant measures have been at his disposal in the past, and, secondly, to protect the debtor insofar as the acts have to be such which the creditor performs in the country of the debtor and which according to the law of that country have the respective effect, hence the debtor always has to be familiar with the latter.

3. What is referred to here is not a cessation of the limitation period as in Article 13 fol, which can be corrected pursuant to Article 17. Rather, the wording of this context relates to an interruption in the traditional meaning. Where the act performed by the creditor in the debtor's country causes only a shorter additional period but not a full new limitation period, that act does not come under Article 19.

4. For several reasons, Bulgaria, the former GDR and Hungary, in particular, spoke out against Article 19 at the diplomatic conference (O. R., 213): First, that article would introduce domestic law into the Convention to an extent to which it would be detrimental to the creation of international uniform laws. Second, this rule would violate the principle of equality and equal chances of the parties if there were reciprocal claims, but only in one country the possibility was given to cause the limitation period to cease to run by acts other than the institution of arbitral or court proceedings, e.g. by mere reminder.

There is doubt as to whether these objections were indeed justified. In the event of claims vis-a-vis foreign debtors there is frequently a payment risk involved. An additional possibility for causing the limitation period to cease to run may, therefore, be useful.

Article 20

(Acknowledgement by debtor)

(1) Where the debtor, before the expiration of the limitation period, acknowledges in writing[1] his obligation to the creditor, a new limitation period of four years shall commence to run from the date of such acknowledgement[2].

(2) Payment of interest or partial performance of an obligation by the debtor shall have the same effect as an acknowledgement under paragraph (1) of this article if it can reasonably be inferred[3] from such payment or performance that the debtor acknowledges that obligation.

1. The practice that the limitation period ceases to run when there is an acknowledgement in writing is *in line with generally applicable principles*. The acknowledgement can be made also in the form of a request for deferment of payment. The proposal to accept as sufficient for the extension of the limitation period also an implied acknowledgement by the debtor (as in 208 German BGB) was rejected at the diplomatic conference (O. R., 68).

2. Compare note 3 on Article 19.

3. *Not every partial performance is to be treated as an acknowledgement of an obligation.* There may be a dispute on whether or not there is a claim at all going beyond the partial performance. In certain circumstances, the debtor wanted to pay off his debts by way of the partial performance.

Article 21

(Extension where institution of legal proceedings prevented)

Where, as a result of a circumstance[1] which is beyond the control of the creditor and which he could neither avoid nor overcome, the creditor has been prevented from causing the limitation period to cease to run[3], the limitation period shall be extended so as not to expire before the expiration of one year from the date on which the relevant circumstance ceased to exist[2].

1. The Limitation Convention refers to a circumstance which has hindered the creditor and which he could not prevent nor overcome. Compare also Article 79 CISG. The Convention does not mention *force majeure* because that term is attributed different substances in diverse legal systems. Such a circumstance might be, for instance, a *standstill of administration of justice* in the debtor's country. Other such circumstances could include the *interruption of communications* between the countries concerned; the *death or incapacity of the debtor* as long as no receiver is appointed; *wrong data* given *by the debtor* as to himself and his address. Concerning fraud see the specific rule of Article 10, paragraph 3.

2. The problem of the extension of the limitation period is solved here in a flexible way. In the event of *force majeure* there will be no automatic extension of the period during which those circumstances remain in effect. Where *force majeure* occurs during the first three years of a 4-year limitation period, it will have no effect. On the other hand, the limitation period can be extended either by a period that is longer or a shorter period than the one during which *force majeure* was in effect. This solution is suited to protect the creditor from disadvantage without unnecessarily extending the limitation period. By no means can the limitation period be extended beyond the general limit of Article 23.

3. This is the case, for instance, when the creditor could not present a claim under Article 13 or institute arbitral proceedings under Article 14 and when he could not perform any other act provided for in this Convention or under domestic law (Article 19). The creditor must have exhausted all of the possibilities given under Article 13 fol.

Modification of the limitation period by the parties

Article 22

(Modification by the parties)

(1) The limitation period cannot be modified or affected by any declaration or agreement between the parties, except in the cases provided for in paragraph (2) of this article[1].

(2) The debtor may at any time during the running of the limitation period extend the period[2] by a declaration in writing to the creditor. This declaration may be renewed[3].

(3) The provisions of this article shall not affect the validity of a clause in the contract of sale which stipulates that arbitral proceedings[4] shall be commenced within a shorter period of limitation than that prescribed by this Convention, provided that such clause is valid under the law applicable to the contract of sale.

1. The Limitation Convention here formulates the principle that it is *inadmissible* for the parties *to modify the limitation period*. This meets the intentions, in particular, of many developing countries which feared that otherwise the respective stronger party would be in a position to impose its will to the detriment of the less strong party. (This is indeed possible when the Limitation Convention is fully excluded pursuant to Article 3, paragraph 3, but, on the other hand, national law will then become effective which may favour both the creditor and the debtor.) By contrast to this rule, 225 German BGB generally allows a shortening of the limitation period by party agreement and 477 German BGB an extension of that period for claims from the delivery of defective goods.

2. The declaration must be in writing and unequivocal. It is valid only when the limitation period has not expired yet. On the other hand, it is not effective when the limitation period has not begun to run, hence already at the time of the conclusion of the contract.

A *similar result* is achieved by *acknowledging an obligation* under Article 20. By contrast, a declaration under Article 22 does not cause the limitation period to cease to run and thus entail a full new period. Rather, it is in the debtor's hands to determine the length by which the period is extended. On the other hand, he accommodates the wishes of the creditor leaving him time for settling the disputed issues without himself having to acknowledge an obligation and throwing away chances.

3. But not beyond the general limit fixed in Article 23.

4. Paragraph 3 contains *one further exception to the principle*. By contrast to paragraph 2 it is not an extension which is referred to but a *shortening of the limitation period* which is brought about not by a one-sided declaration, which would have to be made by the creditor, in this case, but *by an agreement between the parties*. However, the agreement mentioned before is no agreement on a shortening of the limitation period. Rather, it is one that stipulates that, irrespective of the provisions of the Limitation Convention, an agreement of the contract shall be valid which provides for the need to institute arbitral proceedings within a shorter limitation period, than provided for in the Limitation Convention. This presupposes, of course, that such a contractual agreement is admissible under the law applicable to the contract of sale.

General limit of the limitation period

Article 23

(Over-all limitation for bringing legal proceedings)

Notwithstanding the provisions of this Convention[1], a limitation period shall in any event expire not later than 10 years[2] from the date on which it commenced to run under articles 9, 10, 11 and 12 of this Convention.

1. Notwithstanding the provisions of this Convention means notwithstanding the various possibilities to extend the limitation period under Articles 17, 18, 19, 20, 21 and 22.

2. At the diplomatic conference the views on this rule differed for two reasons. On the one hand, there was the opinion that a ceiling for Article 20, acknowledgement of an obligation, and Article 22, extension on the part of the debtor, but possibly also for Article 21, *force majeure*, was not required, indeed undesirable. On the other, the view held by a majority prevailed according to which irrespec-

tive of the circumstances of the individual case a *general limit would be in the interest of the parties and of the courts*, and thus also in that of the States.

There was also concern that the general limit could become effective when, for instance, after the expiration of ten years the court of second or even third instance has to engage again in the legal dispute (O. R., 225). The notion that the Supreme Court could handle a claim, which had not lapsed in the first instance, as having lapsed after ten years was rejected as unfounded, however (O. R., 227).

Consequences of the Expiration of the Limitation Period

Article 24

(Who can invoke limitation)

Expiration of the limitation period shall be taken into consideration[1] in any legal proceedings only if invoked by a party to such proceedings[2].

1. The fact of limitation is not taken into consideration *ex officio* in the court and arbitral proceedings, but only when it is invoked as a plea by one of the parties, i.e. the defendant, (note 2 of Article 25). This approach meets the needs of international trade (c. for instance 222 German BGB). The Limitation Convention does not determine when the plea relating to the expiration of the limitation period will have to be invoked in legal proceedings. This is determined, therefore, according to domestic procedural law. (It does not seem possible to decide this question following the general principles, c. Article 7.) Where the plea relating to the expiration of the limitation period is not treated as a *plea obstructing the proceedings* which has to be put in *before the beginning of the hearings*, it can be raised at any stage of the proceedings up to the conclusion of the hearings.

2. The representatives of a number of States, mostly from Asia and Africa, very much objected to this principle. According to them, the issue of limitation was a *question of law and order* and/or legal policies of a State. Therefore, it could *not be left to the parties* to decide whether or not they wanted to rely on the limitation. The latter would rather have to be taken into account *ex officio* (O. R., 229). This had to be seen against the background of equality before the

court. Obviously, there was concern that some companies might be to inexperienced and might forget to rely on the limitation. On the other hand, the afore-mentioned view was countered expressing that some facts which cause a limitation period to commence to run, cease to run or expire were only known to the parties. Further arguments put forward included the opinion that Article 24 would not hinder a court to point to the fact that the time between the claim's becoming due and the institution of proceedings has expired and to ask whether or not the expiration of the limitation period should be taken into consideration. There might be reasons which may cause a debtor not to rely on the expiration of the limitation period because it is exactly for the sake of his relationship with the plaintiff that he is interested in a decision binding on the merits of the claim.

To ensure that the limitation be taken into consideration *ex officio*, as practiced in some countries, the Limitation Convention in Article 36 provides for any State, when depositing the instrument of ratification or of accession, to make a reservation declaring that it will not apply Article 24 or, to put it in other words: that his courts will *ex officio* take the limitation into consideration.

Article 25

(Effect of expiration of the period; set-off)

(1) Subject to the provisions of paragraph (2) of this article and of article 24[2], no claim shall be recognized or enforced in any legal proceedings[1] commenced after the expiration of the limitation period.

(2) Notwithstanding the expiration of the limitation period, one party may rely on his claim as a defence[3] or for the purpose of set-off[4] against a claim asserted by the other party[5], provided that in the latter case this may only be done[6]:

(a) If both claims relate to the same contract or to several contracts concluded in the course of the same transaction[7]; or[6]

(b) If the claims could have been set off[8] at any time before the expiration of the limitation period.

1. Paragraph 1 formulates the *principle* that after the expiration of the limitation period *claims can no longer be enforced through a court or arbitral tribunal*. What is at issue is not the existence of a *claim* as such, it *does not cease to exist* when the limitation period expires. Therefore, also claims which are barred can still be set off (c. paragraph 2) and/or payments made can be demanded back (c. Article 26). The Limitation Convention does not contain any provisions on whether and how the creditor, in spite of the expiration of the limitation period, can satisfy his claims from a pledge or other secured credits (c. Article 5, subpara. (c)). This has to be decided under national law.

2. The application of this principle presupposes that the debtor relies on the expiration of the limitation period. Where the *debtor omits a plea* knowingly or out of ignorance, the *court will have to decide in the matter*. A debtor may well set great store by that the court determines that there is no claim at all, and urge, therefore, a decision binding on the merits of the claim.

3. Hereunder it is to be understood that a debtor bases his claim, which is barred, on a counterclaim (c. Article 16), provided that the claim was not barred yet at the time it was raised. The difference between a counterclaim and a set-off consists in that the set-off permits the satisfaction of one's own claims only up to the amount in which the other party had asserted and enforced his claim whereas the claims asserted through a counterclaim may go beyond.

4. What is referred to here is limitation. Whether or not a set-off is admissible in this context is determined by the applicable substantive law.

5. One's own claims can be invoked at any stage of the proceedings. Insofar as these claims are to be founded on a counterclaim, the prescriptions of the procedural law of the *lex fori* have to be taken into consideration.

6. This part regulates *two different cases*. A Soviet proposal to replace "or" by "and" had been rejected at the conference.

7. Where the two claims relate to the same contract or to several contracts concluded in the course of the same transaction (c. note 3 of Article 16), there is no time limit. The *set-off* itself is *possible even when the debtor's claim had been in lapse already when the creditor's claim developed*.

8. In this case the two claims will have to have been in existence, able to be set off, i.e. due and barred, without having emerged from the same transaction. Therefore, one could imagine here also the possibility of a *transfer of obligations for the purpose of set-off.*

Article 26

(Restitution of performance after the expiration of the period)

Where the debtor performs his obligation after the expiration of the limitation period, he shall not on that ground be entitled in any way to claim restitution[1] even if he did not know at the time when he performed his obligation that the limitation period had expired.

1. At least he has no right to restitution on the ground that the limitation period had expired already. This provision does not prevent a claim for restitution on other grounds.

The principle of Article 26 once again clarifies, just as already Article 25 in regard to set-off with claims that are barred, that the Limitation Convention proceeds on the limitation of the enforceability by courts, but does not equate the expiration of the limitation period with the lapsing of the claim itself. *The party who performs in spite of limitation, does not perform without a legal ground*. The party who receives in spite of limitation, has not unjustly enriched himself.

Article 27

(Interest)

The expiration of the limitation period with respect to a principal debt shall have the same effect with respect to an obligation to pay interest[2] on that debt[1].

1. There is thus *no independent limitation period for interest*. Compare also Article 20, paragraph 2. (On the question of interest in the international sale of goods compare also Article 78 CISG.)

2. The German BGB (224) in this context refers to the more general term of auxiliary claims rather than interest.

Calculation of the period

Article 28

(Basic rule)

(1) The limitation period shall be calculated in such a way that it shall expire at the end of the day which corresponds to the date on which the period commenced to run[1]. If there is no such corresponding date, the period shall expire at the end of the last day of the last month of the limitation period.

(2) The limitation period shall be calculated by reference to the date of the place where the legal proceedings are instituted[2].

1. By this way of calculation, which can easily be done, the period is practically extended by one day.

2. This provision may become relevant when the commencement and the end of the limitation period are considered on both sides of the date line.

Article 29

(Effect of holiday)

Where the last day of the limitation period falls on an official holiday or other *dies non juridicus*[1] precluding the appropriate legal action in the jurisdiction where the creditor institutes legal proceedings or asserts a claim as envisaged in articles 13, 14 or 15 the limitation period shall be extended so as not to expire until the end of the first day following that official holiday or *dies non juridicus* on which such a claim could be asserted in that jurisdiction.

1. Even though it will certainly occur very seldom that the creditor wants to institute court proceedings on this last day, Article 29 determines that the limitation period in such cases will not expire before the end of the day which follows the official holiday or the "*dies non juridicus*" and on which proceedings can be instituted or claims can be asserted.

International effect

Article 30

(Acts or circumstances to be given international effect)

The acts and circumstances referred to in articles 13 through 19[2] which have taken place in one Contracting State[1] shall have effect for the purposes of this Convention in another Contracting State, provided that the creditor has taken all reasonable steps[3] to ensure that the debtor is informed of the relevant act or circumstances as soon as possible[4].

1. The institution of legal proceedings under the Convention has *international effect* only when it is done in a Contracting State. The Convention, in this context, only refers to relations between the Contracting States. There was a vivid dispute on this issue (O. R., 237 fol) at the diplomatic conference. While a number of delegations obviously were guided by the international law principle of reciprocity, other delegations held the view that it would be more reasonable in the interest of the unification of the limitation provisions and their broadest application to recognize also such acts and circumstances which take place in a non-Contracting State. The principle of reciprocity was fully legitimate in State-to-State relations, but in the relations between economic organizations and companies clarity, legal certainty and uniformity was needed above all.

It is indeed hard to understand why in spite of the institution of proceedings in a non-Contracting State in regard to the same claim in a Contracting State the limitation period should continue to run. Irrespective of whether or not a claim can be asserted in more than one State, it will always be the same claim for which there should be, therefore, not different but only one single, uniform limitation period.

In the end, a minority of participants in the conference prevailed for the vote on the issue "Contracting State or non-Contracting State" ended in a draw 17 : 17 (O. R., 240).

The restriction contained in Article 30 was to exert a certain pressure on the States to accede to the Limitation Convention.

The effects of the institution of legal proceedings in a non-Contracting State are left by the Limitation Convention to the national law.

2. The acts or circumstances designated in Articles 20 through 22 are *not restricted to Contracting States*. The acknowledgement of an obligation which was made in a non-Contracting State will thus be recognized also before a court of a Contracting State as causing the limitation period to cease to run.

This provision of Article 30 has also to be seen in connection with Article 3, paragraph 1 according to which the Limitation Convention is to be applied only when the two parties have their place of business in Contracting States. Court proceedings under Article 13 will only rarely be instituted in third countries. Proceedings under Articles 15, 18 and 19 will regularly take place only in the debtor's country. Only arbitral proceedings under Article 14 - which are of particular relevance in foreign trade - will be held in third countries more frequently.

3. In the majority of cases, the debtor will *ex officio* be informed. Incidentally, the limitation period ceases to run only *when the debtor is informed of it* (c. for instance Article 18).

4. Article 30 was not modified by the Protocol amending the Convention. But insofar as the Limitation Convention applies in regard to the Protocol there will be a *contradiction between Article 3 and Article 30*. Pursuant to the new version of Article 3, the Limitation Convention applies also to the relationship between parties of whom one may have his place of business in a non-Contracting State. But under Article 30, the acts performed in this non-Contracting State have no effect in the other (Contracting) State. Attention was repeatedly drawn to the contradiction at the Vienna Conference in the debate on the Protocol amending the Convention, but in spite of a suggestion by the Secretariat (O. R., 467) it was renounced to adapt Article 30 to the new sphere of application.

PART II

IMPLEMENTATION

Article 31

(Federal States; non-unitary State)

(1) If a Contracting State has two or more territorial units[1] in which, according to its constitution, different systems of law are applicable in relation to the matters dealt with in this Convention, it may, at the time of its signature, ratification or accession, declare that this Convention shall extend to all its territorial units[3] or only to one or more of them, and may amend its declaration by submitting another declaration at any time.

(2) These declarations shall be notified to the Secretary General of the United Nations and shall state expressly the territorial units to which the Convention applies.

(1) If a Contracting State has two or more territorial units[1] in which, according to its constitution, different systems of law are applicable in relation to the matters dealt with in this Convention, it may, at the time of its signature, ratification or accession, declare that this Convention shall extend to all its territorial units[3] or only to one or more of them, and may amend its declaration by submitting another declaration at any time.

(2) These declarations shall be notified to the Secretary General of the United Nations and shall state expressly the territorial units to which the Convention applies.

(3) If a Contracting State described in paragraph (1) of this article makes no declaration at the time of signature, ratification or accession, the Convention shall have effect within all territorial units of that State[2].

(3) If a Contracting State described in paragraph (1) of this article makes no declaration at the time of signature, ratification or accession, the Convention shall have effect within all territorial units of that State[2].

(4) If, by virtue of a declaration under this article, this Convention extends to one or more but not all of the territorial units of a Contracting State, and if the place of business of a party to a contract is located in that State, this place of business shall, for the purposes of this Convention, be considered not to be in a Contracting State unless it is in a territorial unit to which the Convention extends[4].

1. Compare in this context notes on Article 93 CISG.

2. Article III of the Protocol amending the Convention on the Limitation Period in the International Sale of Goods adds a fourth paragraph here.

3. During the drafting of the Limitation Convention the attempt was made to include a so-called *colonial clause*. Under that clause a State could declare that the Convention shall be applicable to "all or any of the *territories for whose international relations it is responsible*". This clause can frequently be found in earlier conventions.

4. This paragraph was added to adapt the Limitation Convention to Article 93 CISG, which, however, may have the effect of restricting the sphere of application of the Limitation Convention.

Article 32

(Determination of the proper law when a federal or a non-unitary State is involved)

Where in this Convention reference is made to the law of a State in which different systems of law apply, such reference shall be construed to mean the law of the particular legal system concerned[1].

1. This article, which was included at the proposal of the United States, takes account of the particularities of non-unitarian States.

The provisions of Articles 31 and 32, which consider the specific situation of federal States, are also in the interest of the other Contracting States of the Limitation Convention because they minimize an uncertainty about the legal situation in establishing contractual relations and their fulfilment with parties in those States.

Article 33

(Non-applicability to prior contracts)

Each Contracting State shall apply the provisions of this Convention to contracts concluded on or after the date of the entry into force of this Convention[1].

1. Compare notes on Article 100 CISG.

PART III

DECLARATIONS AND RESERVATIONS

Article 34[1]

(Declarations limiting the application of the Convention)

(1) Two or more Contracting States[2] may at any time declare[3] that contracts of sale between a seller having a place of business in one of these States and a buyer having a place of business in another of these States shall not be governed by this Convention, because they apply to the matters governed by this Convention the same or closely related legal rules.

(1) Two or more Contracting States[2] which have the same or closely related legal rules on matters governed by this Convention may at any time declare[3] that the Convention shall not apply to contracts of international sale of goods where the parties have their places of business in those States. Such declarations may be made jointly or by reciprocal unilateral declarations.

(2) A Contracting State which has the same or closely related rules on matters governed by this Convention as one or more non-Contracting States may at any time declare that the Convention shall not apply to contracts of international sale of goods where the parties have their places of business in those States.

(3) If a State which is the object of a declaration under paragraph (2) of this article subsequently becomes a Contracting State, the declaration made shall, as from the date on which this Convention enters into force in respect of the new Contracting State, have the effect of a declaration made under paragraph (1), provided that the new Contracting State joins in such declaration or makes a reciprocal unilateral declaration[4].

1. Article 34 was newly drafted in accordance with Article IV of the Protocol amending the Convention.

2. Compare in this context notes on Article 94 CISG.

3. When signing the Convention, Norway declared, and reaffirmed during the act of ratification, that the Limitation Convention will not apply to the contracts it concluded with parties from Denmark, Finland, Iceland and Sweden.

4. The old version of Article 34 only provided for the possibility of paragraph 1, whereas now the enlarged version of Article 94 CISG is included in the Convention. This offers the *opportunity of making unilateral declarations in regard to non-Contracting States*. It was made clear that several States can make both joint and reciprocal unilateral declarations.

Article 35

(Reservation with respect to actions for annulment of the contract)

A Contracting State may declare, at the time of the deposit of its instrument of ratification or accession, that it will not apply the provisions of this Convention to actions for annulment of the contract[1].

1. This provision was included because some States have specific limitation rules for action for annulment for reasons of incapacity, threat or fraud. Also, the CISG does not contain any provisions on the voidness or rescission of sales contracts (note 2 of Article 4).

Article 36

(Reservation with respect to who can invoke limitation)

Any State may declare, at the time of the deposit of its instrument of ratification or accession, that it shall not be compelled to apply the provisions of article 24 of this Convention[1].

1. When a State makes use of this reservation, his courts will *ex officio* take the limitation period into consideration. This reservation was included at the request of those States which consider it an issue of law and order to strictly observe provisions on limitation (c. note 2 of Article 24).

Article 36 bis[1] (Article XII of the Protocol)

(Reservation on application of Convention)

Any State may declare at the time of the deposit of its instrument of accession[2] or its notification under article 43 bis[3] that it will not be bound by the amendments to article 3 made by article I of the 1980 Protocol[4]. A declaration made under this article shall be in writing and be formally notified to the depositary.

1. In adopting this article, the same reservation was provided for as in Article 95 CISG, i.e. the possibility of excluding the application of the Convention to parties in non-Contracting States.

2. In the case of accession it is proceeded according to Article 43 ter.

3. In the case of ratification or accession under Article 43 bis to the old version of the Limitation Convention and simultaneous notification of the accession to the Protocol.

4. Such a State will then be bound by article 3 of the unamended Convention.

Article 37[1]

(Relationship with conventions containing limitation provisions in respect of international sale of goods)

This Convention shall not prevail over conventions already entered into or which may be entered into[2], or which contain provisions concerning the matters governed by this Convention, provided that the seller and buyer have their places of business in States parties to such convention.

This Convention shall not prevail over any international agreement[3] which has already been or may be entered into and which contains provisions concerning the matters governed by this Convention, provided that the seller and buyer have their places of business in States parties to such agreement.

1. Article 37 was newly worded by Article V of the Protocol.

2. Compare here notes on Article 90 CISG.

3. The new version is based on Article 90 CISG because some delegations were concerned that "conventions" could not be as widely interpreted as "international agreement" (O. R., 472).

Article 38

(Reservations with respect to the definition of a contract of international sale)

(1) A Contracting State which is a party to an existing convention relating to the international sale of goods[1] may declare, at the time of the deposit of its instrument of ratification or accession, that it will apply this Convention exclusively to contracts of international sale of goods as defined in such existing convention[2].

(2) Such declaration shall cease to be effective on the first day of the month following the expiration of twelve months after a new convention on the international sale of goods, concluded under the auspices of the United Nations, shall have entered into force[3].

1. The rule of Article 38 takes account of the situation of those States which have ratified the Hague Sales Convention (c. also notes on paras. 2 and 3).

2. The Hague Convention and the Limitation Convention proceed from *different definitions of the term "contract of international sale of goods"* with the result that there are differences in regard to the substantive sphere of application. According to the Hague Convention, the States are called upon to include the provisions of the Convention into their domestic law. Where those States participate unreservedly in the Limitation Convention, this means:

(a) there are different definitions in their law on the contract of international sale of goods, and

(b) sales contracts, which under the national sales law are not considered international, constitute contracts of international sale of goods in regard to the Limitation Convention.

3. Compare notes to Article 99 CISG. That article presupposes, however, that the State which made the declaration has become a Contracting State of the new convention on the international sale of goods. The entering into force of the new convention changes nothing in the legal situation of a State which has made a declaration under Article 38, paragraph 1, Limitation Convention, where the old Hague Convention remains in force for that State.

Article 39

(No other reservations permitted)

No reservations[1] other than those made in accordance with articles 34, 35, 36 bis and 38 shall be permitted.

1. Compare notes on Article 98 CISG. A declaration under Article 31 is not considered a reservation.

Article 40

(When declarations and reservations take effect; withdrawal)

(1) Declarations[1] made under this Convention shall be addressed to the Secretary-General of the United Nations and shall take effect simultaneously with the entry of this Convention into force in respect of the State concerned, except declarations made thereafter. The latter declarations shall take effect on the first day of the month following the expiration of six months after the date of their receipt by the Secretary-General of the United Nations[2].

(1) Declarations[1] made under this Convention shall be addressed to the Secretary-General of the United Nations and shall take effect simultaneously with the entry of this Convention into force in respect of the State concerned, except declarations made thereafter. The latter declarations shall take effect on the first day of the month following the expiration of six months after the date of their receipt by the Secretary-General of the United Nations[2]. Reciprocal unilateral declarations under article 34 shall take effect on the first day of the month following the expiration of six months after the receipt of the latest declaration by the Secretary-General of the United Nations[3].

(2) Any State which has made a declaration under this Convention may withdraw it at any time by a notification addressed to the Secretary-General of the United Nations. Such withdrawal shall take effect on the first day of the month following the expiration of six months after the date of the receipt of the notification by the Secretary-General of the United Nations. In the case of a declaration made under article 34 of this Convention, such withdrawal shall also render inoperative, as from the date on which the withdrawal takes effect, any reciprocal declaration made by another State under that article.

1. Compare notes on Article 97 CISG.

2. A sentence was added here by including Article VI of the Protocol.

3. This provision was taken from Article 97, paragraph 3 CISG, in order to express in more precise terms that the first unilateral declaration cannot become effective as long as the reciprocal second unilateral declaration becomes effective.

PART IV

FINAL CLAUSES

Article 41

(Signature)

This Convention shall be open until 31 December 1975 for signature by all States at the Headquarters of the United Nations[1].

1. Compare notes 1 - 4 on Article 91 CISG.

At the concluding meeting of the diplomatic conference on 14 June 1974 Brazil, Byelorussia, the GDR, Mongolia, Poland, the USSR, Ukraine and Hungary signed the Convention. Bulgaria, Ghana, Costarica, Nicaragua, Norway and Czechoslovakia did so before the period for signature had expired.

Article 42

(Ratification)

This Convention is subject to ratification. The instruments of ratification shall be deposited with the Secretary-General of the United Nations[1].

1. Compare note 6 on Article 91 CISG.

On the situation in regard to ratification see Introductory remarks.

Article 43

(Accession)

This Convention shall remain open for accession by any State. The instruments of accession shall be deposited with the Secretary-General of the United Nations[1].

1. Compare notes on Articles 89 and 91 CISG.

On the situation in regard to accession see Introductory remarks.

Article 43 bis[1] (Article X of the Protocol)

(Accession to the amended version)

> If a State ratifies or accedes to
> the 1974 Limitation Convention
> after the entry into force of the
> 1980 Protocol, the ratification
> or accession shall also
> constitute a ratification[3] or an
> accession to the Convention as
> amended by the 1980 Protocol
> if the State notifies the
> depositary accordingly[2].

1. States can accede simultaneously to both versions of the Limitation Convention. Compare also Article 43 ter.

2. The notification has to be simultaneous and is treated by the depositary as two separate instruments being deposited. Accession to the Protocol pursuant to Article 43 bis is different from that under Article 43 ter in that an instrument of ratification will have to be deposited under Article 43 ter whereas a note will suffice under Article 43 bis.

3. Article X of the Protocol only mentions accession because the Protocol cannot be ratified.

Article 43 ter (Article VIII (2) of the Protocol)

(Accession to the amended version)

> Accession[1] to the 1980 Protocol
> by any State which is not a
> Contracting State to the 1974
> Limitation Convention shall
> have the effect of accession to
> that Convention as amended
> by the Protocol[2], subject to the
> provisions of article 44 bis.

1. A simplified procedure is provided for here, i.e. immediate accession without prior signature followed by ratification.

Accession is to be understood in a broad sense so that the States which have domestic prescriptions for adoption, confirmation or other are also covered. On the situation with regard to accession to the Protocol see Introductory remarks.

2. An accession by a State to the Protocol is at the same time an accession to both the amended and unamended version of the Limitation Convention (c. Article 44 bis).

The accession to the Limitation Convention of 1974 is provided for by the Convention itself and is amended by the Protocol only insofar as accession is also possible if the mechanism of Articles 43 ter and 44 bis is invoked.

Article 44

(Entry into force)

(1) This Convention shall enter into force on the first day of the month following the expiration of six[1] months after the date of the deposit of the tenth instrument of ratification or accession.

(2) For each State ratifying or acceding to this Convention after the deposit of the tenth instrument of ratification or accession, this Convention shall enter into force on the first day of the month following the expiration of six months after the date of the deposit of its instrument of ratification or accession[2].

1. By contrast to the CISG, six months will be sufficient here.

2. Compare notes on Article 99 CISG.

Article 44 bis[1] (Article XI of the Protocol)

(Simultaneous accession to both versions)

Any State which becomes a Contracting Party to the 1974 Limitation Convention, as amended by the 1980 Protocol, shall, unless it notifies the depositary to the contrary, be considered to be also a Contracting Party to the Convention, unamended, in relation to any Contracting Party to the Convention not yet a Contracting Party to the 1980 Protocol[2].

1. The substance of this article should have been included as Article 43 quater.

2. Two variants of access are provided for:

- to the unamended version of the Limitation Convention, pursuant to Article 43 bis and

- to the amended version of the Limitation Convention, pursuant to Article 43 ter.

Such accession is tied to the accession to the respective other version:

- in the case of Article 43 ter automatically, if there is no notice to the contrary, and

- in the case of Article 43 bis by an express declaration.

According to Article 40 of the Vienna Convention on the Law of the Treaties, the same result would be obtained also without an express declaration. Paragraph 5 of that article reads as follows:

"Any State which becomes a party to the treaty after the entry into force of the amending agreement shall, failing an expression of a different intention by that State:

(a) be considered as a party to the treaty as amended; and

(b) be considered as a party to the unamended treaty in relation to any party to the treaty not bound by the amending agreement."

In the relations between the States which are Contracting Parties to both version it will be the respective amended version which is valid.

Article 45

(Denunciation)

(1) Any Contracting State may denounce this Convention by notifying the Secretary-General of the United Nations to that effect.

(2) The denunciation shall take effect on the first day of the month following the expiration of twelve months after receipt of the notification by the Secretary-General of the United Nations[1].

1. Compare notes on Article 101 CISG.

Article 45 bis (Article XIII (3) of the Protocol)

Any Contracting State in respect of which the 1980 Protocol ceases to have effect by the application of paragraphs (1) and (2) of article XIII[1] **of the 1980 Protocol shall remain a Contracting Party to the 1974[2] Limitation Convention, unamended, unless it denounces the unamended Convention in accordance with article 45 of the Convention[3].**

1. These read as follows:

"(1) A Contracting State may denounce this Protocol by notifying the depositary to that effect."

"(2) The denunciation shall take effect on the first day of the month following the expiration of twelve months after receipt of the notification by the depositary."

2. Denunciation of the Protocol only entails a denunciation of the amended Limitation Convention.

3. A denunciation of the 1974 Limitation Convention has no influence on the existence of the Protocol amending it and of the amended version of the 1980 Limitation Convention.

A State which wants to remain a party to the amended version does not have to denounce the unamended version, for the latter automatically ceases to be in effect as soon as all Contracting Parties have acceded to the amended version (c. Article 59, Vienna Treaty Convention).

Article 46

(Official languages)

The original of this Convention, of which the Chinese, English, French, Russian and Spanish texts are equally authentic[1], shall be deposited with the Secretary-General of the United Nations.

1. Compare the respective notes of the final clause of the CISG. By contrast to the CISG, the Limitation Convention was only made out in five languages because at the time of its drafting Arabic was not an official language of the United Nations. The Protocol amending it, however, was adopted also in Arabic. An Arabic version of the Limitation Convention provided by the Secretary-General of the United Nations, unlike the other five versions, is not authentic but is only a translation. That version, however, was approved of by the interested Arab-speaking delegations at the XIIIth session of UNCITRAL held in July 1990.

The Limitation Convention was translated into German with the participation of the FRG, the former GDR and Austria.

INDEX

The capital letters A and B refer to the Sales Convention (A) and the Limitation Convention (B). The numbers printed in bold refer to the articles of the respective Convention, the numbers following the bold print refer to the paragraphs of the commentary upon those articles.

A

Good faith: A 7/5; B 7/1

Goods

carriage: **A 30/3; 31/3; 32; 67/1; 68/13.3.**

insurance during --: **A 32/9; 67/6**

category of: **A 2/7, 8; B 4/1**

conformity of: **A 25/3.4.; 35/2, 4; 60/1.2.**

damage to --before risk has passed: **A 66/1.3.**

damages: **A 75/3, 4, 5**

defect: **A 25/3.4.,; 35/2, 4**

deposit with third parties: **A 87/1.1.**

distance sales: **A 31/5**

documents: **A 34/2; 57/8**

emergency sale: **A 62/2, 88/1.1., 1.2., 2.3., 3**

examination: **A 38/1; 58/9; 82/7**

handing over: **A 34/2**

identification. **A 32/2; 67/11**

lack of conformity: **A 25/3.4.; 35/2; 36/1; 39/1 fol;**
46/3 fol; **B 10/3**

market price: **A 76/2**

markings: **A 32/2; 67/10**

model: **A 35/16**

non-conformity of part of goods: **A 51/1**

packaging of: **A 35/5, 6, 17 :**

perishing or damaging (deterioration) of: **A 66/2; 82; 88**

place of handing over: **A 31/1; 57/9; 58/5.1., 6**

preservation of: **A 85/5.1, 5.2., 5.3.; 86/10.1.; 87; 88**

quality: **A 35/4; 36/1**

quantity: **A 35/3; 36/1**

repair: **A 37/5; 46/7**

reservation of title in: **A 41/2**

responsibility for: **A 36**

restitution of: **A 82/2.2., 4.1.; 84/1, 6**

right to examine: **A 57/8.2.; 58/9.; B 10/4**

sale of --to be preserved: **A 62/2; 63; 88/1.1., 1.2., 4**

M

N

O

T